The Messianic Idea
in Judaism

The Messianic Idea in Judaism

AND OTHER ESSAYS ON JEWISH SPIRITUALITY

GERSHOM SCHOLEM

SCHOCKEN BOOKS • NEW YORK

Michael A. Meyer translated the following essays from the Ger-
man: "Toward an Understanding of the Messianic Idea," "The
Crypto-Jewish Sect of the Dönmeh," "Martin Buber's Interpreta-
tion of Hasidism," "The Tradition of the Thirty-Six Hidden Just
Men," "The Star of David," "The Science of Judaism," "At the
Completion of Buber's Translation of the Bible," "On the 1930
Edition of Rosenzweig's *Star of Redemption*," "The Politics of
Mysticism," and parts of "Revelation and Tradition as Religious
Categories."

Hillel Halkin translated "Redemption Through Sin" from the
Hebrew.

See also "Sources and Acknowledgments," pp. 365-66.

71-770

Contents

Foreword

THE ESSAYS COLLECTED in this volume represent some aspects of my attempts at synthesis over the last thirty-five years. They grew out of my deep involvement with the study of Jewish mysticism in its many ramifications, to which I have devoted my life's work. Starting from attempts to understand the primary sources of Kabbalistic literature, to which hardly any serious attention had been given by Jewish scholarship, I gradually widened my horizons, especially when I came to see the complex relations between Jewish mysticism and Messianism. About half the papers in this book are concerned with this relationship, which I consider of primary importance for an understanding of Jewish history in general and of Jewish mysticism in particular.

This, of course, is not to say that I approached this neglected field without any general ideas—or you may say intuitions—about the subject that attracted me most. For many years I immersed myself in philological studies, not because I had no such general ideas, but rather because I had too many. As a young man, I was intrigued to find out what precisely it was that made Judaism a living thing. I felt challenged by a welter of conflicting ideas, and I wanted to sort out the truth from the figments of my own rather lively imagination. For a long time, this made me reluctant to summarize the results of my studies, before they would be supported by a meticulous probing of detail. It was not until my fortieth year that I found the courage to speak out about topics which, at least for me, had held a strong attraction and fascination. I have discussed some of the larger issues in my major works. The present volume takes up certain of these themes, sometimes enlarging upon them and sometimes trying to distill their essence. This way, the central issues taken up here will, I hope, be brought into sharper focus and, to some extent, be clarified.

The ideas expressed in some of these papers have sometimes been vehemently attacked, and the author has been accused of promoting all kinds of destructive, nihilistic, and what-not tendencies. There is no point in answering such polemics or trying to distinguish between the nonsense attributed to me and those theses I in fact defend. The work has to stand on its own, and its theses will be proved and confirmed by the fruits these new insights into the meaning of Jewish history are likely to produce.

It is often said that this generation is not interested in history and tradition. I find it hard to believe this. At any rate, this book (in which repetitions of certain concepts and issues have intentionally been retained), is addressed to people who have not merely some moderate and far-away interest in the questions of Judaism and its past, but a passionate one. The connection between the renascence of the Jewish people and its historical consciousness is obvious, and has resulted in a new awareness of the dynamics and dialectics of Jewish history. The papers collected in this book are, I venture to hope, living witness to this.

Jewish history has many aspects—paths and bypaths—which were forgotten, lost sight of, and sometimes consciously played down by a galaxy of great scholars who had a one-sided and rather dogmatic idea of what Judaism was and should be. This book is written by a man who believes Judaism to be a living phenomenon, which, although developing under the impact of a great idea, has changed considerably over the long periods of its history and has not yet exhausted its potentialities. As long as it is alive, it will cast off forms and take on new ones, and who are we to predict in what guise they will present themselves? A new period of Jewish history has begun with the holocaust and the foundation of the State of Israel. But by whatever new forms the living consciousness of the Jews will be expressed, the old ones will always be of relevance to those who find in Judaism both a challenge and an answer.

I wish to express my debt of gratitude to my friend and colleague Nahum N. Glatzer, who was instrumental in bringing about this collection, and equally to the translators who have faced no easy task in putting these essays, written originally in Hebrew and German, into English.

GERSHOM SCHOLEM

Jerusalem
November 1970

Toward an Understanding
of the Messianic Idea
in Judaism

I

ANY DISCUSSION OF the problems relating to Messianism is a
delicate matter, for it is here that the essential conflict between
Judaism and Christianity has developed and continues to exist.
Although our discussion will not be concerned with this conflict,
but rather with internally Jewish perspectives on Messianism, it
will be of value to recall the central issue of this conflict. A totally
different concept of redemption determines the attitude to Messianism in Judaism and in Christianity; what appears to the one
as a proud indication of its understanding and a positive achievement of its message is most unequivocally belittled and disputed
by the other. Judaism, in all of its forms and manifestations, has
always maintained a concept of redemption as an event which
takes place publicly, on the stage of history and within the community. It is an occurrence which takes place in the visible world
and which cannot be conceived apart from such a visible appearance. In contrast, Christianity conceives of redemption as
an event in the spiritual and unseen realm, an event which
is reflected in the soul, in the private world of each individual,
and which effects an inner transformation which need not correspond to anything outside. Even the *civitas dei* of Augustine,
which within the confines of Christian dogmatics and in the
interest of the Church has made the most far-reaching attempt
both to retain and to reinterpret the Jewish categories of redemption, is a community of the mysteriously redeemed within an unredeemed world. What for the one stood unconditionally at the
end of history as its most distant aim was for the other the true
center of the historical process, even if that process was henceforth peculiarly decked out as *Heilsgeschichte*. The Church was

convinced that by perceiving redemption in this way it had overcome an external conception that was bound to the material
world, and it had counterpoised a new conception that possessed
higher dignity. But it was just this conviction that always seemed
to Judaism to be anything but progress. The reinterpretation of
the prophetic promises of the Bible to refer to a realm of inwardness, which seemed as remote as possible from any contents
of these prophecies, always seemed to the religious thinkers of
Judaism to be an illegitimate anticipation of something which
could at best be seen as the interior side of an event basically
taking place in the external world, but could never be cut off from
the event itself. What appeared to the Christians as a deeper ap-
prehension of the external realm appeared to the Jew as its liquidation and as a flight which sought to escape verification of the
Messianic claim within its most empirical categories by means of a
non-existent pure inwardness.

The history of the Messianic idea in Judaism has run its course
within the framework of this idea's never-relinquished demand for
fulfillment of its original vision. The considerations I would like
to set forth in what follows concern the special tensions in the
Messianic idea and their understanding in rabbinic Judaism. These
tensions manifest themselves within a fixed tradition which we
shall try to understand. But even where it is not stated explicitly,
we shall often enough find as well a polemical side-glance, or an
allusion, albeit concealed, to the claims of Christian Messianism.
A number of the things which I would here like to sum up briefly
are obvious and hardly constitute an object of learned controversy;
of others, however, this can hardly be said, and much as the history of Messianism has been discussed, there is room for a sharper
analysis of what it is that makes up the specific vitality of this
phenomenon in the history of the Jewish religion. I shall not try
to compete with historical and mythological analyses of the origins
of Messianic belief in biblical texts or in the history of religion in
general; such studies have been undertaken by outstanding scholars
like Joseph Klausner, Willi Staerk, Hugo Gressmann, Sigmund
Mowinckel, and many others.[1] The object of these remarks is not
the initial development of the Messianic idea but the varying
perspectives by which it became an effective force after its crystallization in historical Judaism. In this connection it must be emphasized that in the history of Judaism its influence has been exercised
almost exclusively under the conditions of the exile as a primary
reality of Jewish life and Jewish history. This reality lends its

special coloring to each of the various conceptions with which we shall be dealing here.

Within rabbinic Judaism as a social and religious phenomenon three kinds of forces are active precisely at those points where it is the most alive: conservative, restorative, and utopian. The conservative forces are directed toward the preservation of that which exists and which, in the historical environment of Judaism, was always in danger. They are the most easily visible and immediately obvious forces that operate in this type of Judaism. They have established themselves most effectively in the world of *Halakhah,* in the construction and continuing preservation and development of religious law. This law determined the nature of the Jew's life in exile, the only frame in which a life in the light of Sinaitic revelation seemed possible, and it is not surprising that it drew to itself, above all, the conservative forces. The restorative forces are directed to the return and recreation of a past condition which comes to be felt as ideal. More precisely, they are directed to a condition pictured by the historical fantasy and the memory of the nation as circumstances of an ideal past. Here hope is turned backwards to the re-establishment of an original state of things and to a "life with the ancestors." But there are, in addition, forces which press forward and renew; they are nourished by a vision of the future and receive utopian inspiration. They aim at a state of things which has never yet existed. The problem of Messianism in historical Judaism appears within the field of influence of these forces. To be sure, the conservative tendencies, great and even crucial as their role and their significance were for the existence of the religious community of Judaism, have no part in the development of Messianism within this community. This is not true, however, of the two other tendencies which I characterize as restorative and utopian. Both tendencies are deeply intertwined and yet at the same time of a contradictory nature; the Messianic idea crystallizes only out of the two of them together. Neither is entirely absent in the historical and ideological manifestations of Messianism. Only the proportion between them is subject to the widest fluctuations. Among various groupings within Jewry entirely different points of application for such forces and tendencies are emphasized. There has never been in Judaism a measured harmony between the restorative and the utopian factor. Sometimes the one tendency appears with maximal emphasis while the other is reduced to a minimum, but we never find a "pure case" of exclusive influence or crystallization of one of these tendencies. The reason for this is clear: even the restorative force has a utopian factor, and in utopianism restorative factors are at work. The restorative tendency, per se, even when it understands itself as such—as for example in the case of Maimonides whose statements regarding the Messianic idea I shall shortly discuss in greater detail—is nourished to no small degree by a utopian impulse which now appears as projection upon the past instead of projection on the future. The reason for this, too, is clear. There is a common ground of Messianic hope. The utopianism which presents the Jew of that epoch with the vision of an ideal as he would like to see it realized, itself falls naturally into two categories. It can take on the radical form of the vision of a new content which is to be realized in a future that will in fact be nothing other than the restoration of what is ancient, bringing back that which had been lost; the ideal content of the past at the same time delivers the basis for the vision of the future. However, knowingly or unknowingly, certain elements creep into such a restoratively oriented utopianism which are not in the least restorative and which derive from the vision of a completely new state of the Messianic world. The completely new order has elements of the completely old, but even this old order does not consist of the actual past; rather, it is a past transformed and transfigured in a dream brightened by the rays of utopianism.[2] Thus the dialectically linked tension between the utopian and restorative factors provides us also with deep tensions in the forms of Messianism crystallized in rabbinic Judaism, to say nothing of the interiorization of these impulses in Jewish mysticism. I shall now elaborate several principal structures of these forms and in so doing try to clarify the tensions they express.

II

When the Messianic idea appears as a living force in the world of Judaism—especially in that of medieval Judaism, which seems so totally interwoven with the realm of the *Halakhah*—it always occurs in the closest connection with apocalypticism. In these instances the Messianic idea constitutes both a content of religious faith as such and also living, acute anticipation. Apocalypticism appears as the form necessarily created by acute Messianism.

It is self-evident and needs no justification that the Messianic idea came into being not only as the revelation of an abstract proposition regarding the hope of mankind for redemption, but rather in very specific historical circumstances. The predictions and messages of the biblical prophets come to an equal degree from revelation and from the suffering and desperation of those whom they addressed; they are spoken from the context of situations and again and again have proven effective in situations where the End, perceived in the immediate future, was thought about to break in abruptly at any moment. To be sure, the predictions of the prophets do not yet give us any kind of well-defined conception of Messianism. Rather we have a variety of different motifs in which the much emphasized utopian impulse—the vision of a better humanity at the End of Days—is interpenetrated with restorative impulses like the reinstitution of an ideally conceived Davidic kingdom. This Messianic message of the prophets addresses man as a whole and sets forth images of natural and historical events through which God speaks and in which the End of Days is announced or realized. These visions never involve the individual as such, nor do these declarations claim any special "secret" knowledge gained from an inner realm not accessible to every man. By contrast, the words of the apocalyptists represent a shift in this view of the content of prophecy. These anonymous authors of writings like the biblical book of Daniel, the two books of Enoch, Fourth Ezra, the Baruch apocalypses, or the Testaments of the Twelve Patriarchs—to name only a few documents of this at one time seemingly over-flourishing literature—encase the words of the ancient prophets in a frame which they mold and furnish in their own way.

Here God no longer shows the seer individual instances of historical occurrence or only a vision of history's end; rather he sees all of history from beginning to end with particular emphasis on the arrival of that new aeon which manifests itself and prevails in the Messianic events. The Pharisee Josephus had already seen Adam, the first man, as a prophet whose vision encompassed not only the flood in Noah's day but also the flood of fire at the end of time and thus included all of history.[3] The talmudic Aggadah saw things very much the same: God shows Adam—but also Abraham or Moses—the entire past and future, the current and the final aeon.[4] Likewise, the priest of the End of Days (the priestly Messiah) who appears in the Habakkuk commentary of the Dead Sea sectarians, will be able to interpret the visions of the ancient prophets regarding the total course of the history of Israel as all of their features now become fully visible. In this interpretation of the visions of the ancient prophets or even in the work of the apocalyptists themselves, motifs of current history, which refer to contemporary conditions and needs, are closely intertwined with those of an apocalyptic, eschatological nature, in which not only the experiences of the present exercise an influence, but often enough ancient mythical images are filled with utopian content. As students of apocalypticism have always noted correctly, in this process the new eschatology moves decisively beyond the ancient prophecies. Hosea, Amos, or Isaiah know only a single world, in which even the great events at the End of Days run their course. Their eschatology is of a national kind: it speaks of the re-establishment of the House of David, now in ruins, and of the future glory of an Israel returned to God; also of everlasting peace and the turning of all nations toward the one God of Israel and away from heathen cults and images. In contrast, apocalypticism produced the doctrine of the two aeons which follow one another and stand in antithetical relationship: this world and the world to come, the reign of darkness and the reign of light. The national antithesis between Israel and the heathens is broadened into a cosmic antithesis in which the realms of the holy and of sin, of purity and impurity, of life and death, of light and darkness, God and the anti-divine powers, stand opposed. A wider cosmic background is superadded to the national content of eschatology and it is here that the final struggle between Israel and the heathens takes place. There arise the conceptions of the Resurrection of the Dead, of reward and punishment in the Last Judgment, and of Paradise and Hell, in which notions of individual retribution at the End of Days occur in conjunction with promises and threats addressed to the nation. All these are conceptions which are now closely tied to the ancient prophecies. The words of the prophets, which in their original context appear so clear and direct, henceforth become riddles, allegories, and mysteries which are interpreted—one might say, deciphered—by an apocalyptic homiletic or an original apocalyptic vision. And thus we have the framework in which the Messianic idea now begins its historical influence.

But there is an additional factor. As the meaning of the Greek word indicates, apocalypses are revelations or disclosures of God's hidden knowledge of the End. That is to say, what reached the prophets as knowledge which could hardly be proclaimed with sufficient loudness and publicity, in the apocalypses becomes secret. It is one of those enigmas of Jewish religious history that have not been satisfactorily solved by any of the many attempts at explanation just what the real reason is for this metamorphosis which makes knowledge of the Messianic End, where it oversteps the prophetic framework of the biblical texts, into an esoteric form of knowing. Why does the apocalyptist conceal himself instead of shouting his vision into the face of the enemy power as did the prophets? Why does he load the responsibility for those visions, fraught with danger, on the heroes of biblical antiquity and why does he convey them only to the select or initiated? Is it politics? Is it a changed understanding of the nature of this knowing? There is something disturbing in this transcendence of the prophetic which at the same time carries along with it a narrowing of its realm of influence. It cannot be coincidental that for nearly a millennium this character of apocalyptic knowing has also been preserved by the heirs of the ancient apocalyptists within rabbinic Judaism. For them it takes its place at the side of the gnostic knowledge of the *merkabah,* the throne-world of God and its mysteries which, explosive as this knowledge in itself was, could be reported only in a whisper. Not without reason the writings of the *merkabah* mystics in Judaism always contain apocalyptic chapters.[5] The stronger the loss of historical reality in Judaism during the turmoil surrounding the destruction of the Second Temple and of the ancient world, the more intensive became consciousness of the cryptic character and mystery of the Messianic message, which indeed always referred precisely to the re-establishment of that lost reality although it also went beyond it.

In an almost natural way Messianic apocalypticism orders the old promises and traditions, along with the newly adhering motifs, interpretations, and reinterpretations, under the two aspects which the Messianic idea henceforth takes on and keeps in Jewish consciousness. These two aspects, which in fact are based on the words of the prophets themselves and are more or less visible there, concern the catastrophic and destructive nature of the redemption on the one hand and the utopianism of the content of realized Messianism on the other. Jewish Messianism is in its origins and by its nature—this cannot be sufficiently emphasized—a theory of catastrophe. This theory stresses the revolutionary, cataclysmic element in the transition from every historical present to the Messianic future. This transition itself becomes a problem in that, beginning with the words of the prophets Amos and Isaiah, the really non-transitional character of it is pointed up and emphasized. Isaiah's Day of the Lord (chapters 2 and 4) is a day of catastrophe and is described in visions which stress this catastrophic nature in the extreme. But we learn nothing about how that Day of the Lord, on which previous history ends and on which the world is shaken to its foundations, is related to the "End of Days" (promised at the beginning of chapter 2 of Isaiah) on which the House of the Lord shall be established at the top of the mountains and the peoples flow unto it.

The elements of the catastrophic and the visions of doom are present in peculiar fashion in the Messianic vision. On the one hand, they are applied to the transition or destruction in which the Messianic redemption is born—hence the ascription of the Jewish concept of "birth pangs of the Messiah" to this period. But, on the other hand, it is also applied to the terrors of the Last Judgment which in many of these descriptions concludes the Messianic period instead of accompanying its beginnings. And thus for the apocalyptist's glance the Messianic utopia may often become twofold. The new aeon and the days of the Messiah are no longer one (as they still are in some writings of this literature); rather they refer to two periods of which the one, the rule of the Messiah, really still belongs to this world; the other, however, already belongs entirely to the new aeon which begins with the Last Judgment. But this doubling of the stages of redemption is mostly the result of learned exegesis which seeks to put every saying of the Bible harmoniously into place. In an original vision catastrophe and utopia do not twice follow after each other, but it is precisely by their uniqueness that they bring to bear with full force the two sides of the Messianic event.

However, before I devote a few remarks to these two sides of the Messianic idea as they characterize Messianic apocalypticism, I must preface a word intended to correct a widespread misconception. I am referring to the distortion of historical circumstances, equally popular among both Jewish and Christian scholars, which lies in denying the continuation of the apocalyptic tradition in rabbinic Judaism. This distortion of intellectual history is quite understandable in terms of the anti-Jewish interests of Christian scholars as well as the anti-Christian interests of Jewish ones. It was in keeping with the tendencies of the former group to regard Judaism only as the antechamber of Christianity and to see it as moribund once it had brought forth Christianity. Their view led to the conception of a genuine continuation of Messianism via the apocalyptists in the new world of Christianity. But the other group, too, paid tribute to their own prejudices. They were the great Jewish scholars of the nineteenth and early twentieth centuries, who to a great extent determined the popular image of Judaism. In view of their concept of a purified and rational Judaism, they could only applaud the attempt to eliminate or liquidate apocalypticism from the realm of Judaism. Without regrets, they left the claim of apocalyptic continuity to a Christianity which, to their minds, gained nothing on that account. Historical truth was the price paid for the prejudices of both camps. Attempts to eliminate apocalypticism completely from the realm of rabbinic Judaism have not been lacking since the Middle Ages and in what follows we shall even deal with the most consequential of these attempts, that of Maimonides. Such attempts represent one tendency among other, entirely different ones which have also been active in the history of Judaism. By themselves these attempts can claim no value as a truthful representation of the historical reality of Judaism. For this denial of apocalypticism set out to suppress exceedingly vital elements in the realm of Judaism, elements filled with historical dynamism even if they combined destructive with constructive forces. The idea that all apocalyptic currents of the pre-Christian age flowed into Christianity and there found their real place is a fiction which cannot be maintained against more careful historical examination. Just after the origin of the known apocalypses, especially those of the first pre- and post-Christian centuries, an undiminished mighty stream of apocalypticism rushes forth within the Jewish rabbinic tradition; in part it flows into the channel of the talmudic and aggadic literature, in part it finds its expression in its own literature, preserved in Hebrew and Aramaic. There can be no talk of a discontinuity between these later apocalypses and those ancient ones whose Hebrew originals have until now remained lost and which have only been preserved in translations and in the adaptations of the Christian churches. While one may question to which Jewish circles these independent writings that preserve their pseudepigraphic literary form really belong—nothing in them contradicts the spiritual world of the rabbis even if it is not possible to bring them into close relationship with it—there remains no doubt about the entry of apocalyptic tradition into the House of Study and the range of ideas of the traditional scholars. Here the cover of anonymity is again thrown off, the secretive whisper turns into an open exchange of ideas, into formal instruction, and even into pointed epigrams whose authors, with their often well-known names, take responsibility for their words. The significance of these two sources of rabbinic apocalypticism for an understanding of Messianism in the world of the *Halakhah* cannot be estimated too highly.

I spoke of the catastrophic nature of redemption as a decisive characteristic of every such apocalypticism, which is then complemented by the utopian view of the content of realized redemption. Apocalyptic thinking always contains the elements of dread and consolation intertwined. The dread and peril of the End form an element of shock and of the shocking which induces extravagance. The terrors of the real historical experiences of the Jewish people are joined with images drawn from the heritage of myth or mythical fantasy. This is expressed with particular forcefulness in the concept of the birth pangs of the Messiah which in this case means the Messianic age. The paradoxical nature of this conception exists in the fact that the redemption which is born here is in no causal sense a result of previous history. It is precisely the lack of transition between history and the redemption which is always stressed by the prophets and apocalyptists. The Bible and the apocalyptic writers know of no progress in history leading to the redemption. The redemption is not the product of immanent developments such as we find it in modern Western reinterpretations of Messianism since the Enlightenment where, secularized as the belief in progress, Messianism still displayed unbroken and immense vigor. It is rather transcendence breaking in upon history, an intrusion in which history itself perishes, transformed in its ruin because it is struck by a beam of light shining into it from an outside source. The constructions of history in which the apocalyptists (as opposed to the prophets of the Bible) revel have nothing to do with modern conceptions of development or progress, and if there is anything which, in the view of these seers, history deserves, it can only be to perish. The apocalyptists have always cherished a pessimistic view of the world. Their optimism, their hope, is not directed to what history will bring forth, but to that which will arise in its ruin, free at last and undisguised.

To be sure, the "light of the Messiah" which is to shine wondrously into the world, is not always seen as breaking in with complete suddenness; it may become visible by gradations and stages, but these gradations and stages have nothing to do with the history that has gone before. "It is told of Rabbi Hiyya and Rabbi Simeon that they walked in the valley of Arbela early in the morning and saw the dawn breaking on the horizon. Thereupon Rabbi Hiyya said: 'So too is Israel's redemption; at first it will be only very slightly visible, then it will shine forth more brightly, and only afterwards will it break forth in all of its glory.' "6 Such a belief was very common among apocalyptic calculators in all ages whenever they sought schemata according to which the different stages of the redemption would occur within the frame of the Last Days. But the apocalyptic calculation which relied upon numbers and constellations expresses only one side of this point of view and many teachers repudiated it again and again, not without reason, though with little success. In opposition to it stands the no less powerful sentiment that the Messianic age cannot be calculated. This was most pointedly expressed in the words of a talmudic teacher of the third century: "Three things come unawares: the Messiah, a found article, and a scorpion."7 And with sharper stress on the always possible End, the immediacy to God of each day, we find: "If Israel would repent even for a single day, they would be instantly redeemed and the Son of David would instantly come, for it says (Ps. 95:7): *Today* if you will listen to His voice."8

Such words add to the concept of the spontaneity of the redemption the idea, expressed in numerous moral dicta of the talmudic literature, that there are deeds which, as it were, help to bring about the redemption, somewhat like a midwife at a birth. Whoever does one thing or another (whoever, for example, cites what he has heard, stating the name of his source), "he brings redemption into the world." But here it is not a matter of real causality, only of an already established frame for pointed, sententious formulations which are directed less at the Messianic redemption than at the moral value of the suggested conduct. Indeed, statements of this kind stand totally outside the realm of apocalyptic thought. They present a moralism which must have been welcomed by later reinterpretations of Messianism in the sense of a rational and sensible utopianism. But in fact there can be no preparation for the Messiah. He comes suddenly, unannounced, and precisely when he is least expected or when hope has long been abandoned.

This deep feeling of the impossibility of calculating the Messianic age has produced in the Messianic Aggadah the idea of the occultation of the Messiah, who is always already present somewhere and whom a profound legend, not without cause, allows to have been born on the day of the destruction of the Temple. Beginning at the moment of the deepest catastrophe there exists the chance for redemption. "Israel speaks to God: When will You redeem us? He answers: When you have sunk to the lowest level, at that time will I redeem you."[9] Corresponding to this continually present possibility is the concept of the Messiah who continually waits in hiding. It has taken many forms, though admittedly none more grand than that which, with extravagant anticipation, has transplanted the Messiah to the gates of Rome, where he dwells among the lepers and beggars of the Eternal City.[10] This truly staggering "rabbinic fable" stems from the second century, long before the Rome which has just destroyed the Temple and driven Israel into exile itself becomes the seat of the Vicar of Christ and of a Church seeking dominion by its claim to Messianic fulfillment. This symbolic antithesis between the true Messiah sitting at the gates of Rome and the head of Christendom, who reigns there, accompanies Jewish Messianic thought through the centuries. And more than once we learn that Messianic aspirants have made a pilgrimage to Rome in order to sit by the bridge in front of the Castel Sant' Angelo and thus enact this symbolic ritual.

III

This catastrophic character of the redemption, which is essential to the apocalyptic conception, is pictured in all of these texts and traditions in glaring images. It finds manifold expression: in world wars and revolutions, in epidemics, famine, and economic catastrophe; but to an equal degree in apostasy and the desecration of God's name, in forgetting of the Torah and the upsetting of all moral order to the point of dissolving the laws of nature.[11] Such apocalyptic paradoxes regarding the final catastrophe were accepted even into as sober a text as the Mishnah, the first canonical codification of the *Halakhah*.

In the footsteps of the Messiah [i.e., in the period of his arrival] presumption will increase and respect disappear. The empire will turn to heresy and there will be no moral reproof. The house of assembly will become a brothel, Galilee will be laid waste, and the people of the frontiers will wander from city to city and none will pity them. The wisdom of the scribes will become odious and those who shun sin will be despised; truth will nowhere be found. Boys will shame old men and old men will show deference to boys. "The son reviles the father, the daughter rises up against the mother . . . a man's enemies are the men of his own house" (Micah 7:6). The face of the generation is like the face of a dog [i.e., brazenness will reign]. On whom shall we then rely? On our Father in heaven.[12]

The pages of the Talmud tractate Sanhedrin which deal with the Messianic age are full of most extravagant formulations of this kind. They drive toward the point that the Messiah will come only in an age which is either totally pure or totally guilty and corrupt. Little wonder that in one such context the Talmud cites the bald statement of three famous teachers of the third and fourth centuries: "May he come, but I do not want to see him."[13]

Though the redemption, then, cannot be realized without dread and ruin, its positive aspect is provided with all the accents of utopianism. This utopianism seizes upon all the restorative hopes turned toward the past and describes an arc from the re-establishment of Israel and of the Davidic kingdom as a kingdom of God on earth to the re-establishment of the condition of Paradise as it is foreseen by many old Midrashim, but above all by the thought of Jewish mystics, for whom the analogy of First Days and Last Days possess living reality. But it does more than that. For already in the Messianic utopianism of Isaiah we find the Last Days conceived immeasurably more richly than any beginning. The condition of the world, wherein the earth will be full of the knowledge of the Lord as the waters cover the sea (Isa. 11:9), does not repeat anything that has ever been, but presents something new. The world of *tikkun*, the re-establishment of the harmonious condition of the world, which in the Lurianic Kabbalah is the Messianic world, still contains a strictly utopian impulse. That harmony which it reconstitutes does not at all correspond to any condition of things that has ever existed even in Paradise, but at most to a plan contained in the divine idea of Creation. This plan, however, even with the first stages of its realization, came up against that disturbance and hindrance of the cosmic process known as the "breaking of the vessels" which initiates the Lurianic myth. In reality, therefore, the Last Days realize a higher, richer, and more fulfilled condition than the First Days, and even the Kabbalists remain bound to a utopian conception. The contents of this utopia differ in the various circles. The model of a renewed humanity and of a renewed kingdom of David or of a descendant of David, which represents the prophetic legacy of Messianic utopianism, is often enough combined by the apocalyptists and mystics with a renewed condition of nature and even of the cosmos as a whole. The escapist and extravagant character of such utopianism, which undertakes to determine the content of redemption without having experienced it yet in fact, does of course subject it to the wild indulgence of fantasy. But it always retains that fascinating vitality to which no historical reality can do justice and which in times of darkness and persecution counterpoises the fulfilled image of wholeness to the piecemeal, wretched reality which was available to the Jew. Thus the images of the New Jerusalem that float before the eyes of the apocalyptists always contain more than was ever present in the old one, and the renewal of the world is simply more than its restoration.

In this connection, the talmudic teachers were already faced with the question whether one may "press for the End," that is to say, force its coming by one's own activity. Here we find a deep cleavage of opinion with regard to Messianism. The dream was not always accompanied by the determination to do something for its realization. On the contrary: it is one of the most important characteristics of Messianism that to the minds of a great many there was an abyss here. And this is not surprising since precisely in the biblical texts which served as the basis for the crystallization of the Messianic idea it is nowhere made dependent upon human activity. Neither Amos' Day of the Lord nor Isaiah's visions of the End of Days are deemed the results of such action. Likewise, the ancient apocalyptists, who undertook to disclose the secrets of the End, know nothing of this. In truth, everything is here attributed to God and it is just this that lends a special character to the contradiction between what is and what shall be. The warnings against human action which dares to bring about the redemption have always been most offensive to the revolutionary and to the one who "presses for the End," as the Jewish term would have it. But they do not lack legitimacy, and they are by no means only signs of weakness and possible cowardice (although they may sometimes be that as well).

In Song of Songs 2:7 we find the verse: "I adjure you, daughters of Jerusalem, by the gazelles and by the hinds of the field, do not awaken or stir up love until it is ready." Rabbi Helbo comments: "Four vows are contained here. The Israelites are adjured not to revolt against the kingdoms of the world [the secular powers], not to press for the End, not to reveal their mystery to the nations of the world, and not to come up from exile like a wall [in great masses]. But, if so, why does King Messiah come? To gather in the exiled of Israel."

Thus we read in the old Midrash to the Song of Songs.[14] But likewise the author of Fourth Ezra is exhorted by the angel: "You will certainly not want to hasten more than the Creator" (4:34).

This is the attitude of the spokesmen of that Messianism in Judaism which still placed all hope on unbroken faith in God. It corresponds to and originates from the afore-mentioned conception of the essential lack of relation between human history and the redemption. But we can understand why such an attitude was again and again in danger of being overrun by the apocalyptic certainty that the End had begun and all that was still required was the call to ingathering. Ever and again the revolutionary opinion that this attitude deserves to be overrun breaks through in the Messianic actions of individuals or entire movements. This is the Messianic activism in which utopianism becomes the lever by which to establish the Messianic kingdom. One may, perhaps, formulate the question which produced this division of minds more pointedly. It would then be: Can man master his own future? And the answer of the apocalyptist would be: no. But the enticement to action, the call to fulfillment, is inherent in this projection of the best in man upon his future, which is just what Jewish Messianism in its utopian elements so emphatically set forth.

And it is not surprising that beyond the repudiations and reservations of the theologians, historical recollection and mythical legend together kept alive the memory of the Messianic ventures of Bar Kokhba or of Sabbatai Zevi, who created epochs in the history of Judaism. The legend of Rabbi Joseph de la Reyna, which long enjoyed great popularity,[15] pictures in extreme fashion an individual's enticement to Messianic action, an enticement which must fail because no one is capable of such action. It describes the undertaking of a great teacher in Israel, for whom the redemption is concentrated on shattering only one last barrier. But it must be done by magic, and it must fail for just this reason. This legend of the great magician and Kabbalist who captured Sammael, the devil, and thus could have brought about the redemption if he had not himself fallen under the devil's sway in the process, is a grand allegory on all "pressing for the End." Such Joseph de la Reynas have never been lacking in Jewish life, whether they remained hidden in some corner of the exile or, by exposing their identity and exaggerating their own magic, made the jump into world history.

This Messianic activism, incidentally, lies on that peculiar double line of mutual influence between Judaism and Christianity which goes hand in hand with inner tendencies of development in both religions. The political and chiliastic Messianism of important religious movements within Christianity often appears as a reflection of what is really Jewish Messianism. It is well known how vigorously such tendencies were decried as Judaizing heresies by their orthodox opponents in Catholicism and Protestantism alike. From a purely phenomenological point of view there is doubtless some truth to these reproaches, even if in historical reality these tendencies also arise spontaneously from attempts to take Messianism seriously and from a feeling of dissatisfaction with a Kingdom of God which is to lie within us and not about us. The more Christian Messianism—to use the words of a significant Protestant theologian, who with this formulation no doubt believed he had expressed something most positive [16]—presented itself as "this wondrous certainty of pure inwardness," the more strongly dissatisfaction with this view had to find itself referred back to the Jewish vision. And thus, again and again, such chiliastic and revolutionary Messianism as emerges, for example, among the Taborites, the Anabaptists, or the radical wing of the Puritans, draws its inspiration mainly from the Old Testament and not from Christian sources. To be sure, it is the Christian conviction regarding the redemption which has already come that lends this activism a special seriousness and its special vehemence—and thus its significance in world history. In the Jewish realm, from which it originates, this activism remains singular and strangely powerless precisely because it is aware of the radical difference between the unredeemed world of history and that of the Messianic redemption, as I have explained it above. Parallel to this line, along which Judaism has again and again furnished Christianity with political chiliastic Messianism, runs the other one, along which Christianity, for its part, has bequeathed to Judaism or aroused within it the tendency to discover a mystical aspect of the interiorization of the Messianic idea. To be sure, this aspect comes to the same degree from the inner movement and development of mysticism in Judaism itself, for which the Messianically promised reality must in addition appear as a symbol of an inner condition of the world and of man. It will always remain difficult to decide how much may be said of historical influence with regard to these two channels and how much must be ascribed to immanent movement within each one's own world of ideas.

The interiorization of the redemption remains a problem even where, unlike in Christianity, it did not serve to establish a thesis alleging that in the redemption something like a pure inwardness bursts forth. I have already stressed that it is indicative of the special position of Judaism in the history of religion that it thought nothing of such a chemically pure inwardness of redemption. I do not say: thought little, but thought nothing at all. An inwardness, which does not present itself in the most external realm and is not bound up with it in every way, was regarded here as of no value. According to the dialectics of Jewish mysticism, the drive to the essence was at the same time the drive outward. The re-establishment of all things in their proper place, which constitutes the redemption, produces a totality that knows nothing of such a division between inwardness and outwardness. The utopian element in Messianism refers to this totality and to it alone. Historically, this totality could be viewed with a double glance, cast upon the inner and outer aspect of the world, as in the Lurianic Kabbalah, so long as it was certain that one would not fall victim to the other. But it remains peculiar that this question concerning the inner aspect of the redemption should emerge so late in Judaism—though it finally does emerge with great vehemence. In the Middle Ages it played no role. Perhaps this is connected with the repudiation of the Christian claim which just at that time returned to the notion of the inwardness of redemption and insisted upon it, a notion which was so evidently refuted on the stage of history and therefore, as far as the churches were concerned, had no business being there.

IV

In the above, I have emphasized the two aspects of the Messianic idea which appear in rabbinic Judaism and provide it with on-going apocalyptic inspiration: the catastrophic and the utopian. Yet the figure of the Messiah, in whom the fulfillment of redemption is concentrated, remains peculiarly vague; and this, I think, has good reason. Features of such varying historical and psychological origins are gathered into this medium of fulfillment and coexist within it that they do not furnish a clear picture of the man. One is almost tempted to say that his character is over-determined and therefore has again become uncertain. Unlike Christian or Shiite Messianism, no memories of a real person are at work here which, though they might arouse the imagination and attract old images of expectation, nonetheless are always bound to something deeply personal. Jesus or the Hidden Imam, who once existed as persons, possess the unmistakable and unforgettable qualities of a person. This is just what the Jewish image of the Messiah, by its nature, cannot have since it can picture everything personal only in completely abstract fashion, having as yet no living experience on which to base it.

There is, however, a historical development in this character of the Messiah on which the two aspects stressed here shed a great deal of light. I am referring to the doubling of the figure of the Messiah, its split into a Messiah of the House of David and one of the House of Joseph. This conception of the "Messiah ben Joseph" was again discussed only a few years ago in a very interesting monograph by Siegmund Hurwitz which tries to explain its origins in psychological terms.[17] But I think it can best be understood in terms of those two aspects with which we have been concerned here. The Messiah ben Joseph is the dying Messiah who perishes in the Messianic catastrophe. The features of the catastrophic are gathered together in him. He fights and loses— but he does not suffer. The prophecy of Isaiah regarding the suffering servant of God is never applied to him. He is a redeemer who redeems nothing, in whom only the final battle with the powers of the world is crystallized. His destruction coincides with the destruction of history. By contrast, when the figure is split, all of the utopian interest is concentrated on the Messiah ben David. He is the one in whom what is new finally comes to the fore, who once and for all defeats the antichrist, and thus presents the purely positive side of this complex phenomenon. The more these two sides are made independent and emphasized, the more this doubling of the Messiah figure remains alive for the circles of apocalyptic Messianists even in later Judaism. The more this dualism becomes weakened, the less is the doubling mentioned, and the special figure of the Messiah ben Joseph becomes superfluous and meaningless.

Such mitigations of the dualism occur even in the talmudic literature itself. Much as apocalyptic imagination fascinated many rabbinic teachers, and varied as its continuing influence was in medieval Judaism, more sober conceptions remained alive as well. There were many who felt repulsed by apocalypticism. Their attitude is most sharply expressed by the strictly anti-apocalyptical definition of the Babylonian teacher Samuel of the first half of the third century, which is often referred to in the Talmud: "The only difference between this aeon and the Days of the Messiah is the subjection [of Israel] to the nations." [18] This obviously polemical utterance provides the cue for a tendency with which we shall still have to deal in terms of its effect and its crystallization in the powerful formulations of Maimonides.

Such counter-tendencies have not, however, been able to hamper the continuing effectiveness of radical apocalyptic, utopian currents in Jewish Messianism. On the contrary, one might say that this apocalypticism was deeply rooted in popular forms of Judaism that were widespread during the Middle Ages. The esoteric element increasingly spills out into the popular domain. Apocalyptic productivity stretches from the third century down to the period of the Crusades. Important products of the Kabbalistic literature still clearly manifest the continuing influence of this apocalyptic element, as indeed many of its parts represent a productive continuation of the old Aggadah, though on a new level. We must of course take into account that a number of such products of popular apocalypticism fell victim to rabbinical censorship. This censorship, though not constituted in any institutional form, was no doubt effective. Much that was written in the Middle Ages did not at all suit the fancy of the responsible leadership, and sometimes we learn of ideas and writings, which did not gain entry into the "higher literature," only via fortuitously preserved letters or some hidden quotation. This popular apocalypticism presents itself to us as propaganda literature. In a time of gloom and oppression it seeks to bring consolation and hope, and thereby it necessarily generates extravagances. There is an anarchic element in the very nature of Messianic utopianism: the dissolution of old ties which lose their meaning in the new context of Messianic freedom. The total novelty for which utopianism hopes enters thus into a momentous tension with the world of bonds and laws which is the world of *Halakhah*.

The relationship between the Jewish *Halakhah* and Messianism is indeed filled with such tension. On the one hand, Messianic utopianism presents itself as the completion and perfection of *Halakhah*. It is to perfect what cannot yet find expression in the *Halakhah* as the law of an unredeemed world. Thus, for example, only in Messianic times will all those parts of the law which are not realizable under the conditions of the exile become capable of fufillment. And thus there seems to be no antagonism created at all between what can be provisionally fulfilled in the law and what can only be fulfilled Messianically. The one calls for the other, and the concept of a Messianic *Halakhah* in the Talmud's terms, i.e., one which can be taught and fufilled only in the Days of the Messiah, is by no means merely an empty phrase; it represents a very real content. The law as such can be fulfilled in its total plenitude only in a redeemed world. But there is doubtless another side to the matter as well. For apocalypticism and its inherent mythology tore open a window on a world which the *Halakhah* rather preferred to leave shrouded in the mists of uncertainty. The vision of Messianic renewal and freedom was by its nature inclined to produce the question of what it would do to the status of Torah and of the *Halakhah* which was dependent on it. This question, which the men of *Halakhah* could consider only with misgivings, is necessarily raised by rabbinic apocalypticism. For even if the Torah was regarded as not subject to change, the problem of its practical application in the Messianic age had to emerge within such conceptions as well. And here indeed it was easier to assume that the divine "Yoke of the Torah" would become heavier rather than lighter. For at that time a great deal would become capable of fulfillment for the first time which under the conditions of the exile, in which the *Halakhah* had largely developed, was not at all realizable. At the same time, the conception of a "Torah of the Messiah," as it appears in the talmudic literature, drew in its wake yet another conception: that of a more complete development of the reasons for the commandments, which only the Messiah will be able to explain.[19] Both understanding of the Torah and its fulfillment will thus be infinitely richer than they are now. But along with this, there were bound to be motifs which carried this new understanding to the level of a deeper, even purely mystical comprehension of the world of the law. The greater the assumption of changes in nature or of revolutions in man's moral character—which latter were determined by the extinction of the destructive power of the evil inclination in the Messianic age—the greater did the modification also have to become which under such circumstances affected the operation of the law. A positive commandment or a prohibition could scarcely still be the same when it no longer had for its object the separation of good and evil to which man was called, but rather arose from the Messianic spontaneity of human freedom purely flowing forth. Since by its nature this freedom realizes only the good, it has no real need for all those "fences" and restrictions with which the *Halakhah* was surrounded in order to secure it from the temptations of evil. At this point there arises the possibility of a turning from the restorative conception of the final re-establishment of the reign of law to a utopian view in which restrictive traits will no longer be determinative and decisive, but be replaced by certain as yet totally unpredictable traits which will reveal entirely new aspects of free fulfillment. Thus an anarchic element enters Messianic utopianism. The Pauline "freedom of the children of God" is a form in which such a turning meant leaving Judaism behind. But this was by no means the only form of these conceptions, which appear in Messianism again and again with dialectical necessity. Finally, the anarchic element is also joined by the antinomian potentialities which are latent in Messianic utopianism. (See "Redemption Through Sin.")

The opposition between restorative and purely utopian, radical elements in the conception of the Messianic Torah brings an element of uncertainty into the *Halakhah*'s attitude to Messianism. The battle lines are by no means clearly drawn. Unfortunately, a penetrating and serious study of this relationship of the medieval *Halakhah* to Messianism is one of the most important yet unfulfilled desiderata of the scientific study of Judaism. As far as I can see, no one has taken an interest in doing it. If I may trust my own very incompetent judgment—really only an impression— I would say that many of the great men of *Halakhah* are completely entwined in the realm of popular apocalypticism when they come to speak of the redemption. For a number of them, apocalypticism is not a foreign element and is not felt to be in contradiction to the realm of the *Halakhah*. From the point of view of the *Halakhah,* to be sure, Judaism appears as a well-ordered house, and it is a profound truth that a well-ordered house is a dangerous thing. Something of Messianic apocalypticism penetrates into this house; perhaps I can best describe it as a kind of anarchic breeze. A window is open through which the winds blow in, and it is not quite certain just what they bring in with them. As vital as this anarchic airing may have been for the house of the law, it is certainly easy to understand the reticence and misgivings with which other significant representatives of *Halakhah* regarded everything that makes up Messianic utopianism. Many, as I have said, were deeply involved with apocalypticism; but among many others one can notice an equally deep uneasiness with regard to the perspectives it reveals. As long as Messianism appeared only as an abstract hope, as an element totally deferred to the future which had no living significance for the life of the Jew in the present, the opposition between the essentially conservative rabbinic and the never completely defined Messianic authority, which was to be established from entirely new dimensions of the utopian, could remain without real tension; indeed, there could be attempts to create a certain harmony between such authorities. But whenever there was an actual eruption of such hope, that is to say, in every historical hour in which the Messianic idea entered the mind as a power with direct influence, the tension which exists between these two forms of religious authority immediately became noticeable. These things could be united in pure thought, or at least they could be preserved next to one another, but they could not be united in their execution. Observing the appearance of such tension in the Messianic movements of the twelfth century with their concomitant antinomianism, among the followers of David Alroy in Kurdistan or among those of the Messiah who appeared at that time in Yemen, no doubt influenced Maimonides' attitude when with such great energy he set about to restrict the scope of Messianic utopianism to an absolute minimum.

The emergence of such radical contents in the Messianic idea can be most clearly seen in a medieval work in which *Halakhah* and Kabbalah are very closely intertwined. I am thinking of the book *Ra'ya Mehemna,* which belongs to the most recent layer of the literature that is gathered together in the *Zohar* and which came into being in the last years of the thirteenth or the first years of the fourteenth century. The author, who is a Kabbalist deeply rooted in the *Halakhah,* here deals with the mystical reasons for the commandments and prohibitions of the Torah. But his book is also written out of an acute Messianic expectation which possesses all of the urgency of the imminently impending End. He is not, however, motivated in the least by an interest in the catastrophic aspect of the redemption, of which he has not discovered any new, independent features, but rather in the utopian content which in anticipation he seeks to formulate. Here an anarchic vision of liberation from the restrictions which the Torah has laid upon the Jew in an unredeemed world, and above all in the exile, plays a central role. The author expresses his vision by means of old biblical symbols which now become types for the different status of things in the unredeemed world and in the Messianic age.

These symbols are the Tree of Life and the Tree of Knowledge, or the Tree of Knowledge of Good and Evil, which because its fruit brings about death is also called the Tree of Death. These trees, respectively, control the state of the world, be it the state of Creation as such or of the Torah, which as the divine law governs and determines it. Standing in the center of Paradise and representing higher orders of things, the trees control a great deal more than just existence in the Garden of Eden. Since the Fall of Adam, the world is no longer ruled by the Tree of Life as it had been in the beginning, but by the Tree of Knowledge. The Tree of Life represents the pure, unbroken power of the holy, the diffusion of the divine life through all worlds and the communication of all living things with their divine source. There is no admixture of evil in it, no "shells" which dam up and choke life, no death, and no restriction. But since the Fall of Adam, since the time when the forbidden fruit of the Tree of Knowledge was eaten, the world is ruled by the mystery of this second tree in which both good and evil have their place. Hence, under the rule of this Tree, the world contains differentiated spheres: the holy and the profane, the pure and the impure, the permitted and the forbidden, the living and the dead, the divine and the demonic. Although the Torah, the revelation of God's providence, is in essence one and immutable, it manifests itself in every state of the world in a manner befitting this state. Our comprehension of revelation is presently tied to the Tree of Knowledge and presents itself as the positive law of the Torah and as the realm of the *Halakhah*. Its meaning appears to us now in what is commanded and what is prohibited and in everything which follows from this basic distinction. The power of evil, of destruction and death, has become real in the free will of man. The purpose of the law, which as it were constitutes the Torah as it can be read in the light—or shadow!—of the Tree of Knowledge, is to confine this power if not to overcome it entirely. But in the Messianic redemption the full glory of the utopian again breaks forth, although characteristically and in keeping with the idea of the Tree of Life it is conceived as a restoration of the state of things in Paradise. In a world in which the power of evil has been broken, all those differentiations also disappear which had been derived from it. In a world in which only the pure life still reigns, obstructions to the stream of life, which solidify it in externals and in "shells," no longer have any validity or significance. In the present state of the world the Torah must appear on many levels of meaning; even the mystical meaning, by which the insightful individual is permitted a glance at least into its hidden life and into his own connection with this life, is necessarily bound to the phenomena of even the most external realm. Therefore, in exile, *Halakhah* and Kabbalah always remain mutually related. But when the world will again be subject to the law of the Tree of Life, the face of *Halakhah* itself will change. Where everything is holy there will no longer be need of restrictions and prohibitions, and whatever appear as such today will either vanish or reveal a totally new, as yet undiscovered, aspect of pure positiveness. In this conception, the redemption now appears as the manifestation of something deeply spiritual, as a spiritual revolution which discloses the mystical content and significance of the Torah as its real and true literal meaning. Mystical utopia takes the place of the national and political utopia without actually abrogating it, but as a kernel which has now begun to sprout. The author revels in the contrast between the "Torah of the Exile" and the "Torah of Redemption": the latter alone will disclose the undistorted and living meaning of the entire Torah in its infinite fullness. But he does not elucidate any transition between these two kinds of manifestation or between the conditions in the two states of the world which are expressed in these two aspects of the one "complete Torah of God." The utopian vision in rabbinic Judaism was driven no further than this, and scarcely could have been.

V

If we now move on to an examination of the function of the Messianic idea in connection with the rational tendencies in Judaism we shall reach conclusions very different from those of our previous discussion. These rational tendencies developed within the Jewish philosophy of the Middle Ages, which attempted to prove that Jewish monotheism and the religion of revelation based on it were a consistent system of rational religion and insofar as possible tried to construe them as such. This project of the philosophers and rational theologians of Judaism does not immediately and in the same manner attack all of the realms of Jewish tradition in which the earlier Judaism's convictions of faith had still without any systematic connection been crystallized. But since its development in the period from Saadia Gaon (died 942) to Moses Maimonides (died 1204) and Hasdai Crescas (died 1410), there has been an unmistakable tendency to open up to rational inquiry and hence to rational critique even such realms as were originally the most foreign to it. The Messianic idea is a case in point, and most drastically so in the forms of rabbinic apocalypticism of which we have spoken above.[20]

We here encounter the important fact that the rational tendencies in Judaism pushed the restorative factor in Messianism decidedly into the foreground. With the influential formulation of this tendency by Maimonides restoration becomes the focus of Messianism. By contrast, the utopian element quite peculiarly recedes and is only maintained at a bare minimum. That it is maintained at all is due only to the fact that a utopian element of the prophetic promise in a precise sense, namely the universal knowledge of God, is related to the supreme good of these philosophical doctrines. But this supreme good is the contemplative life which the medieval philosophers, on account of the presuppositions of their Greek philosophical legacy, were bound to regard as the ideal of a fulfilled life. As the history of all three monotheistic religions teaches us, the theoretical contemplation, which on a purely philosophical basis could be set up as the highest value, was easily able to find a connection with the religious sphere. Occupation with the contents of the Torah and the reflection on God's attributes and rule created within Judaism a traditional framework for such an identification of the *vita contemplativa* with concern for the objects and facts of the Jewish religious realm. The fulfillment of God's law was, after all, always closely connected with its study, without which such fulfillment could not even be considered legitimate. It is this idea of study of the Torah which opens up the highest realm of contemplation to the Jewish philosopher, and it is only from here that the world of *Halakhah* was illumined. The active life, which is ordered by the *Halakhah,* finds its complement and consummation in that sphere which Maimonides never doubted was of superior worth. It was possible to develop this idea of the contemplative life as a positive value without any reference to the Messianic idea. And in fact it appears without any such reference as the crowning element at the conclusion of Maimonides' main philosophical work, his *Guide of the Perplexed.* In other words, it is in principle, though only in rare and isolated cases, independently capable of realization even in an unredeemed world. However, a utopian content of this vision is preserved, since in the Messianic age—incidentally, under purely natural conditions—the leisure for such a *vita contemplativa* will take on entirely different dimensions and the contemplative knowledge of God will become everyone's principal concern. The utopian content does not disappear entirely, but it is now only the intensive realization of a state which fundamentally and in its real essence can be already reached under the conditions of our time. Utopianism is preserved in the boundless expansion and increase of the contemplative element. Restorative elements determine everything else.

I must now emphasize that this rational limitation of the Messianic to its restorative components lies not at all in the nature of the rationalistic tendencies in Judaism as such. Rather, it occurs only in its medieval varieties, and there is a great difference here between medieval and modern rationalism which must be maintained against obvious tendencies to efface it. For precisely to the extent that the rationalism of the Jewish and European Enlightenment subjected the Messianic idea to an ever advancing secularization, it freed itself of the restorative element. It stressed instead the utopian element, though in a totally new way that is foreign to the Middle Ages. Messianism became tied up with the idea of the eternal progress and infinite task of humanity perfecting itself. In this process, the concept of progress, itself a non-restorative element, became central for rational utopianism. The restorative factors lost their effect to the degree that the national and historical elements of the Messianic idea were superseded by a purely universalistic interpretation. Hermann Cohen, surely as distinguished a representative of the liberal and rationalistic reinterpretation of the Messianic idea in Judaism as one could find, was driven by his religion of reason into becoming a genuine and unhampered utopian who would have liked to liquidate the restorative factor entirely.

If we ask ourselves why this changed attitude to Messianism in medieval and modern Jewish rationalism came about, the answer seems to me that in the Middle Ages apocalypticism received a significance which by the time of the Enlightenment had completely lost its impact. That tendency, of which Maimonides was the grandest and most influential representative, consciously and with clear intent aimed at the liquidation of apocalypticism in Jewish Messianism. It was deeply suspicious of that anarchic element which I discussed earlier—perhaps on account of a fear of the eruption of antinomian trains of thought, which apocalypticism, in fact, could easily produce. This fear of radical utopianism and its various forms brought about the determined reversion to the restorative factor which lent itself to setting a limit to such eruptions. In Maimonides' environment these were quite real apprehensions, well founded upon historical phenomena of his own experience. In an era like the nineteenth century, by contrast, apocalypticism seemed finally liquidated and possessed, at least for the historical experience of the great Jewish rationalists of this age, no urgency or force whatever. (That they deeply and crucially deluded themselves on this score is another matter.) Nowhere did they reveal any feeling for the immense power of apocalypticism, which was still active in disguised forms, since for them it had become meaningless, empty nonsense. The anarchic element in utopianism no longer frightened the freest among them as something destructive, but rather counted as a positive element in the progress of mankind, which was developing from old forms to ever higher and less restricted forms of human freedom. But in medieval Judaism currents of this kind were without significance. We may say that to the medievals only the radical antipodes possess creative significance for an understanding of the Messianic idea: on the one hand, the apocalyptists; on the other, the liquidators of apocalypticism. The latter group's thinking, whether rooted in *Halakhah* or in philosophy, is ultimately motivated by anti-Messianic impulses and recognizes the dangers inherent in the utopianism of Messianic freedom. It is an error often committed to see only the second tendency in Judaism, though, to be sure, it is represented by the most powerful personalities. It is no less wrong, however, in awareness of the great importance of apocalypticism, to underestimate the effect of that other tendency which aimed at removing the apocalyptic thorn. The particular vitality of the Messianic idea in Judaism resides in the dialectical tension between these two tendencies.

Despite the conception's immense power of attraction, the Messianic idea was formulated only quite late into a positive basic dogma or principle of Judaism. There were a great many enthusiasts among the Jews who rejected in advance any selection of principles whatever, and who demanded equal authority for all components of the tradition. When a selection was made at all, it could remain doubtful whether next to the principles of monotheism and of the authority of the Torah as the norm of life, the Messianic hope as certainty of the redemption could claim an equivalent sanction. It is surely worth noting in this connection that Maimonides, who took this step more decisively than several of his predecessors and who made room for the Messianic idea among his thirteen principles of the Jewish faith, accepted it only together with anti-apocalyptic restrictions.[21] Maimonides, who sought to set down a firm authority for a rather anarchically organized medieval Jewry, was a man of extraordinary intellectual courage. In his nearly standard codification of *Halakhah,* he succeeded in including his own metaphysical convictions as binding norms of religious conduct for the Jews in general, i.e., as *Halakhot,* although crucial parts of these theses have no legitimate basis whatever in the biblical and talmudic sources and are rather indebted to the philosophical traditions of Greece. And just as he is prepared at the beginning of his great work to lend the power of law in the sense of *Halakhah* to his own convictions, thus he acts no less arbitrarily in his radical acceptance of the anti-apocalyptical elements of the talmudic tradition and his decided exaggeration of them in the sense of his own realm of ideas at the end of this work. In the last two passages of his code of laws, in the eleventh and twelfth paragraphs of the "Laws Concerning the Installation of Kings," we find a portrait of the Messianic idea. After we have become acquainted above with several of the formulations of the apocalyptists, it will be of value to look at several essential points of these contradictory remarks.[22] Here we read:

> The Messiah will arise and restore the kingdom of David to its former might. He will rebuild the sanctuary and gather the dispersed of Israel. All the laws will be reinstituted in his days as of old. Sacrifices will be offered and the Sabbatical and Jubilee years will be observed exactly in accordance with the commandments of the Torah. But whoever does not believe in him or does not await his coming denies not only the rest of the prophets, but also the Torah and our teacher Moses.
>
> Do not think that the Messiah needs to perform signs and miracles, bring about a new state of things in the world, revive the dead, and the like. It is not so. . . . Rather it is the case in these matters that the statutes of our Torah are valid forever and eternally. Nothing can be added to them or taken away from them. And if there arise a king from the House of David who meditates on the Torah and practices its commandments like his ancestor David in accordance with the Written and Oral Law, prevails upon all Israel to walk in the ways of the Torah and to repair its breaches [i.e., to eliminate the bad state of affairs resulting from the incomplete observance of the law], and fights the battles of the Lord, then one may properly assume that he is the Messiah. If he is then successful in rebuilding the sanctuary on its site and in gathering the dispersed of Israel, then he has in fact [as a result of his success] proven himself to be the Messiah. He will then arrange the whole world to serve only God, as it is said: "For then shall I create a pure language for the peoples that they may all call upon the name of God and serve him with one accord" (Zeph. 3:9).
>
> Let no one think that in the days of the Messiah anything of the natural course of the world will cease or that any innovation will be

introduced into creation. Rather, the world will continue in its accustomed course. The words of Isaiah: "The wolf shall dwell with the lamb and the panther shall lie down with the kid" (Isa. 11:6) are a parable and an allegory which must be understood to mean that Israel will dwell securely even among the wicked of the heathen nations who are compared to a wolf and a panther. For they will all accept the true faith and will no longer rob or destroy. Likewise, all similar scriptural passages dealing with the Messiah must be regarded as figurative. Only in the Days of the Messiah will everyone know what the metaphors mean and to what they refer. The sages said: "The only difference between this world and the Days of the Messiah is the subjection of Israel to the nations." [23]

From the simple meaning of the words of the prophets it appears that at the beginning of the Days of the Messiah the war between Gog and Magog will take place. . . . [With regard to these Messianic wars and the coming of the prophet Elijah before the End, Maimonides then continues:] Concerning all these things and others like them, no one knows how they will come about until they actually happen, since the words of the prophets on these matters are not clear. Even the sages have no tradition regarding them but allow themselves to be guided by the texts. Hence there are differences of opinion on the subject. In any case, the order and details of these events are not religious dogmas. Therefore a person should never occupy himself a great deal with the legendary accounts nor spend much time on the Midrashim dealing with these and similar matters. He should not regard them as of prime importance,[24] since devoting himself to them leads neither to the fear nor to the love of God. . . .

The sages and prophets longed for the days of the Messiah not in order to rule over the world and not to bring the heathens under their control, not to be exalted by the nations, or even to eat, drink, and rejoice. All they wanted was to have time for the Torah and its wisdom with no one to oppress or disturb them.

In that age there will be neither famine nor war, nor envy nor strife, for there will be an abundance of worldly goods. The whole world will be occupied solely with the knowledge of God. Therefore the Children of Israel will be great sages; they will know hidden things and attain an understanding of their Creator to the extent of human capability, as it is said: "For the earth shall be full of the knowledge of God as the waters cover the sea" (Isa. 11:9).

In these measured words of a great master every sentence has a polemical purpose, whether or not it is openly expressed. Their sober prudence codifies the protest against apocalypticism, against the rampant fantasy of the Aggadists, and against the authors of the popular Midrashim in which the stages of the End and the catastrophes of nature and history which accompany it are described. With a grand gesture all of this is waived aside. Maimonides knows nothing of Messianic miracles or other signs. Negatively, the Messianic age brings about freedom from the enslavement of Israel, and, positively, freedom for the knowledge of God. But to this end it is necessary to abrogate neither the law of moral order (the revelation of the Torah) nor the law of natural order. Neither creation nor revelation undergo any kind of change. The binding force of the law does not cease and the lawful order of nature does not give way to any miracles. For Maimonides, the intervention of heaven on earth constitutes no criterion for the legitimacy of the Messiah and of his mission. He will allow only one criterion: whether the Messiah succeeds in his endeavors.[25] The Messiah must prove his identity to justified skeptics not by cosmic signs and miracles, but by historical success. Nothing in any supernatural constitution of his nature guarantees his success and makes it possible to recognize him with certainty until he has proven his identity.[26] Every crucial aspect of the Messianic age which he inaugurates is emphasized as restorative. Anything leading beyond this, specifically the utopian state of the world, is rejected with a powerful: no. Only contemplation of the Torah and the knowledge of God within a world that otherwise operates entirely according to natural laws remains, as indicated above, the one irreducible utopian element. And this is quite understandable. For Maimonides, the task of man since the Revelation has been clearly defined and man's fulfilling it is not dependent upon the coming of the Messiah. As a state of things here on earth, the Messianic age is no highest good but only a preliminary stage in the final transition to the world-to-come; the immortal soul enters this world after its severance from the body, in proportion to the share of eternity it has gained through rational activity in this life. Thus, since the end of the individual life leads it anyhow to the threshold of the longed-for final state—which in reality is not a future world but an eternal present, the immanent logic of Maimonides' general position does not in the least require an effort to bring about the end of world history in order for man to fulfill his task.[27] Messianism, in fact, is not a postulate of his philosophical thought; regardless of how he may twist it to fit his rationalism, it remains even in this minimal state of utopianism a pure element of the stock of tradition. It is tied to the concerns of Maimonides' systematic thought only via this earlier mentioned highly presumptuous identification of the contemplative life with the knowledge of God demanded by the prophets—but which in the prophetic sense always contained an active and moral element. The Messianic age eases the conditions under which the salvation of the soul can be found in the fulfillment of the Torah and the knowledge of God, but this facilitation is really all that here lends the restorative ideal a faint utopian shimmer.

Maimonides regards the Messianic age as restorative and as a public event realized in the community. It is not to be confused with the conception of the salvation of each individual soul, which has nothing at all to do with the Messianic and can be achieved without its assistance. Earlier writings of Maimonides, above all his *Epistle to Yemen* (1172), directed to a community in which a strong Messianic movement had come into being, show that he had a deep sensitivity for the national elements of this expectation, even where he very carefully tries to weaken them. Here the bitter account of oppressions and persecutions by the nations, which is almost totally eliminated in the rational formulation of his code of law, remains present in his mind, and he consoles the Yemenite Jews by telling them that God will cause the false religions to perish and reveal the Messiah precisely when the nations would least expect it. But Maimonides nowhere recognizes a causal relationship between the coming of the Messiah and human conduct. It is not Israel's repentance which brings about the redemption; rather, because the eruption of redemption is to occur by divine decree, at the last moment there also erupts a movement of repentance in Israel itself. The Messianic restoration, which is tied to no idea of progress toward the redemption, is and remains a miracle—though of course not a miracle that occurs outside of nature and her laws, but a miracle because it has been previously announced by the prophets to affirm God's dominion in the world. The Messianic age is a free-will gift of God, but it is a gift which has been promised, and that raises its beginnings above the level of nature, even if they do occur under natural conditions. Maimonides did not attempt a purely philosophical justification of the Messianic idea on the basis of his ontology or ethics. Man is in principle completely capable of mastering his task and thereby mastering his future—in contrast to the apocalyptists who do not attribute this ability to man. The anti-apocalyptic vision of Maimonides says only that the Messianic age will strengthen man's capability by favorable conditions of universal peace and universal happiness, but not that it will make possible that capability for the first time.

Thus the dramatic element, which lent apocalypticism so much vitality, is, of course, lost.[28] Maimonides does not deny in advance the traditions and prophecies regarding the catastrophic character of the redemption—indeed, he considers them a possibility here and there in his writings—but he decides to forego them. He leaves them as sealed enigmas which will be disclosed only in the events themselves and which allow of no anticipation. He pulls back from this realm and tries to forbid it to everyone else. The monumental simplicity and decisiveness with which Maimonides formulates this attitude in no way vitiates the polemical character of this effort. Maimonides knows that he stands on an advance outpost which has been held only by relatively few before him. He is not concerned about the real continuation of an unbroken tradition but about gaining the acceptance of a new concept of the redemption which is formed from a selection of congenial elements in the tradition. Saadia's *Book of Beliefs and Opinions* still contains the opposite of Maimonides' opinion regarding the Messianic idea, to say nothing of the works of other Messianists of the Middle Ages who must have gone directly *contre coeur* to Maimonides: for example, the detailed presentation of Messianism in Abraham bar Hiyya's *Scroll of the Revealer* from the early twelfth century.[29] But since the time of Maimonides this tendency has not vanished from the forefront of discussions within Judaism.

The rival tendencies of apocalyptic and rationalistic Messianism, as we might expect, define their differences on the basis of contradictory biblical exegeses. Exegesis becomes a weapon in constructing and destroying apocalypses. The apocalyptists can never get enough of biblical sayings which they can relate to the Last Days: to their dawning and their content. They draw upon everything: not just texts which manifestly deal with the Last Days, but a great deal else, and the more the better. The more colorful and the more complete the picture, the greater the possibility of creating a dramatic montage of the individual stages of the redemption and the plenitude of its content. There has been no lack of mystics who on the basis of their assumptions regarding the inherently infinite meaning of Scripture concluded that one of these levels of meaning in every biblical word contained a reference to, or a prefiguration of, the Messianic End. Thus apocalyptic exegesis could be applied without exception. There exists a commentary on the Psalter which carries such interpretation through nearly completely. It stems from the period shortly after the expulsion from Spain when the apocalyptic waves rose especially high in the agitated hearts of the people.[30]

Their opponents do exactly the opposite. As much as possible, they try to refer biblical passages not to Messianic, but to some other circumstances. They detest typology. The predictions of the prophets have for the most part already come to pass in events at the time of Ezra, Zerubbabel, the Maccabees, and the period of the Second Temple in general. Many passages which the one group interprets to refer to the Messiah are interpreted by the other as predictions regarding the destiny of the entire Jewish people (like that famous chapter 53 in Isaiah, which speaks of the suffering servant of God). The second tendency, then, is to restrict the valid scope of the Messianic as much as possible. However, there is also an apologetic impulse at work which must not be underestimated. The representatives of the rational tendencies stood in the forefront of the theological defenses mounted against the claims of the Church. The more biblical exegesis could reduce the purely Messianic element, the better it was for the defenses of the Jewish position which were often made necessary by the application of external force. But the apocalyptists were not in the least interested in apologetics. Their thought has its locus beyond such disputes that occur on the borders, and they are not concerned with fortifying the frontiers. This is no doubt the reason why the statements of the apocalyptists often appear freer and more genuine than those of their opponents who often enough must take into account the diplomatic necessities of anti-Christian polemics and therefore do not always permit penetration to the true motives of their thought. In rare individuals the two tendencies come together. The most important codifications of the Messianic idea in later Judaism are the writings of Isaac Abravanel (ca. 1500) and *The Victory of Israel* by the "High Rabbi Loew," Judah Loew ben Bezalel of Prague (1599). The authors are not visionaries but writers who endeavor to embrace as a whole the legacy of ideas which has been transmitted in such contradictory traditions. Despite their otherwise reticent manner, they richly avail themselves of the apocalyptic traditions.

VI

I have endeavored to shed some light on the significance of two major currents for an understanding of the Messianic idea in Judaism. Only in passing have I touched on the specific forms which the Messianic idea took in the thinking of the Jewish mystics, and I have dealt not at all with the specific problematics which the question of the redemption had to assume in the thought of the Kabbalists for whom Judaism was more than anything else a *corpus symbolicum,* a symbolic representation of the world's reality and of man's task within it. I discuss these matters in the next essay and will not repeat myself here.[31] The Kabbalists were of course concerned with the mystical meaning of the redemption in which the true meaning of the event is revealed for the first time. (Incidentally, in keeping with what I said at the outset, the concept is not thereby in the least divested of its historical, national, and social character.) They too must deal with the question of the restorative and the utopian elements in the redemption: it is they who aften give special emphasis to the relation of the End to the beginning of all things. The restorative factor here very often receives not so much a purely historical character as that of the restoration of an interrupted initial unity and harmony of all things. But it is of course true that a restored unity simply is not the original one, and so it is not surprising that the utopian element, in multiple forms, expresses itself in new formulations or symbols. In the redemption lights shine forth from within the universe which until then had remained hidden inside their source.[32] There are locked-up realms of the divine which will not be opened until that time, and they make the state of redemption infinitely richer and more fulfilled than any initial state.

The utopian content of the Messianic redemption as a non-restorative state of the world is continued in the Jewish mystical tradition of the Kabbalists and Hasidim. It is preserved, above all, in an awareness of the strictly paradoxical nature—from our point of view—of the renewed Messianic existence, about which the mystics have written so much. The arrival of the Messiah himself is tied to impossible, or at any rate highly paradoxical, conditions, probably never expressed in a more melancholy and humanly contorted way than in this sharpened expression of a saying from the *Zohar:* the Messiah will not come until the tears of Esau will be exhausted.[33] Of all the conditions for redemption, truly the most surprising and at the same time the most impossible! For the tears of Esau are those which, according to Genesis 27:38, he shed when Jacob deceived him to gain Isaac's blessing. There has never been a lack of such profound dicta. Among the most famous sayings of this kind are those of Rabbi Israel of Rizhin, that in the days of the Messiah man will no longer quarrel with his fellow but with himself, or his bold suggestion that the Messianic world will be a world without images, "in which the image and its object can no longer be related"—which apparently means that a new mode of being will emerge which cannot be pictorially represented. All these are forms by which the utopian element gives evidence of its continuing power, and the writings of the Kabbalists are full of attempts to fathom its unfathomable depths.

One word more, by way of conclusion, should be said about a point which, to my mind, has generally received too little attention in discussions of the Messianic idea. What I have in mind is the price demanded by Messianism, the price which the Jewish people has had to pay out of its own substance for this idea which it handed over to the world. The magnitude of the Messianic idea corresponds to the endless powerlessness in Jewish history during all the centuries of exile, when it was unprepared to come forward onto the plane of world history. There's something preliminary, something provisional about Jewish history; hence its inability to give of itself entirely. For the Messianic idea is not only consolation and hope. Every attempt to realize it tears open the abysses which lead each of its manifestations *ad absurdum.* There is something grand about living in hope, but at the same time there is something profoundly unreal about it. It diminishes the singular worth of the individual, and he can never fulfill himself, because the incompleteness of his endeavors eliminates precisely what constitutes its highest value. Thus in Judaism the Messianic idea has compelled a *life lived in deferment,* in which nothing can be done definitively, nothing can be irrevocably accomplished. One may say, perhaps, the Messianic idea is the real anti-existentialist idea. Precisely understood, there is nothing concrete which can be accomplished by the unredeemed. This makes for the greatness of Messianism, but also for its constitutional weakness. Jewish so-called *Existenz* possesses a tension that never finds true release; it never burns itself out. And when in our history it does discharge, then it is foolishly decried (or, one might say, unmasked) as "pseudo-Messianism." The blazing landscape of redemption (as if it were a point of focus) has concentrated in itself the historical outlook of Judaism. Little wonder that overtones of Messianism have accompanied the modern Jewish readiness for irrevocable action in the concrete realm, when it set out on the utopian return to Zion. It is a readiness which no longer allows itself to be fed on hopes. Born out of the horror and destruction that was Jewish history in our generation, it is bound to history itself and not to meta-history; it has not given itself up totally to Messianism. Whether or not Jewish history will be able to endure this entry into the concrete realm without perishing in the crisis of the Messianic claim which has virtually been conjured up—that is the question which out of his great and dangerous past the Jew of this age poses to his present and to his future.

The Messianic Idea
in Kabbalism

THE NINETEENTH CENTURY, and nineteenth-century Judaism, have bequeathed to the modern mind a complex of ideas about Messianism that have led to distortions and counterfeits from which it is by no means easy to free ourselves. We have been taught that the Messianic idea is part and parcel of the idea of the progress of the human race in the universe, that redemption is achieved by man's unassisted and continuous progress, leading to the ultimate liberation of all the goodness and nobility hidden within him. This, in essence, is the content which the Messianic ideal acquired under the combined dominance of religious and political liberalism—the result of an attempt to adapt the Messianic conceptions of the prophets and of Jewish religious tradition to the ideals of the French Revolution.

Traditionally, however, the Messianic idea in Judaism was not so cheerful; the coming of the Messiah was supposed to shake the foundations of the world. In the view of the prophets and Aggadists, redemption would only follow upon a universal revolutionary disturbance, unparalleled disasters in which history would be dislodged and destroyed. The nineteenth-century view is blind to this catastrophic aspect. It looks only to progress toward infinite perfection. In probing into the roots of this new conception of the Messianic ideal as man's infinite progress and perfectibility, we find, surprisingly, that they stem from the Kabbalah.

When we study the Messianic ideal we simultaneously study the nature of the Diaspora, the Galut. The medieval Jew thought of redemption as a state that would be brought about by the reversal of all that had produced Galut. The Messianic ideal of the prophets of the Bible and other classical Jewish sources provided no precedent for this view. Both prophets and Aggadists conceived of redemption as a new state of the world wholly unrelated to anything that had gone before, not the product of a purifying development of the preceding state. Hence for them the world unredeemed and the world in process of redemption were separated by an abyss. History was not a *development* toward any goal. History would reach its terminus, and the new state that ensued would be the result of a totally new manifestation of the divine. In the Prophets this stage is called the "Day of the Lord," which is wholly unlike other days: it can only arrive after the old structure has been razed. Accordingly, upon the advent of the "Day of the Lord" all that man has built up in history will be destroyed.

Classical Jewish tradition is fond of emphasizing the catastrophic strain in redemption. If we look at the tenth chapter of the tractate Sanhedrin, where the Talmudists discuss the question of redemption at length, we see that to them it means a colossal uprooting, destruction, revolution, disaster, with nothing of development or progress about it. "The Son of David [the Messiah] will come only in a generation wholly guilty or a generation wholly innocent"—a condition beyond the realm of human possibility. Or "the Son of David will not come until the kingdom is subverted to heresy." These hopes for redemption always show a very strong nationalistic bent. Liberation of Israel is the essence, but it will march in step with the liberation of the whole world.

It is well known that the whole broad area of Messianic expectations which appear in the aggadic tradition and in Midrashim was not deemed worthy of systematic treatment by the great Jewish philosophers and theologians of the Middle Ages (with the sole exception of Saadia Gaon in the tenth century). Thus popular imagination and the religious impulse were left free to dream their own dreams and think their own thoughts, without encountering the opposition of the enlightened part of the community. A whole popular literature grew up in the Middle Ages which prophesied the final apocalyptic war that would bring history to an end, and vividly pictured redemption as the crowning event in the national and communal saga. In this way, Messianic expectation, looked down upon by the intellectual aristocracy, struck roots among the masses of the people, diverting their minds from efforts to solve the problems of the present to the utopian realm of the "Day of the Lord."

The early Kabbalists—from the twelfth century until the expulsion from Spain in 1492—had little to add to the popular myth of redemption, for their faces were turned not to the End of

Days but to the primal days of Creation. They hoped for a particular and mystical redemption for each individual, to be achieved by escaping from the turbulence, perplexity, chaos, and storms of the actual course of history to the beginnings of history.

These early Kabbalists assigned special importance to such questions as: What is the nature of Creation? and: Whence have we come? For they believed that to know the "ladder of ascent," or, more precisely, the ladder of descent, the order of rungs which link all creatures downward from the source of Creation, from God, "the root of all roots," down to our own straitened existence —to know the secret of our beginnings, whence the imperfections of this distorted and dark world in which we are stranded, with all the storms and perturbations and afflictions within it—to know all this would teach us the way back to "our inward home." Just as we have descended, just as every creature descends by its particular path, so is it able also to ascend, and this ascent aims at a return to the origin of Creation and not to its end. Here, then, we have a view of redemption in which the foundations of the world are not moved by great Messianic disturbances. Instead, the world itself is rejected by ascent upon the rungs of the ladder which rises to the heavenly mansions in the bosom of God. The Kabbalist who was prepared to follow this path of inwardness would be liberated and redeemed by the fact that he himself in the depths of his own soul would seek a way of return to God, to the source whence he was hewn.

The masterpiece of Spanish Kabbalism is the *Zohar,* which was written in the last quarter of the thirteenth century in Castile, the central part of Spain. In this book Kabbalah and Messianism are not yet dovetailed into a genuinely organic whole. On the subject of redemption we find utterances that give expression in new form and with the addition of interesting details, but without essential change, to the prophecies of the End recorded in the popular apocalyptic literature referred to above.

The *Zohar* follows talmudic Aggadah in seeing redemption not as the product of inward progress in the historical world, but as a supernatural miracle involving the gradual illumination of the world by the light of the Messiah. It begins with an initial gleam and ends with full revelation: the light of the Messiah.

At the time when the Holy One, blessed be He, shall set Israel upright and bring them up out of Galut He will open to them a small and scant window of light, and then He will open another that is larger, until He will open to them the portals on high to the four directions of the universe. So shall it be with all that the Holy One, blessed be He, does for Israel and for the righteous among them, so shall it be and not at a single instant, for neither does healing come to a sick man at a single instant, but gradually, until he is made strong.

The Gentiles (who are designated Esau or Edom), however, will suffer the opposite fate. They received their light in this world at a single stroke, but it will depart from them gradually until Israel shall grow strong and destroy them. And when the spirit of uncleanliness shall pass from the world and the divine light shall shine upon Israel without let or hinderance, all things will return to their proper order—to the state of perfection which prevailed in the Garden of Eden before Adam sinned. The worlds will all be joined one to another and nothing will separate Creator from creature. All will rise upward by ascents of the spirit, and creatures will be purified until they behold the Shekhinah "eye to eye."

In the last section of the *Zohar,* this prophecy is supplemented by another foretelling the liberation of Israel from all the limitations which the yoke of the Torah has laid upon her in Galut. The author expresses his vision in the imagery of the Tree of Life and the Tree of Knowledge (from which death depends). Since Adam sinned, the world has been governed not by the Tree of Life (as it properly should be) but by the Tree of Knowledge. The Tree of Life is entirely and exclusively holy, with no admixture of evil, no adulteration or impurity or death or limitation. The Tree of Knowledge, on the other hand, contains both good and evil, purity and impurity, virtue and vice, and therefore under its rule there are things forbidden and things permitted, things fit for consumption and things unfit, the clean and the unclean. In an unredeemed world the Torah is revealed in positive and negative commandments and all that these imply, but in the redeemed future uncleanliness and unfitness and death will be abolished. In an unredeemed world the Torah must be interpreted in manifold ways—literal, allegorical, mystical; but in the redeemed future it will be revealed in the pure spirituality of the Tree of Life, without the "clothing" it put on after Adam sinned. It will be wholly inward, entirely holy.

In this conception, redemption becomes a spiritual revolution which will uncover the mystic meaning, the "true interpretation," of the Torah. Thus a mystic utopia takes the place of the national and secular utopia of the early writers. But the author of these latest sections bestows special emphasis on the opposition between the Torah of the Galut and the Torah of the redemption without indicating any transition between them. The two states of the world were still separated by a chasm which history could never bridge.

The efforts of the Spanish Kabbalists had been bent upon a new understanding of Judaism. They re-examined Jewish life, the life of the commandments, the world of the Halakhah, no less than of the Aggadah, delving into the mystery of the Torah, of man's works in this world, of his relation to God. In these matters their convictions had no vital connection with the theme of redemption. But on the heels of the expulsion from Spain, the Kabbalah underwent a pronounced shift which was of momentous consequences for Jewish history generally, even more than for Kabbalah itself. Just as the Kabbalah of the thirteenth century sought to interpret Judaism in a way that would enable a thirteenth- or fourteenth-century man to be a Jew according to the religious conceptions of that period, so after the expulsion from Spain the Kabbalah sought to provide an answer for questions which arose from an event which had uprooted one of the principal branches of Judaism.

But the attempt to reinterpret the nature of the universe and of Judaism in the light of this experience was not made in the years immediately following the catastrophe of 1492. The Kabbalists, like their fellow Jews in general, believed that complete redemption was around the corner. In the expulsion from Spain they saw the beginnings of the "travail of the Messiah"—the beginnings of those disasters and frightful afflictions which would terminate history and usher in the redemption. There was no need for new religious concepts and principles; the end had already come. At any hour, any moment, the gates of redemption might swing open, and men's hearts must now be awakened to meet the future. For the span of one generation, during the forty years after the Spanish expulsion, we find a deep Messianic excitement and tension almost as intense as before the eruption of the Sabbatian movement. Traditional principles remained untouched; the teaching of the early Kabbalah continued without basic change; the important thing now was propaganda, the dissemination of the apocalyptic message.

The master propagandist of this acute Messianism in the generation after the Spanish expulsion was Abraham ben Eliezer ha-Levi, a rabbi from Spain who lived in Jerusalem and was one of the great Kabbalists of his day. On the basis of all Hebrew literature, from the book of Daniel to the *Zohar* and the writings of the medieval sages, he proved that the travails of redemption had already begun in 1492 and would end in full glory in 1531. We have other such ingenious books dating from the same period. The teaching of one of them, *Kaf ha-Ketoret* ("Spoon of Incense"), an anonymous commentary on the book of Psalms (which is extant only in manuscripts), runs like this:

According to the words of the sages the Torah has seventy aspects, and there are seventy aspects to each and every verse; in truth, therefore, the aspects are infinite. In each generation one of these aspects is revealed, and so in our generation the aspect which the Torah reveals to us concerns matters of redemption. Each and every verse can be understood and explained in reference to redemption.

According to this author, every single verse in the Book of Psalms refers to the imminent redemption, and he declares that all the lyrics in the Psalms are battle songs of the final apocalyptic war. That a devout Jew should consider the Psalms as battle hymns is evidence of the depth of the new feelings which had seized the Jews upon the expulsion. But the implication is still that the notions of Galut and redemption do not require new interpretation.

The redemption, however, did not come, only disaster and travail, and all these powerful expectations were frustrated. And in the measure that hope was disappointed in the external world, the spiritual effects of the Spanish expulsion sought expression in the deeper reaches of the soul. The weight of the event gradually sank, as it were, from the outer strata of man to the deeper strata in the soul, to more fertile strata out of which are formed new visions and new symbols. The prophecy of the imminent end waned, and men began to think the matter out anew. Only then did there begin a movement which involved setting up a new religious climate around the ideas of Galut and redemption.

What now took place can be defined as the merging of two hitherto disparate forces—the Messianic theme and Kabbalah—into a unified whole. In other words, the Messianic theme became a productive element in the speculations of the mystics themselves. They began to seek explanations for the expulsion from Spain: What had happened? What brought on the affliction and suffering? What is the nature of this gloomy world of Galut? They sought an answer to such questions in terms of their basic mystical outlook, which regarded all external being as the sign and symbol

of the inward being that speaks through it. And by connecting
the notions of Galut and redemption with the central question of
the essence of the universe, they managed to elaborate a system
which transformed the exile of the people of Israel into an exile
of the whole world, and the redemption of their people into a
universal, cosmic redemption.

The result was that the Kabbalah succeeded in establishing its
predominance over the broad masses of the Jewish people. This
is a phenomenon which has always puzzled scholars. How did a
movement so highly mystical, individual, and aristocratic as the
Kabbalah become a social and historical force, a dynamic power
in history? At least part of the explanation is that the sixteenth-
century Kabbalah found in the expulsion itself a way of answering the most urgent question confronting the Jews of that period:
the nature of Galut and the nature of redemption.

This answer was formulated during the span of a single generation, from 1540 to 1580, by a small, albeit very intense, congregation of saints, devotees, priests, and reformers in the little
Palestinian town of Safed. Since the question of Galut and redemption was everywhere troublesome in the same measure, and
since the various Jewish communities throughout the world were
still more or less homogeneous, it was possible for the definitive
answer given at Safed to be accepted as relevant in all parts of
the Galut.

Of the many systems formulated in Safed, the one which was
most highly respected and which achieved authoritative status,
both among mystics and the masses of the people, was the Kabbalah of Rabbi Isaac Luria Ashkenazi (1534-72), later called the
Ari ("the Lion").

The Ari's basic conceptions are pictorial in character and work
upon the imagination, and though their original formulation was
quite simple, they lent themselves to extremely subtle and profound interpretation. The Galut the Ari's Kabbalah saw as a
terrible and pitiless state permeating and embittering all of Jewish
life, but Galut was also the condition of the universe as a whole,
even of the deity. This is an extremely bold idea, and when the
Lurianic Kabbalists came to speak of it, they shuddered at their
own audacity, hedging it with such deprecatory expressions as
"one might suppose," "as it were," "to stun the ear." Nevertheless, the idea was developed through the three central conceptions
which shape the Lurianic system: limitation, destruction, reparation.

According to the Ari and his school, the universe was created by an action of which the ancients generally were ignorant. God did not reveal Himself overtly in creation, but confined and concealed Himself, and by so doing enabled the world to be revealed. Then came the second act, the fashioning of the universal "emanations," the creations of the worlds, the revelation of the divine as mankind's diety, as the Creator, as the God of Israel.

The original phase of concealment carries many implications. There is voluntary restraint and limitation, something related to the quality of harshness and rigidity in God, for all concentration and limitation imply the functioning of this quality. There is ruthlessness toward Himself, for He exiled Himself from boundless infinity to a more concentrated infinity. There is a profound inward Galut, not the Galut of one of the creatures but of God Himself, who limited Himself and thereby made place for the universe. This is the Lurianic concept of limitation or concentration, *tzimtzum,* which supplanted the simpler idea of creation held by the Spanish Kabbalists.

To the question of how the world came into being the Spanish Kabbalists had proffered their doctrine of emanations. From the abundance of His being, from the treasure laid up within Himself, God "emanated" the *sefirot,* those divine luminaries, those modes and stages through which He manifests Himself externally. His resplendent light emanates from stage to stage, and the light spreads to ever wider spheres and becomes light ever more thickened. Through the descent of the lights from their infinite source all the worlds were emanated and created; our world is but the last and outward shell of the layers of divine glory. The process of Creation is thus something like progressive revelation.

In the system of the Ari, the notion of concentration supplies a greater complexity. In order for a thing other than God to come into being, God must necessarily retreat within Himself. Only afterward does He emit beams of light into the vacuum of limitation and build our world. Moreover, at each stage there is need for both the force of limitation and the force of emanation. Without limitation everything would revert to the divine, and without emanation nothing would come into being. Nothing that exists can be uniform, everything has this basic Janus character—the limiting force and the emanating force, retreat and propagation. Only the concurrence of the two disparate motifs can produce being.

The concept of limitation seems paradoxical, but it has vitality;

it expresses the notion of a living God—a God thought of as a living organism. But let us consider the continuation of this process.

God was revealed in His potencies and His various attributes (justice, mercy, etc., etc.). By these powers through which He willed to effect Creation He formed "vessels" destined to serve the manifestation of His own being. (It is a binding rule that whatever wishes to act or manifest itself requires garbs and vessels, for without them it would revert to infinity which has no differentiation and no stages.) The divine light entered these vessels in order to take forms appropriate to their function in creation, but the vessels could not contain the light and thus were broken. This is the phase which the Kabbalists call the "breaking of the vessels." And what was the consequence of the shattering of the vessels? The light was dispersed. Much of it returned to its source; some portions, or "sparks," fell downward and were scattered, some rose upward.

This "breaking" introduces a dramatic aspect into the process of Creation, and it can explain the Galut. Henceforth nothing is perfect. The divine light which should have subsisted in specific forms and in places appointed for it from the beginning is no longer in its proper place because the vessels were broken, and thereafter all things went awry. There is nothing that was not damaged by the breaking. Nothing is in the place appointed for it; everything is either below or above, but not where it should be. In other words, all being is in Galut.

And this is not all. Into the deep abyss of the forces of evil, the forces of darkness and impurity which the Kabbalists call "shells" or "offscourings," there fell, as a result of the breaking of the vessels, forces of holiness, sparks of divine light. Hence there is a Galut of the divine itself, of the "sparks of the Shekhinah": "These sparks of holiness are bound in fetters of steel in the depths of the shells, and yearningly aspire to rise to their source but cannot avail to do so until they have support"—so says Rabbi Hayyim Vital, a disciple of Luria.

Here we have a cosmic picture of Galut, not the Galut of the people of Israel alone, but the Galut of the Shekhinah at the very inception of its being. All that befalls in the world is only an expression of this primal and fundamental Galut. All existence, including, "as it were," God, subsists in Galut. Such is the state of creation after the breaking of the vessels.

Next comes reparation, the third juncture in the great process:

the breaking can be healed. The primal flaw must be mended so that all things can return to their proper place, to their original posture. Man and God are partners in this enterprise. After the original breaking God began the process of reparation, but He left its completion to man. If Adam had not sinned the world would have entered the Messianic state on the first Sabbath after creation, with no historical process whatever. Adam's sin returned the universe, which had almost been amended, to its former broken state. What happened at the breaking of the vessels happened again. Again the worlds fell. Adam—who at first was a cosmic, spiritual, supernal being, a soul which contained all souls —fell from his station, whereupon the divine light in his soul was dispersed. Henceforward even the light of the soul would be imprisoned in a dungeon with the sparks of the Shekhinah under a single doom. All being was again scattered in Galut. In all the expanse of creation there is imperfection, flaw, Galut.

The Galut of Israel is only the expression—compelling, concrete, and extremely cruel—of this phase of the world before reparation and redemption. The predicament of Israel, then, is not a historical accident but inherent in the world's being, and it is in Israel's power to repair the universal flaw. By amending themselves, the Jewish people can also amend the world, in its visible and invisible aspects alike. How can this be done? Through the Torah and the commandments. These are the secret remedies which by their spiritual action move things to their ordained station, free the imprisoned divine light and raise it to its proper level, liberate the sparks of Shekhinah from the domination of the "offscourings," complete the figure of the Creator to the full measure of His stature, which is now wanting in perfection, "as it were," because of the Galut of the Shekhinah. Through the "discernment" of good and evil, a decisive boundary is fixed between the areas of the holy and the unclean which became mixed up at the original breaking and then again when Adam sinned. Galut, then, is a mission for emendation and clarification. The children of Israel "lift up the sparks" not only from the places trodden by their feet in their Galut, but also, by their deeds, from the cosmos itself.

Every man amends his own soul, and by the process of transmigration that of his neighbor. This is a crucial item in the doctrine of the "selection" of goodness from its exile in the spheres of evil. Belief in transmigration spread as a popular belief only upon the heels of the movement which emanated from Safed from the middle of the sixteenth century onward. The causes are easy to understand. In the system of the new Kabbalists, transmigration was not an appendage but an inextricable basic element. Transmigration, too, symbolized the state of the unamended world, the confusion of the orders of creation which was consequent upon Adam's sin. Just as bodies are in Galut, so also there is inward Galut for souls. And "Galut of souls" is transmigration. Isaiah Horovitz, one of the great Kabbalists of this school, writes: "In the blessing 'Sound Thou a great shofar for our liberation' we pray for the ingathering of the souls scattered to the four corners of the earth in their transmigrations . . . and also in 'Gather Thou our scattered from amongst the nations'; these apply to the ingathering of the Galut of souls which have been dispersed." Every living being is subject to the law of transmigration from form to form. There is no being, not even the lowliest, which may not serve as a prison for the sparks of the "banished souls" seeking restoration from their Galut.

In this system, redemption is synonymous with emendation or restoration. After we have fulfilled our duty and the emendation is completed, and all things occupy their appropriate places in the universal scheme, then redemption will come *of itself*. Redemption merely signifies the perfect state, a flawless and harmonious world in which everything occupies its proper place. Hence the Messianic ideal, the ideal of redemption, receives a totally new aspect. We all work, or are at least expected to work, for the amendment of the world and the "selection" of good and evil. This provides an ideology for the commandments and the life of *Halakhah*—an ideology which connects traditional Judaism with the hidden forces operating in the world at large. A man who observes a commandment is no longer merely observing a commandment: his act has a universal significance, he is amending something.

This conception of redemption is no longer catastrophic: when duty has been fulfilled the son of David, the Messiah, will come of himself, for his appearance at the End of Days is only a symbol for the completion of a process, a testimony that the world has in fact been amended. Thus it becomes possible to avoid the "travails of the Messiah." The transition from the state of imperfection to the state of perfection (which may still be very difficult) will nevertheless take place without revolution and disaster and great affliction.

Here, for the first time, we have an organic connection between the state of redemption and the state preceding it. Redemption now appears not as the opposite of all that came before, but as the logical consequence of the historical process. We are all involved in one Messianic venture, and we all are called up to do our part.

The Messiah himself will not bring the redemption; rather he symbolizes the advent of redemption, the completion of the task of emendation. It is therefore not surprising that little importance is given to the human personality of the Messiah in Lurianic literature, for the Kabbalists had no special need of a personal Messiah. But like all mystics, they were at once conservatives and radicals. Since tradition spoke of a personal Messiah they accepted him while revolutionizing the content of the traditional idea.

We have, then, a complete array of conceptions in the new Kabbalah that show an inner logic. Galut and redemption are not historical manifestations peculiar to Israel, but manifestations of all being, up to and including the mystery of divinity itself. The Messiah here becomes the entire people of Israel rather than an individual Redeemer: the people of Israel as a whole prepares itself to amend the primal flaw. Redemption is a consequence of antecedents and not of revolution, and though the redemption of Israel in the national and secular sense remained a very real ideal, it was widened and deepened by making it the symbol of the redemption of the whole world, the restoration of the universe to the state it was to have attained when the Creator planned its creation.

The new Kabbalah had a very important function in restoring to the Jew his sense of responsibility and his dignity. He could now look upon his state, whether in Galut or in the Messianic hope, as the symbol of a profound mystery which reached as high as God, and he could relate the fundamental experiences of his life to all cosmic being and integration. He saw no contradiction between the nationalist and secular aspect of redemption, and its mystic and universalist aspect. In the conviction of the Kabbalists the former served to adumbrate and symbolize the latter. The anguish of the historical experience of Galut was not blurred by this new interpretation; on the contrary, it may be said to have been emphasized and sharpened. But now there was added a conviction that the secret of Israel's anguish was rooted in the hidden sources of the vital sustenance of all creation.

The Crisis of Tradition
in Jewish Messianism

I

WE HAVE SET a great theme for ourselves at this Eranos Conference: "Tradition and the Present." I should like to examine it here with regard to what seems to me an especially precise and enlightening phenomenon.

There are three ways in which tradition evolves and develops in history. It can be carried forward with a retention of continuity; it can be transformed through a natural process of metamorphosis and assume a new configuration; and finally, it can be subjected to a break which is associated with the rejection of the tradition itself.

In our time it is the break that stands in the foreground. Our attention is directed to the abandonment of tradition, even to the point of its total negation, in the interest of new construction. This break is the possibility most emphasized by those to whom we today listen most readily: the impetuous youth. But in their case as well the question which will force itself upon us during the course of the discussion remains: What persists even after the break? Is the break in a tradition really a break? Does the tradition not somehow manage to continue in new formulas and configurations even if metamorphosis is seemingly rejected? Is there anything that endures through all of this? And can this enduring element be formulated? Before I begin speaking about the specific problematics of the crisis of tradition and the radical forms in which it has appeared in Judaism under certain conditions, I should like to fill in the background against which my exposition will take place.

Historical Judaism represents a classical form of religious community, one which is most emphatically grounded upon tradition and in which tradition was the vehicle of the vital energies which found their expression through it. Six years ago I spoke at length before this same conference on the meaning and the significance of the concept of tradition in Judaism. Here I should first like to review in brief what at that time I developed in larger scope.[1]

The concepts of revelation and tradition constitute two poles around which Judaism has grouped itself during two millennia. In the view that prevailed in the talmudic development of Judaism, revelation and tradition were both manifestations of Torah, of "teaching" on the shaping of human life. Revelation here comes to be regarded as the "Written Torah," which is represented by the Pentateuch, and as the tradition, which as "Oral Torah" serves as its ongoing interpretation, dealing with the possibility for application and execution of the revelation in historical time. The word of God in revelation, which is crystallized in the demands of the law, needs tradition in order to be capable of application. In the course of the history of the Jewish religion these categories of revelation and of the tradition in which revelation is refracted in the medium of history have become clearly established and have thereby pushed out all other forms. Thus there arose a traditionalism par excellence which was, however, accompanied and undergirded by powerful mystical accents.

Revelation in Judaism is considered the voice which resounds from Sinai throughout the world, a voice which, although it can be heard, is not immediately meaningful. Rather it represents simply that which is capable of assuming meaning, which needs interpretation in the medium of language in order to be understood. Thus tradition in Judaism is taken to be the Oral Torah, the voice of God turned into words which only here become capable of interpretation, significant and comprehensible. This, then, is the great line of tradition in Judaism: an attempt to render the word of God utterable and usable in a way of life determined by revelation.

In juxtaposition to all of this in the history of Judaism stands Messianism in its manifold facets. It represents the intrusion of a new dimension of the present—redemption—into history, which enters into a problematic relation with tradition. The Messianic idea required a long period of time until it could emerge in post-biblical Jewish literature as the product of very diverse impulses, which in the Hebrew Bible still exist side by side without connection or unity. Only after the Bible did such varying conceptions as that of an ideal state of the world, of a catastrophic collapse of history, of the restoration of the Davidic kingdom, and of the "Suffering Servant" merge with the prophetic view of the "Day of the Lord" and a "Last Judgment." Initially, Messianism runs counter to the revelation idea of the Torah. It does not originate as a continuation or a further development of the idea of a law which obligates the living, or of a tradition regarding its applicability, say, in the End of Days. Rather it comes from a different source. It has its origins in a historical experience, and above all in the counterpart of this experience present in the imagination of the Jews.

Two elements are combined in the Messianic idea and they determine the historical configurations which Messianism has assumed in Judaism. These two elements are the restorative and the utopian. Conceiving the content of redemption as a public occurrence, which takes place at the end of history or even beyond it, affecting the collectivity and not the individual, Messianism could be, in the first place, the return to a primeval period, to a state of things which in the course of history, or perhaps even from the very beginning, became decadent and corrupt and which needs restoration, reconstitution, or reintegration. Redemption in this restorative sense means the restoration of a pristine state and, as such, contains an obvious conservative element. Here it is a matter of reinstituting a connection with something that was lost and that will be regained in the redemption. In contrast we find the second element, which was bound to enter into natural conflict with the first. It represents the conception of redemption as a phenomenon in which something emerges which has never before existed, in which something totally new is unmistakably expressed. These two elements appear clearly both in the theology of the Jews and in the historical forms of an at times acute Messianism. Of course these restorative and utopian elements in the Messianic idea could exist side by side as long as it was simply a hope that was projected into the distant future, an affirmation of faith that corresponded to no real experience. As long as the Messianic hope remained abstract, not yet concretized in people's experience or demanding of concrete decisions, it was possible for it to embody even what was contradictory, without the latent contradiction being felt.

In this form the belief in the future redemption itself became a piece of tradition; the state of tension it produced with the other segments of the tradition could be silently passed over or rhetorically veiled. In the imagination which gave shape to these things the still unrealized restorative and utopian elements could live peacefully side by side or together with each other; for the imagination connects images and seeks to create bridges and roads between them. Thus Messianism could take over even a conservative attitude and in this way become part of the tradition. Messianic activity, however, could hardly do this. The moment that Messianism moved from the realm of affirmation of faith, abstract doctrine, and synthesizing imagination into life and took on acute forms, it had to reach a point where the energies that lay dormant in these two elements would emerge into conflict with each other—the conflict of the tradition of the past versus the presence of redemption.

It is for this reason that in Jewish theology there has not been the problem of a conflict between Messianism and tradition. The Messianic idea, even if it was not developed logically from the idea of tradition, was regarded as compatible with it. Only where historical experience stirred people's hearts could such experience also find a quasi-theological expression in which the crisis of tradition then very quickly erupted within Messianism.

Thus the obvious question of the status of the Torah in the Messianic world was treated by the early Jewish literature (the Talmud, the Midrash, and the apocalypses) in purely imaginative fashion: in wishful dreams, in projections of the past upon the future, and in utopian images which relegated everything new to a time yet to come. These images are more the products of hopes and desires than of historical experiences. Admittedly, here and there some scholars—Victor Aptowitzer with great emphasis [2]— have asserted that certain historical experiences have played a role in the formation of these conceptions; for example, the actions of the Hasmoneans of the second and first pre-Christian centuries, which wide circles viewed unsympathetically. Likewise, it has often enough been claimed that the polemical disputes with Paulinism and the early Christian conceptions of the redemption reactively influenced the development of Messianic ideas in Judaism itself. However, these theories seem to me unsubstantiated and dubious, although I naturally would not deny that Paulinism represents a genuine crisis of tradition within Jewish Messianism that is analogous to the one we must still analyze here more closely in the case of Sabbatianism. But the reactive influence of this crisis upon the development of Jewish conceptions is highly hypothetical in view of the early Church's exceedingly rapid break with Judaism.

Therefore a conception of the redemption, which was not the product of Messianic experience (or anti-experience), required an essentially conservative notion which did not embody any conflict, let alone one that would have insisted upon any such conflict. In the sense of these speculations the redemption instead represents a more complete development of everything that previously was only partially capable of execution—but not its abrogation. This holds true for the familiar literary documents of early Messianism such as the Midrashim.

At times the Messiah who brings about the redemption is viewed simply as a Moses of the new aeon, a Moses redivivus,[3] and the question arises whether the parallel can be pursued any further. Is the Messiah as a new Moses who leads his people out of exile into the world of redemption also perhaps the giver of a Torah for the time of the redemption? Is the Torah and its radiation outward via the tradition the final word of God to Israel or is there in the Messianic or apocalyptic view a new revelation, a new form of the word of God? The Bible knows of no crisis of this kind. Isaiah (2:3) does know that at the End of Days "from Zion goes forth the Torah and the word of the Lord from Jerusalem." But it is simply Torah, not old Torah and not new Torah. It is the untouched Torah, which has not yet known any crisis and which in the prophetic vision is seen in its full development. Related to this is the notion, widely found in the rabbinic literature, that the Torah of the Messianic age will solve the contradictions and difficulties which now exist in regard to several points. On this issue the sources of Jewish tradition are nearly all clear. There is progress in the understanding of the Torah which in the Messianic age reaches its height. But the idea of a radical change or a questioning of the traditional element was eliminated and was not even perceived as a real possibility. "Since the Days of the Messiah represent the religious and political consummation of the national history and, however idealized, still belong to the world in which we live, it is only natural that in the Messianic age the Torah not only retain its validity but be better understood and better fulfilled than ever before." [4] W. D. Davies, who has devoted a valuable study to the position of the Torah in the Messianic Age [5] and on whom I have drawn to a considerable extent here, has rightly noted that even the new covenant, of which Jeremiah is the first to speak (31:31ff.) and which then plays such a large role in the sectarian writings of the Dead Sea Community, was not counterpoised as a contradiction to the old tradition but as its final establishment in the hearts of all mankind, as its final interiorization.

One more factor must be stressed if we would understand why there could not originally be any awareness of a possible conflict between tradition and Messianism. As long as the historical process in which the Torah became the bedrock and life element of Judaism remained in flux, this positive factor of giving shape to life within the realm of the Torah made it possible to draw the productive energies inward. This process, which in the course of more than five hundred years had created the "tradition" itself, left no room for questions affecting the value or validity of this positive element of building a life under the law of the Torah. Only where this process reached its climax did such questions gain historical urgency, and even then, as I have already indicated, only when a new concrete element intruded as happened in the case of acute and activist Messianism.

Quite logically, the infinite estimation of the Torah in its two aspects of "written" and "oral" Torah produced the conception of its essential immutability, even if the interpretation of this immutability could in the course of generations become subject to highly diverse conceptions, especially in the case of the Kabbalists.[6] According to Davies, "The fully developed (rabbinic) Judaism revealed to us in our sources was not a soil in which the belief in any radical changes in the existing Torah was likely to grow nor a soil which would welcome a new kind of Torah."[7] This statement, however, holds up for the world of tradition only as long as the Messianic idea remains an abstraction. Here the only kind of Torah that could be foreseen was a more complete one, but not a radically new form of the Torah. For this reason it is frequently emphasized that in the future the precepts of the Torah will be followed ever more strictly.

In contrast, as early as the Talmud we find hyperboles which express a utopian vision and suppose a Messianic status of the Torah in which certain demands of the law lose their force. In such cases the hyperbolic nature of the statements is evident. "All sacrifices will be abolished except for the offering of thanksgiving", "all prayers will be abolished except for the prayer of thanksgiving."[8] "All festivals will one day be abolished, except for Purim which will never be abolished. . . . Rabbi Eleazar said:

'Also the Day of Atonement [*Yom ha-Kippurim*] will never be abolished.' " [9] The contrast between the holiest and the relatively least significant of all holidays—which likely also involves a pun —is quite characteristic. The pun is both witty and dangerous for it rests on the equivalent sound present in both the name of the most holy and thoroughly ascetic holiday of the Jewish calendar, *Yom Kippurim,* and Purim, a day of joy. The Day of Atonement, which is now a day of fasting, of the utmost self-restraint, and of return to God, will one day be "like Purim," and we have to remember that in rabbinic tradition Purim is a kind of Jewish carnival. Thus a utopian element emerges here which splits apart the Day of Atonement and equates it with its opposite. To be sure, these are statements that are made almost in passing.

Though still remaining in the purely speculative exegetical and literary realm, a remark concerning Psalm 146:7 goes much further. It decisively removes the words "The Lord releases the prisoners" from the previous undialectical interpretation according to which the tradition will be completely fulfilled in the Messianic age and, in most descriptions of it, shine forth with undiminished radiance. The Hebrew words of the Psalm lend themselves as well to a more daring but still faithful translation as: "The Lord dissolves the commandments" or "The Lord allows the forbidden" (*mattir isurim* instead of *mattir asurim*). "What does this mean? Some say: 'All animals which were forbidden [to be eaten] in this world God will one day again allow, as was the case until the time of Noah. And why, in fact, has He forbidden them? In order to see who would accept His words and who would not. In the time to come, however, He will allow everything which He has forbidden.' " This view is indeed immediately followed by another according to which even in the Messianic age the unclean animals will not be allowed.[10] Little wonder that such passages, which were quoted gleefully by Christian apologists and anti-rabbinic polemicists, always disturbed conservative spirits and brought about protests and opposition. It remains unclear from which layer of the Midrash they originate.

Such cannot be said of a no less disputed interpretation which often appears in the sources. It understands Isaiah 51:4, "For Torah shall go forth from Me," as: "A *new* Torah shall go forth from me." [11] There seem to have been manuscripts of the Bible in which the verse existed in this form. Here we find the conception of a new Torah which some then associated with the Torah that the Messiah himself would teach.[12] We are not told whether this new Torah is a reinterpretation of the old without its rejection or whether it represents an internal break, a new combination of the elements which constitute it. Both conceptions were possible and in fact are expressed in the different readings in which the Torah is cited. But as long as such statements could be found only in books and corresponded to no situation which could provide their contents with historical actuality, their ambiguity and equivocality bothered hardly anyone at all.

We must make mention of an additional element as well. What I have called the imaginative conceptions and portraits of the Messianic age, which were embodied in the literature, represent no active promotion of such Messianic strivings. There seems to be hardly any bridge here leading from imagination to activity. The historian Gerson D. Cohen has recently stressed the great and totally consistent rabbinic opposition to Messianic movements during the 1600 years between the destruction of the Temple and the Sabbatian movement.[13] We know of many Messianic movements in Judaism during this long span of time. But ever since the collapse of the Messianic resistance to Rome led by Bar Kokhba (Kosba) in the first half of the second century, which led to the ruin of the Jewish community in many parts of Palestine, they have always been geographically limited and remained without historical effect. Generally they were lay movements which emerged in every conceivable part of the Diaspora and only in the rarest instances received the support of the local rabbinical authorities. In most cases such movements provoked resistance and were eliminated—which can to a large extent be explained by the circumstances I have outlined here. The preservers of the traditional element—and in the Jewish Middle Ages that meant the bearers of rabbinical authority—perceived in these acute Messianic outbreaks an element of nonconformity which endangered the continuity of the authoritative tradition. Such apprehensions that acute Messianism would lead to a crisis, as also their fear of the anarchic element in Messianic utopianism which they did not acknowledge, without question play a large role in this nearly unanimous opposition to the rabbis. There were many good reasons for this: concern for the stability of the community, concern for the fate of the Jews after a disappointment as suggested by historical experience, combined with a deep-rooted aversion to the "Forcers of the End," as those people are called in Hebrew who could not wait for the arrival of the Messiah but thought to do something for it themselves. All of these factors operate in the direction of removing Messianism into the realm of pure faith and inaction, leaving the redemption to God alone and not requiring the activity of men. The bearers of religious authority, no less than the heads of the communities who were responsible to the powers reigning in the non-Jewish environment, were forced into a position of political quietism on account of the conditions necessary for sustaining Jewish life in the exile, and for many of them it then became second nature.

If in this connection I have spoken of "lay movements," I use the word "lay" not in opposition to priestly, but to learned rabbinic authority to which representation and interpretation of the tradition were entrusted. After the destruction of the Temple, Judaism no longer recognized a priesthood exercising any real functions and it reserved only a few insignificant liturgical and social privileges to the descendants of priestly families in the male line.

The aggressiveness, the revolutionary element which is part and parcel of the Messianic movements, was bound to scare away the bearers of authority. In turning itself against the status quo, such a movement also called into question its subjection to the existing structure of traditional forms. Thus we find in the reports of the chroniclers no lack of complaints about an attitude of rejection, and even an inclination to break with elements of the tradition, as we have it attested for the movement of David Alroy in Kurdistan in the twelfth century.[14] The more intensive the outbreak and the larger the arena in which such a movement took place, the more clearly was a new situation created in which traditional exegeses were no longer as important as the confrontation with historical realities.

In the history of Jewish Messianism there are two possibilities which determine the content of an actually experienced redemption and the manner of dealing with the emotional states it produces.

A crisis in the tradition which finally leads to its abrogation could receive its direct impulse from the outside, i.e., from an element which demanded confrontation with it. This is abundantly true of the religious strategy of Paul when, as we know from the *Acts of the Apostles,* in the interest of Christian propaganda he had to forgo demanding of the gentile Christians that they keep the law or accept its obligation. This impulse from the outside did not arise out of any immanent logic which might have forced Paul himself, after accepting Christ as a Redeemer, to break with the law and its tradition in his own life. However, especially in the seventh chapter of *Romans,* it then received a far-reaching dialectical and downright antinomian justification in the logic whereby Christ could be proclaimed the "End of the Law" (Rom. 10:4). Here for the first time the crisis of the tradition is explained out of the inner dynamic of the redemption itself in which the considerations that led to this theology have become unimportant and have receded completely into the background.

On the other hand, a development could take place on the basis of a Messianic experience which opened up new perspectives in the concept of Torah itself. In this instance the Torah as such was not abrogated by calling into question the validity of the law on account of the influence of propagandistic considerations. Rather the antinomian tendencies, which constitute the eruption of the utopian elements in Messianism, were built into the Torah itself. The boldness and radicality with which this was done compares very well with the paradoxes of Pauline theology. The significant interest which this development has for the history of religions rests upon the fact that, in contrast to the very sparse documentation that exists for the movement accompanying these processes in early Christianity, we can here study the relevant processes in the full light of history and with manifold documentation. I am speaking of the Sabbatian movement, to which I shall devote the remainder of my remarks. It was the movement which, beginning in 1665, first encompassed the collective Jewish community and later broke into radical and sectarian forms, and into forces smoldering beneath the surface—in all of this affecting wide circles of the Jewish people in Europe and the Near East.

In Sabbatianism as well as in early Christianity the sudden appearance of the redemption, which is experienced as real and full of meaning, creates the element that releases the crisis of tradition. The Messiah has arrived, in whatever guise he may appear. In the light of such experience, what happens to the validity of the tradition which both at the time of Paul and at the time of Sabbatai Zevi had reached high points of its development: in the middle of the first century in the complete development of Pharisaic Judaism and in the seventeenth century in the complete development of the Kabbalistic world of ideas within rabbinism? The differences between Paulinism and Sabbatianism are great, but the kinship of the basic structures, their antinomianism and the crisis theologies they rapidly developed, should be neither overlooked nor mistaken.

It will be advisable to review briefly the facts which serve as the foundation for our further considerations. By the middle of the seventeenth century Kabbalistic mysticism had become a historical force within the rabbinic tradition, and to a large extent influenced and determined not only the thinking of those circles most affected by religion but, in its consequences, the entire Jewish community as well. This later Kabbalah, as it developed in classical forms in Safed in Palestine in the sixteenth century, was in its whole design electric with Messianism and pressing for its release;[15] it was impelling a Messianic outburst which, as it turned out, came approximately one generation after the reception of this Kabbalah by the Judaism of that time. The movement that went forth from Safed required about three generations to gain general acceptance. But after that, one generation, fully imbued with these Messianic conceptions, was enough to create a situation in which a Messiah who seemed to fit these ideas could find a wide-ranging echo. This was true in the case of Sabbatai Zevi from Smyrna who lived from 1626 to 1676 and who, under especially dramatic circumstances, in the year 1665 ignited a Messianic movement which began in Palestine and from this center reached out to the entire Diaspora. In the history of post-Christian Judaism it represents by far the most significant and extensive Messianic movement. Within it impulses that arose out of the historical situation of the Jews and out of the dynamics of Messianism itself were entwined with others that referred to the personality of the central figure of the Messiah. For the consciousness of the Jewish masses the specifically personal element was almost from the beginning covered by a thick web of legends which had little or nothing to do with the real figure, but which met their religious needs and accommodated traditional and widespread notions. These notions set forth how one should regard the signs which would accompany the coming of the Messiah and his activity. The real Sabbatai Zevi, however, whose figure we can today draw quite precisely,[16] scarcely fits the scheme. That just such a man could become the central figure of this movement is one of the greatest enigmas posed by Jewish history.

Sabbatai Zevi was a strange kind of saint and far removed from the type a conservative Jew would have acknowledged or even apperceived as the Messiah. He was not a Messiah who represented the consummation of the tradition in the conservative

sense and he was certainly not a conqueror who could have made
the kings of the world tremble. He was a man affected by the
most severe mental imbalance, who tottered between heights of
ecstasy and depths of melancholy in steeply alternating manic-
depressive stages. He was a rabbinically educated Jew, well versed
in the talmudic tradition and deeply entwined in the world of the
Kabbalah. He was highly unusual in only one respect: in moments
of religious exaltation he tended to commit bizarre acts which
violated the law. He enjoyed performing deeds which involved a
violation of the law, or effecting fantastic demonstrations as if they
were particularly meaningful religious ceremonies. In such acts
he apparently found a certain meaning which they were to bear
in the mystical process of the reintegration of all things. Carrying
out such functions, which he dared to do only in ecstatic moments
and without later being able to explain them, was hardly likely to
win him adherents.

The type of the "holy sinner" did not belong to the stock of
the Messianic tradition in Judaism. As a matter of fact, from his
first appearance in Smyrna in 1648 until his proclamation as the
Messiah in Gaza in 1665, Sabbatai Zevi had *not one* adherent
who would have regarded him as the Messiah. He was laughed
at, declared insane, or pitied. No one cared about him until
under especially peculiar circumstances he found a young rabbi of
the Talmud schools in Jerusalem who had settled in Gaza.
Nathan of Gaza had intensively studied the Talmud and the
Kabbalistic mysticism of his time and possessed significant powers
of imagination. In March 1665 he had had a vision in which this
peculiar Sabbatai Zevi, who he must often have seen on the
streets of Jerusalem, appeared to him as the Messiah. For his
part, Nathan convinced the much older man, who was plagued
by self-doubt and was struggling with the demons in his own soul,
that his mission was legitimate. As the prophet of the Messiah he
then embarked upon a wide range of activity and produced that
great outburst of Messianism which in the eyes of the Diaspora
Jews was substantiated precisely by the appearance of a true
prophet—and Nathan of Gaza was considered such—confirming
the mission of the Messiah.

In a very short time the movement overwhelmed Jewish communities from Yemen and Persia to England, Holland, Russia,
and Poland. It produced something to which the custodians of
the tradition had paid all too little attention but which to the
historian is quite comprehensible: the experience of redemption as

a historical event is anticipated in the experience of redemption as an emotional reality and appears in broad circles with such force that this anticipation is even capable of surviving the conflict. For disappointment in the historical world was ineluctable and was bound to conflict with the religious experience which took place on a different level. The fantastic wave of enthusiasm which swept up Jewish communities for an entire year created a mental reality which had not been anticipated by the rabbis or considered in the ancient books. After one year came the catastrophe: in September 1666 Sabbatai Zevi was brought before the Sultan in Adrianople and given the choice of upholding his Messianic claims and suffering martyrdom, or of converting to Islam. He preferred apostasy from Judaism which for him in some strange manner seemed to confirm the paradoxical claim of his Messianic mission, a final step of holy sinfulness, in fact, its apotheosis. From that point on a choice between the two levels of outer and inner experience was unavoidable.

We can estimate how strong the force of this Messianic eruption was if we consider that even this act of apostasy from Judaism and conversion to Islam—the most scandalous act imaginable from the viewpoint of faithful Jews—did not immediately lead to the total collapse of the high expectations. All other movements were destroyed by historical disappointment and left no trace in Jewish consciousness; we know about them only through the testimony of chroniclers. But here the transforming power of the movement was so strong that significant groups accepted even this totally unprecedented step of the Messiah, one of which no one had ever previously read in the ancient literature, and indicated they were ready to justify it out of these very writings. Suddenly there opened before the eyes of the "believers"—as the followers of Sabbatai Zevi called themselves—a new view of the ancient writings and documents of the tradition. Now it appeared to the theologians—or one might say ideologues—of the Sabbatian movement that all the pages of the old books really spoke of nothing other than the necessary apostasy of the Messiah, who was required to complete his mission by passing or descending into the underworld of the nations. For the sparks of the holy which are scattered among all peoples must be brought home if everything is to return to its proper place and the redemption thereby be completed. Induced by a historical event, the conception of the Messiah suffers a dialectical ruin. His mission takes on a destructive and paradoxical quality which must come into full effect before the positive part of the redemption can become visible. The figure of the Messiah himself takes on a sinister character which calls into question every traditional value. One cannot overlook the abyss which yawns between the figure of the Messiah who died for his cause upon the Cross and this figure who became an apostate and played his role in this disguise. Nonetheless, like the former, this ambiguous and treacherous twilight figure also exercised a seductive fascination.

II

We have become acquainted with the situation which posed the question of how the crisis of tradition would develop in such an acute Messianic outburst. This crisis emerged especially in the circle of the most determined "believers" in direct connection with attempts to understand the apostasy of the Messiah as a mission which leads into realms inaccessible to believing Jews; realms which the Messiah alone can penetrate and even there complete the mission of redemption. The apostasy of the Messiah necessarily produced a division. Those who regarded the verdict of history and of the exterior world as decisive—because everything exterior also symbolically expresses the inner state—had to turn away from such a Messiah. For some, anticipation of the redemption had become so vivid in their experience that they could endure the dialectical split between exterior and interior experience. But most could not remain loyal to this Messiah who seemed to have disowned himself and betrayed his mission.

Thus Sabbatianism became a heretical movement within Judaism which in Central and Eastern Europe continued to proliferate down to the beginnings of the age of Emancipation in the first part of the nineteenth century while in Turkey, though now dying out, it has preserved itself even down to the present. It took on the forms of a sect operating in the underground of the ghetto, at first treated mainly with silent rejection by the Jewish authorities in the communities, and then in increasing measure vehemently persecuted by them. At first the crisis of tradition appears in an implicit antinomianism which in the radical wing of the "believers" later turns into an explicit one. This process is supported with concepts from the Jewish tradition itself and formulated in a thoroughly Jewish way of thinking. With amazing rapidity this crisis of tradition finds significant expression in the literature of the "believers." The decisive formulations were crystallized as early as the years 1667–79. They by no means appear in the very small group which, while Sabbatai Zevi was still alive, imitated him by apostatizing to Islam, thinking the actions of the Messiah exemplary and obligatory also upon his followers. Rather they appeared just in those circles of "believers" who sought to give their new Messianic consciousness expression within the Jewish community and without taking symbolic steps of separation from it. Sabbatai Zevi himself, who in the last decade of his life led a double life as Muslim and Jew, did indeed possess a very lively imagination and he remained very influential in circles that were close to him personally. But he did not have the ability to formulate his concepts with persuasive force. This was left to the prophets, especially to Nathan of Gaza, and to the theologians of this group.

After 1683, the year of the mass conversion of several hundred families in Salonika, there arose in that city the sect of the Dönmeh (literally: Apostates), as they were simply called by the Turks, whose members were ostensibly Muslim but in reality crypto-Jewish Sabbatians who felt themselves obligated to carry through in their lives that imitation of Sabbatai Zevi which I just mentioned.[17] This sect maintained itself for more than 250 years, and several of its most important writings have only very recently come into the hands of scholars. They sought to solve the conflict between the exterior and their interior worlds, which their faith laid bare, by attaching themselves on the outside to the unredeemed world of Islam but on the inside to a mystical, Messianic Judaism which very soon assumed orgiastic-anarchic features. The theological capacity for formulating the crisis of tradition was, however, already forged earlier, and by men who never left the framework of Judaism. They had to justify the same contradiction which loomed in the first Christian generation after the death of Jesus between the apparent reality which knew nothing of any Messianic transformation of the world and their Messianic faith which daily expected the return of the Messiah in his glory. Just as at that time the theology of Christianity emerged from this contradiction, so in this case there arose the theology of Sabbatianism which was all too long neglected by Jewish historiography. Thus it is that the three most upsetting and astonishing texts which document this transformation and crisis of tradition were unable to induce any scholar before my generation to read them.

Here are three men and three texts which show what is possible in an atmosphere saturated with the tradition and the concepts of Judaism when the situation is felt to be revolutionary. The first name that must be mentioned is that of Nathan of Gaza, who died in Skoplje (Turkish: Üsküp), Macedonia in 1680, and who appeared in his writings both as prophet and theologian—a very rare combination in the history of religions. He elaborated his ideas in numerous open letters and treatises, but especially in a manuscript the Hebrew title of which (*Zemir Aritzim;* cf. Isa. 25:5) implies: "Overthrow of the Enemy Forces" or "Overthrow of the Tyrants," i.e., of those who hinder redemption.[18] It was written about 1670. The second author is Abraham Miguel Cardozo (1627–1706) who was born into a crypto-Jewish Marrano family in Spain, returned to Judaism in Venice in 1648, and whose attachment to the Sabbatian movement grew out of Marrano currents of thought. For him the apostasy of the Messiah represented a kind of highest justification of the apostasy of the Spanish Marranos in 1391 and 1492. Under the influence of the prophet Nathan, with whose writings he was familiar, he composed in Tripoli (North Africa) as early as 1668—two years after the conversion of Sabbatai Zevi—a long open letter entitled *Magen Abraham* ("Shield of Abraham").[19] His later writings scarcely exceed the sharpness with which his ideas were formulated here. The third author is Israel Hazan from Kastoria in Macedonia, a student and for many years the secretary of Nathan of Gaza. We possess from his hand a commentary to a large number of psalms which he composed about 1678–79 in Kastoria; it is one of the most moving personal documents of Sabbatianism. He interprets every psalm either as a lament of the Messiah who has apostatized in fulfillment of his mission and speaks of his destitution and his hope, or as a triumphal ode for the redemption which has begun and for the upheavals which are associated with it.[20] All of these writings were composed while Sabbatai Zevi was still alive or shortly after his death. They prove how quickly the crisis of Jewish tradition manifested itself within this acute Messianism, while in the case of Paul this crisis received literary expression only about fifteen years after the death of Jesus.

Of what sort, then, are the currents of thought which are presented here and are repeated and varied in manifold ways in the later literature of the Sabbatians, both of those who remained within Judaism and of the Dönmeh? In this case we are not concerned with the question of how the apostasy of the Messiah was explained as a necessary descent into the realm of darkness. Our authors do not doubt the legitimacy of Sabbatai Zevi's Messianic mission nor its paradoxical character. The question which agitates the "believers" is: What about the Torah and everything associated with it now that the Messiah has appeared in the flesh and our hearts are filled with this experience? Something must now follow for our lives in the immediate future and even more after his expected return from those realms of darkness. In addition, the new eyes with which the "believers" read the old books had revealed to them that those books, in fact, spoke throughout of that seeming apostasy of the Messiah which no one had noted there until it actually came about. Thus they searched for conceptions and symbols in which that unnoticed crisis of tradition, which had come to life in the feelings of the Sabbatians, could have manifested itself. The attitude of Sabbatai Zevi, even before his apostasy, had made clear to them that the Messiah himself at particular moments stood above the way of life prescribed by tradition, violated it in a downright challenging fashion in several of his actions, and thus showed himself a figure standing at the boundary between the validity of the old law and the coming into view of a new level of the Torah's fulfillment. By his concrete appearance the problem of the validity of all previous tradition had become acute. As proof of their faith, Sabbatai Zevi had demanded of a few adherents that they transgress certain prohibitions which were in themselves incomprehensible and meaningless but were expressed with great emphasis in the Torah, such as eating the fat of animals (Lev. 7:23 ff.), a ritual gesture of decidedly symbolic nature since it was not connected with any sensual gratification.[21] After his apostasy he had also required a number of the "believers" to take this same step. Thus from the beginning the problem was not limited to the figure of the Messiah himself but —as some of our authors put it—was posed for all those who came from the same "root" as the soul of the Messiah and were designated "the kin of the Messiah."

As early as 1668 Cardozo expressed this crisis in a radical formulation: "The Torah as it now exists [or: as it is now observed] will not exist in the Messianic age." [22] For him the reason is clear: at that time the world will be cleansed of every defect and be restored to its original state or *tikkun*. Since fulfillment of the precepts of the Torah serves as the instrument of this reintegration—a fundamental teaching of the Lurianic Kabbalah—the status of the Torah must necessarily change in the Messianic world where the reasons for this fulfillment lose their force. According to later Kabbalistic lines of thought, the Messiah, more than bringing about the redemption, signalizes in symbolic fashion the conclusion of a process which we realize ourselves through our actions. Once we have carried through this process of the integration of all things in their original place—and it is a mystical process in the interior of the cosmos—then the redemption will appear entirely of itself and conclude this process in the exterior realm as well. Once the interior world is put in order, the exterior must manifest it also: it is put into effect because everything exterior is nothing more than a symbol of the interior. Cardozo says:

The two Torahs [the Written and the Oral] correspond to the situation of a person who has fallen "from a high roof into a deep well." Whoever plunges from a height down to the ground, his body becomes bruised all over and he needs various medicaments and cures until all of his 365 blood vessels and 248 organs [i.e., his entire physical organism] are healed. The same is true of events in the upper [divine] lights which are the mystical figure of the Creator. These lights are the precepts of the Torah whose number not by chance corresponds to the number of organs in the human body which they are supposed to cure if wounded or broken. Just as someone who has become injured or wounded must abstain from foods and beverages which could harm him and must keep to his diet for as long a time as an experienced physician prescribes, so it is also with the observance of the commandments. When the new era and the time of healing will have come and brought about the ascension of the holy sparks [of the divine light] to their original place, the patient will surely no longer have need of the prescriptions of the physician nor of the diet affecting foods and beverages which previously would have hurt him. And this analogy holds directly for the status of the commandments which correspond to the physician's cures. For at that time the lights and all worlds will surely arise to their former level, which of course will become possibe only in the days of the redeemer; he has the power of restoring all worlds because he himself is the first Adam [in his Messianic reincarnation].[23]

At the end of this exposition Cardozo manifestly casts aside the traditional Lurianic conception of the character and the function of the Messiah, which corresponds to his own analogy, in favor of an extravagant conception, widely found among the Sabbatians, according to which the mystical abundance of power resident in the Messiah himself brings the process of healing salvation to its conclusion. According to Cardozo, this gradual advance in the process of salvation manifests itself in the giving

of the Torah and its commandments in different stages according
to the requirements of various generations; some commandments
had already been given to Adam, others to Noah and his sons,
still others to Abraham, until finally Israel received the Torah in
its entirety "in order to purify all the holy sparks, cleanse them
from their admixture [with the unholy powers] and raise them up
to their point of origin, for they possess the ability and power to
raise those sparks up into the primeval thoughts [of God] since
they themselves originate there."

However, in this exposition of the function of the Torah and
the concrete fulfillment of the commandments, Cardozo at other
points makes a clear distinction between the Written and the Oral
Torah. Leaning upon the mystical speculations of the Kabbalists,
he no longer takes the Written Torah to mean what it meant to
the Talmudists, i.e., a realm circumscribed by the Bible itself, containing concrete commandments and prohibitions to which the
oral law added only further, more explicit statements. Following
the mystics, the Written Torah, the revelation as such, is seen as
not calling for concrete execution in any realm of application
whatever. The Torah becomes applicable only through the medium
of the Oral Torah in which the word of God is appropriated to the
contingencies of its fulfillment. The concept of the Oral Torah,
identical with that of the tradition, encompasses the actual historical tradition of rabbinic Judaism, of the historical form of
Judaism which the Kabbalists sought to interpret. Thus there could
be a differentiation here: the crisis of tradition, which the beginning of the redemption was bound to bring about, could con-
ceivably remain limited to the realm of the Oral Torah if the
Written Torah were understood as an essentially mystical realm
of pure revelation, of the absolute word of God which by nature
is immutable—though it may be received in different ways by
those who hear it. In this view, the translations of the absolute
word into humanly intelligible words capable of articulation
already belong to the realm of tradition; they represent a permuta-
tion into something that can be spoken and fulfilled. The written
law in the normal sense, as a readable book and concrete instruction, thereby becomes itself an initial manifestation of the Oral
Torah. Only in this sense does a crisis take place even within the
written law, since in the Messianic age the letters which constitute the Written Torah will become subject to different combinations and thus take on new meanings, or at least their old combinations will be interpreted in an entirely new way.[24]

Likewise in the writings of the Sabbatians the differentiations in the concept of the Torah play a part when its position in the Messianic age is to be defined. Cardozo explicitly states that the crisis of the Torah affects the forms of the tradition, of the Oral Torah. For the six orders of the Mishnah and its sixty tractates in which the tradition was first codified correspond to its status in a cosmic order, or rather disorder, which has its symbolic expression in Israel's exile. He therefore has good reason to refer to a passage in the *Zohar* which gives a mystical interpretation of a verse in the Midrash regarding the beginning of the redemption: "The heart does not reveal it to the mouth." Originally this meant that the date of the Messianic redemption was hidden.[25] One cannot find out anything about the redemption until it begins. However, this was interpreted mystically to mean that where the heart, i.e., the heart of the Torah as the secret, absolute word of God, becomes manifest it no longer needs the mouth of tradition by which it has hitherto expressed itself. Where the inner mystical essence breaks forth undisguised and no longer needs any intermediary, the masking expression which veiled this "heart" becomes unnecessary. Whereas the talmudic eschatology expected an infinitely rich development of the oral law in the Messianic age, for Cardozo the law will be "no longer necessary"; [26] in fact, it undergoes a distinct transvaluation, as we shall see shortly.

In their endeavor to develop the crisis of tradition out of the concepts of the tradition itself the Sabbatians were able to refer back to symbols of the earlier Kabbalistic literature whose implicit antinomianism had for more than three hundred years hardly aroused any attention, let alone protests. But now, in the excitement of the Messianic uprising and in the hands of the Sabbatians, these symbols showed their explosive power in shattering the tradition. There are, above all, three typological descriptions which recur here again and again, and which originate in the most recent layer of the *Zohar*. In these sections, especially in the "Faithful Shepherd" (*Ra'ya Mehemna*), and in the *Tikkune Zohar,* an extensive commentary to the first chapters of Genesis composed as an independent volume, these typological figures are used at many points and are varied in the most diverse ways. They are:

1. The figure of the two trees of Paradise, the Tree of Life and the Tree of the Knowledge of Good and Evil.
2. The figure of the two pairs of the tablets of the law which Moses received at Sinai. For when Moses came down

from the mountain with a pair of tablets and was forced to witness the dance of Israel around the golden calf they had made in his absence, he smashed them upon the ground. Only later, after Israel had again been humbled by Moses' anger, did he receive a second pair of tablets whose content is conveyed in the Torah (Exod. 34).

3. The figure of the six days of the week and the Sabbath as archetypes of world history which runs its course in a great cosmic week and a Sabbath which follows thereafter.[27]

Let us examine the conceptions lying behind these figures.

What do the two trees in Paradise represent? Already in biblical metaphor wisdom, identified by Jewish tradition with Torah, is designated as Tree of Life (Prov. 3:18); thus opens the whole realm of typology. The trees in Paradise are not merely physical trees; beyond this they point to a state of things which they represent symbolically.[28] In the opinion of the Jewish mystics both trees are in essence one. They grow out into two directions from a common trunk. Genesis tells us that the Tree of Life stood in the center of Paradise, but it does not indicate the exact position of the Tree of Knowledge. The Kabbalists took this to mean that it had no special place of its own but sprouted together with the Tree of Life out of the common matrix of the divine world. The two trees are different aspects of the Torah, which have their common origin in revelation. The Tree of Life represents that aspect which has hitherto been unrealizable because, due to the sin of Adam, it remained virtually hidden and inaccessible, and we do not know the taste of its fruits. The law which is concealed in the life of this tree is that of a creative force manifesting itself in infinite harmonies, a force which knows no limitations or boundaries. The paradisaic life under this law never came into being. The sin of Adam was that he isolated the Tree of Life from the Tree of Knowledge to which he directed his desire. Once the unity of the two trees in men's lives was destroyed, there began the dominion of the Tree of Knowledge. No longer did unitary gushing, unrestrained life prevail, but the duality of good and evil in which the Torah appears in this aspect of revelation. Since the expulsion from Paradise, in the exile in which we all now find ourselves, we can no longer apperceive the world as a unified whole. The Tree of the Knowledge of Good and Evil under whose law the world now stands corresponds to a condition of this world in which distinctions must be made before the unity of life can be regained: the distinctions between good and evil, commandment and prohibition, holy and profane, pure and impure. For the author of those sections of the *Zohar* the two trees were not only, as they were for the other Kabbalists, symbols of the *sefirot,* of the manifestations of God in Creation, of which the Tree of Knowledge represented the tenth and last *sefirah,* but beyond this they were models for two possible forms of life in the light of revelation. Of course at the present only the one is tangible and capable of fulfillment. Precisely out of those very distinctions and limitations man is to restore the lost form and the violated image of the divine in himself and thus bring the Tree of Knowledge, with which he is mystically associated, to its full development. This Torah of the Tree of Knowledge is, however, nothing other than the world of tradition which represents the law of the unredeemed world since the expulsion from Paradise. Only the redemption, breaking the dominion of exile, puts an end to the order of the Tree of Knowledge and restores the utopian order of the Tree of Life in which the heart of life beats unconcealed and the isolation in which everything now finds itself is overcome. Thus the inner logic of this conception of the dominion of the Tree of the Knowledge of Good and Evil as the legitimate form of revelation in an unredeemed world had to regard the redemption itself as a return home to Paradise where all things will again be in their true place. Although it is not a matter of a physical return to a geographical Paradise, it is in any case life in a state of the world which corresponds to that of Paradise or in which Paradise, for its part, expands into the world. The Torah of the Messianic age will then be that of the Tree of Life, which no longer knows anything of all those separations and limitations. This Torah is still revelation and, in Kabbalistic terms, an evolution of the divine name; but it has nothing further to do with the form under which we have known it until now. It is a utopian Torah for a utopian state of the world. The Sabbatians saw in such a vision no contradiction to acknowledging the forms of the tradition, i.e., those of historical Judaism, for the period of exile. Without question this thinking of the Jewish Messianic heretics is structurally connected closely to that of the spiritualistic sects in Christianity. It was not, however, influenced by them in its specific historical appearance and formulation, which remained entirely Jewish.

According to the conception of the Sabbatians, who here again followed the intimations of these same sections of the *Zohar,* such a state of redemption, of liberation from exile, was achieved at the time of the revelation on Sinai. It is not surprising that when this typological thinking was applied to the exodus from Egypt—the very archetype of exile—revelation should seem the opportunity of redemption. But Israel, which was to receive this revelation, was not equal to the opportunity and it lapsed into worship of the golden calf. Thereupon the Torah under the aspect of the Tree of Life, which would have made up the content of the revelation, reverted to its hidden state, and the tradition, the Oral Torah which encompassed the real revelation like a husk enclosing a kernel, began its dominion under the aspect of the Tree of Knowledge; only in this form could it be realized in history.

At this point the figure of the two trees in Paradise is brought into relation with that of the two pairs of tablets of the law. The first tablets, which were given to Moses before the people lapsed into the heathen cult of the golden calf, were the laws for a redeemed world and represented a revelation of the Tree of Life. They were the law of freedom. To this the spiritualistic exegesis of the *Tikkune Zohar* applied the famous passage of the Mishnah regarding these first tablets of which the Torah says (Exod. 32:16): "And the tablets were God's work, and the writing was God's writing, incised, *harut,* upon the tablets." The word *harut,* however, can also be read as *herut,* which means freedom.[29] While the talmudic exegesis still understood this reading to mean that it was precisely the study of the Torah which lent true freedom, a freedom under the law, the mystical interpretation of the *Zohar* saw it as the freedom of the redemption expressed through the Torah on the first set of tablets. This idea is taken up and stressed by both Nathan of Gaza and Cardozo. No one has yet read the Torah of the Tree of Life which was inscribed on the first tablets. Israel was entrusted only with that second set of tablets, and they render the Torah as it is read under the dominion of the Tree of Knowledge and Differentiation, which is also called the Tree of Death.[30] But with the redemption the first tablets will again be raised up; they will be a Torah in which the restoration of the state of Paradise is associated with a utopia that as yet has never been, that as yet has never been capable of realization. In this exegesis of the *Zohar* we can already notice the unconcern with a passage of the Torah such as Exodus 34:1 which says explicitly that the second set of tablets contained the same words as the first. It did not matter. The parallel between the trees in the primeval history of man and the tablets in the story of the revelation was simply too seductive for the radicals of mysticism.

The third typology is that which saw a parallel between the

course of world history and the history of the Creation. A day for God, according to one interpretation of a verse in Psalms, is a thousand years. Thus the six thousand years of world history correspond to the six workdays leading up to the great cosmic Sabbath, to redemption on the seventh day of the universe. Like a good Jewish exegete, Cardozo argues—even though he carries this exegesis over into heresy—that other laws hold on the Sabbath than on a workday. The activities of the workday are to a large extent prohibited on the Sabbath and other activities take their place. Whoever performs the actions of a workday on the Sabbath violates the law. But on the cosmic Sabbath the Tree of Life reigns, and not the Tree of Knowledge. "Thus there clearly follows from all of this that, with the onset of the order of the Tree of Life on the great cosmic Sabbath, not only shall we no longer need to observe the order of the six weekdays, which corresponds to the mode of life prescribed in the six orders of the Mishnah. But beyond this, everyone who wants to serve God as he does now [i.e., by the traditional way of life] will in those days [of the Messiah] be called a desecrator of the Sabbath and a destroyer of the plantings [i.e., a downright heretic]."[31] The Mishnah is the first codification of the oral Torah and the six orders into which it is divided by subject constitute the framework of *halakhic* Judaism. The author of the above-mentioned parts of the *Zohar* indulged abundantly in remarks regarding the inferiority of the Mishnah; he opposes it to the mystical order of life of the Kabbalah and to the Messianic abrogation of those aspects of the Torah which it contains. Cardozo, who was very much attracted by these seditious passages, in his above-mentioned formulation simply drew the consequences. He presents us with the palpable intrusion of implicit antinomianism into the world of tradition. What was commandment becomes downright prohibition. And from here it was only a short step to a further consequence, of which we have yet to speak: acts that had previously been prohibited now become not only permissible but are even considered holy.

However Cardozo, who remained loyal to the tradition in his personal observance, established a safeguard within these channels of thought which put off any explicit antinomianism, at least for a transitional period. As long as the Messiah has not returned from his mission into those realms where Cardozo does not dare to follow him, believing that they can be entered only by the Messiah—he decisively rejected mystical apostasy for anyone other than the Messiah himself—so long does the tradition retain its undiminished validity. The restoration of the true figure of man, Adam, is not complete as long as the Redeemer himself remains in the world of the "husks," of the powers of the "other side," where he gathers up the holy sparks. With his return, which corresponds to the New Testament conception of the parousia, the law of the renewed world—the Torah of the Tree of Life—will come into effect. Thus the world of the tradition is liable to collapse at any time, and for the Sabbatians the reasons for this collapse have been given long before it actually takes place. According to the immanent logic of their conceptions, its crisis cannot be averted.

The real Adam is restored in the figure of the Messiah and now begins his career in a renewed world which stands under the law of freedom. In the writings of the Sabbatians hidden conflicts come to light on this issue and are expressed, for example, in the differences between the positions of Cardozo and Nathan of Gaza. The Messiah could be conceived as one who has completely mastered the Tree of Knowledge and its Torah, and from this experience, which is that of the Jew in exile as well as that of suffering mankind, pushes forward into the new realms of the Tree of Life. He could appear as the heir of the millennia who thereby gives the redemption a plenitude which it might have never had if Adam had not succumbed to temptation. For according to the Lurianic Kabbalah the first opportunity for redemption presented itself to Adam on the day of his creation. Had Adam decided otherwise on the proposition of the serpent, the redemption of all worlds would already have begun then and the first Sabbath would also have been the last—the final cosmic Sabbath. But whether the Adam who would never have tasted the fruit of the Tree of Knowledge would have been richer than the one who went through this experience could remain doubtful. In fact we find, especially in the writings of Nathan of Gaza, a very different conception of the Messiah which stands in opposition to this one. According to Nathan's view, the soul of the Messiah was from the first and since the beginning of the world inextricably bound up with the Tree of Life and was never subjected to the law of the Tree of Knowledge. Thus he always stood beyond good and evil, commandment and prohibition, because he never left the state of Paradise. Only from our perspective do his actions often seem reprehensible, illicit, and scandalous, when in truth they conform to the laws of his origin.[32] He must be measured by other criteria. But this is not to say that passage through the world of tradition, which is incumbent upon all other holy souls and soul-sparks, does not exist at all for the Messiah. In the pre-natal history of his soul— about which Nathan of Gaza relates astonishing things—as well as in his earthly career, he represents the rebellious element which stems from his root and is bound by no tradition, the "holy serpent" which from the very beginning struggles against its rival. Motifs which the *Zohar* carries through in a variety of ways the Sabbatians combine into a coherent imagery of antinomianism. It is by no means disobedience or apostasy which appears in this abrogation of the Torah, but rather a changed situation of the world.[33] When Adam was driven from Paradise and came under the law of the Tree of Knowledge, he had need of clothing and raiment in his exile into the world because in his present situation he could no longer reveal his naked essence. The same is true of the Godhead, the Shekhinah, who manifests herself in the Torah and who accompanies Israel on their way through exile. She too needs clothing that must cover her real nature. In exile the Shekhinah wears the sombre dress of mourning. The pure spirituality of the Torah requires the physical garments of the commandments and prohibitions. An unveiled Torah would be the Torah of the Tree of Life. But the Torah of the Tree of Knowledge is a veiled Torah and its garments are identical with the tradition, with the Judaism of the commandments and the *Halakhah,* with Judaism as it is known by history. At the time of redemption it will no longer need these garments since that redemption will signify a restoration of the state of Paradise in which Adam and Eve stood naked within the context of the pristine life. In exile the inner Torah was unrecognizable, or rather recognizable only by great initiates. But in the redemption it will be visible to every man. Cardozo says: "When the dross of the husks is removed [i.e., after the reintegration of all things], the world will no longer need to keep those garments in good condition." This keeping in good order, however, is nothing other than the fulfillment of the commandments and prohibitions; in their stead "the Torah will youthfully renew itself."

Following upon these trains of thought we find as early as Nathan of Gaza and Cardozo the appearance of an additional motif which in the Sabbatian heresy of the seventeenth and eighteenth centuries proves to be very effective, but also especially offensive and objectionable: the abrogation of sexual taboos, and of the incest prohibition in particular, as indices of the Messianic Torah. Here the crisis of tradition achieves a symbolically very visible, if also scandalous, expression. The restrictions which originate in the curse of woman after the Fall lose their force in the Messianic world. These restrictions, however, according to a talmudic interpretation,[34] are above all of a sexual character. In Cardozo's view, Eve might, at least in principle, have belonged to several men while she was still in Paradise. In the redemption this promiscuity, be it animal or paradisaic, will be restored, as it were, on a new and hitherto unattained level. The restorative and utopian elements interpenetrate here in a most characteristic fashion. The abrogation of the sexual taboos finds its expression in heretical rituals. When fulfilling each commandment, the pious Jew says a blessing. But according to the new Messianic formulation, introduced by Sabbatai Zevi himself, he says: "Praised be He who permits the forbidden," a formula which the defenders of Jewish tradition rightly regarded as the epitome of this revolutionary heresy. As so often in the history of spiritualistic sects, the sexual taboos provided a point of application at which Messianic freedom—through libertinism—could find its confirmation and concrete content. Orgiastic rituals were preserved for a long time among Sabbatian groups, and in the circles of the Dönmeh until about 1900. As late as the seventeenth century a festival was introduced called Purim that was celebrated at the beginning of spring. It reached its climax in the "extinguishing of the lights" and in an orgiastic exchange of wives. That such rituals, which anticipated the Messianic utopia, struck at the heart of the strict sexual morality of the Jewish tradition is obvious. And in fact the bitter struggle against the Sabbatians began in earnest only when the performance of such rituals, about which the Sabbatian texts could leave no doubt, became known to wider circles. Here was an obvious reversal of values that could destroy the moral structure of the Jewish communities.

Especially embittering in this regard was the behavior of a certain Baruchya Russo who about the year 1700 was the leader of the most radical wing of the Sabbatians in Salonika. The Torah knows of thirty-six prohibitions that are punishable by "extirpation of the soul." Varying speculations existed as to the meaning of this punishment, but one thing was clear: it involved particularly heinous sins.[35] Half of them are the prohibitions against incest mentioned in the Torah (Lev. 18). Baruchya not only declared these prohibitions abrogated but went so far as to transform their contents into commandments of the new Messianic Torah.[36]

The new Torah is designated the Torah of *atzilut,* the Torah of the highest condition of the world, as opposed to the Torah of *beriah,* the Torah of the sensual creaturely world which exists before the redemption. This pair of concepts also originates in the *Tikkune Zohar.*[37] There, however, the meaning is somewhat different. The "Torah of Creation" represents the aspect of the one absolute Torah in which it exoterically presents itself to us in the circumstances of our world; the "Torah of the World of Emanation" represents the Torah on the mystical level, the Torah read with the eyes of the Kabbalist. The creaturely Torah with its explicit commandments and prohibitions is the shell enfolding a mystical kernel which the Kabbalist can reveal. But as early as the Kabbalah of Safed there is a shift in the meaning of this mystical Torah. It contains not only the mysteries of the Kabbalah, but also the law of pure spirituality which will one day be revealed, a kind of *Evangelium Eternum* as the Franciscan spiritualists understood this concept. As the word of God, this Torah of *atzilut* existed even in the earliest aeons in the form of combinations and permutations of the name of God and of lights which shine forth with this name. But even before the Creation of the lower, visible world, it was woven into the world of divine emanation as its determining power. It had not yet, however, become—one could say: flowed into—that applicable Torah as which it appears in our world of Creation.

The higher form of the Torah could also easily take on a Messianic dimension in which at the final redemption it could appear as a higher revelation replacing the existing Torah. In such fashion this pair of concepts was closely identified with the two trees discussed earlier. To be sure, this Torah is still not accessible since it can become visible only in a world transformed in every respect, even externally. Such was the opinion of Nathan of Gaza and his circle. His disciple Israel Hazan of Kastoria says: "Only at the second and final appearance of the Messiah [the parousia] shall we who have the true faith [in the mission of the Messiah Sabbatai Zevi] apprehend the mystery of our holy Torah, the Torah of *atzilut,* from the mouth of the Most High." [38] For whereas the previous forms of the Torah come from the tenth *sefirah, malkhut,* or the central *sefirah, tiferet,* this final form of revelation will originate in the first *sefirah,* the highest manifestation of the Godhead which in the *Zohar* is called "the Holy Ancient One," *atika kadisha.* This Torah will be the gift of God to the redeemed world and will replace that Torah which was given in the desert under the conditions of a desolate, unredeemed world. Instead of reading the word of God in the form of the Torah of Moses as it has come down to us, we shall receive the gift of reading it as the Torah of *atzilut* which the Messiah one day will teach us. In other words: as yet he has not taught it, even though he has already—before his apostasy— made his first appearance. We stand in an in-between realm, in transition between the two phases of the Messiah's mission. The Torah of *atzilut* is thus not identical with the teaching of the historical Sabbatai Zevi, either before or after his apostasy. At that moment it could not even have been described or conceived and therefore could be transmitted only in the most general terms. Only after the passage of thirty years, long after the death of Sabbatai Zevi, was that further step taken whereby Baruchya set up his nihilistic Torah as the content of the teachings propounded by Sabbatai Zevi. From that point on the Torah of *atzilut* becomes the symbol of a Messianic, anarchic Judaism, even in the circles of those sectarians who remain in the confines of Judaism. This new Judaism has in principle already completed the inner break with the Jewish tradition even where it continues to draw sustenance from it, and it has confirmed that break by symbolic acts and rituals.[39]

The Sabbatian "believers" felt that they were champions of a new world which was to be established by overthrowing the values of all positive religions. And so, from the pen of their last significant leader, Jacob Frank, who appeared as a successor to Baruchya in Poland in 1756, we have a watchword which matchlessly expresses the situation of these mystical "soldiers" in the army of the Messiah: "Soldiers are not allowed to have a religion." [40] In its positive valuation of both the situation of the soldier and the lack of religion in the service of a mystically understood world revolution, this statement represents the extreme consequence to which a Messianic crisis of tradition, erupting in the very heart of Judaism, could lead. The old mystical Kabbalistic symbols in which this crisis was formulated disappeared. What remained was a wild revolt against all traditions, a movement that found a new, popular content in the biblical books and translated them into a totally untheological, even vulgar language. And all this was happening in the generation directly preceding the outbreak of the French Revolution, the event which left in its wake an intense crisis of a totally different sort, one that shook the very foundations of the realm of Jewish tradition.

Redemption Through Sin

I

No CHAPTER IN the history of the Jewish people during the last
several hundred years has been as shrouded in mystery as that of
the Sabbatian movement. On one point, at least, there is no
longer any disagreement: the dramatic events and widespread religious revival that preceded the apostasy of Sabbatai Zevi in 1666
form an important and integral part of Jewish history and deserve
to be studied objectively, to the exclusion of moralistic condemna-
tions of the historical figures involved. It has come increasingly
to be realized that a true understanding of the rise of Sabbatianism
will never be possible as long as scholars continue to appraise it
by inappropriate standards, whether these be the conventional beliefs of their own age or the values of traditional Judaism itself.
Today indeed one rarely encounters the baseless assumptions of
"charlatanry" and "imposture" which occupy so prominent a place
in earlier historical literature on the subject. On the contrary: in
these times of Jewish national rebirth it is only natural that the
deep though ultimately tragic yearning for national redemption to
which the initial stages of Sabbatianism gave expression should
meet with greater comprehension than in the past.

In turning to consider the Sabbatian movement after Sabbatai
Zevi's conversion to Islam, however, we are faced with an entirely different situation. Here we find ourselves still standing
before a blank wall, not only of misunderstanding, but often of
an actual refusal to understand. Even in recent times there has
been a definite tendency among scholars to minimize at all costs
the significance of this "heretical" Sabbatianism, with the result
that no adequate investigation yet exists of its spiritual founda-
ions, its over-all impact on eighteenth-century Jewry, or its ulti-

mate fate. It is impossible, in fact, to read any of the studies that have been done in these areas without being astounded by the amount of invective directed against the leaders and adherents of the various Sabbatian sects. Typical of this approach is David Kahana's *A History of the Kabbalists, Sabbatians, and Hasidim* (in Hebrew), but the angry moralizing that characterizes this volume has not been confined to any one historical school; rather, it has been shared by writers of widely differing points of view, secular as well as religious. The problem itself, meanwhile, remains as recondite as ever.

Two enormous difficulties, therefore, confront the student of the Sabbatian "heresies": on the one hand, there are the obstacles posed by the sources themselves, and on the other, those created by the attitude generally taken toward them. To a great extent, moreover, these two sets of difficulties have always been related.

Why should this be so?

The Sabbatian movement in its various shadings and configurations persisted with remarkable obstinacy among certain sectors of the Jewish people for approximately 150 years after Sabbatai Zevi's conversion. In a number of countries it grew to be powerful, but for various reasons, internal as well as external, its affairs were deliberately hidden from the public eye. In particular, its spokesmen refrained from committing their beliefs to print, and the few books that they actually published concealed twice what they revealed. They did, however, produce a rich literature, which circulated only among groups of "believers" (*ma'aminim*)—the term by which Sabbatian sectarians generally chose to refer to themselves, down to the last of the Dönmeh in Salonika and the last Frankists in the Austro-Hungarian Empire. As long as Sabbatianism remained a vital force within the Jewish ghetto, threatening to undermine the very existence of rabbinic Judaism, its opponents labored ceaselessly to root it out and systematically destroyed whatever of its writings came into their possession, "including [even] the sacred names of God [*azkarot*] which they contain," as the bans upon them read. As a result many of their writings were lost without a trace, and had it been left solely up to the rabbinical authorities nothing would have come down to us at all except for certain tendentiously chosen fragments quoted in anti-Sabbatian polemics. In addition, although an extensive religious literature was still to be found in the hands of Frankists in Moravia and Bohemia at the beginning of the nineteenth century, the children and grandchildren of these "believers" in Prague and other Jewish centers themselves attempted to obliterate every shred of evidence bearing on their ancestors' beliefs and practices. The well-known philosopher and historian of atheism Fritz Mauthner has preserved the following interesting story in his memoirs [1]: in the declining days of the movement in Bohemia, Frankist "emissaries" came to his grandfather (and undoubtedly to other members of the sect as well) and requested that he surrender to them a picture of "the Lady" and "all kinds of writings" which he had in his possession. The emissaries took them and left. The incident took place sometime during the 1820's or 1830's. In spite of all this, at least two large manuscripts from these circles have survived.

One must therefore bear in mind that in dealing with the history of Sabbatianism powerful interests and emotions have often been at stake. Each for reasons of his own, all those who have written on the subject in the past shared one belief: the less importance attributed to it, the better.

Authors and historians of the orthodox camp, for their part, have been anxious to belittle and even distort the over-all role of Sabbatianism in order to safeguard the reputations, as they have conceived of them, of certain honored religious figures of the past. Such apologetics have had their inevitable effect upon the writing of history, as has the fundamental outlook of their proponents, tending as it does to idealize religious life in the ghetto at the expense of completely ignoring the deep inner conflicts and divisions to which not even the rabbis were necessarily immune. To acknowledge the Sabbatianism of eminent rabbis in Jerusalem, Adrianople, Constantinople, or Izmir, Prague, Hamburg, or Berlin, has been in the eyes of such authors to openly impeach the integrity of an entire body of men who were never supposed to be other than learned and virtuous defenders of Jewish tradition. Given such an attitude, it is hardly to be wondered at that one should instinctively avoid the kinds of inquiry that might lead to the discovery of heretical opinion, to say nothing of actual licentiousness, in the most unlikely places. One might cite endless examples of this kind of mentality in historical literature dealing with rabbinical and congregational life in the eighteenth century, and in at least one case, A. L. Frumkin's *A Historical Account of the Scholars of Jerusalem* (in Hebrew), the author goes so far as to "acquit" some of the most dedicated Sabbatians we know of of the "scandal" of heterodoxy!

Secularist historians, on the other hand, have been at pains to de-emphasize the role of Sabbatianism for a different reason. Not only did most of the families once associated with the Sabbatian movement in Western and Central Europe continue to remain afterwards within the Jewish fold, but many of their descendants, particularly in Austria, rose to positions of importance during the nineteenth century as prominent intellectuals, great financiers, and men of high political connections. Such persons, needless to say, could scarcely have been expected to approve of attempts to "expose" their "tainted" lineage, and in view of their stature in the Jewish community it is not surprising that their wishes should have carried weight. Furthermore, in an age when Jewish scholarship itself was considered to be in part an extension of the struggle for political emancipation, the climate for research in so sensitive an area was by no means generally favorable. In consequence, those Jewish scholars who had access to the wealth of Sabbatian documents and eyewitness reports that were still to be found early in the century failed to take advantage of the opportunity, while by the time a later generation arrived on the scene the sources had been destroyed and were no longer available even to anyone who might have desired to make use of them.

The survivors of the Frankists in Poland and of the Dönmeh or "Apostates" in Salonika formed yet a third group having a direct interest in disguising the historical facts. These two Sabbatian sects, both of which formally renounced the Jewish religion (the Dönmeh converting to Islam in 1683, the Frankists to Catholicism in 1759), continued to adhere to their secret identities long after their defection from their mother faith; the Dönmeh, in fact, did not disappear until the present generation, while in the case of the Frankists, whose history in the course of the nineteenth century is obscure, it is impossible to determine at exactly what point in time they were finally swallowed up by the rest of Polish society. There is reason to suspect that until the eve of World War II many original manuscripts and documents were preserved by both these groups, particularly by a number of Frankist families in Warsaw; but how much of this material may yet be uncovered, and how much has been purposely destroyed by its owners in order to conceal forever the secret of their descent, is in no way ascertainable.

Nevertheless, the total picture is not as dark as it may seem to have been painted: despite the many efforts at suppression, which supplemented, as it were, the inevitable "selective" process of time itself, a considerable amount of valuable material has been

saved. Many of the accusations made against the "believers" by
their opponents can now be weighed (and more often than not
confirmed!) on the basis of a number of the "believers'" own
books which were not allowed to perish. Little by little our
knowledge has grown, and although many of the historical details
we would like to know will undoubtedly never come to light at
all, there is reason to hope that this important chapter in Jewish
history will yet be fully written. In any event, it is clear that a
correct understanding of the Sabbatian movement after the apostasy of Sabbatai Zevi will provide a new clue toward understanding the history of the Jews in the eighteenth century as a
whole, and in particular, the beginnings of the Haskalah [En-
lightenment] movement in a number of countries.

I do not propose in this article to trace the outward history
of Sabbatianism in its several manifestations over the century and
a half in which it retained its vitality, nor (although I can hardly
conceal my opinion that the entire movement was far more widespread than is generally conceded even today) do I mean to debate the question of whether this or that particular individual
was or was not a Sabbatian himself. Suffice it to say that the
sources in our possession, meager as they are, make it perfectly
clear that the number of Sabbatian rabbis was far greater than
has been commonly estimated, greater even than was believed by
that anti-Sabbatian zealot Rabbi Jacob Emden, who has almost
always been accused of exaggeration. In the present essay, however, I shall put such questions aside and limit myself to the area
that has been the most sadly neglected in the entire field, namely,
the origins and development of Sabbatian thought per se.

If one accepts what Heinrich Graetz and David Kahana have
to say on the subject of Sabbatian theology, it is impossible to
understand what its essential attraction ever was; indeed, if it is
true, as both these writers claim, that the entire movement was a
colossal hoax perpetrated by degenerates and frauds, one might
well ask why a serious historian should bother to waste his time
on it in the first place. And if this is the case with Sabbatianism
in general, how much more so when one ventures to consider
what is undoubtedly the most tragic episode in the entire drama,
that of the Frankists, the psychological barriers to the understanding of which are incomparably greater. How, for instance,
can one get around the historical fact that in the course of their
public disputation with Jewish rabbis in Lvov in 1759 the members of this sect did not even shrink from resorting to the no-

torious blood libel, an accusation far more painful to Jewish sensitivities than any of their actual beliefs? A great deal has been written about this incident, particularly by the eminent historian Meir Balaban, in whose book, *On the History of the Frankist Movement* (in Hebrew), it is exhaustively dealt with. Balaban, who makes the Lvov libel a starting point for his over-all inquiry, reaches the significant conclusion that there was no organic connection between it and the Frankist "articles of faith" presented at the disputation. The members of the sect, in fact, were reluctant to make the accusation at all, and did so only at the instigation of the Catholic clergy, which was interested in using them for purposes of its own, having nothing to do with their Sabbatian background. That they finally agreed to collaborate in the scheme can be explained by their desire to wreak vengeance on their rabbinical persecutors.[2]

Thus, though the behavior of the Frankists at Lvov must certainly be judged harshly from both a universal-ethical and a Jewish-national point of view, it is important to keep in mind that the blood libels against the Jews (the indications are that there was more than one) do not in themselves tell us anything about the inner spiritual world of the sect, in all of whose literature (written one and two generations after the Lvov disputation) not a single allusion to such a belief is to be found. The truly astonishing thing is that although several important texts of Frankist teachings actually do exist, not a single serious attempt has so far been made to analyze their contents. The reason for this is simple. Graetz and A. Kraushar, two reputable scholars, one of whom wrote a full-length study of Jacob Frank and his Polish followers, were both of the opinion that there was no such thing as a Frankist "creed," and that *The Sayings of the Lord (Slowa Pańskie)* which has come down to us in a Polish version alone, was incoherent nonsense. According to Kraushar, Frank's sayings are "grotesque, comical, and incomprehensible," while Graetz, whose attitude toward all forms of mysticism is well known, could hardly have been expected to show much insight into the religious motivations of the sect. Balaban, on the other hand, is mainly concerned with the outward history of the Frankists up to the time of their mass conversion, and his reconstruction of their theology is based solely on the positions publicly taken by them in their disputations with the rabbis. It is his reliance on these "articles of faith," in fact, which were actually far from accurate reflections of the Frankists' true beliefs, that leads him to conclude that after 1759 the history of the sect was "determined more by the personalities of Jacob Frank and his disciples than by any intrinsic religious relationship to Judaism."

I myself cannot agree with Balaban on this point, and in the following pages I shall attempt to show, at least summarily, that Sabbatianism must be regarded not only as a single continuous development which retained its identity in the eyes of its adherents regardless of whether they themselves remained Jews or not, but also, paradoxical though it may seem, as a specifically *Jewish* phenomenon to the end. I shall endeavor to show that the nihilism of the Sabbatian and Frankist movements, with its doctrine so profoundly shocking to the Jewish conception of things that the violation of the Torah could become its true fulfillment (*bittulah shel torah zehu kiyyumah*), was a dialectical outgrowth of the belief in the Messiahship of Sabbatai Zevi, and that this nihilism, in turn, helped pave the way for the Haskalah and the reform movement of the nineteenth century, once its original religious impulse was exhausted. Beyond this, I hope to make the reader see how within the spiritual world of the Sabbatian sects, within the very sanctum sanctorum of Kabbalistic mysticism, as it were, the crisis of faith which overtook the Jewish people as a whole upon its emergence from its medieval isolation was first anticipated, and how groups of Jews within the walls of the ghetto, while still outwardly adhering to the practices of their forefathers, had begun to embark on a radically new inner life of their own. Prior to the French Revolution the historical conditions were lacking which might have caused this upheaval to break forth in the form of an open struggle for social change, with the result that it turned further inward upon itself to act upon the hidden recesses of the Jewish psyche; but it would be mistaken to conclude from this that Sabbatianism did not permanently affect the outward course of Jewish history. The desire for total liberation which played so tragic a role in the development of Sabbatian nihilism was by no means a purely self-destructive force; on the contrary, beneath the surface of lawlessness, antinomianism, and catastrophic negation, powerful constructive impulses were at work, and these, I maintain, it is the duty of the historian to uncover.

Undeniably, the difficulties in the face of this are great, and it is not to be wondered at that Jewish historians until now have not had the inner freedom to attempt the task. In our own times we owe much to the experience of Zionism for enabling us to detect in Sabbatianism's throes those gropings toward a healthier national existence which must have seemed like an undiluted nightmare to the peaceable Jewish bourgeois of the nineteenth century. Even today, however, the writing of Jewish history suffers unduly from the influence of nineteenth-century Jewish historiography. To be sure, as Jewish historians we have clearly advanced beyond the vantage point of our predecessors, having learned to insist, and rightly so, that Jewish history is a process that can only be understood when viewed from *within;* but in spite of all this, our progress in applying this truth to concrete historical situations, as opposed to general historiosophical theories has been slow. Up to the present* only two men, Siegmund Hurwitz in his *From Whither to Where* (in Hebrew) and Zalman Rubashov [Shazar] in his essay "Upon the Ruins of Frankism" (in Hebrew), have shown any true appreciation of the complexities of Sabbatian psychology, and their work has by and large failed to attract the attention it deserves.

And now, one last introductory comment. In dismissing the need for objective research on the Sabbatian and Frankist movements, it has often been asserted that since the phenomena in question are essentially pathological, they belong more properly to the study of medicine than to the study of history. Indeed, an article on "Frank and His Sect in the Light of Psychiatry" (Bychowski, *Ha-Tekufah,* Vol. XIV) has actually been published, but it only succeeds in demonstrating how incapable such an approach is of dealing satisfactorily with the problem. From the standpoint of sexual pathology it can hardly be doubted that Frank himself was a diseased individual, just as there can be no question that at the center and among the ranks of the Sabbatian movement (as in all radical movements that spring from certain particular tensions, some of which are not so far removed from those of "ordinary" life) it would be possible to find cases of marked mental aberrance. But what is the significance of all this? We are not, after all, so much concerned with this or that prominent Sabbatian personality as with the question of why such people were able to attract the following that they did. The diagnosis of a neurologist would be of little value in determining why thousands of human beings were able to find a spiritual home in the labyrinth of Sabbatian theology. We must refuse to be deluded by such convenient tags as "hysteria" or "mass psychosis," which

* This essay was written in 1935.

only confuse the issue at the same time that they provide an ex-
cuse for avoiding it and comfortably reassure one of one's own
comparative "normality." It is undoubtedly true that Jacob Frank
was every bit the depraved and unscrupulous person he is supposed to have been, and yet the moment we seriously ponder his
"teachings," or attempt to understand why masses of men should
have regarded him as their leader and prophet, this same individual becomes highly problematic. Even more than the psychology of the leader, however, it is the psychology of the led that
demands to be understood, and in the case of Sabbatianism, a
movement built entirely upon paradoxes, this question is crucial
indeed. Whatever we may think of Sabbatai Zevi and Jacob
Frank, the fact is: their followers, while they were certainly not
"innocents"—if there was one thing lacking in the paradoxical
religion of the Sabbatians it was innocence!—were sincere in
their faith, and it is the nature of this faith, which penetrated to
the hidden depths and abysses of the human spirit, that we wish
to understand.

II

As a mystical heterodoxy Sabbatianism assumed different and
changing forms: it splintered into many sects, so that even from
the polemical writings against it we learn that the "heretics"
quarreled among themselves over practically everything. The word
"practically," however, must be stressed, for on one essential, the
underlying ground of their "holy faith," as they called it, the
"believers" all agreed. Let us proceed then to examine this common ground of faith as it manifested itself both psychologically
and dogmatically.

By all accounts, the Messianic revival of 1665–66 spread to
every sector of the Jewish people throughout the Diaspora. Among
the believers and penitents a new emotion, which was not restricted to the traditional expectation of a political deliverance of
Israel alone, began to make itself felt. This is not to say that hope
for a divine liberation from the bondage and degradation of exile
was not an important element in the general contagion, but
rather that various psychological reactions which accompanied it
soon took on an independent existence of their own. Prior to
Sabbatai Zevi's apostasy, great masses of people were able to believe in perfect simplicity that a new era of history was being
ushered in and that they themselves had already begun to inhabit

a new and redeemed world. Such a belief could not but have a profound effect on those who held it: their innermost feelings, which assured them of the presence of a Messianic reality, seemed entirely in harmony with the outward course of events, those climactic developments in a historico-political realm that Sabbatai Zevi was soon to overthrow by means of his miraculous journey to the Turkish sultan, whom he would depose from his throne and strip of all his powers.

In the generation preceding Sabbatai Zevi's advent the rapid spread of the teachings of Rabbi Isaac Luria and his school had resulted in a grafting of the theories of the Kabbalists, the *de facto* theologians of the Jewish people in the seventeenth century, onto the traditional Jewish view of the role and personality of the Messiah. Mystical Lurianic speculations about the nature of the redemption and "the restored world" (*olam ha-tikkun*) which was to follow upon its heels added new contents and dimensions to the popular Messianic folk-myth of a conquering national hero, raising it to the level of a supreme cosmic drama: the redemptive process was now no longer conceived of as simply a working-out of Israel's temporal emancipation from the yoke of the Gentiles, but rather as a fundamental transformation of the entire Creation, affecting material and spiritual worlds alike and leading to a rectification of the primordial catastrophe of the "breaking of the vessels" (*shevirat ha-kelim*), in the course of which the divine worlds would be returned to their original unity and perfection. By stressing the spiritual side of the redemption far more than its outward aspect the Kabbalists of the Lurianic school, though by no means overlooking the latter, gradually converted it into a symbol of purely spiritual processes and ends. As long as the Messianic expectancies they encouraged were not put to the test in the actual crucible of history, the dangers inherent in this shift of emphasis went unnoticed, for the Kabbalists themselves never once imagined that a conflict might arise between the symbol and the reality it was intended to represent. To be sure, Lurianic Kabbalah had openly educated its followers to prepare themselves more for an inner than for an outer renewal; but inasmuch as it was commonly assumed that the one could not take place without the other, the procedure seemed in no way questionable. On the contrary: the spread of Lurianic teachings, so it was thought, was in itself bound to hasten the coming of the historical Redeemer.

The appearance of Sabbatai Zevi and the growth of popular faith in his mission caused this inner sense of freedom, of "a world made pure again," to become an immediate reality for thousands. This did not of course mean that Sabbatai Zevi himself was no longer expected to fulfill the various Messianic tasks assigned him by Jewish tradition, but in the meantime an irreversible change had taken place in the souls of the faithful. Who could deny that the Shekhinah, the earthly presence of God, had risen from the dust?

"Heretical" Sabbatianism was born at the moment of Sabbatai Zevi's totally unexpected conversion, when for the first time a contradiction appeared between the two levels of the drama of redemption, that of the subjective experience of the individual on the one hand, and that of the objective historical facts on the other. The conflict was no less intense than unforeseen. One had to choose: either one heard the voice of God in the decree of history, or else one heard it in the newly revealed reality within. "Heretical" Sabbatianism was the result of the refusal of large sections of the Jewish people to submit to the sentence of history by admitting that their own personal experience had been false and untrustworthy.

Thus, the various attempts to construct a Sabbatian theology were all motivated by a similar purpose, namely, to rationalize the abyss that had suddenly opened between the objective order of things and that inward certainty which it could no longer serve to symbolize, and to render the tension between the two more endurable for those who continued to live with it. The sense of contradiction from which Sabbatianism sprung became a lasting characteristic of the movement: following upon the initial paradox of an apostate Messiah, paradox engendered paradox. Above all, the "believers," those who remained loyal to their inward experience, were compelled to find an answer to the simple question: what could be the value of a historical reality that had proved to be so bitterly disappointing, and how might it be related to the hopes it had betrayed?

The essence of the Sabbatian's conviction, in other words, can be summarized in a sentence: it is inconceivable that all of God's people should inwardly err, and so, if their vital experience is contradicted by the facts, it is the facts that stand in need of explanation. In the words of a Sabbatian "moderate" [3] writing thirty years after Sabbatai Zevi's apostasy: "The Holy One, blessed be He, does not ensnare even the animals of the righteous, much less the righteous themselves, to say nothing of so terribly deceiving an entire people. . . . And how is it possible that all of

Israel be deceived unless this be part of some great divine plan?" This line of argument, which was adopted by many persons from the very beginning of the Sabbatian movement, is known to have impressed even the movement's opponents, who were equally disinclined to find fault with the entire Jewish people and sought instead some other explanation for what had happened.

During the century and a half of its existence Sabbatianism was embraced by those Jewish circles which desired to prolong the novel sensation of living in a "restored world" by developing attitudes and institutions that seemed commensurate with a new divine order. Inasmuch as this deliberately maintained state of consciousness was directly opposed to the outlook of ghetto Jewry as a whole, of which the "believers" themselves formed a part, the latter of necessity tended to become innovators and rebels, particularly the radicals among them. Herein lay the psychological basis of that spirit of revolt which so infuriated the champions of orthodoxy, who, though they may at first have had no inkling of the lengths to which it would be ultimately carried, rightly suspected it from the outset of striving to subvert the authority of rabbinic Judaism. Herein, too, lay the basis of all future efforts to construct a Sabbatian theology, to the consideration of which we must now turn our attention.

In the history of religion we frequently encounter types of individuals known as "pneumatics" (*pneumatikoi*) or "spiritualists" (*spirituales*). Such persons, who played a major role in the development of Sabbatianism, were known in Jewish tradition as "spiritual" or "extra-spirited" men or, in the language of the *Zohar,* as "masters of a holy soul." These terms did not refer to just anyone who may have had occasion in the course of his life to be "moved by the spirit"; rather, they applied only to those few who abode in the "palace of the king" (*hekhal ha-melekh*), that is, who lived in continual communion with a spiritual realm through whose gates they had passed, whether by actually dwelling within it to the point of abandoning their previous existence, or by appropriating from it a "spark" or "holy soul," as only the elect were privileged to do. One so favored was in certain respects no longer considered to be subject to the laws of everyday reality, having realized within himself the hidden world of divine light. Naturally, spiritualistic types of this sort have always regarded themselves as forming a group apart, and hence the special sense of their own "superiority" by which they are characterized: from their lofty perspective the world of material affairs tends to look lowly indeed. Here, then, we have all the prerequisites for the sectarian disposition, for the sect serves the *illuminati* as both a rallying point for their own kind and a refuge from the incomprehension of the carnal and unenlightened masses. The sectarians regard themselves as the vanguard of a new world, but they do not therefore need to renounce the parent religion which inspired them, for they can always reinterpret it in the light of the supreme reality to which they owe their newly discovered allegiance.

For a number of reasons, which cannot be gone into here, such spiritualists were rarely allowed to develop within the Jewish community after the period of the Second Temple. In part this was a consequence of Christianity, to which many of them ultimately passed; but even when they continued to exist within Judaism itself, it was always as isolated and unorganized individuals. It is a well-known fact, for instance, that spiritualism particularly abounds in the domain of religious mysticism; and yet, as the history of Kabbalism amply demonstrates, despite the opposition between conventional religion and the ecstasy, at times even abandon, of the pneumatic, medieval Judaism was capable of absorbing the latter into its orbit. Such was not the case, however, with either Christianity or Islam: here the conflict broke out openly and fiercely on numerous occasions, and the spiritualist sects which it produced went on to play important roles in the development of new social and religious institutions, often giving birth, albeit in religious guise, to the most revolutionary ideas. To take but one example, historical research during the last several decades has clearly shown the direct connection between Christian sectarianism in Europe and the growth of the Enlightenment and the ideal of toleration in the seventeenth and eighteenth centuries.

The existence of similar forces in Jewish history, on the other hand, has been all but neglected by the historians, an oversight facilitated by the fact that Jewish spiritualism has either long been outwardly dormant or else, as in the case of Kabbalism, has always preferred to work invisibly and unsystematically beneath the surface. Indeed, as long as Jewish historiography was dominated by a spirit of assimilation, no one so much as suspected that positivism and religious reform were the progeny not only of the rational mind, but of an entirely different sort of psychology as well, that of the Kabbalah and the Sabbatian crisis—in other words, of that very "lawless heresy" which was so soundly excoriated in their name!

In the Sabbatian movement, which was the first clear manifestation (one might better say *explosion*) of spiritualistic sectarianism in Judaism since the days of the Second Temple, the type of the radical spiritualist found its perfect expression. To be sure, *illuminati* of the same class were later prevalent in Hasidism too, particularly during the golden age of the movement; but Hasidism, rather than allow itself to be taken over by such types, forced them after a period of initial equivocation to curb their unruly spirituality, and did so with such success that it was able to overcome the most difficult and hazardous challenge of all, that of safely incorporating them into its own collective body. Unlike Sabbatianism, whose followers were determined to carry their doctrine to its ultimate conclusion, it was the genius of Hasidism that it knew where to set itself limits. But the Sabbatians pressed on to the end, into the abyss of the mythical "gates of impurity" (*sha'are tum'ah*), where the pure spiritual awareness of a world made new became a pitfall fraught with peril for the moral life.

Here, then, were all the materials necessary to cause a true conflagration in the heart of Jewry. A new type of Jew had appeared for whom the world of exile and Diaspora Judaism was partly or wholly abolished and who uncompromisingly believed that a "restored world," whose laws and practices he was commanded to obey, was in the process of coming into being. The great historical disappointment experienced by the Sabbatian had instilled in him the paradoxical conviction that he and his like were privy to a secret whose time had not yet come to be generally revealed, and it was this certainty which, in Hebrew literature of the period, imparted a special meaning to his use of the terms "believer" and "holy faith," the peculiar shadings of which immediately inform us that we are dealing with a Sabbatian document even when there is not the slightest allusion therein to Sabbatai Zevi himself: by virtue of his "holy faith" in the mysterious realignment of the divine worlds and in the special relationship to them of the Creator during the transitional period of cosmic restitution (*tikkun*), the "believer," he who trusted in the mission of Sabbatai Zevi, was exalted above all other men. Hidden in the "believer's" soul was a precious jewel, the pearl of Messianic freedom, which shone forth from its chamber of chambers to pierce the opaqueness of evil and materiality; he who possessed it was a free man by power of his own personal experience, and to this inner sense of freedom, whether gotten during the mass revival that preceded Sabbatai Zevi's apostasy, or afterwards, in the ranks of the "holy faith," he would continue to cling no matter how much he knew it to be contradicted by the outward facts.

All Sabbatian doctrine had as its aim the resolution of this contradiction. The conflict was bitterly clear. Those who were disillusioned by Sabbatai Zevi's apostasy were able to claim that nothing had really changed: the world was the same as ever, the exile was no different than before; therefore the Torah was the same Torah and the familiar Kabbalistic teachings about the nature of the Godhead and the divine worlds remained in force. A great opportunity had perhaps existed, but it had been missed; henceforth the one recourse was a return to Israel's traditional faith in its God. The "believers," on the other hand, could say in paraphrase of Job, "our eyes have beheld and not another's": the redemption had begun indeed, only its ways were mysterious and its outward aspect was still incomplete. Externals might seem the same, but inwardly all was in the process of renewal. Both the Torah and the exile had been fundamentally altered, as had the nature of the Godhead, but for the time being all these transformations bore "inward faces" alone.

The Sabbatian movement soon developed all the psychological characteristics of a spiritualist sect, and before long many of its followers proceeded to organize themselves along such lines. The persecutions against them on the part of various rabbinical and congregational authorities, their own special feeling of apartness and of the need to preserve their secret, and the novel practices which their beliefs eventually compelled them to pursue, were all factors in bringing this about. I do not propose to dwell at length on the history of any of these groups, but I do wish to emphasize briefly at this point that large numbers of Jews, especially among the Sephardim, continued to remain faithful to Sabbatai Zevi after his conversion. Even such opponents of Sabbatianism as Jacob Sasportas, who claimed that the followers of the movement were now an "insubstantial minority," was forced to admit on other occasions that the minority in question was considerable indeed, particularly in Morocco, Palestine, Egypt, and most of Turkey and the Balkans. Most of the Sabbatian groups in these areas maintained constant contact with each other and kept up a running battle over the correct interpretation of their "holy faith." From these regions came the first theoreticians of the movement, men such as Nathan of Gaza, Samuel Primo, Abraham Miguel Cardozo, and Nehemiah Hayon, as well as the believers in "voluntary Marranism," who went on to form the sect of the Dönmeh in Salonika. In Italy the number of Sabbatians was smaller, though it included some of the country's most important Kabbalists; within a generation after its appearance there, Sabbatianism had dwindled into the concern of a few rabbis and scholars (chief among them Rabbi Benjamin Cohen of Reggio and Rabbi Abraham Rovigo of Modena), in whose hands it remained for a century without ever penetrating into wider circles. In Northern Europe Sabbatianism was also restricted at first to small groups of adherents, devotees of such "prophets" as Heshel Zoref of Vilna and Mordecai of Eisenstadt in Hungary, but after 1700, following the commencement of a "Palestinian period" during which organized Sabbatian emigrations to the Holy Land took place from several countries, the movement spread rapidly through Germany and the Austro-Hungarian Empire. In Lithuania it failed to take root, but in Podolia and Moravia it became so entrenched that it was soon able to claim the allegiance of many ordinary Jewish burghers and small businessmen (according to Jacob Emden, the numerical value of the Hebrew letters in the verse in Psalms 14, "There is none that doeth good, not even one," was equivalent to the numerical value of the letters in the Hebrew word for Moravia!) In Prague and Mannheim Sabbatian-oriented centers of learning came into being. The influence of the "graduates" of these institutions was great; one of them, in fact, was the author of the heretical treatise *Va-Avo ha-Yom El ha-Ayin* ("And I Came This Day Unto the Fountain") which provoked so much furor at the time of the controversy surrounding Jonathan Eibeschütz (1751) and led to a polemical "battle of the books" which has enabled us to trace the identities of many Sabbatians of whom otherwise we would have known nothing at all. In the middle of the eighteenth century many of the Sabbatians in Podolia converted to Christianity after the example of their leader Jacob Frank, but still others remained within the Jewish fold. Finally, a Sabbatian stronghold sprang up again in Prague, where Frankism was propagated in a Jewish form. After 1815, however, the movement fell apart and its members were absorbed into secular Jewish society, like the Frankist ancestors of Louis Brandeis.

It is now time to turn our attention to the actual content of the spiritualism of these Sabbatian groups, for although the details of their theosophical teachings cannot be understood by anyone not already familiar with the intricacies of Kabbalistic speculation in both the *Zohar* and the writings of the Lurianic school, other vital questions which concerned them, as well as their doctrine of the Godhead in its more general form, can be rendered intelligible even to those who are not fully versed in the esoteric side of Jewish mystical thought.

III

The question which first confronted the "believers" after the apostasy of Sabbatai Zevi, and one to which they never ceased returning, was of the following order: since by all external tokens the redemption had already been at hand, and since the Messiah, the authenticity of whose mission was beyond doubt, had actually revealed himself to his people, why had he forsaken them and his religion, and why had the historical and political deliverance from bondage which was to have naturally accompanied the cosmic process of *tikkun* been delayed? To this a paradoxically compelling answer was quickly offered: the apostasy of the Messiah was itself a religious mystery of the most crucial importance! No less an authority than Maimonides himself, it was argued, had stated that the actual details of the redemptive process were not to be known in advance; and although the truth of the matter was that everything that had happened was fully alluded to in the Holy Scriptures, these allusions themselves could not be correctly understood until the events they foretold had come to pass. All might be found to have been predicted in the relevant prophecies and legends, which Nathan of Gaza, and even more so Abraham Cardozo, now proceeded to expound in the form of a new doctrine to which Sabbatai Zevi himself apparently subscribed.[4]

As long as the last divine sparks (*nitzotzot*) of holiness and good which fell at the time of Adam's primordial sin into the impure realm of the *kelipot* (the hylic forces of evil whose hold in the world is particularly strong among the Gentiles) have not been gathered back again to their source—so the explanation ran —the process of redemption is incomplete. It is therefore left to the Redeemer, the holiest of men, to accomplish what not even the most righteous souls in the past have been able to do: to descend through the gates of impurity into the realm of the *kelipot* and to rescue the divine sparks still imprisoned there. As soon as this task is performed the Kingdom of Evil will collapse of itself, for its existence is made possible only by the divine sparks in its midst. The Messiah is constrained to commit "strange acts" (*ma'asim zarim;* a concept hereafter to occupy a central place in Sabbatian theology), of which his apostasy is the most startling; all of these, however, are necessary for the fulfillment of his mission. In the formulation of Cardozo: "It is ordained that the King Messiah don the garments of a Marrano and so go unrecognized by his fellow Jews. In a word, it is ordained that he become a Marrano like me." [5]

Before proceeding to take a closer look at this bold and heretical doctrine, one might well dwell for a moment on Cardozo's own words, which provide in my opinion an invaluable clue to the motivation behind it, as they do in fact to nearly every other feature of the Sabbatian movement as well. Underlying the novelty of Sabbatian thought more than anything else was the deeply paradoxical religious sensibility of the Marranos and their descendants, who constituted a large portion of Sephardic Jewry. Had it not been for the unique psychology of these reconverts to Judaism, the new theology would never have found the fertile ground to flourish in that it did. Regardless of what the actual backgrounds of its first disseminators may have been, the Sabbatian doctrine of the Messiah was perfectly tailored to the needs of the Marranic mentality. Indeed, we know for a fact that Abraham Cardozo, one of the movement's most successful proselytizers, was of definite Marrano origin—he was born in Spain in 1627—a particular which goes far to explain the remarkable zeal and sincerity with which he defended the new doctrine. Historians in our own day have pointed out at length the degree of contradiction, of duplicity and duality, which was involved in the religious consciousness of the Marranos. For these undercover Jews "to don the garments of a Marrano" was by no means an unjustifiable act; in its defense they were fond of citing the story of Queen Esther, as well as various other biblical fragments and verses. Formal apostasy had never been considered by them to represent an irreconcilable break with their mother faith. And now along came a religious metaphysic which exalted just such a form of life to the highest possible level by attributing it to the person of the Redeemer himself! Certainly all kinds of implications, which we shall deal with later on, were contained in this original idea. Let us examine it more closely.

To begin with, the new doctrine could no longer be harmonized with the traditional Messianic folk-myth held to by the Jewish masses unless room could be found in the latter for such a "contradiction in terms" as the apostasy of the Redeemer. At first it was no doubt believed that the Messiah's descent into the realm of the *kelipot* was but an incidental aspect of his mission, "as happened to King David [when he sojourned] with Achish King of Gath," but it soon came to be realized that such an extraordinary event must occupy the center of any Messianic schema, which if necessary would have to be rebuilt around it: if the Messiah's task indeed contained a tragic element, as was now being proposed, support for this belief would have to be found in the sources and attitudes of Jewish tradition. What now took place in Sabbatianism was similar to what happened in Christianity at the time of the apostles, the chief difference being the shifting of the tragic moment in the Messiah's destiny from his crucifixion to his apostasy, a change which rendered the paradox in question even more severe. And to this novel conception another was soon added, one which indeed had a basis in aggadic literature, but whose hidden implications had gone unnoticed as long as no pressing reality had existed to force its application outside of the domain of pure theory and imagination; this was the notion that the King Messiah was to give "a new Torah" and that the commandments of the Law (*mitzvot*) were to be abrogated in Messianic times. Speculations of this nature could be found in various Midrashim and Aggadot, but possessed no particular authority and were easily challenged by means of other exegetical passages to the opposite effect, with the consequence that, in Jewish tradition, the entire question had hitherto been allowed to remain in abeyance. Even those visionaries who dreamt through the ages of a new Word of God in a redeemed world did not, in fact, particularly connect this idea with the activities of the Messiah himself, and it was not until it was seized upon by the new "Marranic" doctrine that its latent explosive power was revealed.

The doctrine of the necessary apostasy of the Messiah did not originate in the realm of literature, but was rather rooted in new religious feelings that had come to exist. It was only after the initial manifestation of these that the effort to justify them on the basis of authoritative sources began, and with truly remarkable results, for practically overnight a new religious language was born. From bits and pieces of Scripture, from scattered paradoxes and sayings in the writings of the Kabbalah, from all the remotest corners of Jewish religious literature, an unprecedented theology of Judaism was brought into being. The cynicism of most Jewish historians toward these "inanities" does not reveal any great understanding of what actually took place. Suddenly we find ourselves confronted by an original Jewish terminology, far removed from that of Christianity, yet equally determined to express the contradictions inherent in the life of the Redeemer and in redemption itself. Striking as it did a hidden wellspring of deep religious emotion, one can hardly deny that this gospel must have possessed a powerful attraction, nor that it often managed to inject new meanings into familiar phrases and figures of speech with a fascinating profundity. Such a dialectical eruption of new forces in the midst of old concepts is rare indeed. Because Graetz and other historians insisted on regarding its articulation as being nothing more than a pretext for a monstrous debauchment of moral and spiritual values, they completely overlooked its true significance. To be sure, the doctrine of an apostate Messiah did serve as a pretext too, but it was also a great deal more; and had it not appealed (and by virtue of its very paradoxicality!) to vital components in the spiritual make-up of the Jew, and above all to his sense of spiritual mission, it would never have succeeded in attracting a following in the first place. This missionary ideology reached a peak in the writings of the Lurianic Kabbalah, which strove to inculcate in every Jew a sense of duty to "elevate the sparks" and so help bring about the ultimate *tikkun* of the Creation.

Here the 53rd chapter of Isaiah played a key role, for as it was now reinterpreted the verse "But he was wounded because of our transgressions" was taken to be an allusion not only to the Messiah ben Joseph, the legendary forerunner of the Redeemer who according to tradition was to suffer death at the hands of the Gentiles, but to the Messiah ben David as well, who "would be forceably prevented from observing the Torah." By a play on words, the Hebrew *ve-hu meholal,* "but he was wounded," was interpreted as meaning "from sacred he [the Messiah] will be made profane [*hol*]." Thus,

all Gentiles are referred to as profane [*hol*] and *kelipah,* and whereas Israel alone is called sacred, all the other nations are profane. And even though a Jew commit a transgression, as long as he remains a Jew among Jews he is called sacred and an Israelite, for as the rabbis have said, "Even though he has sinned, he is still an Israelite." It follows that there is no way for the King Messiah to be made profane except he be removed from the Community of Israel into another domain.

Many similar homilies were written on the rest of the chapter, especially on the verse, "And he made his grave with the wicked." Yet another favorite verse was Deuteronomy 33:7 ("And this for Judah, and he said: Hear, Lord, the voice of Judah, and bring him unto his people"), which was assumed to allude to the Davidic Messiah of the House of Judah, whose destiny it was to be taken from his people (hence Moses' prayer that God bring him back to them).[6] Endless biblical verses were cited to prove that the Messiah was fated to be contemned as an outcast and criminal by his own people. Clothed in Messianic radiance, all the typical arguments of the Marranos were applied to Sabbatai Zevi:

And similar to this [the apostasy of Sabbatai Zevi] is what happened to Esther, who was the cause of great salvation to Israel; for although most of the people, being ignorant, most certainly despised her for having given herself to an idol-worshiper and a Gentile in clear violation of the bidding of the Torah, the sages of old, who knew the secret [of her action], did not regard her as a sinner, for it is said of her in the Talmud: "Esther was the ground of the entire world."

In the same vein, the familiar aggadic saying that "the last Redeemer will be as the first" was taken to mean that just as Moses lived for many years at the court of Pharaoh, so the Messiah must live with "the Turk," for as the exile draws to a close the Messiah himself must be exiled to atone for Israel's sins.

Next came the turn of the *Zohar*, and here too, with the help of major or minor distortions, a world of new symbols was made to emerge, such as the figure of "the king who is good within but clothed in evil garments."[7] In vain it was argued against this interpretation that the passage does not refer in this context to a king at all, much less to the Messiah; the image, so expressive in its obscurity, penetrated deep into the Sabbatian consciousness where it remained for generations to come. Two other writers whose works were mined in this fashion were Rabbi Judah Loew ben Bezalel of Prague and Rabbi Joseph Taitatsak of Salonika, one of the emigrés from Spain in 1492: the former was found to have cryptically predicted that the Messiah would be bound to the world of Islam, while the latter was supposed to have stated, "when the rabbis said that the Son of David would not come until the kingdom was entirely given over to unbelief [Sanhedrin 97a], they were thinking of the Kingdom of Heaven, for the Shekhinah is destined to don the garments of Ishmael."[8] In

a word, the attempt to justify the belief that the fall and apostasy
of the Messiah were necessary actions was carried out assiduously
and successfully and led to the composition of many homilies,
treatises, and books, some of which have not yet been recovered
from their resting places. Endless vindications and defenses of the
new doctrine were brought from practically every corner of
Jewish literature. At first the tendency was to assert that although
the Messiah's conversion had been forced upon him, it was quali-
tatively to be considered as a deliberate act; gradually, however,
this motif disappeared, and the emphasis came to be placed
squarely on the paradox that the Messiah should convert of his
own free will. The descent into the *kelipot* was, indeed had to be,
a voluntary one.

It was at this point that a radically new content was bestowed
upon the old rabbinic concept of *mitzvah ha-ba'ah ba-averah,* literally, "a commandment which is fulfilled by means of a transgression." Once it could be claimed that the Messiah's apostasy was in
no way a transgression, but was rather a fulfillment of the commandment of God, "for it is known throughout Israel that the
prophets can do and command things which are not in accord with
the Torah and its laws," [9] the entire question of the continued
validity of the Law had reached a critical stage. We know that
even before his apostasy Sabbatai Zevi violated several of the
commandments by eating the fat of animals and administering it
to others,[10] directing that the paschal sacrifice be performed outside of the Land of Israel, and cancelling the fast days. His followers soon began to seek explanations for these acts, and here began
a division which was to lead eventually to an open split in the
movement.

IV

The new doctrine of the necessary apostasy of the Messiah was
accepted by all the "believers." In fact, it proved to be symbolically richer than was at first assumed, for it expertly expressed the
contradiction between the outward reality of history and the inward reality of the "believers'" lives. It was now no longer to
be wondered at that the outward deliverance had been delayed, for
this could be explained by the mystic principle of "good within
but clothed in evil garments." In turn, however, other questions
arose which the doctrine of necessary apostasy was in itself insufficient to answer.

First of all, it was asked, what was the nature of the Messiah's act? Was it intended to be an exemplar for others? Were all Jews enjoined to follow suit? Or was it essentially inimitable and to be looked upon as a theoretical model only?

Second, what was the nature of the transitional period during which the Messiah was in the clutches of the *kelipot?* Could it properly be called the redemption or not? Since it was agreed by all that the Shekhinah had "risen from the dust," where was the Shekhinah now? Did it still make sense to speak of her "exile" and to mourn for her? What exactly was the relationship of inwardness to outwardness in the present age?

Third, what was the status of the Torah during this period? Had a new aspect of it been revealed? How was the principle of *mitzvah ha-ba'ah ba-averah* to be understood? Could it not be argued that the change which had taken place in the relationship of the divine worlds necessitated a corresponding change in the performance of the commandments, the purpose of which had been to restore the harmony of the old, unredeemed cosmos that had been shattered by the primordial sin? Was not the Lurianic Kabbalah in its traditional form now outdated?

These were the principal dilemmas which were to shape the development of Sabbatianism in the course of the following hundred years, and in several countries to transform it from a Messianic movement into a nihilistic movement operating within a religious framework. And just as these questions were themselves mutually related, so the nihilism which resulted from them was to be characterized by its internal unity and consistency.

Here, then, it is necessary to distinguish between two opposing Sabbatian factions which emerged from the clashes of opinion surrounding these disputed points, as well as from differing interpretations of the theosophical "mystery of the Godhead" (*sod ha-elohut*) revealed by Sabbatai Zevi to his disciples: a moderate and rather piously inclined wing of the movement on the one hand, and a radical, antinomian, and nihilistic wing on the other. (Both of these factions, in turn, contained many subdivisions, but here we are concerned only with the more general features of each.) In the case of some Sabbatians, who have left us no completely candid record of their feelings, it is difficult to determine to which of these two camps they belonged.[11] As might naturally be expected, in face of the persecutions against them the "believers" were not often in a position to expound their beliefs undisguisedly, and certainly not to permit them to appear in

print. This was particularly true of the nihilists, who had good
and compelling reasons for concealing their doctrines.

Moderate Sabbatianism, which we shall consider first, was a
view shared by many rabbis and was represented by men like
Nathan of Gaza, Abraham Cardozo, and Abraham Rovigo. Of
these three, Cardozo and Rovigo are the more valuable sources,
especially the former, a large number of whose many treatises
have survived thanks to the refusal of his disciples in London,
Turkey, and Morocco to burn them in compliance with the injunctions of the rabbinical courts.

According to the "moderates," the apostasy of the Messiah was
not intended to serve as an example for others. To be sure, Sabbatai Zevi had done what was necessary, but to attempt to follow
in his footsteps was to belie the significance of his act, which was
performed in behalf of everybody. In the words of Isaiah 53:
"The Lord hath made to light on him the iniquity of us all."
Strictly speaking, "all were [originally] under the obligation to
convert," but God in His mercy permitted the apostasy of the
Messiah to atone for the sins of his people. Besides being strange
and scandalous in its nature, Sabbatai Zevi's conversion was in a
class by itself and was not an object of imitation. The Jew was
expected to remain a Jew. True, a new world-era had undoubtedly
been ushered in, the spiritual worlds had undergone *tikkun,* and
their structure was now permanently altered; nonetheless, as long
as the redemption did not manifest itself outwardly in the realm
of objective events in history, as long as the external bondage
continued and the phenomenal world remained unchanged, no
aspect or commandment of the Torah was to be openly tampered
with except for the small number of innovations, such as the
cancellation of the fast of *Tish'ah be'Av* (the day of the destruction of the Temple), which had been proclaimed by the Messiah
and his prophets as symbolic tokens of the redemption's commencement. Even on this point, however, there was disagreement,
for several Sabbatians, including Abraham Rovigo himself, decided to reinstate the fast after a period of hesitation lasting a
number of years during which they disregarded it—not because
they had "gone back" on their beliefs, but because of the questionable nature of the practice itself, as witnessed by the fact that
Rovigo's disciple Mordecai Ashkenazi had been bidden by a *maggid* or "spiritual intelligence" to desist from it. On the whole, it
was the view of the "moderates" that during the transitional
period under way the *kelipot* still retained a good deal of their

power, which could only be eliminated by continued performance of the *mitzvot*: the "façade" of rabbinic Judaism must be allowed to remain temporarily standing, although great changes had already taken place within the edifice. One unmistakable testimony to this inner transformation was the abandonment by many of the "moderates" of the mystical meditations (*kavvanot*) of Isaac Luria. The first to discontinue their use was Nathan of Gaza, whose reasons for doing so were as follows:

The *kavvanot* of the Lurianic Kabbalists were inward actions of thought designed to relate the performance of given commandments or prayers to specific stages in the dynamic chain of the divine worlds and thereby to reintegrate the latter by helping to restore them to the places they had occupied before their catastrophic fall. Thus, each *kavvanah* was a spiritual act demonstrating that the outward undertaking which occasioned it harmonized invisibly with the over-all structure of the cosmos. Now, however, with the advent of the Messiah, this structure had changed. The sense of inner freedom possessed by the "believers" was not a subjective illusion, but was caused by a real reorganization of the worlds illuminating the soul, as a result of which the Lurianic *kavvanot* had become obsolete. This in turn led to a re-evaluation of the entire Lurianic Kabbalah, and on occasion both Nathan of Gaza and Abraham Cardozo went so far as to direct veiled criticisms at Isaac Luria himself. Nathan, for example, writes: "In the present age it is no longer in order to read the *tikkunim* composed by Rabbi Isaac Luria of blessed memory and his disciples, nor to meditate according to their *kavvanot,* for the times have changed. The *kavvanot* of Rabbi Isaac Luria were meant for his own age, which was [like] an ordinary day of the week, whereas now it is the eve of the Sabbath, and it is not proper to treat the Sabbath as though it were a weekday." [12] Elsewhere he writes: "My meaning is that the *kavvanot* discovered by our teacher Rabbi Isaac Luria, may his saintly and righteous memory be blessed, are no longer appropriate to our own time, because the raising up [of the divine worlds] has entered a new phase, so that it would be like employing *kavvanot* intended for a weekday on the Sabbath. Therefore, let everyone beware of using them, and likewise let none of the *kavvanot* or homilies or writings of Rabbi Isaac Luria be read henceforward, for they are abstruse and no living man has understood them except Rabbi Hayyim Vital, who was a disciple of the master [Isaac Luria] for several years, at the end of which he surpassed him in knowledge." [13] In a similar vein: "It is no longer in order to perform the midnight vigil, that is, to weep and mourn for the exile of the Shekhinah, for she has already begun to rise from the earth, so that whoever mourns for her is a blunderer and attracts the company of that guilty [demon] Lilith, since it is she who now weeps and wails." Many other passages like these could be cited. As a matter of course Cardozo hastened to compose a new series of updated *kavvanot,*[14] but these were never to prove popular with his fellow Sabbatians, who either gave up the practice of mystical meditations entirely, or else, like many of the Hasidim who came after them, took to composing their own as they individually saw fit.

It was generally held by all the Sabbatians that now, on the "eve of the Sabbath," the mystery of the Godhead (*sod ha-elohut*) that had eluded the rabbis, philosophers, and Kabbalists throughout the ages was finally to be revealed. This was not to say that the secret had not been hinted at by the last of the Gnostics living in the Tannaitic period, who cryptically concealed it in the pages of the *Zohar* and in several Aggadot, particularly those known as the *aggadot shel dofi* or "offensive Aggadot," which had served as milestones for the contemplation of the mystics and as obscure hints at the mysteries during the dark night of exile. But the true meaning of these had been overlooked; nor could it be fully comprehended until the End of Days. On the other hand, although the "mystery of the Godhead" was yet to be revealed in its entirety, a part of it had now been made known. Here again a rejection of Lurianism and the substitution of a new Sabbatian Kabbalah in its place were involved.[15] The first written exposition of the new system, which was to be subject to a great many differing inferences and interpretations, was the small tract *Raza de-Mehemanuta* ("The Secret of the Faith") which was orally dictated by Sabbatai Zevi to a disciple after his apostasy.[16] Its effect was to prefix yet another stage to the theogonic speculations of the Kabbalists, for it treated (and quite remarkably) of the mysterious inner life of the Godhead before its *tzimtzum* or primordial contraction, whereas Lurianic Kabbalah had dealt only with the counter-expansion of the deity once the *tzimtzum* had taken place.

We have already seen in regard to their doctrine of the apostate Messiah that the Sabbatians were not in the least bit chary of paradoxes, and indeed, their theological reflections on the true nature of "the Faith" and its history in Israel reveal a dialectical daring that cannot but be respected. Here we are given our deepest glimpse yet into the souls of these revolutionaries who regarded themselves as loyal Jews while at the same time completely over-turning the traditional religious categories of Judaism. I am not of course speaking of a feeling of "loyalty" to the Jewish re-ligion as it was defined by rabbinical authority. For many, if not for most Sabbatians, the Judaism of the rabbis, which they iden-tified with the Judaism of the exile, had come to assume an en-tirely dubious character. Even when they continued to live within its jurisdiction it was not out of any sense of positive commit-ment; no doubt it had been suited to its time, but in the light of the soul-shaking truth of the redemption that time had passed. Taking into account all that has been said here, it is hardly surprising that this attitude should have existed. What is surpris-ing, however, indeed astoundingly so, is the nature of the spiritual world that the Sabbatians should have stumbled upon in the course of their search through the Bible for "the mystery of the God-head" which exilic Judaism had allowed to perish, for here we are confronted with nothing less than the totally unexpected re-vival of the religious beliefs of the ancient Gnostics, albeit in a transvalued form.

The Gnostics, who were the contemporaries of the Jewish Tannaim of the second century, believed that it was necessary to distinguish between a good but hidden God who alone was worthy of being worshiped by the elect, and a Demiurge or creator of the physical universe, whom they identified with the "just" God of the Old Testament. In effect they did not so much reject the Jewish Scriptures, whose account of events they conceded to be at least partly true, as they denied the superiority of the Jewish God, for whom they reserved the most pejorative terms. Salvation was brought to mankind by messengers sent by the hidden God to rescue the soul from the cruel law or "justice" of the Demiurge, whose dominion over the evil material world, as testified to by the Bible, was but an indication of his lowly status. The hidden God Himself was unknown, but he had entrusted Jesus and the gnostic faithful with the task of overthrowing the "God of the Jews." As for the claim of both Jews and orthodox Christians that the God of Israel who created the world and the transcendent God of goodness were one and the same, this was a great false-hood which stood in the way of true gnosis. This kind of "meta-physical anti-Semitism," as is well known, did not vanish from history with the disappearance of the gnostic sects, but continued to reassert itself within the Catholic Church and its heretical off-shoots throughout the Middle Ages.

"The mystery of the Godhead" which Sabbatianism now "dis-covered" and which it believed to be identical with "the mystery of the God of Israel" and "the faith of Father Abraham," was founded entirely on a new formulation of this ancient gnostic paradox. In the version made current by Cardozo it was ex-pounded as follows:

All nations and philosophers have been led by irrefutable laws of the intellect to acknowledge the existence of a First Cause responsible for setting all else in motion. Given the fact, therefore, that anyone capable of logical reasoning can demonstrate to his own satisfaction that such a Cause exists, what need is there for it to be specially revealed to mankind? What possible religious difference can such a revelation make when we are no less the wiser without it? The answer is, none at all. The First Cause, which was worshiped by Pharaoh and Nimrod and the wise men of India alike, is not the concern of religion at all, for it has nothing to do with the affairs of this world or its creation and exerts no influence on it for good or for bad. The purpose of a divine revelation must be to make something known which cannot be grasped by the intellect on its own, something which has spe-cifically religious value and content. And indeed, this is precisely the case with the Jewish Torah, which does not dwell at all on that Hidden Principle whose existence can be adequately proven by the intellect, but speaks only of the God of Israel, *Elohei Yis-rael,* who is the creator of the world and the first emanation to proceed from the First Cause. This God, in turn, has two aspects, or "countenances" (*partzufim*), one male and one female, the latter being known as the Shekhinah; He alone it is who creates and reveals Himself and redeems, and to Him alone are prayer and worship to be rendered. It is this paradox of a God of re-ligion who is distinct from the First Cause that is the essence of true Judaism, that "faith of our fathers" which is concealed in the books of the Bible and in the dark sayings of the Aggadot and the Kabbalah. In the course of the confusion and demoraliza-tion brought on by the exile this mystery (of which even Chris-tianity was nothing but a distorted expression) was forgotten and the Jewish People was mistakenly led to identify the impersonal First Cause with the personal God of the Bible, a spiritual dis-aster for which Saadia Gaon, Maimonides, and the other philoso-

phers will yet be held accountable. It was thus that the words of
the prophet Hosea, "For the Children of Israel shall sit solitary
many days without a king" (3:4), came to be fulfilled. At the
exile's end, however, Israel's God will reveal Himself once more,
and this secret is a source of precious comfort to the "believers."

Here we have a typically gnostic scheme, only inverted: the
good God is no longer the *deus absconditus,* who has now become
the deity of the philosophers for whom there is no room in
religion proper, but rather the God of Israel who created the world
and presented it with His Torah. What daring labyrinths of the
spirit are revealed in this new creed! What yearnings for a re-
generation of faith and what disdainful negation of the exile!
Like true spiritual revolutionaries, with an unfeigned enthusiasm
which even today cannot fail to impress the reader of Cardozo's
books, the "believers" unflinchingly proclaimed their belief that
all during the exile the Jewish People had worshiped a powerless
divinity and had clung to a way of life that was fundamentally
in need of reform. When one considers how wildly extravagant
all this may appear even now, it is easy enough to appreciate the
wrath and indignation with which such a theology was greeted
by the orthodox camp in its own day. Determined to avoid a full-
scale revolution within the heart of Jewry, the rabbinical traditionalists and their supporters did all they could to drive the
"believers" beyond the pale. And yet in spite of all this, one can
hardly deny that a great deal that is authentically Jewish was embodied in these paradoxical individuals too, in their desire to
start afresh and in their realization of the fact that negating the
exile meant negating its religious and institutional forms as well
and returning to the original fountainheads of the Jewish faith.
This last practice—a tendency to rely in matters of belief upon
the Bible and the Aggadah—grew to be particularly strong among
the nihilists in the movement. Here too, faith in paradox reigned
supreme: the stranger the Aggadah, the more offensive to reason
and common sense, the more likely it was to be seized upon as a
symbol of that "mystery of faith" which naturally tended to
conceal itself in the most frightful and fanciful tales.

I have alluded to the fierce discussions that broke out among
the Sabbatians over the issue of how "the mystery of the Godhead" was to be interpreted. Several of the elucidations of the
doctrine that are known to us differ substantially from the version
given by Cardozo, who devoted his very best speculative powers

to the question. All of these treatises employ the terminology of the *Zohar* and the Lurianic Kabbalah, but proceed to attribute to it meanings that are entirely their own. Among the speculations on the subject that have come down to us in detail are those of Nehemiah Hayon, Samuel Primo, and Jonathan Eibeschütz. Despite their division of the Godhead into three hypostases (*part-zufim*), the First Cause or "Holy Ancient One" (*atika kadisha*), the God of Israel or "Holy King" (*malka kadisha*), and the Shek-hinah, all of these writers sought to uphold the essential dynamic unity of the divinity. The central problems as they saw them— problems, be it said, which did not exist for non-Sabbatian Kabbalah at all—were first of all to determine the nature of the relationship, the "three knots of faith" as they called it, between the First Cause, the God of Israel, and the Shekhinah, and secondly to establish the exact content of the new revelation concerning the essence of the God of Israel. Characteristic of the approach of these Sabbatian "moderates" was their stubborn refusal to leave any room in their gnostic theories for a doctrine of divine incarnation. Indeed, the literature of "moderate" Sabbatianism is in general filled with violent denunciations of Christianity and of the Christian dogma of the Trinity.[17]

According to several of the "moderates," "the mystery of the Godhead" had not yet been fully revealed:[18] during the original Messianic revival of 1665-66, they argued, there had been an initial revelation which it was permitted to freely make known, but now, during the period of transition, eclipse, and uncertainty the situation was no longer the same. The Shekhinah had indeed "begun to rise," but "she has still not returned to her place entirely, for had she returned we would no longer be in exile." These words were written by Abraham Rovigo more than thirty years after Sabbatai Zevi's apostasy, of the mystic meaning of which he had absolutely no doubt, and they illustrate in a nutshell the psychology of "moderate" Sabbatianism while at the same time solving the riddle of how so many rabbis who were confirmed "believers" nevertheless managed to remain in their rabbinical posts. The redemption had truly begun, but it was a gradual process: "[It proceeds] step by step. In the end the Holy One, blessed be He, will raise her from the dust." This was not to say that the Shekhinah had not already begun to rise of her own accord, but "as long as He does not lift her up Himself it is said that she is still in exile." It goes without saying that those who subscribed to this view were obliged to keep up all the traditional practices of exilic, i.e., historic, Judaism. Even the midnight vigil for the Shekhinah was ultimately reintroduced.

In a word, at the same time that it was completely transforming the historic inner world of Judaism in its own unique manner, "moderate" Sabbatianism continued to adhere to traditional Jewish observance not for the sake of mere camouflage, but as a matter of principle. The inward crisis which every "moderate" underwent was permitted little or no outward expression, and inasmuch as such an objectification of his feelings was barred by either the exigencies of the situation or the compunctions of his own religious consciousness, he was forced to retreat even further into himself. But although the new sense of inner freedom bore purely inner consequences, we can nevertheless rely on the judgment of those anti-Sabbatian polemicists who saw perfectly clearly that the inward devastation of old values was no less dangerous or far-reaching than its outward manifestation. Whoever reads such a volume as Rabbi Jonathan Eibeschütz' *The Book of the Eternal Name,* [19] a treatise on "the mystery of the Godhead" composed in the traditional style of talmudic dialectics, will readily see what abysses had opened up in the very heart of Judaism. From these were to come the deluge: pure founts of salvation and spiritual rebirth to the one camp, gross waters of corruption and shameless sacrilege to the other.

V

We have seen how the principal feature of "moderate" Sabbatian doctrine was the belief that the apostasy of the Messiah was *sui generis.* The Messiah must go his lonely way into the kingdom of impurity and "the other side" (*sitra ahra*) and dwell there in the realm of a "strange god" whom he would yet refuse to worship. The enormous tension between the subjective and the objective which had developed in the ranks of his followers had so far found a legitimate expression in this one act alone. Whereas Sabbatai Zevi had actually done strange and objectionable things in the name of the holy, the celebration of this paradox among the "believers" was restricted to the domain of faith. "Moderate" Sabbatianism drew a circle around the concept of "strange holiness" and forbade itself to enter: it was indeed the Messiah's fate to scandalize Israel by his deeds, but it was decidedly his fate alone.

Once drawn, however, the line was clearly difficult to maintain. The more ardent "believer" found himself becoming increasingly restive. Was he to abandon the Messiah entirely just when the latter was engaged in the most bitter phase of his struggle with the power of evil? If the spark of the redemption had been experienced by all, why should not all do as the Redeemer? How could one refuse to go to his aid? And soon the cry was heard: Let us surrender ourselves as he did! Let us descend together to the abyss before it shuts again! Let us cram the maw of impurity with the power of holiness until it bursts from within.

Feelings such as these formed the psychological background for the great nihilistic conflagration that was to break out in the "radical" wing of the Sabbatian movement. The fire was fed by powerful religious emotions, but in the crucial moment these were to join forces with passions of an entirely different sort, namely, with the instincts of anarchy and lawlessness that lie deeply buried in every human soul. Traditionally Judaism had always sought to suppress such impulses, but now that they were allowed to emerge in the revolutionary exhilaration brought on by the experience of redemption and its freedom, they burst forth more violently than ever. An aura of holiness seemed to surround them. They too would be granted their *tikkun,* if only in the "hindparts of holiness."

Ultimately, too, the disappointing course of external events had a telling effect. Though he possessed the heroic soul of the warrior Bar Kokhba,[20] Sabbatai Zevi had not gone forth to do battle on the Day of the Lord. A yawning chasm had appeared between inner and outer realities, and once it was decided that the former was the truer of the two, it was only to be expected that the value of the latter would increasingly come to be rejected. It was precisely at this point that Messianism was transformed into nihilism. Having been denied the political and historical outlets it had originally anticipated, the new sense of freedom now sought to express itself in the sphere of human morality. The psychology of the "radical" Sabbatians was utterly paradoxical and "Marranic." Essentially its guiding principle was: Whoever is as he appears to be cannot be a true "believer." In practice this meant the following:

The "true faith" cannot be a faith which men publicly profess. On the contrary, the "true faith" must always be concealed. In fact, it is one's duty to deny it outwardly, for it is like a seed that has been planted in the bed of the soul and it cannot grow unless it is first covered over. For this reason every Jew is obliged to become a Marrano.

Again: a "true act" cannot be an act committed publicly, before the eyes of the world. Like the "true faith," the "true act" is concealed, for only through concealment can it negate the falsehood of what is explicit. Through a revolution of values, what was formerly sacred has become profane and what was formerly profane has become sacred. It is no longer enough to invent new mystical meditations (*kavvanot*) to suit the changed times. New forms of action are needed. Prior to the advent of the Redeemer the inward and the outward were in harmony, and this is why it was possible to effect great *tikkunim* by means of outwardly performing the commandments. Now that the Redeemer has arrived, however, the two spheres are in opposition: the inward commandment, which alone can effect a *tikkun,* has become synonymous with the outward transgression. *Bittulah shel torah zehu kiyyumah:* the violation of the Torah is now its true fulfillment.

More than anything else, it was this insistence of the "radicals" on the potential holiness of sin—a belief which they attempted to justify by citing out of context the talmudic dictum (Nazir 23b) "A transgression committed for its own sake is greater than a commandment not committed for its own sake"—which alienated and offended the average Jew and caused even the "believers" themselves to undergo the severest of conflicts.

In the history of religion, whenever we come across the doctrine of the holiness of sin it is always in conjunction with one or another spiritualistic sect. The type of the pneumatic, which I have previously discussed, is particularly susceptible to such a teaching and it is hardly necessary to point out the connections that exist between the theories of nihilism and those of the more extravagant forms of spiritualism. To the pneumatic, the spiritual universe which he inhabits is of an entirely different order from the world of ordinary flesh and blood, whose opinion of the new laws he has chosen to live by is therefore irrelevant; insofar as he is above sin (an idea, common to many sectarian groups, which occasionally occurs in the literature of Hasidism as well) he may do as the spirit dictates without needing to take into account the moral standards of the society around him. Indeed he is, if anything, duty-bound to violate and subvert this "ordinary" morality in the name of the higher principles that have been revealed to him.

Although individuals with inclinations in this direction existed in Judaism also, particularly among the Kabbalists, up to the time of the Sabbatians their activities were confined entirely to the level of pure theory. The most outstanding example of such speculative or virtual "spiritualism" to be found in Kabbalistic literature is the *Sefer ha-Temunah* ("The Book of the Image"), a mystical treatise written in early thirteenth-century Spain, in which it is stated that the Torah consists of a body of spiritual letters which, though they remain essentially unchanged, present different appearances to the reader in different cosmic aeons (*shemitot*). In effect, therefore, each aeon, or *shemitah,* possesses a Torah of its own. In the current *shemitah,* which is ruled by the divine quality of *din,* stern judgment or rigor, the Torah is read in terms of prohibitions and commandments and even its most mystic allusions must be interpreted in this light. In the coming aeon, however, which will be that of *rahamim,* divine mercy, the Torah will be read differently, so that in all probability "what is prohibited now will be permitted then." Everything depends on the particular aeon and the divine quality (or attribute) presiding over it. Sensing the dangers inherent in such a doctrine, certain Kabbalists, such as Moses Cordovero, attempted to dismiss it as entirely unworthy of consideration. But it was precisely those works that propounded it, such as the *Sefer ha-Temunah* and the *Sefer ha-Kanah,* which influenced the Sabbatians tremendously.

To the theory of the cosmic aeons the Sabbatians assimilated a second, originally unrelated concept. The *Zohar* itself does not recognize or, more exactly, does not utilize the idea of the *shemitot* at all (a fact that was instrumental in making it suspect in the eyes of later Kabbalists), but in two later additions to the *Zoharic* corpus, the *Tikkunei ha-Zohar* and the *Ra'ya Mehemna,* a great deal is said on the subject of four emanated worlds, the World of *atzilut* or "Emanation," the World of *beriah* or "Creation," the World of *yetzirah* or "Formation," and the World of *asiyah* or "Making," which together comprise the different levels of spiritual reality. In connection with these we also occasionally hear of a "Torah of *atzilut*" and a "Torah of *beriah,*" the meanings of which are not entirely clear.[21] By the time of the Kabbalists of the School of Safed, however, we find these latter terms employed in a definite sense to indicate that there are two aspects of the one essential Torah, i.e., the Torah as it is understood in the supernal World of *atzilut* and the Torah as it is understood in the lower World of *beriah.* What the Sabbatians now did was to seize this idea and expound it in the light of the theory of cosmic aeons. The Torah of *beriah,* they argued, borrowing a metaphor from the *Zohar* (I, 23), is the Torah of the unredeemed world of exile, whose purpose it was to serve as a garment for the Shekhinah in her exile, so that whoever observed its commandments and prohibitions was like one who helped clothe the Shekhinah in her state of distress. The Torah of *atzilut,* on the other hand, is the "true" Torah which, like "the mystery of the Godhead" it makes manifest, has been in a state of concealment for the entire period of the exile. Now that the redemption has commenced it is about to be revealed, and although in essence it is identical with the Torah of *beriah,* its way of being read will be different, thus, all the commandments and prohibitions of the Torah of *beriah* will now be reinterpreted by the light of the World of *atzilut,* in which (to take but one example), as is stated in several Kabbalistic sources,[22] there is no such thing as forbidden sexual practices. It was in this manner that assertions made in a completely different spirit and in terms of a wholly different understanding of the concepts "World of *atzilut"* and "Torah of *atzilut"* were pressed into service by the "radical" Sabbatians as slogans for their new morality.[23]

The concept of the two Torahs was an extremely important one for Sabbatian nihilism, not least because it corresponded so perfectly to the "Marranic" mentality. In accordance with its purely mystical nature the Torah of *atzilut* was to be observed strictly in secret; the Torah of *beriah,* on the other hand, was to be actively and deliberately violated. As to how this was to be done, however, the "radicals" could not agree and differing schools of thought evolved among them. It is important to keep in mind that we are dealing here with an eruption of the most diverse sorts of emotion. The Gordian knot binding the soul of the exilic Jew had been cut and a vertigo that ultimately was to be his undoing seized the newly liberated individual: genuine desires for a reconsecration of life mingled indiscriminately with all kinds of destructive and libidinal forces tossed up from the depths by an irrepressible ground swell that undulated wildly between the earthly and the divine.

The psychological factors at work were particularly various in regard to the doctrine of the holiness of sin, which though restricted at first by some of the "believers" to the performance of certain specified acts alone, tended by virtue of its own inner logic to embrace more and more of the Mosaic Law, especially the

biblical prohibitions. Among the leaders of the Dönmeh the antinomian blessing composed by Sabbatai Zevi, "Blessed art Thou O
Lord our God, King of the universe, who permittest the forbidden
[*mattir isurim*]," * became a byword.[24] In fact, two somewhat
contradictory rationalizations of antinomian behavior existed side
by side. On the one hand there were those who said: in the world
of redemption there can be no such thing as sin, therefore all is
holy and everything is permitted. To this it was retorted: not at
all! what is needed rather is to totally deny the *beriah,* "Creation"
(a word that had by now come to denote every aspect of the old
life and its institutions), to trample its values underfoot, for only
by casting off the last vestiges of these can we truly become free.
To state the matter in Kabbalistic terms, the one side proposed to
withhold the sparks of holiness from the *kelipot* until they perished from lack of nourishment, whereas the other insisted that the
kelipot be positively filled with holiness until they disintegrated
from the pressure. But in either case, and despite the many psychological nuances which entered into the "transgression committed
for its own sake" and the sacred sin, all the "radicals" were united
in their belief in the sanctifying power of sin itself "that dwelleth
with them in the midst of their uncleannesses," as they were fond
of interpreting the phrase in Leviticus 16:16.

It would be pointless to deny that the sexual element in this
outburst was very strong: a primitive abandon such as the Jewish
people would scarcely have thought itself capable of after so many
centuries of discipline in the Law joined hands with perversely
pathological drives to seek a common ideological rehabilitation.
In the light of what happened there is little to wonder at when
we read in the texts of rabbinical excommunications dating from
the eighteenth century that the children of the "believers" were to
be automatically considered bastards, just as it is perfectly understandable that these children and grandchildren themselves should
have done everything in their power to obscure the history of their
descent. One may readily grant, of course, as Zalman Rubashov
justly observes in his study of the Frankists, that "every sectarian
movement is suspected by the church against which it rebels of
the most infamous misconduct and immorality," a conclusion
which has led to the hypothesis that such accusations invariably
tell us more about the depraved fantasies of the accusers than they

---

* A pun on the blessing in the morning prayer, "Blessed art Thou O
Lord our God, King of the universe, who freest those who are in bondage
[*mattir asurim*]." [Translator's note.]

do about the actual behavior of the accused.[25] It is Rubashov's opinion, indeed, that although the conduct of the Frankists was "in itself adequate cause for indignation and amazement," there is also "every reason to assume that as a matter of course it was greatly exaggerated." As valid as the general rule may be, however, the plain facts of the matter are that in the case of the "radical" Sabbatians there was hardly any need for exaggeration. As Nahum Sokolow has pointed out in a note to Kraushar's history of Frankism,[26] no matter how thoroughly fantastic and partisan the allegations of the anti-Sabbatians may seem to us, we have not the slightest justification for doubting their accuracy, inasmuch as in every case we can rely for evidence on the "confessions" of the "believers" themselves, as well as on a number of their apologias which have come down to us in both theoretical and homiletical form.

All this has recently been confirmed by an unexpected discovery. For many years—well into the present age, in fact—the Sabbatians in Salonika, the Dönmeh, regularly held a celebration on the twenty-second day of the Hebrew month of Adar known as "the Festival of the Lamb," the exact nature of which was kept a carefully guarded secret until some of the younger members of the sect were finally prevailed upon to reveal it to outsiders. According to their account the festival included an orgiastic rite called "the extinguishing of the lights." From what we know of this rite it probably came to Salonika from Izmir, for both its name and its contents were evidently borrowed from the pagan cult of "the Great Mother" which flourished in antiquity and continued to be practiced after its general demise by a small sect of "Light Extinguishers" in Asia Minor under the cover of Islam.[27] There can be no question that the Dönmeh took over this ancient bacchanalia based on immemorial myths and adapted it to conform to their mystical belief in the sacramental value of exchanging wives,[28] a custom that was undoubtedly observed by other "radicals" in the movement as well.

The history of Sabbatian nihilism as a mass movement rather than as the concern of a few isolated Jewish scholars who "donned the fez" like Sabbatai Zevi, began in 1683, when several hundred Jewish families in Salonika converted to Islam "so as to conquer the kelipah from within." From this point on organized Sabbatian nihilism appeared in four main forms:

1. That of the "believers" who chose "voluntary Marranism" in the form of Islam. The research that has been done on

the subject of the Dönmeh, particularly the studies of Abraham Danon [29] and Solomon Rosanes, [30] definitely establishes that the sect was purely Jewish in its internal character, not, of course, in the accepted rabbinical sense, but rather in the sense of a mystical heresy. The apostasy of the Dönmeh aroused violent opposition among the "moderates," for reasons which I have already made clear.

2. That of the "believers" who remained traditional Jews in outward life while inwardly adhering to the "Torah of *atzilut.*" Several groups of such individuals existed in the Balkans and Palestine (beginning with the arrival there of Hayyim Malakh), and afterwards, in the eighteenth century, in Northern and Eastern Europe, where they were concentrated particularly in Podolia and in such nearby towns as Buczacz, Busk, Gliniany, Horodenka, Zhólkiew, Zloczow, Tysmenieca, Nadworna, Podhaice, Rohatyn and Satanow, but also in other countries, especially Rumania, Hungary, and Moravia.

3. That of the Frankists who "Marranized themselves" by converting to Catholicism.

4. That of the Frankists in Bohemia, Moravia, Hungary, and Rumania, who chose to remain Jewish.

Despite the differences between these groups, all of them were part of a single larger entity. Inasmuch as it was believed by all the "radicals" that externals were no indication of true faith, apostasy was not a factor to come between them. A Jew in the ghetto of Prague, for example, who went on publicly observing the commandments of the "Torah of *beriah*" while at the same time violating them in private, knew perfectly well that the "believer" in Warsaw or Offenbach who had recently been baptized "for mystical reasons" was still his brother, just as fifty years earlier Sabbatians in Northern Europe had continued to remain in close touch with the Dönmeh in Salonika even after their conversion to Islam. Essentially, the "radicals" all inhabited the same intellectual world. Their attitudes toward the Torah, the Messiah, and "the mystery of the Godhead" were identical, for all that they assumed new and unusual forms among the Frankists.

VI

The systematic violation of the Torah of *beriah* was considered by the "radical" Sabbatians to be the principal attestation of the new epoch ushered in by Sabbatai Zevi. But exactly how was one to distinguish between what belonged to the lower World of *beriah* and its Torah, and what belonged to the higher World of *atzilut* and its Torah? Here opinion was divided. Baruchya Russo, better known as Berahya or Berochia, the leader of the radical wing of the Dönmeh in the beginning of the eighteenth century, preached to his followers that even the thirty-six transgressions deemed worthy by the Torah of the ultimate punishment of *karet,* i.e., being "cut off" from Israel and from God (a category that included all the forbidden sexual practices), were aspects of the Torah of *beriah* only.[31] By the same token it was decreed permissible to eat of the sinew of the thigh-vein, for with the advent of the Messiah "Jacob's thigh has been restored." * [32] In the opinion of some, who based their argument on a passage from the *Zohar,* refraining from the sinew of the thigh-vein and fasting on *Tish'ah be-Av* were mutually connected observances: "As long as it is forbidden to eat on *Tish'ah be-Av* it is forbidden to eat the sinew of the thigh-vein, and when it is permitted to eat on *Tish-'ah be-Av* it is permitted to eat the sinew of the thigh-vein." [33] Others went still further: "It is widely known that belonging to these sects are those who believe that [with the advent of the Messiah] the Torah has been nullified [*betelah*] and that in the future it will be [read] without [reference to] the commandments, for they say that the violation of the Torah has become its fulfillment, which they illustrate by the example of a grain of wheat that rots in the earth." [34] In other words, just as a grain of wheat must rot in the earth before it can sprout, so the deeds of the "believers" must be truly "rotten" before they can germinate the redemption. This metaphor, which appears to have been extremely popular, conveys the whole of sectarian Sabbatian psychology in a nutshell: in the period of transition, while the redemption is still in a state of concealment, the Torah in its explicit form must be denied, for only thus can it too become "concealed" and ultimately renewed.

There were, however, even more extreme cases than these. Jacob Emden relates how he was told by a rabbinical associate of great learning, the Rabbi of the Amsterdam Ashkenazim, that

---

* The prohibition against eating the sinew of the thigh-vein is to be found in Genesis 32, which tells of Jacob's wrestling with the angel: "Therefore the children of Israel eat not the sinew of the thigh-vein which is upon the hollow of the thigh unto this day; because he touched the hollow of Jacob's thigh, even in the sinew of the thigh-vein" (32:33). [*Tr. Note*]

when he was in Zhólkiew he became involved with one of these heretics, a man named Fishl Zloczow, who was expertly versed in the
entire Talmud, which he knew practically by heart, for he was in the
habit of shutting himself up in his room in order to pore over it, never
ceasing from his studies (for he was a wealthy man) nor engaging in
idle conversation. He would linger over his prayers twice as long as
the Hasidim of olden times and was considered by all to be a most
pious and ascetic individual. Once he came to him [i.e., to Emden's
informant] in order to confess his sins and revealed that he belonged
to the sect of Sabbatai Zevi, that he had eaten leavened bread on the
Passover, and so forth, carrying on contritely all the while as though
he had truly repented of his deeds. Soon afterwards, however, he was
caught in the act of committing grave transgressions of the Law and
was excommunicated by the rabbis of Lithuania and Volhynia. When
asked why he had not continued his hidden sins in private instead of
[committing acts that led to his exposal] in public . . . he replied that
on the contrary, the more shame he was forced to suffer for his faith,
the better it was.[35]

Here we are confronted with the type of the "believer" in its most
paradoxical form, and, significantly, the individual in question was
no ordinary Jew, but was rather conceded to be an excellent rabbinic scholar by an eminent authority who was in a position to
know. One could hardly wish for a more perfect example of the
nihilistic rejection of the Torah of *beriah,* which in this case was
studied for the sole purpose that it might be better violated in
spirit! The Jewish world was indeed showing signs of inner
decay if types such as these were able to make themselves so easily
at home in its midst. And yet underneath all these vagaries there
was obviously a deep-seated desire for something positive which
for lack of suitable conditions under which to function had come
to nought.

Illustrative parables and homilies were also brought to bear on
the doctrine of the sacred sin itself, and the reader cannot fail to
notice that they are more than just paradoxical and highly offensive
sayings. They breathe an entirely new spirit. "The patriarchs came
into the world to restore [*le-takken*] the senses and this they did
to four of them. Then came Sabbatai Zevi and restored the fifth,
the sense of touch, which according to Aristotle and Maimonides
is a source of shame to us, but which now has been raised by him
to a place of honor and glory." [36] As late as the beginning of the
nineteenth century we find a fervent "believer" in Prague commenting in connection with the verse in Psalms 68, "Thou hast
ascended on high, Thou hast led captivity captive," that the captive

in question is the spiritual Torah of *atzilut,* which is called a "prisoner" because it was captured by Moses and forced to dwell in the prison cell of the material Torah of *beriah:*

Such is the case with the inner Torah, for the outer is in opposition to the inner . . . and must be annihilated before the inner can be freed. And just as a woman from Ishmael [i.e., from a Moslem country] feels as though she has been freed from her confinement when she comes to Edom [i.e., a Christian country] . . . so continuing [to live] in Israel under the Torah of *beriah* is called captivity, nor can she be given in marriage under the Torah of *beriah* but only in Edom, whereas in Israel one must remain a virgin—and [he who is able to, let him] understand.

The cryptic Frankist allusions at the end of this passage to Christianity and to "remaining a virgin" are rather obscure, but it is evident from the whole how strongly the rejection of the lower, or material, Torah of *beriah* continued to be upheld by Sabbatian Jews right down to the movement's last years. Elsewhere the author of the above,[37] a thoughtful and deeply religious individual, explains that the commonly expressed belief that "no mischief can befall the righteous man [Prov. 12:21] nor can he be a cause of sin" must be understood in the light of the Torah of *atzilut* to mean that no matter how sinful the acts of the righteous may appear to others they are in fact always fully justified in themselves. He then adduces a number of astute mystical reasons for the necessity of certain transgressions, such as eating on the fast days, which he defends by arguing that fasting is a kind of spiritual "bribe" given to the *kelipot* and as such is not in keeping with the pure spiritual nature of the Torah of *atzilut.*

As to the ultimate step of apostasy, the arguments presented by the "radicals" in its behalf closely resemble those brought forward by the "moderates" to vindicate the apostasy of Sabbatai Zevi himself. We happen to have in our possession an illuminating document bearing on the disputes that arose over this question among the "believers" in the form of a homily by the well-known Sabbatian Nehemiah Hayon on the verse (Deut. 29:17), "Lest there be among you man, or woman, or family, or tribe, whose heart turneth away this day from the Lord our God, to go serve the gods of those nations; lest there should be among you a root that beareth gall and wormwood." [38] The paradoxical solution arrived at by Hayon toward the close of his long discourse, which I quote here in abbreviated form, is an invaluable reflection of the perplexity and deep inner conflict experienced by those Sabbatians who were unable to choose between the "radical" and "moderate" positions:

It is supposed among those versed in esoteric lore that the redemption can be brought about in either one of two ways: either Israel will have the power to withdraw all the sparks of holiness from [the realm of] the *kelipah* so that the *kelipah* will wither into nothing, or else the *kelipah* will become so filled with holiness that because of this repletion it must be spewn forth. . . . And this [fact], that the coming of the redemption can be prompted in one of two ways, was what the rabbis of blessed memory had in mind when they said that the Son of David would come either in a generation that was entirely guiltless (meaning when Israel by virtue of its good deeds had withdrawn all the sparks of holiness from the *kelipah*), or else in a generation that was entirely guilty (meaning when the *kelipah* had become so filled with holiness that it split its maw and perished). . . . And it is in consequence of this thesis that many, though their intentions are good, have mistakenly said, "Let us go worship other gods that we may fill the *kelipah* to bursting that it die." . . . Nay, do not reason with yourself, "Since it is impossible for all to become guiltless so as to withdraw the holiness from the *kelipah,* it is better that I become a sinner and so hasten the doom of the *kelipah* in that way that it might die and salvation might come," but rather "Wait for the Lord and keep His way" [Ps. 37:34]: it is better that you endure the length of the exile and look to salvation than that you sin by worshipping other gods in order to bring on the redemption. This brings us to the meaning of the verse, "Lest there be among you a root that beareth gall and wormwood [29:17], and it come to pass when he heareth the words of this curse [etc.; 29:18]. In other words, when he hears the words of the curse that is threatened . . . he turns away his heart from God and blesses himself in his heart [29:18], saying: "What Moses has written is true" . . . but [he thinks that] if he does not turn away his heart from God and if his intentions are good, that is, if he means to quench the *kelipah* by giving it holiness to drink, then certainly no evil will befall him, but on the contrary, God will turn the curse into a blessing. And this is the meaning of the words "and he blesses himself in his heart," for he says to himself, "I am sure that no harm will befall me . . . because I did not turn my heart [from God] . . . and because my intentions are good . . . [namely] to water the *kelipah,* the thirsty one, with the holiness that I extend to her that she may partake of it and die. It is of such a one that Moses said, "The Lord will not be willing to pardon him" [29:19]. . . . Even though his intentions were good and he only desired to hasten the redemption, he cannot be forgiven. . . . Nor does [the principle of] "A transgression committed for its own sake" [is greater than a commandment not committed for its own sake] apply here, since there [in its original context] it refers to an ordinary sin, as in the case of Jael [in killing Sisera; Judg. 4], whereas here, where it is a question of worshiping other gods, the Lord will not be willing to pardon him. . . . They [who act on this mistaken assumption] are powerless to destroy the *kelipah;* on the contrary, he [who attempts to fill the *kelipah* with holiness] will remain stuck in its midst, and this is why it is said that the Lord will not be willing to pardon him. . . . There is also another possible explanation [of the verse], namely, that when Moses said that the Lord would not be willing to pardon him he was not pronouncing a curse . . . but was thinking the following: . . . since he [the deliberate sinner] believes in his heart that God will not account his actions as sins, but will rather reward them . . . it is inconceivable that he should ever repent for he does not believe he has done wrong . . . How then can the Holy One, blessed be He, forgive him? On the contrary, each time [he sins] he only angers Him the more . . . by thinking that he has done good instead of evil . . . and by saying that the greater a sinner he is the more he hastens the coming of the redemption. Such a one undoubtedly incurs the full power of the curse, since he deliberately violates all its injunctions. . . . "And the Lord shall separate him unto evil out of all the tribes of Israel" [29:20]. . . . But perhaps one can interpret the meaning of the text as follows: since such a person intends his deeds to redound to the benefit of all Israel . . . if after sinning and passing through the *kelipah* he reconsiders and repents completely, he undoubtedly succeeds in raising up many sparks from the *kelipah,* just as in the case of the human body when one is administered an emetic he does not simply vomit up the drug itself, but rather having opened his mouth proceeds to spew forth both the drug and everything that was near it. And so it is with the *kelipah:* sometimes it gains power over a man whose soul is great and does him harm, but as soon as he repents he spews forth all that was within him. And this is what Solomon meant when he said [Eccl. 8:9] there is a time when one man rules another to do him harm.[39] [But since] There is a time [for such things] and miracles do not happen every hour, therefore Moses warns that one should not place himself in this peril. . . . "And the Lord shall separate him unto evil"; in other words, if he [the deliberate sinner] has been a cause of evil he is singled out [for judgment] from the tribes of Israel, for [it is a *halakhic* principle that] one cannot commit a transgression for another by proxy even if one has been authorized to do so, much less if one has not been, so that having gone [and committed evil] of his own accord, there is no doubt that the evil which results [from his actions] will not be imputed to Israel as a whole. But if he does good—that is, if he repents wholeheartedly and raises up sparks from Israel by virtue of his repentance—then all the tribes of Israel have a part in this good; it is only in the evil that they do not have a part.

Likely as not, this entire passage has an autobiographical basis. In any event, it is clear that the attitude of its author toward the "voluntary Marranos" whose conversion he decries yet understands so well is far from being hostile or vindictive.

One of the strongest factors in the development of a nihilistic mentality among the "radicals" was their desire to negate an objective historical order in which the exile continued in full force and the beginnings of the redemption went unnoticed by all but the "believers" themselves. Understandably, during the period now in question this antipathy toward outward reality remained confined to the area of religion alone, the world of ghetto Jewry still being sufficiently stable to preclude its active politicalization. Prior to the French Revolution, indeed, there was no connection between the ideas of Sabbatianism and the growing undercurrent of discontent with the *ancien régime* in Europe. It was only when changing times had widened the "believers'" horizons and revealed to them the existence of more tangible ways of affecting the course of history than the violation of the Torah of *beriah* that they too began to dream of revolutionizing the structure of society itself. In a sense this was to mean the restoration to Jewish Messianism of its traditional political content, which, as I have shown, the Sabbatian movement transformed beyond recognition. As long as external conditions were not conducive to this, even the "radicals" remained politically unaware, nor were they able to conceive of any other method of revitalizing Jewish life than the subversion of its most sacred values; but it is not surprising that once the opportune moment arose the essentially this-worldly emphasis of Jewish Messianism which Sabbatianism had striven to suppress should have come to be stressed again. I shall have more to say on this important subject; first, however, I would like to comment on a related matter, one which will serve as yet another example of the uniquely paradoxical dialectic of Sabbatian thought: its attitude toward Palestine.

Immediately after the collapse of the initial Messianic expectations aroused by Sabbatai Zevi, scattered groups of Sabbatians began to express their opposition to the idea of emigration to the Holy Land. As has now been established, Nathan of Gaza himself was of the opinion that "for the time being it is best not to go to the Land of Israel." [40] But this point of view did not go unchallenged. A number of "believers," especially after 1700, attempted to demonstrate by mystical reasons that in the light of Sabbatian doctrine emigration was indeed desirable after all. Individuals from both the circle of Abraham Rovigo and the whole band of "Hasidim" centered around Rabbi Judah Hasid actually settled in Palestine as a result of specifically Sabbatian aspirations. One belief that was current at the time was that on the occasion of Sabbatai Zevi's second advent, which would take place forty years after his "concealment," a true mystical knowledge of his nature would be revealed to those of his followers, and only to those, who were living in the Holy Land.[41] Sabbatian nihilists like Hayyim Malakh, who were contemporaries of such groups, also were in favor of going to the Land of Israel, from which they too undoubtedly expected special revelations to come; in addition, they may have felt that there was an advantage to violating the Torah of *beriah* on the most consecrated ground of all, on the analogy of "conquering the queen in her own home." As late as the middle of the eighteenth century Sabbatian nihilists in Podolia still had contacts and acquaintances in Palestine,[42] while a number of the emissaries sent by the Palestinian Jewish community to raise funds in the Diaspora were Sabbatian scholars who acted on the side both as secret propagators of the faith and as contacts between "believers" in different localities. Many of these, such as the author of *The Book of the Adornment of Days,* a beautiful and detailed description (in Hebrew) of the life of a Kabbalist devotee all through the year, were undoubtedly "moderates," but regarding many others we will probably never know exactly where they stood. Toward the middle of the eighteenth century, however, a reaction took place, so that we find a distinct anti-Palestinian bias setting in throughout the movement. Whether or not the anti-Palestinian sermon cited by Jacob Emden in his *Edut be-Ya'akov* (44b) is really the handiwork of Jonathan Eibeschütz is uncertain, but in any case there can be no question of its being a total fabrication, inasmuch as similar ideas to those expressed in it can be found in other Sabbatian documents which Emden could not possibly have seen.[43] Among the Frankists an astonishing and clear-cut ideology of Jewish territorialism (as distinct from Palestine-centered tendencies) developed at about this time, apparently as a result of Frank's own personal ambitions. In a word, on the very eve of its absorption of new political ideas Sabbatian nihilism completely reversed its previously positive evaluation of the role of the Land of Israel, so that when shortly afterward it began to speak the language of a revived political Messianism and to prophesy the rebirth of the Jewish nation as one outcome of an impending world revolution, there was no longer any real interest on its part in the idea of the Land of Israel as a national center. As stated by the Frankist writer in Prague whom we have already had occasion to quote, Israel's exile is not a consequence of its sins at all, but is rather part of a plan designed to bring about the destruction of the *kelipot* all over the world, so that "even if several thousands or tens-of-thousands of Jews are enabled to return to the Land of Israel, nothing has been completed." According to the same author this new doctrine of the exile is "a secret mystical principle which was hidden from all the sages until it was [recently] revealed in Poland." And thus we see how in the final stages of Sabbatianism the intrinsic nature of the exile came to be reconsidered in an entirely new light.

The figure of Sabbatai Zevi himself was also recast by the passage of time, becoming entirely mythical: gradually the element of historical truth was diminished until nothing was left but a legendary hero who had inaugurated a new epoch of world history. Even in Sabbatai Zevi's lifetime one of his first disciples, Abraham Yakhini, could write of him (in his book *Vavei ha-Amudim*) "Just as one of the seventy faces of the Torah is concerned entirely with the resurrection of the dead, as is to be seen in [the commentaries of] the *Zohar* on several chapters [of the Pentateuch], [the allusions to the resurrection in] the other chapters being inaccessible to us because of the limitations of our intellects, so one of the seventy faces of the Torah is concerned entirely with the Messiah, our lord and master, may his majesty increase,[44] and shortly, when he reveals himself to us [completely], we shall be privileged to understand the entire Torah in this way." It is little wonder that the concrete historical figure of Sabbatai Zevi came to be transformed by his followers in much the same manner as Jesus' was by his, if not more so, since his conversion into a mythological figure was even more complete. Like the early Christians, in fact, the "radicals" eventually came to believe that the Messiah had not been a mere superior human being, but an incarnation of God Himself in human form. This new interpretation of "the mystery of the Godhead" was accepted by all the "radical" groups down to the last of the Frankists and was considered by them to be the most profound mystic truth in their entire body of doctrine. Whence it came cannot yet be determined: perhaps from the collective memory of thousands of Marranos, perhaps from Christian books or anti-Christian polemics, or perhaps from the "believers'" own inner conflict, the paradoxical cause of which—an apostate Messiah—may have led them to adopt the same paradoxical solution that a like contradiction—a crucified Messiah—produced in yet another group of Jews caught in the toils of religious turmoil. And perhaps, too, all of these factors combined to work together.

The doctrine of an incarnate God, which immediately became a bone of contention between the "radicals" and the "moderates" in the Sabbatian camp, was limited at first to the figure of Sabbatai Zevi himself. According to one view, when the redemption began, "the Holy One, blessed be He, removed Himself upward and Sabbatai Zevi ascended to be God in His place." [45] Since in the Sabbatian faith "the Holy One, blessed be He" was synonymous, as we have seen, with "the God of Israel," this meant that Sabbatai Zevi had now assumed the latter's title and become "the Holy King." [46] Before long, however, the "believers" in Salonika replaced this teaching with another: "the Holy King" had Himself been incarnated in the person of the Messiah in order to restore the world and nullify the Torah of *beriah*. It was in this form that the doctrine was accepted by the Sabbatian nihilists in Podolia. A prayer of theirs that has come into our possession reads, "May it be Thy will that we prosper in Thy Torah and cling to Thy commandments, and mayst Thou purify my thoughts to worship Thee in truth . . . and may all our deeds in the Torah of *atzilut* [meaning: transgressions!] be only for the sake of Thy great name, O Señor Santo,[47] that we may recognize Thy greatness, for Thou art the true God and King of the universe, our living Messiah who wast in this earthly world and didst nullify the Torah of *beriah* and didst reascend to Thy place to conduct all the worlds." [48]

But this doctrine of a single incarnation did not long remain unaltered in turn. Apparently among the Sephardic converts to Islam the belief developed that the leaders of the "believers" in every age were reincarnations of Sabbatai Zevi. Whether this actually meant that these leaders—particularly Baruchya, who was one of the foremost promulgators of the new belief—were thought to be, or considered themselves, divine incarnations no less than the Messiah himself is not entirely clear, but there are good reasons for believing that the gospel preached by Jacob Frank at the beginning of his career was nothing but this Sephardic teaching with a number of modifications to suit his own personality, and Frank himself, though he never said so in so many words, was correctly understood by his disciples to imply that he personally was the living God once again incarnated on earth. Not without a certain "consistency" the Frankists held that each of the three hypostases of the Godhead had its individual incarnation in a separate Messiah: Sabbatai Zevi, whom Frank was in the habit of referring to simply as "The First One," had been the embodiment of "the Ancient Holy One," Frank himself was the personification of "the Holy King," and the third hypostasis, the Shekhinah, variously known in the writings of the Kabbalah as "the Kingdom" (*malkhut*), "the Lady" (*matronita*), "the Maiden," and "the Doe," was to appear in the form of a woman. It is hard not to associate this last novelty—a female Messiah, referred to by Frank as "the Virgin," who was yet to be revealed and whose task it would be to complete the work of the redemption— with the influence of certain mystical Christian sects prevalent at about this time in Eastern Europe that believed in a triad of saviors corresponding to the threefold nature of God and in a feminine incarnation of the Sophia, the Divine Wisdom or Holy Spirit. With one of these groups, in fact, the "Philipovicites" in Rumania and the Ukraine, the Frankists were in such close contact that one of its former leaders publicly defended them before the Catholic authorities of Poland.

Interpreted in this manner the redemption was a process filled with incarnations of the divinity. Even the "radicals" in Prague who clung to their Jewish identity and strove to defend their beliefs by means of Jewish concepts and sources were won over to this view, and although their hostility to Christianity as an institution knew no bounds, references to "the mystery of the incarnation" can be found throughout their literature. The anti-Sabbatian polemicists who accused the "believers" of corporealizing the idea of God were perfectly right in their assertions, but this fact, which seemed to them a damning admission of weakness, was in reality their opponents' greatest source of pride! "Because the Godhead has a body the sting of death is gone," wrote one "believer." On the surface it would seem that the exaggerated spirituality of the World of *atzilut* and the yearning to see God in the flesh that was evidenced by the doctrine of a Messianic incarnation were two mutually opposed tendencies, and yet, after all that has been said here, it should not be difficult to see that underlying both was the struggle of a new sensibility toward life to express itself by means of a religious vocabulary inherited from the old. In such cases the paradox is always the only solution.

In summary, the five distinguishing beliefs of "radical" Sabbatianism are:

1. The belief in the necessary apostasy of the Messiah and in the sacramental nature of the descent into the realm of the *kelipot*.
2. The belief that the "believer" must not appear to be as he really is.
3. The belief that the Torah of *atzilut* must be observed through the violation of the Torah of *beriah*.
4. The belief that the First Cause and the God of Israel are not the same, the former being the God of rational philosophy, the latter the God of religion.
5. The belief in three hypostases of the Godhead, all of which have been or will be incarnated in human form.

These theses amply demonstrate, in my opinion, that in the onward course of the Sabbatian movement the world of traditional Judaism was shattered beyond repair. In the minds of those who took part in this revolutionary destruction of old values a special susceptibility to new ideas inevitably came to exist. Well might the "believers" have asked how long their newly released energies and emotions were to go on being aimlessly squandered. Were their lives required to be dominated by paradoxes forever?

But just as the character of the Sabbatian movement was dictated by the circumstances of the movement's birth, so, in turn, it was to dictate the circumstances of the movement's disintegration and death. For as the "believers" had meant to fire the sparks of holiness with the *kelipot,* so they were to wander in the blackest of blind alleys; and as they had wished to "play" with "the other side," the dark side of life, so they were to dance in the devil's own arms. And last and most ironically of all: as they had hastened to come to the aid of the Redeemer—"to do as he did for strange are his deeds, to worship as he worships for his worship is alien" (Isa. 28:21)—so they were to be induced in the end to play into the hands of a man like Jacob Frank.

VII

Jacob Frank (1726-91) will always be remembered as one of the most frightening phenomena in the whole of Jewish history: a religious leader who, whether for purely self-interested motives or otherwise, was in all his actions a truly corrupt and degenerate individual. Indeed, it might be plausibly argued that in order to completely exhaust its seemingly endless potential for the contradictory and the unexpected the Sabbatian movement was in need of just such a strongman, a man who could snuff out its last inner lights and pervert whatever will to truth and goodness was still to be found in the maze-like ruins of the "believers'" souls. Even if one is willing to concede that the doctrine of the sacred sin, the *mitzvah ha-ba'ah ba-averah,* was not lacking in certain insights, there can be no question but that these were thoroughly debased upon coming in contact with the person of Frank. But just as the "believers" had deliberately chosen to follow that dangerous path along which nothing is impossible, so it was perhaps precisely this that attracted them to Frank, for here was a man who was not afraid to push on to the very end, to take the final step into the abyss, to drain the cup of desolation and destruction to the lees until the last bit of holiness had been made into a mockery. His admirers, who themselves fell far short of him in respect of this ability, were won over by his intrepidness, which neither the fear of God nor the terrors of the bottomless pit were able to daunt, and saw in him the type of the true saint, a new Sabbatai Zevi and an incarnate God.

If the full truth be told, however, even after one has taken into account Frank's unscrupulous opportunism, his calculated deceits, and his personal ambitions, none of which really concerns us here, he remains a figure of tremendous if satanic power. True, neither the promises and pledges with which he allured his disciples, nor his visionary schemes for the future that was to follow the general cataclysm of the times seem particularly impressive today, although of his territorialist program it may at least be said that besides revealing his own lust for power it expressed in a bizarre yet unmistakable manner the desire of his followers for a reconstruction of Jewish national and even economic existence; [49] and yet for all the negativism of his teachings, they nonetheless contained a genuine creed of life.

Frank was a nihilist, and his nihilism possessed a rare authenticity. Certainly, its primitive ferocity is frightening to behold. Certainly too, Frank himself was not only an unlettered man, but boasted continually of his own lack of culture. But in spite of all this—and here is the significant point—we are confronted in his person with the extraordinary spectacle of a powerful and tyrannical soul living in the middle of the eighteenth century and yet immersed entirely in a mythological world of its own making. Out of the ideas of Sabbatianism, a movement in which he was apparently raised and educated, Frank was able to weave a complete myth of religious nihilism. This, surely, is worthy of attention.

Frank was not an original speculative thinker, but he did have a decided talent for the pithy, the strikingly illustrative, and the concretely symbolic expression. Despite their nihilistic content his sayings in *The Sayings of the Lord (Slowa Pańskie)* are not very different in form from those of many famous Hasidic Zaddikim, and for all his despotic nature he possessed a hidden poetic impulse which appears all the more surprising in the light of his customary savagery. Even Kraushar, who like his predecessors was intent on emphasizing everything that seemed incoherent or grotesque in Frank's recorded sayings, was forced to admit that on occasion they show vigor and imagination. For my own part, I fail to see how any sensitive individual who reads the many excerpts published by Kraushar from *The Sayings of the Lord* with a degree of understanding—something which it is far from impossible to do—can contemplate them without emotion. But how many have even troubled to make the effort? [50]

Frank was particularly gifted at the creation of new images and symbols, and in spite of its popular coloration his language is full of mystical overtones. Of the terminology of the Kabbalah he rarely made use, at times even criticizing the Sabbatian sectarians in Podolia for their continuing absorption in Kabbalistic ideas which he called "madness." [51] Anyone familiar with "radical" Sabbatian thought, however, can readily detect its continued presence beneath the new verbal façade. Thus, in place of the familiar Sabbatian "three knots of the faith" we now have "the Good God," "the Big Brother who stands before the Lord," and "the Virgin," terms which are highly suggestive for all their earthy quality. The *kelipah,* the Torahs of *beriah* and *atzilut,* the sparks of holiness, indeed all the conceptual usages that are basic to Sabbatian theological discourse, have disappeared entirely, to be replaced by a completely exoteric vocabulary. Even the figure of Sabbatai Zevi has greatly declined in importance. The world of Sabbatianism itself, on the other hand, remains intact, or rather, has reached that ultimate stage of its development where it verges on self-annihilation.

In the following pages I will attempt to present an over-all view of Frank's religious teachings, to the extent, that is, that they can be fully reconstructed from his many sayings, and in a form that they apparently did not completely attain until after his conversion to Catholicism. Although they will occasionally seem to contradict one another, they are for the most part mutually consistent. The somberness of their world or, more accurately, world-ruin, did not in fact encourage a great deal of variety, although this did not prevent the "believers," including even the traditionalists among them in Prague, from finding a dark fascination in its tidings, which Frank himself brutally summed up in a single brusk remark: "It is one thing to worship God—and quite another to follow the path that I have taken." [52]

According to Frank, the "cosmos" *(tevel)*, or "earthly world" *(tevel ha-gashmi)* as it was called by the sectarians in Salonika, is not the creation of the Good or Living God, for if it were it would be eternal and man would be immortal, whereas as we see from the presence of death in the world this is not at all the case.[53] To be sure, there are "worlds" which belong to "the Good God" too, but these are hidden from all but the "believers." In them are divine powers, one of whom is "the King of Kings," [54] who is also known as "the Big Brother" and "He who stands before the Lord." [55] The evil power that created the cosmos and introduced death into the world, on the other hand, is connected with the feminine, and is most probably composed of three "gods" or "Rulers of the World," one of whom is the Angel of Death. In any case, it is these "Rulers," all of whom have been incarnated on earth in human form,[56] who block the path leading to "the Good God," [57] who is unknown to men, for mystic knowledge of Him has as yet been revealed to no one, nor has the holy soul *(nishmata)* that emanates from Him been in any creature, not even in Sabbatai Zevi.[58] In the current aeon there are three "Rulers of the World": "Life," "Wealth," and "Death," the last of which must be replaced by "Wisdom" [59]—a task, however, that is not easily accomplished, for although "Wisdom" is in some mysterious manner connected to "the Good God," the latter is still not able to reveal Himself to mankind, "for the world is in the thrall of laws that are no good." [60]

Hence, it is necessary to cast off the domination of these laws, which are laws of death and harmful to mankind. To bring this about, the Good God has sent messengers such as the patriarchs "who dug wells," [61] Moses, Jesus, and others, into the world. Moses pointed out the true way, but it was found to be too difficult, whereupon he resorted to "another religion" and presented men with "the Law of Moses," whose commandments are injurious and useless. "The Law of the Lord," on the other hand—the spiritual Torah of the Sabbatians—"is perfect" (Ps. 19:8), only no man has yet been able to attain it.[62] Finally, the Good God sent Sabbatai Zevi into the world, but he too was powerless to achieve anything,[63] because he was unable to find the true way.[64] "But my desire is to lead you towards Life." [65] Nevertheless, the way to Life is not easy, for it is the way of nihilism and it means to free oneself of all laws, conventions, and religions, to adopt every conceivable attitude and to reject it, and to follow one's leader step for step into the abyss.[66] Baptism is a necessity, as Frank said prior to his conversion, "because Christianity has paved the way for us." [67] Thirty years afterwards this same "Christian" observed: "This much I tell you: Christ, as you know, said that he had come to redeem the world from the hands of the devil, but I have come to redeem it from all the laws and customs that have ever existed. It is my task to annihilate all this so that the Good God can reveal Himself." [68]

The annihilation of every religion and positive system of belief—this was the "true way" the "believers" were expected to follow. Concerning the redemptive powers of havoc and destruction Frank's imagination knew no limits. "Wherever Adam trod a city was built, but wherever I set foot all will be destroyed, for I came into this world only to destroy and to annihilate. But what I build, will last forever." [69] Mankind is engaged in a war without quarter with the "no-good" laws that are in power—"and I say to you, all who would be warriors must be without religion, which means that they must reach freedom under their own power and seize hold of the Tree of Life." [70] No region of the human soul can remain untouched by this struggle. In order to ascend one must first descend. "No man can climb a mountain until he has first descended to its foot. Therefore we must descend and be cast down to the bottom rung, for only then can we climb to the infinite. This is the mystic principle of Jacob's Ladder, which I have seen and which is shaped like a V." [71] Again, "I did not come into this world to lift you up but rather to cast you down to the bottom of the abyss. Further than this it is impossible to descend, nor can one ascend again by virtue of one's own strength, for only the Lord can raise one up from the depths by the power of His hand." [72] The descent into the abyss requires not only the rejection of all religions and conventions, but also the commission of "strange acts," [73] and this in turn demands the voluntary abasement of one's own sense of self, so that libertinism and the achievement of that state of utter shamelessness which leads to a *tikkun* of the soul are one and the same thing.

"We are all now under the obligation to enter the abyss" [74] in which all laws and religions are annihilated.[75] But the way is perilous, for there are powers and "gods"—these being none other than the three "Rulers of the World"—that do not let one pass. It is necessary to elude them and continue onward, and this none of the ancients were able to do, neither Solomon,[76] nor Jesus, nor even Sabbatai Zevi. To accomplish this, that is, to overcome the opposing powers, which are the gods of other religions, it is imperative that one be "perfectly silent," [77] even deceitful. This is the mystic principle of "the burden of silence" (*masa' dumah;* Isa. 21:11), i.e., of maintaining the great reserve that is becoming to the "believer" (a new version of the original Sabbatian injunction against appearing as one really is!). Indeed, this is the principle of the "true way" itself:

"Just as a man who wishes to conquer a fortress does not do it by means of making a speech, but must go there himself with all his forces, so we too must go our way in silence." [78] "It is better to see than to speak, for the heart must not reveal what it knows to the mouth." [79] "Here there is no need for scholars because here belongs the burden of silence." [80] "When I was baptized in Lvov I said to you: so far, so good! But from here on: a burden of silence! Muzzle your mouths!" [81] "Our forefathers were always talking, only what good did it do them and what did they accomplish? But we are under the burden of silence: here we must be quiet and bear what is needful, and that is why it is a burden." [82] "When a man goes from one place to another he should hold his tongue. It is the same as with a man drawing a bow: the longer he can hold his breath, the further the arrow will fly. And so here too: the longer one holds his breath and keeps silent, the further the arrow will fly." [83]

From the abyss, if only the "burden of silence" is borne, "holy knowledge" will emerge. The task, then, is "to acquire knowledge," "and the passageway to knowledge is to combine with the nations" [84] but not, of course, to intermingle with them. He who reaches the destination will lead a life of anarchic liberty as a free man. "The place that we are going to tolerates no laws, for all that comes from the side of Death, whereas we are bound for Life." [85] The name of this place is "Edom" or "Esau," and the way to it, which must be followed by the light of "knowledge" (gnosis) and under the "burden of silence" through the depths of the abyss, is called "the way to Esau." [86] This was the road taken by Jacob the patriarch, "the first Jacob," all of whose deeds prefigured those of "the last Jacob"—Jacob Frank. "Esau" too was foreshadowed by the Esau of the Bible, though only in a veiled way: "Esau the son of Jacob was but the curtain that hangs before the entrance to the king's inner chambers." [87] Herein lies the mystical principle of the wells dug by the patriarchs, as well as the mystic content of the story (Gen. 29) of how Jacob came to a well that had already been dug, rolled the stone from its mouth, and encountered Rachel and her father Laban. Another who found the passage to "Esau" was the sorcerer Balaam.[88] "Esau" belongs to the realm of the Good God where the power of death is made nought, and it is also the dwelling place of "the Virgin," she who is called Rachel in the biblical stories about Jacob [89] and is elsewhere known as "the beautiful maiden who has no eyes." [90] She it is who is the real Messiah (who cannot, contrary to traditional opinion, be a man) and to her "all the king's weapons are surrendered," [91] for she is also the much sought-after "Divine Wisdom" [92] or Sophia who is destined to take "Death's" place as one of the three "Rulers of the World." For the present, however, she is hidden in a castle and kept from the sight of all living creatures;[93] all the "strange acts," in comparison with which the "strange fire" offered before the Lord by Aaron's two sons (Lev. 10) was but a trifle, are committed for the sole purpose of reaching her.[94] Again, she is the "holy serpent" who guards the garden,[95] and he who asked what the serpent was doing in Paradise was simply betraying his ignorance.[96] As of yet, the place of "Esau," the home of "the Virgin" and of true salvation, has not been attained by anyone, but its hidden light will first be revealed to the "believers," [97] who will have the distinction of being its soldiers and fighting on its behalf.[98]

These are some of the main features of Frank's teaching. It is a veritable myth of religious nihilism, the work of a man who did not live at all in the world of rational argument and discussion, but inhabited a realm entirely made up of mythological entities. Indeed, to anyone familiar with the history of religion it might seem far more likely that he was dealing here with an antinomian myth from the second century composed by such nihilistic Gnostics as Carpocrates and his followers than that all this was actually taught and believed by Polish Jews living on the eve of the French Revolution, among whom neither the "master" nor his "disciples" had the slightest inkling that they were engaged in resuscitating an ancient tradition! Not only the general train of thought, but even some of the symbols and terms are the same! And yet, none of this seems as surprising as it may appear to be at first glance when we reflect that no less than the Frankists, the Gnostics of antiquity developed their thought within a biblical framework, for all that they completely inverted the biblical values. They too believed that Esau and Balaam were worshipers of "the Good God," they too converted the serpent in the Garden of Eden into a symbol of gnosis, salvation, and the true "Divine Wisdom" that guided men to freedom from the evil rule of the Demiurge by teaching them to disobey his laws and institutions, and they too held that the Law of the good and "alien" God, which enjoined the commission of "strange acts," was directly opposed to the Law of Moses, which was largely the promulgation of the irascible Creator.

Frank's ultimate vision of the future was based upon the still unrevealed laws of the Torah of *atzilut* which he promised his disciples would take effect once they had "come to Esau," that is, when the passage through the "abyss" with its unmitigated destruction and negation was finally accomplished. In seeking to elucidate this gospel of libertinism I can do no better than to quote a passage from the excellent book on Gnosticism by the philosopher Hans Jonas in which he discusses the development of a libertinist ethic among the nihilistically minded pneumatics of the second century:[99]

The spiritualist morality of these pneumatics possessed a revolutionary character that did not stop short of actively implementing its beliefs. In this doctrine of immoralism we are confronted both with a total and overt rejection of all traditional norms of behavior, and with an exaggerated feeling of freedom that regards the license to do as it pleases as a proof of its own authenticity and as a favor bestowed upon it from above. . . . The entire doctrine rests on the concept of an "extra spirit" as a privilege conferred upon a new type of human being who from here on is no longer to be subject to the standards and obligations that have hitherto always been the rule. Unlike the ordinary, purely "psychic" individual, the pneumatic is a free man, free from the demands of the Law . . . and, inasmuch as it implies a positive realization of this freedom, his uninhibited behavior is far from being a purely negative reaction. Such moral nihilism fully reveals the crisis of a world in transition: by arbitrarily asserting its own complete freedom and pluming itself on its abandonment to the sacredness of sin, the self seeks to fill the vacuum created by the "interregnum" between two different and opposing periods of law. Especially characteristic of this over-all mood of anarchy are its hostility towards all established conventions, its need to define itself in terms that are clearly exclusive of the great majority of the human race, and its desire to flout the authority of the "divine" powers, that is, of the World-rulers who are the custodians of the old standards of morality. Over and above the rejection of the past for its own sake, therefore, we are faced here with an additional motive, namely, the desire to heap insult on its guardians and to revolt openly against them. Here we have revolution without the slightest speculative dissemblance and this is why the gospel of libertinism stands at the center of the gnostic revolution in religious thought. No doubt, too, there was in addition to all this an element of pure "daredeviltry" which the Gnostic could proudly point to as an indication of his reliance on his own "spiritual" nature. Indeed, in all periods of revolution human beings have been fond of the intoxicating power of big words.

All of this is fully applicable to both "radical" Sabbatianism in general and to the Frankist movement in particular; the mentality that Jonas describes could not possibly, indeed, assume a more radical form than Frank's nihilistic myth. It goes without saying, of course, that in a given age myth and reality do not always coincide, and in the case of the Frankists the former was undoubtedly the extremer of the two, even if Frank himself was not far from living up to it in actual practice, as emerged from the manuscript of *The Chronicles of the Life of the Lord* which one of the Frankist families permitted Kraushar to use and which afterwards vanished. But in any event the significant point is the fact that the myth should have been born at all and that a considerable number of ghetto Jews should have come to regard it as a way to "political and spiritual liberation," to quote the words used by the educated Frankist Gabriel Porges in Prague to describe the movement's aims to his son after Frank himself was no longer alive. Clearly, for the Jew who saw in Frankism the solution to his personal problems and queries, the world of Judaism had been utterly dashed to pieces, although he himself may not have traveled the "true way" at all, may even, in fact, have continued to remain outwardly the most orthodox of observers.

VIII

We will apparently never know with any certainty why most of the Sabbatians in Podolia followed Frank's lead and became Catholics while their counterparts in Western Europe, who for the most part also regarded Frank as their spiritual leader, chose to remain Jews. Our knowledge in this area, which is of such crucial importance to an understanding of Jewish history in the countries in question, is practically nil and we must content ourselves with mere speculation. Possibly the decisive factor was the differing social structures of the two groups. The majority of the Sabbatians in Podolia were members of the lower class and few (which is not to say none at all) of those who converted were educated individuals. The Sabbatians in Germany and the Austro-Hungarian Empire, on the other hand, were largely from a more wealthy background and many of them were men of considerable rabbinical learning. As is frequently the case with religious sects, Sabbatianism was transmitted by entire families and not just by isolated individuals. Even today records exist to prove that a number of families, some of them quite prominent, which were known for their Sabbatian allegiances about 1740, were still clinging to "the holy faith" over sixty years later. For such groups traditional Judaism had become a permanent outer cloak for their true beliefs, although there were undoubtedly different viewpoints among them as to the exact nature of the relationship. Not all were followers of Frank, albeit the Frankists in Prague were spiritually the strongest among them and were extremely active in disseminating their views. Most probably those Sabbatians who had once been disciples of Rabbi Jonathan Eibeschütz were also to be found in this category. In any case, the fact remains that among these groups the number of conversions was very small. Many of their adherents may have desired to reach "the holy gnosis of Edom," but few were willing to pass through the gates of Christianity in order to do so.

On the whole, however, in the years following Frank's death the various Sabbatian groups still in existence continued to develop along more or less parallel lines. Four principal documents bearing on this final phase of Sabbatianism have come down to us: *The Book of the Prophecy of Isaiah* written by an apostate "believer" in Offenbach;[100] a long sermon on the *alenu* prayer published by Wessely from a lengthy Frankist manuscript;[101] several Frankist epistles as presented in substance by Peter Beer;[102] and a commentary on the book *En Ya'akov* that came into the possession of Dr. H. Brody, when he was Chief Rabbi of Prague. All of these sources share the same world, differing only in that the first speaks in praise of baptism and heaps "prophetic" imprecations on the Jewish people, its rabbis and officials, whereas the others,

written by Jews, preserve silence on these topics. Also found in
the volume containing the commentary on the *En Yd'akov* was a
Frankist commentary on the *hallel* prayer, the joyous faith and
emotion of which are genuinely moving.[103] The man who wrote
these few pages was a pure and immaculate spirit and his jubilant
profession of "the redemption and deliverance of his soul" is obviously deeply felt. Like most of the Sabbatians in the West, he
may never have met Frank face to face, but on the other hand,
the author of *The Prophecy of Isaiah,* who did, also believed him
to be the incarnation of the Living God, "the true Jacob who
never dies," and clung to this feeling of salvation throughout his
life.

In all of these documents the Frankist myth has lost much of
its radical wildness. Most of its component parts are still recognizable in the form of "profound mysteries" that are to be revealed only to the prudent, but these too have undergone
considerable modification. In many places, for instance, Frank's
insistence that the "believers" were literally to become soldiers is
so completely allegorized that it loses both its logic and its paradoxicality. The most striking change, however, is that while the
doctrine of "strange acts" remains, and continues to be associated
with the appearance of "the Virgin" or "the Lady," there is no
longer the slightest reference to any ethic of libertinism. Here
radicalism has retraced its steps and returned from the moral
sphere to the historical. Even if we suppose that the authors of
these documents were careful not to reveal themselves entirely in
their writings—an assumption that many of their cryptic allusions
would indeed seem to bear out—it is nonetheless apparent that
libertine behavior is no longer considered by them to be a binding
religious obligation. Instead there is an increased effort to understand the "strange acts" of the religious heroes of the past, particularly of the characters in the Bible, a book which the
"believers" no less than the orthodox regarded as the ultimate
authority; here too, however, the emphasis falls on vindicating
such cases in theory rather than on imitating them in practice. In
Offenbach, it is true, certain scandalous acts continued to be performed on no less than the Day of Atonement itself,[104] but this
had degenerated into a mere semblance, whereas "in good faith"
among themselves the "believers" were no longer in the habit of
carrying on such practices. As for the mystic principle of the
"conjugation" of masculine and feminine elements in the divine
worlds that had played so large a role in the unorthodox Kabba-

listic theories of the nihilists and the "radicals," this too, to judge by the sources in our possession,[105] was now "toned down." All in all, while the idea of violating the Torah of *beriah* remained a cardinal principle of "the holy faith," its application was transferred to other areas, particularly to dreams of a general revolution that would sweep away the past in a single stroke so that the world might be rebuilt.

Toward the end of Frank's life the hopes he had entertained of abolishing all laws and conventions took on a very real historical significance. As a result of the French Revolution the Sabbatian and Frankist subversion of the old morality and religion was suddenly placed in a new and relevant context, and perhaps not only in the abstract, for we know that Frank's nephews, whether as "believers" or out of some other motive, were active in high revolutionary circles in Paris and Strasbourg. Seemingly, the Revolution had come to corroborate the fact that the nihilist outlook had been correct all along: now the pillars of the world were indeed being shaken, and all the old ways seemed about to be overturned. For the "believers" all this had a double significance. On the one hand, with the characteristic self-centeredness of a spiritualist sect, they saw in it a sign of special divine intervention in their favor, since in the general upheaval the inner renewal and their clandestine activities based on it would be more likely to go unnoticed. This opinion was expressed by Frank himself[106] and was commonly repeated by his followers in Prague.[107] At the same time that the Revolution served as a screen for the world of inwardness, however, it was also recognized as having a practical value in itself, namely, the undermining of all spiritual and secular authorities, the power of the priesthood most of all. The "believers" in the ghettos of Austria, whose admiration for certain doctrines of the Christian Church (such as Incarnation) went hand in hand with a deep hatred of its priests and institutions, were particularly alive to this last possibility. Here the fashionable anti-clericalism of the times found a ready reception. In great and enthusiastic detail the Frankist author of *The Prophecy of Isaiah* describes the coming apocalypse which is destined to take place solely that the Jewish people might be reborn, repudiate its rabbis and other false leaders, and embrace the faith of "the true Jacob" as befits "the People of the God of Jacob." To the commentator on the *hallel* prayer writing in Prague, the verse in Psalms 118, "The right hand of the Lord is exalted," meant that "if the right hand of the Lord begins to emerge, the deceitful left hand of Esau and his priests and the deceitful sword will retire"—an allusion, of course, to the combined rule of the secular and ecclesiastical powers. Throughout this literature apocalyptic ideas mingle freely with the political theories of the Revolution, which were also intended, after all, to lead to a "political and spiritual liberation," to cite that illuminating and undeservedly neglected phrase with which the Frankists in Prague, as we have seen, defined the aims of their movement.

All this culminated in the remarkable case of "the Red Epistle," of 1799, a circular letter written in red ink and addressed by the Frankists in Offenbach, the last Mecca of the sect, to a large number of Jewish congregations, exhorting them to embrace "the holy religion of Edom." The theoretical part of this document—approximately the last third of it—is highly interesting. Here, in a single page, the epistlers summarize their beliefs without a single overt reference to Christianity, the word "Edom," as we have seen, possessing a more specialized meaning in their vocabulary. Besides bearing all the markings of the Frankist myth, the epistle contains the familiar ingredients of the Sabbatian homily as well, particularly in its audacious exegeses of biblical stories, Midrashim and Aggadot, passages from the *Zohar,* and Kabbalistic texts. In sum, an entire mystical theory of revolution. The passage that I am going to quote exemplifies perfectly the thinking, style, and cryptic manner of expression of this type of Frankist literature:[108]

Know that "it is time for the Lord to work, [for] they have made void Thy law" [Ps. 119:226] and in this connection the rabbis of blessed memory have said [Sanhedrin 97a] [that the Messiah will not come] "until the kingdom is entirely given over to heresy," [this being the mystical meaning of the words in Leviticus 13:13] "it is all turned white and then he is clean," [109] and as is explained in the book *Zror ha-Mor* [110] his servants are clean too. For the time has come that Jacob [was referring to when he] promised "I will come unto my Lord unto Seir" [Gen. 33:14], for we know that until now he has not yet gone thither; [111] and he [who will fulfill the verse] is our Holy Lord Jacob, "the most perfect of all" [*Zohar,* II, 23a] and the most excellent of the patriarchs, for he grasps both sides [*Zohar,* I, 147a], binding one extreme to the other [112] until the last extreme of all. But although last, he who will rise upon earth and say, "Arise O Virgin of Israel," is not least [i.e., he is more important and favored than the first Jacob]. Nay, he is certainly not dead,[113] and it is he who leads us on the true way in the holy religion of Edom,[114] so that whoever is of the seed of Abraham, Isaac and Jacob must follow in their path, for they have shown the way that their sons are to take at the End of Days, Abraham by descending to Egypt [Gen. 12], Isaac [by journeying] to Abimelech [Gen. 26], and Jacob, the most excellent of the patriarchs, by leaving Beersheba and going to Haran [Gen. 28] [that is], by leaving the faith [of his fathers] and the Land of Israel for another realm of impurity, as is explained in the *Zohar;* [115] for the *Zohar* explains that the redemption must be sought in the most evil place of all.[116] Then he came to the mouth of the well [117] [Gen. 29] and found Rachel and rolled the stone from the mouth of the well and came to Laban and worked for him [in the realm of evil] and brought out his own portion. And afterwards he went to Esau [Gen. 32], but he was still not done [with his task], for although he rolled the stone [from the well] they rolled it back again [118] [Gen. 29:3], and therefore he could not go to Seir [the place where there are no laws] and all this was but to prepare the way for the last Jacob [Frank], the most perfect of all, at the End of Days. For as the *Zohar* explains,[119] the first Jacob is perfect, but the last Jacob is perfect in everything, and he will complete [Jacob's mission in] everything. And it is said [in allusion to this] in the *Zohar:* "Until a man comes in the form of Adam and a woman in the form of Eve and they circumvent him [i.e., the serpent] and outwit him," [120] and so forth. Therefore, we must follow in his path, for "the ways of the Lord are right, and the just do walk in them" [Hos. 14:10], and though there is a burden of silence [about this] and the heart must not reveal [what it knows] to the mouth,[121] it is nonetheless written [Isa. 42:16], "And I will bring the blind by a way that they know not, in paths that they know not I will lead them, I will make darkness light before them and rugged places plain." And here it was that Jacob "honored his Master," and so forth [namely, by standing in the realm of evil]—and look in the *Zohar* [I, 161b, where these words are to be found].[122] And herein will be [found the mystical meaning of the verses] "Lord, when Thou didst go forth out of Seir, When Thou didst march out of the field of Edom" [Judg. 5:14] and "Who is this that cometh from Edom?" [Isa. 63:1], for as is [stated] in the *Tanna debe Eliyahu,*[123] there will come a day when the angels will seek the Lord and the sea will say "He is not in me" and the abyss will say "He is not in me." Where then will they find him? In Edom, for it is said, "Who is this that cometh from Edom?" And they who follow him into this holy religion and cling to the House of Jacob [Frank] and take shelter in its shadow—for it is said [Lam. 4:20], "Under his shadow we shall live among the nations" and [Mic. 4:2] "Come ye and let us go up to the mountain of the Lord and the House of the God of Jacob; and He will teach us of His ways, and we will walk in His paths"—to them it will be granted to cling to the Lord, for they [the ways of the Lord] are a way of life to those who find them. And it is written [Deut. 4:29], "From thence ye will seek the Lord thy God and thou shalt

find him." Why does the text emphasize "from thence"? Because light
will be made known from darkness [*Zohar,* III, 47b], as it is written
[Mic. 7:8], "Though I sit in darkness, the Lord is a light unto me."

The government officials who intercepted copies of this epistle
rightly suspected its authors of being hidden revolutionaries, but
for the wrong reason: The many obscure references to an individual called "Jacob" led them to surmise that they were in
reality dealing with—the Jacobins, who in this manner were supposed to spread their radical propaganda among the Jews of the
ghetto. An investigation was ordered on the spot. The authorities
who conducted it in Frankfurt and Offenbach, however, did not
delve beneath the surface of the affair and were quickly satisfied
that it involved nothing more than an intrigue to swindle and ex-
tort money from ignorant Jews. In our own day, a historian who
has published their official report, rather naïvely concludes by
remarking, "and so the ridiculous theories of a Frankist plot which
had proved so alarming to these imperial bureaucrats were at last
laid to rest," [124] thereby failing to realize himself that on a deeper
level the authorities' suspicions were fully if unwittingly justified!
Had they bothered to read and understand not just the debtors'
notes of Frank's children in Offenbach which were in the possession of the town's bankers and moneylenders, but also *The
Prophecy of Isaiah* that had been composed within the four walls
of the "court" itself, they would have been amazed to discover
how ardently these Frankist "Jacobins" yearned for the overthrow
of the existing regime.

The hopes and beliefs of these last Sabbatians caused them to
be particularly susceptible to the "millennial" winds of the times.
Even while still "believers"—in fact, precisely because they were
"believers"—they had been drawing closer to the spirit of the
Haskalah all along, so that when the flame of their faith finally
flickered out they soon reappeared as leaders of Reform Judaism,
secular intellectuals, or simply complete and indifferent skeptics.
We have already noted how deeply rooted the Sabbatian apathy
toward orthodox observance and Jewish tradition in general was.
Even the "moderates" tended to believe that the commandments
were for the most part meant to be observed only in the Land of
Israel and that "in the exile there is no punishment [for not observing them], even though there is still as always a reward [if
they are kept]" [125]—a doctrine that was ultimately to have a catastrophic effect on all traditional ties and to help prepare the way
for the philosophy of assimilation. A man such as Jonas

Wehle, for example, the spiritual leader and educator of the Sabbatians in Prague after 1790, was equally appreciative of both Moses Mendelssohn and Sabbatai Zevi, and the fragments of his writings that have survived amply bear out the assertion of one of his opponents that "he took the teachings of the philosopher Kant and dressed them up in the costume of the *Zohar* and the Lurianic Kabbalah." [126] It is evident from the commentary on the *En Ya'akov* and from the letters that were in Peter Beer's possession that men like Wehle intended to use the Haskalah for their own Sabbatian ends, but in the meanwhile the Haskalah went its way and proceeded to make use of them.

Indeed, even for those "believers" who remained faithful to their own religious world and did not share the enthusiasm of the Prague Frankists for the "School of Mendelssohn," the way to the Haskalah was easily traveled. It was surely no accident that a city like Prossnitz, which served as a center for the Haskalah in Moravia upon the movement's spread there one generation earlier, was also a bastion of Sabbatianism in that country. The leaders of the "School of Mendelssohn," who were neither Sabbatians themselves, of course, nor under the influence of mysticism at all, to say nothing of mystical heresy, found ready recruits for their cause in Sabbatian circles, where the world of rabbinic Judaism had already been completely destroyed from within, quite independently of the efforts of secularist criticism. Those who had survived the ruin were now open to any alternative or wind of change; and so, their "mad visions" behind them, they turned their energies and hidden desires for a more positive life to assimilation and the Haskalah, two forces that accomplished without paradoxes, indeed without religion at all, what they, the members of "the accursed sect," had earnestly striven for in a stormy contention with truth, carried on in the half-light of a faith pregnant with paradoxes.

The Crypto-Jewish Sect of the Dönmeh (Sabbatians) in Turkey

I

THE PHENOMENON with which I shall deal in the following pages represents one of the strangest and most paradoxical episodes in the history of the Jewish religion. It concerns the existence of an important religious group which nearly three hundred years ago voluntarily left Judaism, or rather the religious framework of the social and religious organization of the Jewish people. Its members became formally Muslims but remained Jews at heart —though Jews of a most peculiar kind. They continued as a separate entity, preserving their Jewishness in this twofold existence. Deeply motivated, even fanatical adherents of a Jewish mystical heresy, they succeeded in maintaining their identity almost untouched for more than two hundred and fifty years. Moreover, with amazing success they shrouded everything pertaining to their beliefs and religious practices with an impenetrable veil of secrecy. There are few sects in the recent history of religions like the crypto-Jewish sect of the Dönmeh. It has existed for centuries, been known both in its environment and, later, through the literature, yet scholars have had very little trustworthy information on which to proceed. It is therefore not surprising that reports concerning the sect in the scholarly literature on religions are most sparse. This has been true less because of lack of interest than because of the extreme paucity of information that was available to the outside world.

Since Abraham Danon, more than sixty years ago, spoke to the Paris Orientalists' Congress on "une secte judéo-musulmane en Turquie"—which contained the first reliable, if somewhat narrowly circumscribed material—there has really been only one other study: the 1926 review by Vladimir Gordlevsky in *Islamica* of the discussion carried on in 1924 in the Turkish press concerning the Dönmeh, at the time of the Greco-Turkish population exchange. A Turkish book by the well-known publicist Ibrahim Alâettin Gövsa, which appeared in 1938 or 1939, relied for its information on the Dönmeh principally upon this same discussion in the press. This is also true of Abraham Galanté's *Nouveaux documents sur Sabbetaï Sevi; organisation et us et coutumes de ses adeptes,* which appeared in Istanbul in 1935. These two studies contain nothing that is really new. If I now take up the discussion once again, I do so because in the last years, and especially since 1948, for the first time significant portions of the sect's so anxiously guarded secret literature have found their way to Israel and have there given rise to a spate of studies and publications. Thus we can now speak of this peculiar phenomenon with a very different knowledge of sources and circumstances. I hardly need mention that this represents only the beginning of real research into this sect.

As has always been known, the origins of the Dönmeh lie in the great Messianic eruption which took place in Judaism during the years 1665–66. This movement, which crystallized around the figures of the widely acclaimed pseudo-Messiah, the learned Kabbalist Sabbatai Zevi (1626-76), and his prophet and theologian Nathan of Gaza (1644-80), represents far and away the most significant Messianic movement in Diaspora Jewish history. While earlier movements of this type, which have never been lacking, were consistently limited in scope and duration and produced no lasting effect, this was decidedly not the case with the so-called Sabbatian movement. Its roots lay deep in an organic connection of national and popular apocalypticism with mystical ideas. Since the expulsion from Spain this complex of ideas had increasingly gained dominance in the Judaism of the period, so that when a Messianic eruption occurred, the conditions of the time were bound to secure for it an unprecedented echo and the largest effect. The prejudiced Jewish historiography of former generations wanted to minimize as much as possible the significance of this eruption, the depth from which it emerged, and the breadth of its effect. Only the research of the last twenty years has thoroughly swept away these prejudices and taught us to evaluate properly, on the basis of detailed study of manuscript sources, the great significance of this movement, which at one time embraced equally all parts of the Jewish Diaspora. In a work published in Hebrew in 1957, I undertook a comprehensive presentation.

The movement was assured of a special response because it originated in Palestine. There the prophet of Gaza recognized the Kabbalist Sabbatai Zevi, who had come from Smyrna to Jerusalem, as the Messiah. Until this time no one had taken his Messianic pretensions seriously (which, incidentally, Sabbatai had voiced only sporadically). Nathan was now convinced by his own ecstatic visions of the legitimacy of these pretensions. In that deeply agitated year, from October 1665 to November 1666, the movement possessed mass strength of great proportions; the most diverse elements joined together. There developed a movement of penitence of rare intensity, which was regarded as a kind of final effort to draw closer the Messianic redemption. It united with lively apocalyptic expectations which, nourished by ancient texts and traditions, gave up their literary and abstract character to assume acute forms and display their alarming power over the consciousness of large circles of Jews. All too easily perspectives became distorted as the frenzied proclamation of a redemption about to begin was accompanied by all the phenomena of a mass movement. The emotional impetus of the masses already anticipated what was actually supposed to follow only later, albeit in the most immediate future. The consummation of the Messianic redemption became for many an inner reality before it became a historical one, and thus the basis was laid for an inevitable conflict when the historical reality failed to materialize.

Moreover, the personality of Sabbatai Zevi exercised an extraordinary fascination, even apart from the aura of miracle and legend with which the credulous mentality and hopes of the masses soon surrounded it. At least for the circle of his closest adherents he was clearly an ascetic and mystic, who in periodic seizures of ecstasy, euphoria, and enthusiasm felt it his special vocation to place himself beyond the limits of religious law and thus to present Judaism with the heretofore entirely anomalous image of the "holy sinner." He combined a utopian vision of a new Judaism (an anarchic tendency which is quite appropriate to Messianism) with an equally outspoken inclination to invent bizarre and ludicrous rituals that took over items of the Jewish tradition, such as festival rites, but stood them on their head. All of this he did with the claim to a renewed Messianic authority which was supposed to override the traditional, sober authority of the rabbinic *Halakhah*.

The excitement reached its climax when at the beginning of 1666 the Messiah went to Constantinople where his supporters expected him to remove the crown from the head of the Sultan and inaugurate the new Messianic era. It is little wonder that Hebrew books appeared at that time which bore the date: "the first year of the renewal of prophecy and of the Kingdom." The Turkish authorities arrested the Messianic pretender to the throne, but to everyone's surprise did not execute him. Until September 1666 they held him captive near Gallipoli. There, although a prisoner of the state, he was allowed (apparently through bribery) to hold court; he received delegations from near and far which assured him of the support and recognition of their communities, among them the most outstanding and influential centers of Jewish life.

This unreal drama produced a deep impression on the believers. The fast day of the Ninth of Ab, commemorating the destruction of the Temple, was declared by Messianic edict the official birthday of the Messiah and thus proclaimed a joyous festival. The enthusiasm, especially of Turkish Jewry, knew no bounds, and the admonitory voices of isolated opponents and "non-believers" remained without effect. Thus it was a totally unanticipated catastrophe when these tense expectations were struck down by the news that Sabbatai Zevi, led before the Divan in Adrianople on September 16, 1666, in the presence of the Sultan had purchased his life by conversion.

The disarray of the believers was indescribable. But the excitement had run much too deep and was much too firmly rooted for disappointment to liquidate the movement. Large groups of his adherents continued to follow him without leaving Judaism. Nathan of Gaza, who possessed a remarkable ability to reinterpret old texts, produced a new theory which received considerable support. This theory asserted that the consummation of Israel's Messianic redemption from exile has its own tragic dialectic. It is contingent upon the Messiah himself venturing among the nations in order to fulfill a mystical mission: to liberate and "elevate" the sparks of holiness and the holy souls which are to be found also outside of Israel. For such a mission it is not enough to stand within the realm of the holy and to extract holy powers even from the realms of impurity; rather to this end it is necessary to pass into its domain oneself. Thus there is a kind of exile of the Messiah himself who, as it were, cuts himself off from his holy roots or exiles himself from them in order to fulfill the redemption. So we have here a completely new, albeit heretical, Jewish variation of the ancient conception of the *descensus ad inferos*. The apostasy of the Messiah is a necessary act in the fulfillment of his mystical, and also of his historical function. The Messiah has not really become a Turk; rather he is now as ever a Jew. Only henceforth he lives on two levels—the exoteric and the esoteric one—which until his return in the full splendor of Messianic dominion must remain in contradiction.

This theory fit very nicely the actual behavior of Sabbatai Zevi. His double life as Muslim and Jew was tolerated for a number of years by a Turkish government that at first expected much from this important convert. Just as before, believing Sabbatians made pilgrimages to Adrianople, and the above-mentioned theses of the heretical Messianism were widely disseminated through a large number of works circulating in manuscript. A kind of Jewish Messianic underground movement came into being which, despite very understandable opposition and persecution by the official rabbinic authorities, nonetheless maintained itself in many groups and in many lands of the Diaspora. Even the death of Sabbatai Zevi, who after being finally exiled to Albania died in the autumn of 1676 in Dulcigno (Ulcinj), was unable to change things. The Messiah has not really "died," he has only "gone into occultation." In any case, the doctrine of reincarnation, as it was commonly accepted by the Kabbalists, allowed the supposition that the Messiah wandered through many forms from Adam down to his most recent one. In the nineteenth century the Dönmeh assumed eighteen such reincarnations of the soul of Adam and the Messiah.

The dilemma that confronted the adherents of Sabbatai Zevi after 1666 is of decisive significance for the origins of the Dönmeh sect. Should the apostasy of the Messiah be considered a border case not to be imitated or should it serve as an example for the "believers"? In other words: can the belief in the Messianic mission of Sabbatai Zevi be reconciled with remaining inside the framework of the historical Jewish community or does it demand following his lead? The first possibility results in an underground movement which to the outside world seems strictly rabbinic but is inwardly Sabbatian, that is to say, from a Jewish point of view heretical. The second possibility produces the same result but with a Turkish Muslim façade. The overwhelming majority of the Sabbatians stuck to the first of these alternatives and thus played an important role in the spiritual ferment which gripped European Jewry in the next three or four generations. Their fate does not concern us here; I have dealt with it at length in the preceding essay. A minority, however, took up the second alternative. Its

representatives lived in Salonika (the most important center of
Sephardic Judaism in Turkey), in Adrianople, and in Constantinople. They were in close contact with the apostatized Messiah,
especially before his exile to Albania in January 1673. Sabbatai
Zevi's own attitude was ambivalent. Under normal circumstances
he seems mostly, though not always, to have forgone persuading
his adherents to convert, even if here and there he uttered the
opinion that the majority of Israel would have to accept the turban. But in his enthusiastic manic periods, which sometimes
extended to several weeks, he demanded conversion. We know that
to this end he more than once invited influential scholars among
his adherents to Adrianople and was saddened if they did not
comply with his demand, which he sometimes issued in a highly
official manner in the Sultan's presence. We are in possession of
a most dramatic report which at first hand relates one such
incident.

II

The number of these first adherents of Sabbatai Zevi who were
prepared to follow him all the way reached about 200 families
during the lifetime of the Messiah, most of them from the Balkans, but some also from Smyrna and Brusa. It appears also that
they received from him the earliest instructions concerning the
conduct of their lives in the form of such a double existence as
voluntary Marranos. During these first years fluctuations often
occurred when a number of such "believers" would after a certain
time, especially after the death of Sabbatai Zevi, return to Judaism,
as did, for example, Sabbatai Zevi's own brother, Elijah Zevi. But
in general this group constituted a very tightly knit sect which
counted among its members a considerable number of very
learned Kabbalists and rabbis whose families later enjoyed special
status as the oldest segment of the Dönmeh. The connection between them and the "believers" who remained within Judaism
was close. (The term "believers"—ma'aminim—was used by all
varieties of the adherents of Sabbatai Zevi to distinguish themselves from the "deniers"—kofrim—as they called those Jews
who denied the legitimacy of the Messianic mission of Sabbatai
Zevi.) The converts regarded themselves as an aristocratic group
of the elect because they had received a call with which the others
were not honored, or which they had rejected. We possess in
manuscript a commentary to the Book of Psalms which was composed in this circle of Sabbatai Zevi's adherents in Adrianople

about 1679, i.e., only a short time after his death. Although it is
written by an author who himself had not converted, the commentary provides us with a deep insight into the attitude of this
group to mystical apostasy. The author seems relieved that he
was spared this "test," as he calls it, but he nevertheless speaks
with highest respect about those of whom it was demanded and
who submitted to it themselves.

Within the earliest group of the Dönmeh a document was
circulated in Sabbatai Zevi's name, which precisely determines the
mood and manner of life of these new Marranos. Whether it was
composed by himself or only at his behest, he personally appears
in the concluding remarks, speaking in the first person. These are
the "Eighteen Commandments" *(incommendanças),* the text of
which we possess in Spanish and which were accepted by all the
Dönmeh as the basis for their conduct. It is noteworthy in this
connection that the number eighteen plays a prominent role both
in Jewish tradition and also among the Sufis, especially among the
order of the Mevlevis, the dancing dervishes. The eighteen commandments correspond to the "Eighteen Benedictions" which is
the basic prayer of the daily Jewish liturgy; eighteen also possesses
the numerical value of the Hebrew word *hai,* "living." Thus Jews
like to give to charitable causes in sums of eighteen or multiples
thereof. Among the dervishes eighteen represents the holiest
number of all. Although we cannot say for sure, it is possible that
the choice by the Dönmeh was determined by a conscious regard
for this special character of the number eighteen. Abraham Danon
was the first to familiarize himself with these commandments
(although Theodor Bendt had earlier seen them in somewhat
garbled form). With marked Sabbatian variations, they repeat
the Ten Commandments, the prohibition of fornication being formulated in an especially ambiguous fashion which rather re-
sembles a counsel of prudence. Since, as we shall see, the
Sabbatians regarded the sexual restrictions of the Torah as abolished, this is certainly not coincidental. Other commandments
regulate the twofold life style of these *ma'aminim* in their relations with Jews and Turks. Their tenor does not hide an aversion
to Islam, although the commandments enjoin them to its precepts.
The conclusion also takes into consideration the (much larger)
group of Sabbatai Zevi's original adherents who remained Jews.
Regarding them it says: "Announce to our comrades, who are
ma'aminim but have not yet entered into the mystery of the turban, which is the battle [against impurity], that they keep both

the external and the purely spiritual Torah from which they are
to detract nothing until the time of the revelation [the ultimate
redemption at the parousia of the Messiah]. Then they shall come
under the Tree of Life and all will become angels." This same
state of things is reflected by the prohibition against forcibly converting any one of the "believers" to the "faith of the turban."
Intermarriage with Turks is here expressly forbidden. Later texts
of these commandments, while keeping all the essentials, moderate
the sharply anti-Turkish and anti-Islamic remarks.

The Jewish communities of European Turkey in these years
were often still full of open or secret adherents of Sabbatai Zevi
or, as he was known in Islam, Mehmed Aziz Effendi. After his
death their main center moved to Salonika. There, some time
later, the widow of the Messiah—his last wife, Jochebed (in
Islam: Aisha), whom he had married only two years before his
death in Albanian exile—had returned to her family. Her father,
Joseph Filosof, was among the most respected rabbis of Salonika.
Together with the respected scholar Solomon Florentin and with
Barzilai, one of the first disciples of Sabbatai Zevi from the days
of his youth, he stood at the apex of the powerful Sabbatian group
in Salonika. The widow proclaimed her brother Jacob Querido the
mystical vessel in which the soul of Sabbatai Zevi had taken up
its abode.

While we possess many reports and documents dealing with
the way in which the Sabbatian movement sought to cope with the
circumstances created by the terrible disappointment and to master
them through a heretical theology, we have no trustworthy information concerning the powerful ferment which took place during
these years, especially in Salonika. Relevant documents still known
in other Sabbatian circles around 1700 must be regarded as lost.
Whereas in other places other leaders of the movement developed
ideas which furthered or justified the "believers'" remaining
within the historical community of Judaism, here more extreme
tendencies gained dominance. Some of the leaders received revelations which were regarded by the Sabbatians who remained Jews
as the work of the devil who had led them astray. In consequence
of these revelations, in the year 1683—not 1687 as earlier assumed—a group of about 200 to 300 families converted en
masse. They were led by Joseph Filosof and Solomon Florentin, although the driving spirit was Jacob Querido. The more
precise circumstances of the mass apostasy have not previously
become known. However, we possess evidence that here too inter-

vention of the Turkish authorities after Querido's appearance as prophet resulted in the conversion which the most important leaders announced in the presence of the Sultan. Henceforth the apostates organized themselves as a separate group which accepted those earliest Eighteen Commandments as binding also upon itself. This of course meant that they would as before seek inwardly to preserve their Jewish character and their religious convictions, which remained Jewish though largely transformed into a mystical heresy. Smaller groups in Adrianople, Constantinople, and elsewhere followed the lead of Salonika, which remained the center of the new organization. At first, incidentally, a large number of Sabbatians remained Jewish even in Salonika. But nonetheless the Dönmeh group multiplied by conversion and through migration of Sabbatian families from abroad. In the course of time, probably in the second half of the eighteenth century, Polish Sabbatians also joined them, and as late as 1915 there was a group of Dönmeh families known as *Lechli,* i.e., Poles.

While the Turkish authorities no doubt greeted this mass conversion to Islam with joy and looked forward to its having great effect upon Turkish Jewry, they were soon forced to realize that these were by no means genuine converts who were willing to be absorbed into the Turkish nation. To be sure, the neophytes testified to their ardor for the new religion when Jacob Querido with several supporters in 1689–90 undertook the pilgrimage to Mecca, on which, incidentally, he died. But it soon became evident that the converts—called Dönmeh, i.e., "converts," by the Turks of Salonika—only married among each other. Not only did they reject equally intermarriage with Jews and with Turks, but even in their social life they avoided as far as possible any contact with outsiders. All the more close-knit were the relations within the group itself. Nevertheless, they must have taken up some contacts with mystical tendencies in Islam, especially with certain orders of dervishes. Sabbatai Zevi had already been accustomed to living in a dervish monastery on his visits to Constantinople during the first years after his conversion and to being on friendly terms with the mystical lyricist Mehmed Niyazi. And it can hardly be doubted that there were early secret ties between the order of the Bektashi and the Dönmeh. It is known that among the Bektashi orders the doctrine of *takiye* (dissimulation) was widely practiced; it permitted the adherents of even radical mystical heresies in Islam to appear to the outside world as a wholly orthodox segment of the Sunni community in order to avoid persecution. It is also known that their enemies always claimed this duplicity of the Bektashi and accused them of it. Often they also added the even more far-reaching accusation that the Bektashi, or at least certain of their subgroups, secretly subscribed to a religious nihilism. Now it is just this theory and practice of *takiye* which, though here for purely internal Jewish reasons, determined the Dönmeh's way of life in which the external appearance stood in radical contradiction to what they taught and stood for. Their common status as a mystical heresy with often extreme aberrations was bound to create sympathy between these two groups. Perhaps it is also no accident that the cemetery of the most extreme group of the Dönmeh, with the grave of its leader Baruchya Russo (in Islam: Osman Baba), was located in the immediate vicinity of the Bektashi monastery of Salonika. According to Dönmeh tradition, moreover, aside from several groups of Sabbatian families which still later joined them from Poland, a number of Turkish and Greek non-Jewish families also passed over and joined one of their subsects.

Nonetheless, the Jewish character of the Dönmeh was preserved in all matters of consequence, as they now closed themselves off from the outside; it was a very easy thing to do because of their close proximity and steady contact with the vibrant Jewish milieu of Salonika. Although the Dönmeh wanted to live according to their own ways, despite all their heretical convictions they did not at all intend to break completely with the traditional patterns of rabbinical Judaism. Like all Sabbatians, they distinguished between two different aspects of Torah. The one is called the Torah of the creaturely world, the Torah of *beriah,* by which is meant the manifestation of revelation as it is represented in the lower realms and most especially in the unredeemed state of the world. In other words, this is the historical form of the talmudic rabbinical Judaism of the *Halakhah.* The second aspect is called the Torah of spirituality (literally: of the world of emanation, the Torah of *atzilut*) and represents its mystical substantiality wherein it may be comprehended in the upper worlds, but also in the state of redemption. The Messiah replaces the validity of the "creaturely" by that of the "spiritual" Torah which in essence, i.e., in their language, are after all only a single Torah. Because of the confusion created by the fact that while the Messiah has already appeared he has not yet completely fulfilled his mission, the two states of the world overlap and exist side by side. There are spheres of life in which, according to the Sabbatians, the spiritual mystical Torah already reigns, representing anarchic freedom. But there are other spheres, those of civic life, as it were, wherein the "Torah of Creation," befitting the exile, will reign until the parousia of the Messiah. The result was that, although the Dönmeh knew a level of life on which the new law was already in effect, namely, in the most inward and concealed realms, especially of festivals and their rituals in which the new reality finds expression, in many other respects they still maintained the old forms of the tradition. No doubt also after their conversion, they sought to preserve as many of these forms as possible. Their scholars studied the ancient writings and in disputes they utilized talmudic law. For more than two hundred years they never had recourse to Turkish courts. We know for certain that as actual knowledge of the Talmud decreased among them, they would for generations—up to the 1860's—always secretly seek out one of the most respected rabbis of Salonika who decided for them all doubtful cases that arose on the basis of talmudic law. We are familiar with the names of a number of such "judges" of the Sabbatians from the circle of the "non-believers." Only an investigation by the Turkish authorities (concerning which there may still be material in the Turkish archives), prompted by a denunciation of them in 1858 (others say 1864), induced the leaders of the Dönmeh to be more careful and to break off these clandestine relations with rabbinic authorities. In 1915 their archives still contained compendia of the talmudic law and handwritten decisions of their rabbinic confidants concerning questions posed to them by the circle of the Dönmeh.

During the first fifty years of their history, when the religious excitement and the expectation of a final reincarnation of Sabbatai Zevi were at their strongest, a number of splits occurred in the new sect which led to the formation of three main groups or subsects which strictly separated themselves from each other. Following tradition, they also did not intermarry, although their leaders made use of common plans and counsels when matters arose concerning the protection of vital Dönmeh interests. This was of special importance when it became necessary to use bribes in order to fend off the curiosity of high Turkish officials who would have liked to get behind the mysteries of the sect; at least once or twice formal investigations were instituted by governors of Salonika who had become suspicious. Regarded with mistrust and disdain by the Turks because of their double lives despite their often declared loyalty, and with no less lively aversion persecuted by the

Jews of Salonika as apostates, they closed their ranks that much tighter and for a long time found in their secret ritual the emotional satisfaction that they had been chosen as the true Israel.

The splits which I mentioned above were always connected with claims of new leaders. The earliest groups of the "believers" rejected the claims of Jacob Querido. A schism resulted: the "Jacobite" group split off and remained loyal to its leader and his successors. But a schism also occurred in the opponents' camp. Around 1700 Baruchya Russo (or Osman Baba), the son of one of the most respected and learned of the apostates, born shortly after Sabbatai Zevi's death, was proclaimed to be his reincarnation. As in early Christianity, there developed also among the followers of the Sabbatian movement a mystical theology, better: Christology of the incarnation of God in the person of the Messiah, which was picked up by the radical wing of the Sabbatians. About 1716 Baruchya himself was proclaimed such a divine incarnation. A lively propaganda issued forth from Salonika via emissaries to the other centers of European Jewry. At the time it created a great stir in many important Jewish communities and in several places it struck roots. We know of representatives from Polish Sabbatian groups who initiated contacts with Baruchya and accepted his theology of incarnation. Within the circle of the Dönmeh itself there arose a great deal of opposition to these claims and the extremism, bordering on nihilism, which accompanied them. Baruchya died in 1720 and was honored by his subsect as divine. Until the population exchange of 1924 his grave remained the object of special veneration. After his death, his son, who lived nearly to the time of the French Revolution (he died in 1781), and his descendants conducted the sect in much the same spirit. Baruchya's opponents declared him a dull-witted epileptic who had been used as a tool by one of the first Sabbatians. Understandably, his adherents were of a quite different opinion: according to them, he was "a very learned man of rare beauty." It is not at all unlikely that the literature of radical mystical antinomianism has its origins in his personal inspiration, although one cannot be certain since most of it must at present be considered lost. At that time this literature spread from Salonika all the way to Prague, Frankfurt am Main, and Mannheim— to name only a few places. Certain Sabbatian manuscripts contain peculiar sayings transmitted in Baruchya's name. His adherents were later designated by their opponents as the sect of the *Onyolou* (of the "ten paths"), by which was meant, apparently,

that they were regarded as syncretists who wanted to bring together the paths of the various religions and had introduced foreign elements into the sect's original stock of beliefs. It must
remain open to question whether Islamic, Christian, and Jewish-
Kabbalistic doctrines were really interwoven here, except for the
doctrine of incarnation which we know they did accept. Insofar
as documents concerning this particular subgroup have been preserved, they lack any provable influence of foreign theologoumena. Naturally this is even truer of other Dönmeh groups. The
justification of their *takiye,* which was common to all Sabbatians,
hardly constitutes such a specific element of syncretism and may
as easily be considered a parallel to the Sufi conceptions as the
result of Sufi-Bektashi influence. It is naturally not beyond the
realm of possibility that this polemical designation, *Onyolou,*
does contain a certain measure of truth.

The circles of the Dönmeh which recognized neither Jacob
Querido nor Baruchya remained faithful to the original authority
of Sabbatai Zevi and his first prophets. After unsuccessful attempts to reach a rapprochement with the Jacobites, during the
second quarter of the eighteenth century they organized themselves
into a third subsect. In Salonika and Adrianople these various
sects were known by different designations. The older reports
from the nineteenth and the beginning of the twentieth centuries
speak of Izmirlis (Smyrnians, i.e., the earliest adherents and those
who share their point of view) or Kavalieros, Jakubis, and Koniosos. In the later reports, especially since the move to Turkey, the
three sects are most often called Jakubis, Koniosos or Karakash
(the sect of Baruchya), and Kapandshis or Papulars. The last
word means "the old ones," and probably refers to those who
wanted to uphold the old tradition of Sabbatai Zevi himself without any new additions.

Most of the older reports agree in their fairly precise determination of the relative social status of the three subsects. The adherents of Jacob Querido were mostly officials in Salonika; the Kapandshis or, according to other reports, Izmirlis were large- and
middle-scale merchants and in their most recent generations also
produced a great many Turkish professionals: physicians and law-
yers. In the early period all of the barbers of Salonika belonged
to this group and saw to it that the three subsects were differentiated from each other by different styles of haircuts and by the
manner in which they shaved their heads or their beards. The
lowest social position was held by the Karakash; they were poor

artisans, cobblers, stocking weavers, day laborers, porters, and the like. All of this holds true for the outward circumstances of the Dönmeh between 1870 and 1920; with advancing emancipation and disintegration the social stratification naturally also shifted. Especially the first two sects, in which the manifestations of disintegration advanced relatively most rapidly, contributed many individuals to the intelligentsia of the Young Turks. The position of the Karakash improved and they have meanwhile become mostly merchants, especially in the textile trade of Istanbul.

The membership figures given for the Dönmeh during recent generations vary a great deal. The earliest report, that of the Danish orientalist Karsten Niebuhr from the year 1784, gives their number as about 600 families. Since most of the families had a great many children, the number rose in the course of time before the consequences of inbreeding made themselves felt. The estimates of various observers from 1850 to 1924 range from 5,000 to 10,000 souls. (Some even go as high as 15,000 for the total number in Turkey about 1914.) Thus they constituted approximately half of that portion of the population of Salonika designated in the censuses as Turkish, the great majority of the inhabitants being Jews and Greeks. The Jacobites and Izmirlis, by the way, lived in closed-off quarters, real estate which, according to their tradition, had been made available by the Turkish government in reward for their conversion. The Karakash also mostly lived together, even if not to the same degree. The secret synagogues of the various groups were located in houses that stood in the center of the Dönmeh quarters and were completely unrecognizable from the outside. These synagogues, or rather meeting places, possessed none of the paraphernalia of a synagogue such as an ark for the Torah or a raised reading desk. Yet, while the Dönmeh recited the prescribed prayers of Islam in the nearby mosques—which especially the first two sects were careful to do—the real religious worship, which reflected their genuine convictions, took place in the synagogues. The conduct of the services and of religious life in general was in the hands of the Hodjas or Hakhamim, as according to Sephardic custom their rabbis were called. As long as the Dönmeh remained centered in Salonika—about 2000 of them were supposedly scattered in various provinces of Turkey around 1900—they used Turkish in their relations with outsiders, although only later (from 1870 on) did it become also in increasing measure the language they spoke at home. For most of their history they used Judeo-Spanish when speaking to each other as also, we can now say with certainty, in composing their later literature. The knowledge of Hebrew continued for a long time among them, which, considering the ready availability of Jewish teachers in Salonika, is not too surprising. But in the course of time this knowledge markedly decreased. Still, Hebrew script was employed—though in a peculiarly deformed cursive—as late as the nineteenth and twentieth centuries.

It is especially interesting that as knowledge of Hebrew declined among the masses of the Dönmeh, the prayers, which originally were entirely in Hebrew and remained so until late in the nineteenth century, were rendered in a phonetic transcription corresponding to the sound values of Judeo-Spanish but using Hebrew characters. This would therefore indicate that although the prayers were still recited in Hebrew, they were no longer understood; the historical spelling of Hebrew as a Semitic language no longer elicited comprehension. The prayer books were copied in an unusually small format, similar to what we know of the prayer books intended for the Spanish Marranos because in this way they could be more easily hidden. Every family probably received such a copy of the most important prayers. For more than two hundred years they were successful in preventing any outsider from obtaining the text of their liturgies, and one had to rely completely on guesswork. Only two short prayers for the beginning and end of a certain fast day fell by chance into Danon's hands seventy years ago. The Dönmeh preserved an impenetrable silence concerning all their true practices and beliefs. They thereby contributed a great deal themselves to the wild rumors and stories about them which circulated among the Jews of Salonika. Not until 1935 did the text of such a handwritten prayer book become known. It was donated to the Hebrew University Library in Jerusalem by a family which had moved from Salonika to Smyrna and had decided finally to relinquish its Dönmeh past. In 1942 I published this text. We were greatly surprised at the time to discover that we were here dealing with purely Jewish prayers put together from the most important and popular sections of the Sephardic *siddur* and *mahzor*. However, important and far-reaching changes were made in order to use every opportunity to express faith in Sabbatai Zevi as the Messiah. In place of the traditional orthodox Jewish credo consisting of the Thirteen Principles of Maimonides, which are recited at the end of the morning service, we find here a particularly valuable Sabbatian credo. Wherever the traditional prayers or psalms speak of God's commandments, the Dönmeh prayers speak of "belief." The mystical value of belief for these Sabbatians has replaced the real activity of fulfilling the commandments, which for them has become no longer possible or valid. This transformation of Jewish religious elements into purely spiritual ones does not, however, in the least do away with national accents. No part of these prayers would make the reader even dream that these worshipers were Muslims. It will be of interest to present this credo here in translation:

I believe with perfect faith in the faith of the God of truth, the God of Israel who dwells in [the *sefirah*] *tiferet*, the "glory of Israel," the three knots of faith which are one.

I believe with perfect faith that Sabbatai Zevi is the true King Messiah.

I believe with perfect faith that the Torah, which was given through our teacher Moses, is the Torah of truth, as it is written: And this is the Torah which Moses placed before Israel, as ordered by God through Moses. It is a Tree of Life to them that hold fast to it and its supporters will be happy . . . [here follow several biblical verses extolling the Torah].

I believe with perfect faith that this Torah cannot be exchanged and that there will be no other Torah; *only the commandments have been abolished,* but the Torah remains binding forever and to all eternities.

I believe with perfect faith that Sabbatai Zevi, may his majesty be exalted, is the true Messiah and that he will gather together the dispersed of Israel from the four corners of the earth.

I believe with perfect faith in the resurrection of the dead, that the dead shall live and shall arise from the dust of the earth.

I believe with perfect faith that the God of truth, the God of Israel, will send the rebuilt sanctuary from above down to us [on the earth] beneath, as it is said: Unless God build the house, those that build it labor in vain. May our eyes see and our heart rejoice and our soul sing for joy, speedily in our days. Amen.

I believe with perfect faith that the God of truth, the God of Israel will reveal Himself in this [earthly] world [called] *tevel,* as it is said: For they shall see, eye to eye, the Lord returning to Zion. And it is said: And the glory of God will be revealed and all flesh shall see it, for the mouth of the Lord has promised it.

May it be pleasing before Thee, God of truth, God of Israel who dwells in the "glory of Israel," in the three knots of faith which are one, to send us the just Messiah, our Redeemer Sabbatai Zevi, speedily and in our days. Amen.

It is clear that the author of this credo, which surely dates from the earliest period of the sect, has taken over the mystical theory of the first Sabbatians regarding the "three knots of faith," meaning the three manifestations of the Godhead in the hidden world of emanation (of the ten *sefirot*) which have little to do with the Christian trinity. But he does not in the least connect them with a doctrine of the incarnation of one of these configurations or knots of the Godhead in the person of Sabbatai Zevi. Rather he believes—and this too is in keeping with the earliest Sabbatian theology, especially that of Nathan of Gaza—that at the parousia of the Messiah God will visibly appear. All of his principles correspond to the conceptions with which we are familiar from those Sabbatians who remained Jewish. Mystical apostasy plays no role here whatever and has no special significance except for the emphatic conviction concerning the abolition of the ceremonial laws which were valid only before Sabbatai Zevi. This fits in well with the fact that this document came from a family that belonged to the Kapandshis (Izmirlis), who did not tolerate any later additions to their original stock of beliefs. A prayer book belonging to the sect of Baruchya would naturally have looked completely different. After all, they invoked Baruchya himself by his Hebrew name as God incarnate. In the above-mentioned prayer book no more than an occasional deep sigh points to the fact that the worshipers are practicing their religion only in secret. In an addition to one of the ancient Jewish prayers a yearning is expressed for the time "when Thy faith will be public"—i.e., not secret as it is now. Later manuscripts from this circle contain these and similar prayers already in Judeo-Spanish translation.

The discoveries of recent years show that Judeo-Spanish was the basic literary language of the Dönmeh. It was often assumed that this literature was irretrievably lost, especially after Solomon Rosanes reported that the archives of at least one of the three main groups, the Izmirli, was destroyed in the major fire that hit Salonika in 1917. This assumption clearly underestimated the conservatism which, especially in a sect that could not easily allow its productions to appear in print, resulted in many families preserving copies of important texts in their personal possession. As it was, not a single such text, to the best of my knowledge, reached the hands of outsiders before 1924; the sect still held closely together.

Of course signs of disintegration had begun to manifest themselves since about 1875 when the Dönmeh youth launched a revolt demanding, on the one hand, closer ties with the Turkish nation, and on the other, a European education, which at that time meant above all knowledge of French culture. From the beginning, Dönmeh played a significant role in the Committee for Progress and Unity, the organization of the Young Turk movement, which had its origins in Salonika. Among those who participated were freethinkers—especially from the sect of the Jakubis and Izmirlis—who upon the breakdown of their old sectarian convictions developed a totally negative and enlightened attitude toward the religious world, as well as devout Sabbatians who combined their Turkish patriotism and nationalism with Jewish Messianic utopianism. Thus, for example, we have reliable evidence that Djavid Bey, one of three ministers from the circle of the Dönmeh in the first Young Turk government and an important leader of the Young Turk party, played a leading role in the organization of the Karakash sect. In fact he belonged to the most important family of this group, the Russo family, direct descendants of the incarnate god Baruchya Russo or Osman Baba. In this connection it must be mentioned that most of the Dönmeh families carefully nurtured their family traditions and continued the secret use of Hebrew and Judeo-Spanish first names and surnames in addition to their official Turkish ones. These were the names by which they were not only known among one another, but by which they would one day be known in Paradise. Still very recently, members of the Dönmeh intelligentsia during intimate conversations would confide their full Jewish names to their Jewish visitors or, with a knowing glance, they would scribble it in Hebrew on their Turkish calling cards. Assimilation to their Turkish environment advanced with extraordinary rapidity among the Dönmeh after their resettlement robbed them of contact with a Jewish milieu. Yet to this day there is still a core of orthodox Sabbatians who steadfastly maintain their faith. Such a core persists above all among the Karakash group, which was the last to enter into the stream of the new life and which seems still to possess a religious organization. As a result of mixed marriages, lack of interest, and determined assimilation, the other two groups are moving more rapidly toward disintegration. But even among these there are a number of tradition-oriented and committed families. This is the less surprising as we have multiple evidence that, immediately preceding the population exchange, the heads of the Dönmeh in Salonika attempted to gain permission from the Greek government to declare themselves again openly as Jews and thus to remain in Salonika. When their request was refused, several Dönmeh families handed over or sold manuscripts in their possession to Jewish friends. These friends, however, have not as yet made them

known publicly—if indeed they survived the destruction of Greek
Jewry by the German authorities during World War II. Yet we
may confidently expect that documents of historical importance
will still be forthcoming from this source. As a result of similar
events, a large number of Dönmeh manuscripts of the nineteenth
century, especially from the Izmirli group, reached Israel and are
now to be found especially in the library of the Hebrew University in Jerusalem and in the Ben-Zvi Institute for Research on the
Jewish Communities in the Middle East, which is connected with
the University. By contrast, only a single manuscript has become
known from the sect of Baruchya. It reached New York a few
decades ago and contains Judeo-Spanish Kabbalistic miscellanea
plus outlines for Sabbatian sermons for one of their main holidays; there are also several invocations and poems which may stem
from the middle of the eighteenth century. The author of one of
these poems appeals to *mio dio Baruch Yah* to save him. This
fits in with a series of other documents concerning the belief in
Baruchya which we possess from Jewish sources of the eighteenth
century. It is to be hoped that additional texts from this group,
which may yet turn up—surely such material may still be found
in the possession of a number of Karakash families in Istanbul—
will shed even brighter light on the close connection that existed
between this group and the last significant outburst of Sabbatian
activity among the Jews of Poland.

The so-called Frankist movement, which in 1759 led to a
mass conversion of Polish Sabbatians to Catholicism, found recruits among the Podolian adherents of Baruchya. Their leader,
Jacob Frank, who held court in Offenbach until his death in 1791,
carried on the tradition of Baruchya with whose followers he had
come into close contact in Salonika. He frequently refers to him
in his discourses, and the Frankish sect which he founded was for
generations nothing other than a particularly radical shoot of the
Dönmeh, only with a Catholic façade. Relations between the centers of the two sects in Salonika and Warsaw must have continued
until late in the nineteenth century. I personally know of an instance that occurred even after 1920, in which a Dönmeh visiting
Vienna confided to a Jewish friend that they maintained steady
relations with certain seemingly orthodox Catholic families in
Warsaw. But whereas the followers of Baruchya were still totally
wrapped up in the language of Kabbalistic symbolism and mythology, Jacob Frank threw all this out and proclaimed to his followers in popular and uncommonly robust form the antinomian

and nihilistic doctrines of the radical Sabbatians. He regarded
Sabbatai Zevi and Baruchya as the "first two" who had brought
knowledge of the true God into the world, but whose mission he
himself had now come to conclude. Along with its influence on
the Young Turk movement, this connection with Polish Frankism
and the impetus it gave it is the most important historical consequence of the sect. Here its Messianic, utopian, and anarchic elements led to the disintegration of old ties and the search for a
new content and freedom.

But let us turn again to the Dönmeh manuscripts published
by Yitzhak Ben-Zvi, Moshe Attias, Yitzhak R. Molkho, Rivka
Shatz, and myself. As I indicated earlier, these manuscripts come
from the Izmirlis who now often refer to themselves as Kapandshis. Two literary genres predominate. A series of manuscripts
containing songs turned up, including a very considerable wealth
of religious hymns, about 500 all together. Attias and I published
one of these manuscripts, containing 244 such songs, in 1948.
These manuscripts contain both songs from the earliest stock of
the liturgy which was still common to the various sects—citations
from one of them are to be found in Frankist manuscripts!—and
songs which one of the most important leaders of this group composed for them. A number of the earliest songs are still composed
in Hebrew and a small number are Turkish (in Hebrew characters), among them several songs that were. taken over from dervish orders. But the great mass of the songs, including those which
go back as far as the first or second generation of the sect, is in
Judeo-Spanish. Attias has been able to identify the previously completely unknown Judah Levi Toba as the author of a great many
of them. This author is also responsible for the detailed mystical
homilies, also in Judeo-Spanish, which are extant for several portions of the Torah. The homilies dealing with the Torah portion
lekh lekha (Gen. 12-17) were published in a Hebrew rendition
by Molkho and Mrs. Shatz in 1960. (An equally extensive manuscript for the first portion of the Torah, Bereshit, is extant in a
manuscript of the Hebrew University.) Like the songs of Judah
Levi Toba, this published prose text is of the greatest importance
for the understanding of the religious conceptions of the author
and his group. It also enables us to determine the period of his
life with a fairly high degree of precision. The editors and even
Mrs. Shatz, in her otherwise very valuable study on this text, still
assumed that he belonged to the first generation of the Dönmeh
and wrote shortly after 1700; apparently, he lived toward the end

of the eighteenth and the beginning of the nineteenth century. He mentions the year 1783 as a year of catastrophe for Islamic rule, and in fact this was the year in which the Ottoman Empire lost the Crimea, the decisive turning point bringing on the decline of Turkish power. Closer analysis of these homilies will also allow the identification of the author with an important leader of the Dönmeh who in Izmirli tradition had until then been known only by his Turkish name Dervish Effendi. It will be worth while to examine this point here briefly.

From the beginning, their Jewish opponents accused the Dönmeh of practicing ritual fornication and free love in their secret gatherings. Although such reproaches are most common in religious polemics, especially those conducted against gnostic and mystical sects, in this case there was good reason to assume that a great deal of truth lay behind the accusations. We have massive and weighty evidence for it from contemporary sources. Even the tradition of the Dönmeh itself affirmed, in only thinly veiled fashion, the existence of orgiastic rituals on certain festivals which served as the high points of their religious life. As late as 1910 young Dönmeh confided to their Jewish fellow students that these celebrations were still practiced. In conversation with a respected visitor from Israel in 1942, a physician who had settled in Smyrna admitted that his grandfather had participated in ritual wife swapping in Salonika. As late as 1900 there was a generally known tradition among the Dönmeh according to which Dervish Effendi, the leader of the Izmirlis around 1800, was not only a great Kabbalist but openly advocated the mystic doctrine of holding wives in common and practicing ritual fornication; he even undertook to find support for it in the *Zohar* and the Kabbalah. Now the text which has recently become accessible to us fits these data concerning Dervish Effendi most precisely, and it is unlikely that we are here dealing with two different members of the same sect in the same period. When the Dönmeh spoke of their leaders with Jewish friends, they used the Turkish names. But in their writings the Hebrew names are used almost exclusively. Judah Levi Toba does indeed present these theories at numerous points in his homilies, using Kabbalistic language and argument of justification. It is quite obvious that in interpreting the Kabbalistic texts or even the biblical accounts in this spirit, he turned them completely upside down and distorted them.

At any rate, we learn here precisely how the theory of Messianic sexual anarchy and promiscuity, which so offended the morals of pious Jews, was supported by "the ancient books." We know that Baruchya and his successors declared the incest prohibition of the Torah abolished; they invoked the ascendancy of the Torah of *atzilut* in which all prohibitions of this kind were supposed to be, on the contrary, positive commandments. The comments of Toba on this subject constitute one of the most revealing documents in which gnostic antinomianism is supported from Jewish sources using Jewish modes of exegesis. They prove the power of the emotional explosion behind these exegeses. The author ascribes this new revelation to Sabbatai Zevi himself and relates an entire legend about the circumstances which enabled this new reading of the "law" to so pervert the old understanding of the Torah. The whole text rests upon the attempt to draw the consequences for the theology and morals of the "believers" from the above-mentioned twofold manifestation of the historical and the spiritual Torah. King Manasseh, who ordered the execution of the prophet Isaiah, was right! For Isaiah dealt on the level of the Torah of *beriah,* but King Manasseh dealt on the higher level which no longer recognizes a distinction between pure and impure, allowed and forbidden, because on that level everything negative has already disappeared, or been transformed into its opposite. The biblical report of Elisha's visit to the woman from Shunem is treated as a paradigm of ritual fornication—almost like those antinomian Gnostics of whom Epiphanius reports that they credited Elisha with fondling demons and begetting children by them. Even among the songs that we now know, there are some which were manifestly intended for celebrations of this kind and which employ the symbolism of eating, the table, the opening of the rose, "providing," and "lending." In such table songs Toba employs a symbolism which in his prose writings leaves no doubt about its sexual character; he celebrates the "permission of the prohibited" which has now become a sacred activity. In his homilies he proclaims the formula: "Freedom is the secret of the spiritual Torah," a proposition which is less concerned with the Paulinian thesis of the freedom of God's children than with the theory of mystical libertinism. "Soldiers are released from the commandments"—this paradoxical slogan also recurs among the Polish sayings of Jacob Frank, where it receives its most radical nihilistic formulation. Toba's use of it is evidence of its being an early proposition of the Dönmeh. For the soldiers, in Dönmeh terminology, are none other than they themselves, who have sallied forth to do battle with the *kelipah,* the demonic and the impure power which must be destroyed by seeking it out in its own domain.

According to Vladimir Gordlevsky, the Dönmeh brought these conceptions, and especially the orgiastic rituals of the "extinguishing of the lights," to Salonika from underground circles in oriental Jewry where they supposedly led a hidden existence for centuries. I do not believe that this conjecture is well founded. Since he did not know the Kabbalistic literature, Gordlevsky fell victim to the error that the *Zohar,* the holy book of the Kabbalists, really contained the libertine gnostic theses which the Dönmeh derived from it. In actual fact we are dealing with developments within Judaism that show how every acute and radical Messianism that is taken seriously tears open an abyss in which by inner necessity antinomian tendencies and libertine moral conceptions gain strength. The history of the Sabbatian movement, and especially of its radical wing, the Dönmeh, can serve as a paradigm for this insight common to all scholarly study of religions. There will never be a dearth of parallels. Thus, for example, the antinomian theory of the Dönmeh corresponds quite closely to that of the radical wing of the Ismailis as it was set forth in Alamut in Persia after the great Messianic eruption of 1164. Just as the Messiah allowed the forbidden, so here the Imam "removed from you the yoke of the duties of the *shari'a* [the traditional framework of Islam] and brought you to the status of *kiyama,* resurrection." This state of *kiyama* in which the Nizari branch of the Ismailis lived, is regarded as being above the law, as entry into a realm which the Sabbatians would have designated that of the spiritual Torah of *atzilut.* Here too the symbol of entry into the new state of *kiyama* was the public violation of the fast of Ramadan and the imbibing of wine. The inner logic is the same, even if there is no historical connection between the two phenomena.

As we have seen, the libertine theories of the Dönmeh are not the possession of a single group; aside from the extensive attempt to justify them, Toba hardly added anything new. The festival of the 21st Adar, at which especially the "extinguishing of the lights" was practiced, is already mentioned around 1750 among the Sabbatian festivals celebrated by the followers of Baruchya. Only the date is not mentioned in the earliest festival calendars of the sect, which still originated in Adrianople. The day was, however, celebrated in like manner by all of the Dönmeh sects.

Yet there is something novel in the Kabbalistic system which this author presents and on which he also builds his songs. The most important theologian of the first Sabbatian generation was the prophet Nathan of Gaza, who until his death in 1680 propagated his convictions on the Balkan peninsula. He died in Üsküb (Skoplje) three years before the great apostasy and his memory as well as his writings enjoyed the Dönmeh's highest regard. This is the less surprising since, although himself remaining a Jew, he defended the theory of mystical apostasy for those who were called to it. The case of the second outstanding theologian of the movement was quite a different matter. Abraham Miguel Cardozo (1626-1706), who was born a Marrano, became one of the most resolute opponents of mystical apostasy. In his last years he wrote tirelessly against the Dönmeh of Salonika, regarding them as the foolish victims of demons. According to his own testimony, his relations with the sect's members were extremely tense; the sect rejected and fought his particular system of Sabbatian theology. However, in the course of time these polemics must have been forgotten. After his death, not only did Cardozo's writings find access to the sect—it is difficult to say when, perhaps only after 1750—but also the picture of his personal relations to Sabbatai Zevi and the earliest apostates underwent a change. In the writings and poems of Toba he now appears together with Nathan as the friend and ideologue of the sect itself. Toba amalgamates the thoroughly different Kabbalistic systems of Nathan and Cardozo and produces from them a most peculiar new system which contains his own special touch: the libertine element, totally foreign to Cardozo. Thus, a hundred years after the great conversion, the struggles were completely forgotten. In Toba's group Cardozo's writings were studied, copied, and in part even translated into Judeo-Spanish; important texts of Cardozo have just recently come to light again through such manuscripts in Dönmeh possession. It seems that Judah Levi Toba was the last significant religious figure of the Dönmeh. At his time familiarity with the orthodox Kabbalistic and heretical Sabbatian literature was still widespread and those who heard his homilies were able, at least in part, to follow his very abstruse trains of thought. Sabbatian Messianic convictions had struck really deep roots in the spiritual life of the sect. Thus, supported by a gnostic antinomian theory and deeply interwoven with it, this faith was able to survive old Turkey. But disintegration set in when the modern life of new Turkey created a wish for assimilation among most of the Dönmeh. With that, the fate of the sect was probably sealed. Attempts were made to persuade them to re-join the Jewish community. But they remained without effect although some of the Dönmeh had retained a certain romantic longing and inclination toward their Jewish past, even where their faith in Sabbatai Zevi had been lost. Nonetheless, the continuing existence of believing Sabbatians among them is attested down to the present. In the spring of 1960 one of my informants, a Turkologist, held conversations with the religious head, the Hodja, of the remaining Karakash groups which he had succeeded in contacting. From him he received important information relating to the present condition of the Dönmeh. This leader of the Dönmeh had heard of the group in Israel which is studying and trying to understand the Sabbatian movement as one of the most important phenomena of Jewish history and of the history of religions. He was convinced that this group must in reality consist of secret adherents of Sabbatai Zevi! Only in this way could he account for our interest.

A Sabbatian Will
from New York

THE DOCUMENT I present in the following pages is a rather peculiar one, and it is doubtful whether any other of its kind has been written or, at any rate, if written, has been preserved. This is the last will of Gottlieb Wehle, a member of the Sabbatian sect in Prague, who later (1849) settled in America as a member of a group of Sabbatian families about whose emigration we have the monograph of Miss Josephine C. Goldmark: *Pilgrims of '48 . . . a family migration to America* (1930). He settled and died in New York (1881) and it is there that the will was written. According to the genealogy of the Wehle family which was compiled and published by his son, Theodore Wehle, in 1898, Gottlieb Wehle, the great-uncle of the late Justice Louis Dembitz Brandeis, and a first cousin of Zacharias Frankel, one of the founders of the modern *Wissenschaft vom Judentum* (Science of Judaism), was born in Prague on July 27, 1802. Since the first part of the will was written on the testator's sixty-first birthday and the second part one year later, it was composed in 1863-64. It is, therefore, the latest document written by a Jewish Sabbatian who obviously never abandoned the basic tenets of the doctrine which he was taught in his father's house. This, of course, points to a fundamental difference between Wehle's pronouncement on Sabbatianism and the records in the memoirs of Moses Porges (von Portheim) of his experiences as a youth in the Sabbatian milieu at Prague and Offenbach.[1] It is difficult to fix the precise date of the composition of Porges' memoirs, but they must have been written about the same time as Wehle's will when Porges was a very old man. He was twenty years older than Gottlieb Wehle whose father is mentioned in his narrative. Porges retained some knowledge of the darker side of the sectarian life in Offenbach, a knowledge denied to Wehle who obviously knew only about the positive and highly respectable side of Sabbatian life and teaching, and apparently wrote in good faith when he called the widespread tales about the sect a fabric of lies and calumnies. Moses Porges, who emphasizes both sides of the picture—the high moral standard of the last Jewish followers of Sabbatai Zevi and Jacob Frank as well as the continued practice (if in extenuated form) of objectionable rites by Jacob Frank's sons—did not sever all connection with the sect after his return to Prague in 1800, as, according to another communication to Dr. Stein, he was not altogether certain whether there was not something more behind the whole affair than met his youthful eye.[2] But after 1820-30 he gave up the whole sectarian ideology, whereas Wehle's sympathy for the doctrine of his ancestors is quite undisguised. His granddaughters, the Misses Pauline and Josephine Goldmark, of New York, who kindly presented me, in 1938, with a copy of the "theoretical" part of the will, told me that the testator's daughter, their aunt Mrs. Julia Oettinger, who died only some twenty years ago, assured herself that every member of the family received a copy of the will as a testimonial to their Sabbatian origin of which she was still extremely proud. She still considered Eva Frank, whose picture in miniature was held in the family for more than a hundred and twenty years [3] in great reverence, to have been a saint, apparently on the strength of the family tradition.

The Wehles were one of the aristocratic old Jewish families of Prague and took a leading part in the Sabbatian, and later Frankist,[4] group, which at the time attracted considerable attention and whose importance has not yet been sufficiently evaluated. The father of the testator, Aaron Beer Wehle (1750-1825) and particularly the testator's two uncles, Jonas Wehle of Prague (1752-1823) and Emanuel Wehle of Gitschin (Jičin), were outstanding personalities among the Bohemian and Moravian Sabbatians, the two last-mentioned generally being considered spiritual leaders of the sect in its last stage of development. His father's sister Roesel Eger (died, 1831) was a well-known Sabbatian "prophetess" [5] and all of them made several pilgrimages to Offenbach, the last Mecca of Sabbatianism from 1786 to 1816.

In an old English missionary journal of the time [6] I have found a very interesting account of the Wehles and their Sabbatian beliefs written by the missionary J. Nitschke, who visited Bohemia in August and September, 1818, and met Aaron Beer Wehle * whom he calls "a venerable old man." At first he found

---

* He calls him Aaron Wohle, probably a misprint.

great reluctance on Wehle's part when he started to ask him questions about the sect, but in a second talk Wehle "and his friend and former preceptor of his children, Benedikt Patschotsch," became quite friendly and gave him many explanations about their "society" (i.e., the organization of the sect) which at the time still existed and displayed some activity as Nitschke was told by them. As a matter of fact, we know that just about that time they succeeded in drawing into the orbit of their society the young student of medicine Dembitz, the grandfather of Louis Dembitz Brandeis. The missionary, who expected to find in the Sabbatian Jews secret adherents of Christianity, relates that he was not a little disappointed to find "that they are still real Jews," although the other Jews hated and despised them and accused them of all kinds of terrible things and crimes—the usual hint of orgiastic depravity which common opinion in the ghetto ascribed to the sect. They acknowledged Jesus as a great reformer of their nation but not as more than that. Nitschke testifies to their high moral character, their adherence to Kabbalism, and their possession of secret writings about their doctrine. Thus we have here a first-hand witness on the atmosphere in which the author of the Sabbatian will of 1864 grew up. We learn that his teacher was an active member of the group. Nitschke did not know or did not mention that Baruch Petschotsch (as he is called in the genealogy of the Wehle family) was the husband of Aaron Beer Wehle's eldest daughter, Amalie (1792-1864) and was, therefore, Gottlieb Wehle's brother-in-law. The will from New York still reflects the teaching of the Prague conventicle, as we know it from the letters of one of its leaders (presumably Jonas Wehle) which have been included in Peter Beer's volume on the Kabbalah [7] and from the important commentary on the talmudic Aggadot which is now preserved in the Schocken Library in Jerusalem.

Most interesting is the testimony of the author to the Sabbatian leanings of his ancestors, not only of his father, about whose membership in the sect there was never an argument, but also of his grandfathers and great-uncles. It is well known that Sabbatianism in the eighteenth century was in a large measure a "family religion," that is to say, was confined primarily to certain families (some of them very famous ones) where it struck deep roots and was preserved with astounding tenacity as a secret doctrine. Jacob Emden published in 1752 a list of people in Prague who were considered by his informants to be the heads of the

Sabbatian group there.[8] This list contains also the names of two scholars of great renown, Rabbi Jonah Landsopher and Rabbi Ephraim ben Aaron Beer (Wehle), whom their descendant in the present will numbers proudly among his crypto-Sabbatian ancestors. Gottlieb Wehle's knowledge is derived without doubt from family tradition and not from Emden's writings and serves therefore to corroborate Emden's rumors.[9]

Most descendants of Sabbatian stock tried to obliterate the fact as far as possible, and this tendency accounts for the scarcity of our knowledge of who's who in later Sabbatianism.[10] In contra-distinction to this attitude, Gottlieb Wehle, far from being ashamed of Sabbatianism, admonishes his children not to forget their noble pedigree. Whereas in Prague about 1870 nobody would have dared to mention the connection of a respectable family with the sectarians, the cousin in the New World sees in Sabbatianism a revolt against petrified orthodoxy and the obscur-antist fanaticism of the rabbis, and therefore something of which to be proud. Having grown up in the last generation of the sect, after it came into touch with the new atmosphere of the French Revolution and of Enlightenment, he does not know of its darker side which was (it seems) silently dropped about 1800. As far as our scant knowledge goes, the "Society" of the Sabbatian sec-tarians was dissolved in the 1820's; emissaries went from town to town and from family to family and collected the secret writ-ings of the sect, most of which have for this reason disappeared. Both the philosopher Fritz Mauthner, another descendant of a Sabbatian family, and Moses Porges mention this.[11] The Sabbat-ians, including those who clung to their Messianic hopes and dreams of the great role of the sect in the past, became "new Jews," as several observers have remarked, i.e., supporters of the reform movement or indifferent to religion altogether. And this certainly happened to the Wehles. The son of Jonas Wehle was, in 1832, among the founders of the first Reform Congregation in Prague which invited Leopold Zunz as preacher. The will of Gott-lieb Wehle shows the same blend of Sabbatianism and Neology. Yet in 1845 we have the last testimony about the sect in Prague by Wolfgang Wessely who was in close touch with their remnants —he began to publish "Letters of a Sabbatian" who, although un-named, can be identified with Jonas Wehle's son-in-law. His in-troductory remarks to Wehle's letters, written only a short time before Gottlieb Wehle's emigration to the U.S., reflects the mood of the will. He says: "Since [Peter Beer's information about the sect, i.e., since 1822] no further account of it has been published, although it has not altogether ceased to exist. It gives, however, only weak indications of life, the former radical opposition of its members to [rabbinical] Judaism having been mitigated. It seems the members are content with a kind of crypto-Sabbatianism and, indulging in memories of their former apostles and their holy mission, they remain in a state of passivity." [12] The will of Gottlieb Wehle is the last evidence we possess of this state of mind.

Text of the Will (in translation)

In the name of God, the Ruler of Human Destiny!
My dear, beloved children,

I start today a document, the commencement of which I put off for many years. With every year, however, it is more pressing. Alas, far too often the frailty of the human being becomes more evident, so that it eventually appears impossible to make arrangements which before would have been only too easy.

Every human being is affected by a certain timidity—I do not want to call it cowardice—which prevents him thinking of the moment when he will have to leave all that is dear and beloved to him here below. Every father of a family feels forced, on reaching a certain age, especially when tragic events occur in his family or kin, to realize that he also is not secure against a sudden recall from the stage; and that it is therefore advisable, as long as he commands ripe and mature sense, to convey to his children and relatives, with cool and clear mind, his last "Testament." In ordinary life this is known as "making his will," meaning the writing down of dispositions and arrangements by a wealthy father; directing how his personal and real estate are to be divided after his departure. But there are matters besides chattels and fortunes of which a father wishes to talk seriously to his children when departing this life. I cannot say anything definite concerning the state of my possessions and their disposition. I can say nothing definite, as these change daily, though I may have something to announce about it later.

I had the unspeakable sorrow to see my brother Simon, his wife Rosi (née Porges)[1] and three children die in my arms of cholera in December, 1831, within the short period of three days. My sister Fanny, married to Dr. Dembitz from Pressburg[2] in Hungary, I lost in December, 1840, and my brother Adolf, the doctor, in April, 1840. My brother Simon lived to be thirty-five, my sister Fanny forty, and my brother Adolf barely forty. You my dear children celebrate today my birthday, my sixty-first.[3] This number is a warning to me. May the Lord for your sake grant me as many years as I am able to contribute to your well-being!

It is well known to you my dear children that, influenced by the repeated popular demonstrations in Prague against the Jews, I decided to leave the Continent, the country and the town where I and also you were born; where my ancestors throughout the centuries lived an honorable life agreeable to God; where they suffered innocently and so greatly for their belief and their nationality. It is not granted to me to share with them the clod of earth, where they rest in peace.

You did not know my venerable father, who departed from us in August, 1825, when I was twenty-three.[4] My beloved mother who died in December, 1838, may perhaps be dimly remembered by my beloved children Lotti and Tini.

Not having a picture gallery of ancestors, like the European nobility, which may cost thousands of dollars and still be only copies of bad originals, I will introduce you to my gallery of ancestors, which does not give portraits of art, but instead names and character sketches, which are faultless and blameless. Your descent from such men cannot be but a cause of satisfaction and pride for you. Your ancestors did not bear titles of Barons and Counts, they held no high rank in the State service; they were only Jews, offspring and descendants of the oldest and most venerable race. Your ancestors were not heroes who acquired their high positions by the sword, by treacherous assassination or by intrigues; or who started their career as highwaymen or footpads.

Your descent is from the two greatest, most venerable and most celebrated families of the great and cultured community of Prague: My late father Aaron Beer, of the famous family Wehle, my late mother,[5] a daughter of Bermann Simon Frankel Spiro [6]— apparently indicating that they came from Speyer; my father's mother, born Landsopher (Sopher means in Hebrew "Notary" or "Writer," apparently formerly a position of honor among Jews) the only daughter of Jona-Emanuel Landsopher.[7] My grandfather Rabbi Hersch Wehle [8] had two brothers, Ephraim [9] and Isaac. Ephraim, the father of Rabbi Wolf Wehli, was the grandfather of your mother [10] and father of Ernest (Ephraim) and Samuel Wehli. My father's brothers and uncle were Emanuel

(Reb Mendel of Gitschin) and Jonas (Reb Jona),[11] Dr. Hermann Wehle and his brothers Adam, Joseph and Max (Klarenberg), the children of uncle Jonas.[12] You may remember the children of uncle Emanuel, namely Luise Klarenberg,[13] Fanny Dawidels and perhaps Rosa.

The pedigree of my parents is known in Prague since centuries —all these ancestors were noted for their biblical and talmudical learning, for their practice of charity, their honest and blameless way of living, their wealth and inoffensiveness. These are only general traits, which may seem strange to you, as you are removed from those circles, where these gentle-folk have always been mentioned with the greatest respect. They were the dignitaries of Bohemian Jewry. The writings of that period are still widely famed in Jewish-theological circles, and they will remain so. Well known are literary works by old Jonas Landsopher and old Ephraim Wehle under the title: *Ephraim's Vintage.*[14] To these gentle-folk who had a clear conception and a higher urge, the dry study of the Talmud, the aim of which was only sophistry and mental acuteness, did not suffice.[15] That portion of the Talmud, which deals with morals, metaphysics and religion, was neglected by the greater part of their contemporaries; the systems and opinions concerning these theological principles,[16] remained unnoticed! Now your ancestors declared all the old and new writings concerning the Talmud as wrongly exploited by sophistical and astute commentators; that they were only the outer shell and peel of the true Judaism, which instead represented doctrines that were the quintessence and symbol of Judaism, higher than the discussions, debates, questions and solutions of old and long forgotten laws about offerings and food. In consequence your ancestors were decried as heretics by many hypocritical, so-called public educators, who called themselves rabbis. They were slandered and persecuted by them. These hypocrites [17] dared even from the pulpit to stir up the people against them, under the pretext that the principles and doctrines of this "sect" as they called them, had much in common, even the same tendencies,[18] as the Christians. They mesmerized the listeners, even publishing pamphlets containing the most impudent and gross calumnies, which were distributed with lightning speed throughout the greater part of Europe. Persecuted by these hypocrites and zealots, these "heretics, soharites [19] and Sabbatians" endured the intolerance with gentle resignation, without asking the authorities for their proffered protection.[20]

Strangely enough, even the most fanatical opponents had to admit their high intelligence, blameless way of life, strict morality, honesty, and charity; in fact all the virtues of a good citizen.[21]

With pious and gentle resignation the persecuted ones suffered this intolerance. They were moved by their resolve to establish the principles of revealed religion, its high purposes and the future destiny of their nation.[22] They gladly resigned their perfect knowledge of the Talmud because they were seeking for the spirit of religion. They arranged their theological studies in the spirit of the Bible and various other old theological scriptures known under the generally ill-reputed name of Kabbalah. They placed higher the doctrines of this secret lore than the dead ceremonies, and tried to revive the spirit contained in them.[23]

"That man, being an image and masterpiece of God will again return to the perfect state, as he was when he left the Creator's hand; that he will be free from all sickness of body, mind, and soul; that he will be again innocent as before the Fall, free from vice and sin" [24]—this was roughly the program of their endeavors and perception of God, the aim of their studies. Moreover, as God acts only indirectly, a chosen, consecrated Messiah is necessary as deputy of his highest Master.[25] As now, according to the Kabbalistic principles, man is only the tool of Providence through which it acts, therefore the smallest act of one chosen for this highest charge may be of greatest importance. Thus these ill-reputed gentle-folk endeavored to prepare and qualify for this great aim and purpose by the highest moral standards. They welcomed this misinterpretation of their belief as an opportunity [26] for bringing a sacrifice for their high aspirations, and indeed did so on the altar of their creed.

One year has passed and again I am firmly reminded that we frail men do not know what the morrow may bring. My sixty-second birthday has passed and it was a moderately happy one. Two months ago my dear sister [27] had to undergo a second dangerous operation. Eight days later my brother Moritz took his leave, perhaps never to return. Such two depressing events were not calculated to cheer me on my sixty-second birthday. The speedily failing strength of my long-ailing sister, her premonition of approaching release, had a most depressing effect upon me. I tried to fight this melancholy and depression—I repeated to myself again and again: Thy work is not yet completed, thou hast still many tasks to finish before thou canst consider thy work as ended.

Indeed, I still deem it necessary sometimes to think of the moment when I will have to leave you all, my beloved ones. And perhaps it may come so quickly, or maybe I will be in a mental and physical condition when it may be impossible for me to express to you my last wishes. Why should I go from out of your midst without saying my last "farewell"; without taking a kind leave, as it is usual if one parts even for a short time?

As on the occasion of every farewell, I shall at my last parting look to another "Meet Again." I am, my dear children, absolutely sure of it; I have no doubt to overcome. I would maintain with mathematical certainty—if that expression were acceptable: There is a God and man is His image. This image, Man, cannot be condemned to destruction and putrefaction! When you will be reading these lines and perhaps, to my sorrow, some of you with skeptical thoughts, then I will have realized my aspirations, I will know and perceive that the Creator has not endowed man with mind and soul only to let him live and die unhappy, yes unhappier than the lowliest animal! Should it be the only privilege of man over an animal, that he may develop his mind, to embellish the world, eventually to transform it by inventions into a Paradise only to leave it after a short sojourn without any hope of a life after death? Or should it be only by accident that the best and most gentle people, without their fault, drag with sorrow and anxiety through this life during the few years of their existence, and then with the ending of life disappear into nothingness? An inner voice—if we do not suppress it forcefully—tells us: there is a life after this life. How this mental life is constituted we do not know—but the faith in a further life implies the capacity for eternal life. My dear children! believe firmly in this true and blessed faith—without it you will be always unhappy, with it never.

Do not be ashamed of this happy faith of your great ancestors. Say with pride that you feel the germ of this eternal life in you. He who wishes to deprive you of this faith which forms my firm conviction, would rob you of your greatest treasure. He is certainly not your friend. He is not the man who would dare fix his gaze on a future existence. It would mean that he would have to spend his life earnestly on improvement and repentance. But this inclination to good is lacking with most men, and they find it easier to throw a veil over their past and their future.

The Neutralization
of the Messianic Element
in Early Hasidism

I

I CANNOT LAUNCH into a lecture devoted to the memory of Joseph Weiss without first recalling the figure of the man whose premature death we mourn. Professor Weiss was not only my pupil for many years, he was one of the most outstanding and colorful among those in whose spiritual and scholarly formation and development I had a hand. I considered him in many ways the closest of my pupils, and the dialogue between us, a dialogue in the true sense of a term so much abused nowadays, went on for nearly thirty years. When he came to Jerusalem in 1940 he was a young man of wide interests and reading who was groping for his way. Growing up in Budapest, he had eagerly taken up what Hungarian, German, and Jewish literature and philosophy had to offer. From a non-observant Jewish background, he was early attracted by Jewish learning and ritual and fought his way to the study of the primary sources of Judaism. This thirst for a deeper understanding of the spiritual universe of Judaism never left him, and the dramatic conflicts within the Jewish world, first in Hungary and later in Israel, contributed much to his acute awareness of the issues involved. His keen sense of dialectical situations prevented him from taking an easy and all too comfortable or, I should rather say, unambiguous stand in those controversies. Moreover, there was an additional conflict in himself between his unmistakable tendency to put things in a radical way and his contemplative bent of mind. I might say indeed that he was torn between these two. He was a Zionist, but a very strange one who at times, overwhelmed by his own doubts, would deny his own convictions. He was extremely critical of orthodoxy but there was in him a strong streak of sympathy for Neturei Karta attitudes.

In his personal life, periods of strict observance alternated with periods of open indifference to ritual. At all times, however, he remained passionately concerned with Judaism as a religious phenomenon and its meaning or rather its meanings—for he never could bring himself to agree with those who are in possession of a ready and explicit definition. His indecision in matters that called for a definite stand made him often very shy in his personal relations with people, but when he trusted and opened up to you, he proved to be a man of extraordinary personal charm, even in his perplexities.

I spoke of his being torn by conflicting tendencies in his mind, but he was utterly single-minded in his scholarly pursuit and commitment. Twenty-five years ago he had already set himself a definite task and he never permitted himself to deviate from it. This task was the exploration of the Hasidic movement from its beginnings to its spiritual climax in the figure of Rabbi Nahman of Brazlav, whose enigmatic personality and even more enigmatic teachings had held the most powerful fascination for Weiss ever since he first came into contact with the group of his followers in Jerusalem many years ago. Only an exceptional personality such as that of Rabbi Mordecai Joseph Leiner of Izbitsa could arouse his scholarly interest in the generations after Rabbi Nahman's death. It was the outbreak of tremendous spiritual power and originality in the early Hasidic movement struggling for recognition and ascendency in ever wider circles which captivated his imagination and led him to concentrate on its history and phenomenology. Almost everything he published was concerned with these problems. He immersed himself deeply in the study of the sources. He brought to his work that particular intensity and power of penetration which characterized his mind. Because of the many doubts and scruples deriving from his inner struggles, he published relatively very little, but many of his papers are distinguished by high originality and some of them have made a great impact on the study of Hasidism. At the same time, they were bound to arouse controversy by their bold and sometimes daring theses and I admit that I am one of those who not infrequently had protracted discussions with him about some of his major contentions. He has laid the groundwork for extended and deep studies especially of Rabbi Nahman of Brazlav, and their outcome was anticipated with the greatest hopes. His premature death has put an end to all these labors, but the haunted figure of Joseph Weiss will remain with those who knew him, admired his depth and insight, and sympathized with his sufferings and tribulations.

II

The exploration of Hasidism in its most creative period, of its origins, history, and meaning has occupied scholars of the last two generations, and, as I have said, this was the center of Joseph Weiss' research. In honoring his memory I wish to take up the discussion of one of the fundamental issues which all historians of Hasidism have encountered on their way and which has been viewed by quite a few of them as one of the keys to an understanding of the movement. This is the Messianic element in early Hasidism, i.e., from Israel Baal Shem to the pupils of the Maggid of Mezritch at the end of the eighteenth century. Was Messianism at the center of the movement, was it one of the prime elements that pervaded its teaching, as it had the teachings of the Lurianic school of Kabbalah which formed the basis of Hasidic doctrine? Or did it disappear as an essential part in the formation of the movement and its doctrine, so that we can speak of a "liquidation" of Messianism as a living force? Or should we rather take a more dialectical view and speak of the transformation which it underwent, and which brought about a profound change to be defined not so much as the liquidation, but as the neutralization of this element? It is obvious that, whatever the answer to this question, it is a matter of great consequence to the view one will take of the basic character of Hasidism. The controversy on this point has been lively, I would even say impassioned. Of course, I do not refer here to the apologists of the movement belonging to the Hasidic camp itself, who decline to take note of issues arising from the fact of historical development, because for them there is no such thing, and Hasidism in their eyes has remained essentially unchanged throughout its history. Among modern scholars, men of such widely differing perspectives as Simon Dubnow and Martin Buber [1] have supported the view that Hasidism in its classical period was a liquidation of Messianism as an acute, immediate force, a liquidation which constituted a reaction to the destructive outbreak of Messianism in the Sabbatian movement.

Buber said quite fittingly on the teaching of Hasidism that "it has proclaimed in the strongest and clearest manner: there is no definite, exhibitable, teachable, magic action in established formulae and gestures, attitudes and tensions of the soul, that is effective for redemption; only the hallowing of all actions without distinction . . . possesses redemptive power. Only out of the redemption of the everyday does the All-Day of redemption grow." In the same connection, he says of the liquidation of personal Messianism in Hasidism—an interpretation with which I cannot agree —as follows: "The Hasidic message of redemption stands in opposition to the Messianic self-differentiation of one man from other men, of one time from other times, of one act from other actions. All mankind is accorded the co-working power, all time is directly redemptive, all action for the sake of God may be Messianic action. But only unpremeditated action can be action for the sake of God. The self-differentiation, the reflection of man to a Messianic superiority of this person, of this hour, of this action, destroys the unpremeditated quality of the act. Turning the whole of his life in the world to God and then allowing it to open and unfold in all its moments until the last—that is man's work towards redemption."

The diametrically opposite position has been taken up by Ben Zion Dinur in his study on the beginnings of Hasidism. He sees the movement as permeated by the strongest of Messianic impulses from its very start and at the same time makes it a kind of forerunner of Zionism.[2] A more diluted and restrained version of this view has recently been presented by Isaiah Tishby in a long paper, "The Messianic Idea and Messianic Trends in the Growth of Hasidism."[3] A third view, emphasizing the neutralization of Messianism as a historical force, was adopted by me in the chapter on Hasidism in *Major Trends in Jewish Mysticism*. This view was shared by Joseph Weiss in his own studies on "the Beginnings of Hasidism" and on the contemplative mysticism of the Maggid.[4] It has been partly accepted by Tishby, but in part it has also come under fire from him. I intend to offer a restatement of my argument by considering the evidence. It should be clear from the outset that I do not speak of the later period of Hasidism starting around 1800 which was not entirely lacking in the resurgence of Messianic claims or impulses in connection with some outstanding Hasidic leaders such as Jacob Yitzhak Horovitz, the "Seer of Lublin," his pupils Jacob Yitzhak, the "saintly Jew" of Pshizha, and David of Lelov, and, overshadowing them all, the figure of Nahman of Brazlav, the great-grandson of Israel Baal Shem, whose life was doubtlessly pervaded by a sense of Messianic vocation and whose teaching is strongly imbued with Messianic elements, even though much of it is expressed in a veiled and roundabout manner.

Let me quote some sentences about our problem which I wrote thirty years ago:

One can say that after the rise and collapse of Sabbatianism there were only three ways left open to the Kabbalah, in addition to that of accepting the contradictions in which the new believers and adherents of Sabbatai Zevi had become hopelessly enmeshed. One was to pretend that nothing in particular had happened. That was actually what a good many orthodox Kabbalists tried to do. They continued in the old way without bothering much about new ideas. . . . Another way was to renounce all attempts to create a mass movement, in order to avoid a repetition of the disastrous consequences which had followed the most recent of these attempts. That was the attitude of some of the most important representatives of later Kabbalism who entirely renounced the more popular aspects of Lurianism and tried to lead the Kabbalah back from the market place to the solitude of the mystic's place of retreat. . . . Finally, there was a third way, and that is the one which Hasidism took, particularly during its classical period. Here the Kabbalah did not renounce its proselytizing mission; on the contrary, Hasidism—a typical revivalist movement—aimed from the beginning at the widest possible sphere of influence. . . . Hasidism represents an attempt to preserve those elements of Kabbalism which were capable of evoking a popular response, but stripped of the Messianic flavor to which they owed their chief successes during the preceding period. That seems to me the main point. Hasidism tried to eliminate the element of Messianism—with its dazzling but highly dangerous amalgamation of mysticism and the apocalyptic mood—without renouncing the popular appeal of later Kabbalism. Perhaps one should rather speak of a "neutralization" of the Messianic element. I hope I shall not be misunderstood. I am far from suggesting that the Messianic hope and belief in Messianic redemption disappeared from the hearts of the Hasidim. That would be utterly untrue. . . . But it is one thing to allot a niche to the idea of redemption, and quite another to have placed this concept with all it implies in the center of religious life and thought. This was true of the theory of *tikkun* in the system of Lurianism and it was equally true of the paradoxical Messianism of the Sabbatians; there is no doubt what idea moved them most deeply, motivated them, explained their success. And this is precisely what Messianism had ceased to do for the Hasidim.[5]

It is the position stated in these paragraphs that I wish to defend here. When I wrote the above passages, I thought they expressed my viewpoint clearly and distinctly, to use Cartesian language. But apparently, to judge from Professor Isaiah Tishby's criticism, there is room for elucidation and amplification.

If we wish to understand the issue of Messianism in the Hasidic movement and the precise meaning of my thesis regarding the neutralization of this element, it should be clear from the start what such a thesis does *not* imply. The Hasidim were orthodox Jews in the sense that they accepted the whole of Jewish teaching crystallized in rabbinic, philosophical, or Kabbalistic tradition and certainly accepted the thirteen articles of Maimonides' credo, including the Messianic one, as part and parcel of their religious universe. They were prepared to repeat in a routine manner any formulation or statement about the Messiah himself, about the Messianic age and the ways and means by which it might be brought about, in short, any traditional matter. They would not have found any real difficulty in contradictory statements, but would have given them a harmonizing twist according to accepted homiletical procedure. All their books are full of stuff of this kind. But I dare say—and I consider this the core of the present discussion—that there is a decisive difference between things they say because they are generally accepted and repeated, and those in which their specific contribution, their essential interests, and their originality of mind come to the fore. Jewish literature is of course full of books in which no originality and no specific contribution is to be found. But we are concerned with the phenomenon of *Hasidism* where it is truly legitimate to ask the question of what constitutes its originality. For this is not immediately evident. The relation between Hasidic literature and the Kabbalah of the Lurianic school is a case in point. Hasidic books are deeply steeped in metaphysical and moral traditions stemming from Kabbalistic lore, so much so indeed that some authors have denied any *doctrinal* originality to Hasidism and looked for it not in the sphere of thought but in the irrational sphere of the personality, the *Gestalt* of the great Hasidic leaders, the Zaddikim. This was Buber's view, for instance, and it strangely coincided with the view of orthodox panegyrists of Hasidism, though from a totally different angle. This is an oversimplification of the true situation, as will be presently shown. As a matter of fact, a serious effort of analysis is needed to define the points where Hasidism and Lurianic Kabbalism part ways. And it is in the field of Messianism that such points of departure exist and will be found to be of special significance. I might add that analysis, far-reaching as its results may be, is not everything. It is also a matter of knowing where the accents actually lie, what is mere repetition and what is a new turn. This, it should be obvious, depends in no small measure on the historical sense or, in other words, the vision of the historian.

Tishby has said, in a paper in which he again tries to stress the Messianic elements in earlier Hasidism, that "a decisive answer to this question [of Messianism] depends only on information concerning the actual position of Messianic ideas in the Hasidic movement in the early stages of its development, after a study of extant sources with no prior assumptions whatsoever either for or against." [6] Reading the same sources, however, we have come to very different conclusions regarding their meaning and interpretation within the context of our investigation and it appears that there are more "prior assumptions" in his reading of the sources than he is willing to admit.

In this connection much has been made of a letter written by the Baal Shem around 1752 from Rashkov in the Ukraine to his brother-in-law R. Gershon of Kuty who had settled in the land of Israel some years earlier. This letter has even been hailed by Simon Dubnow as "the manifesto of Hasidism" which to me seems a somewhat rash statement.[7] Among other things the Baal Shem tells of a visionary "ascent of the soul" to heaven which he experienced in September 1746. Such experiences, as he has testified himself, came to him not infrequently, and he was able to induce them by his own volition. But the trip to heaven described in this letter surpassed everything he had experienced before. "I went up stage after stage until I entered the palace of the Messiah where Messiah studies Torah with all the Tannaites and the Zaddikim and I became aware of very great rejoicing of which I did not know the meaning and I thought that it might be because of my decease from this world [in this ecstasy]. But later it was intimated to me that I was not yet to die, for they in heaven enjoy it when I perform acts of *yihud* on earth by meditating on their teachings. But the true nature of this rejoicing I do not know to this very day. And I asked Messiah: when will he come, and he answered: until your teaching will spread throughout the world." This short answer is found in a text of the letter purported to be in his own handwriting and preserved by one of the grandchildren of Rabbi Israel of Rizhin.[8] The text, however, published by his close pupil Rabbi Jacob Joseph of Polnoye in 1781, gives a more expanded version of the Messiah's answer which in style and content has an authentic ring.[9] It reads:

By this you shall know it: when your doctrine [his way of teaching] will be widely known and revealed throughout the world and what I taught you will be divulged outwards from your own resources. And they too will be able to perform acts of meditative unification and ascents like you. And then all the "husks" [the powers of evil] will perish and the time of salvation will have come. And I—continues the Baal Shem—was bewildered because of this answer and I was greatly aggrieved by the enormous length of time until this would be possible.

I find it difficult to interpret this paragraph as a testimony to an acute Messianic element in the Baal Shem's activity. On the contrary, Messianism as a driving power and immediate hope can no longer be reckoned with. The coming of the Messiah is relegated to a distant future. The answer, far from encouraging the Baal Shem's Messianic expectations—if he had any at all—saddens and depresses him. It is a promise which holds out no Messianic fulfillment for the Baal Shem's own times. The exact connection between the nature of his way of teaching and future redemption remains unexplained and undefined. It has even been assumed that the paragraph might not refer at all to the specific teaching of the Baal Shem in religious matters but to the proliferation of such magical practices as *yihudim* and ecstatic trips to heaven [10] which, after all, are not characteristic for Hasidism. For it is not these esoteric practices which constitute Hasidism's claim to fame. Actually they played a very marginal role in the movement after the Baal Shem's own lifetime. But I doubt whether such an assumption or suggestion is acceptable. The letter speaks *expressis verbis* of the Baal Shem's teaching or doctrine, *limmud*, and not of esoteric practices. Moreover, as a proclamation of the movement's Messianic character the letter would seem strangely out of focus, for nobody knew of its existence during the most creative period of the movement. It was a private communication of no general appeal which never reached its final destination and remained with the Rabbi of Polnoye whom the Baal Shem had asked to take it to Eretz Yisrael where he had planned to go, though eventually he canceled his journey. There is no reason to assume that the letter was known among the Hasidim before it was published. Nor am I inclined to Tishby's opinion that the very fact of its publication proves that more than twenty years after the Baal Shem's death Rabbi Jacob Joseph took a positive attitude to the Messianic tendencies in Hasidism. "Messianic tendencies" is a phrase that should be clearly defined in the context of our discussion. If it means affirmation of the traditional belief it is a truism, but if it refers to acute Messianic tension in Hasidism—and this is what the controversy is about—then it is without foundation. The extensive writings of the Rabbi of Polnoye himself, who was the most intimate pupil of the Baal Shem, refute this assumption, Tishby's assertion to the contrary notwithstanding.[11]

But before we take up such questions of doctrinal analysis, one more point should be stressed. It is a widespread error to interpret Messianic calculations as an indication of acute Messianism or high Messianic tension. In some cases, such as an author devoting a whole book to demonstrate a certain date for the coming of redemption, this may be true.[12] But in general it is no more than a common device used by many preachers and moralists to hold out consolation to their contemporaries by establishing a date for redemption within their own lifetime. True, the followers of Sabbatai Zevi eagerly applied such calculations, but in their case the Messianic tension was already there. The appearance of such devices in sermons and moralistic tracts is in itself no proof of such tension. Ninety years ago, there was a writer in Jerusalem, David Cohen of Vilna, who for many years used to send out a pamphlet calculating Messianic *gematriot* for the following year. These were homiletical gimmicks and no more. In the literature of Hasidism, speculations of this kind do not occupy any significant place whereas they are to be found in not a few books by non-Hasidic authors of that period written in the traditional vein of Lurianic Kabbalism.[13] For our considerations, this whole question is altogether irrelevant.

III

Here, then, the question must be answered: which *are* actually the relevant considerations in this context? To this I would reply: those points where, in addition to repeating the old formulae (which is often done), significant changes have been introduced into older doctrines and concepts. I maintain that such changes have occurred in two spheres, the first being that of Lurianic Kabbalism and particularly its doctrine of *tikkun* or restoration; the second, that of heretical Sabbatian theology. Both had a great impact on Hasidism, the one openly and admittedly, the other hidden and unacknowledged. What these changes have in common is precisely that element which concerns us here, namely the elimination of the acute Messianic tension or Messianic reference which it had in the primary sources and its transference onto another plane where the sting of Messianism has been neutralized. Our sources for such an analysis are threefold: authentic traditions about the Baal Shem himself and his doctrinal sayings, the extensive writings of Jacob Joseph of Polnoye and of Dov Baer, the Maggid of Mezritch, including those of their immediate pupils. Speaking of *authentic* tradition I deliberately discard as later elaborations, reformulations, and even inventions such sayings of the Baal Shem as first appear only after approximately 1815, when the last disciples of the Maggid had died. Wholesale fabrication of sayings of the Baal Shem has been a feature of later Hasidic writings and is most striking in the voluminous writings of Rabbi Eisik Yehiel of Komarno (1806-74). I shall not enlarge here on such points of *Quellenkritik*. What, to my mind, stands out in all these changes which I propose to discuss, is the inner consistency which lends to early Hasidic teaching a novel face even where it purports to be nothing but a continuation of the old teaching.

In the Lurianic Kabbalah and in Sabbatianism, Messianism was no longer a general utopian hope of a more or less abstract character, but an actual force that determined the essential character of those two great movements. I have shown elsewhere [14] that it was this element of Messianic action inherent in the life of the Jew which was the very life of Luria's doctrine, which decided its overwhelming success and which inevitably brought about the violent explosion of Messianism in the Sabbatian movement, where the revolutionary aspects of Messianism were brought into the open. Hasidism, without changing the outward façade of Lurianic teaching and terminology, introduced such subtle but effective changes as would eliminate the Messianic meaning of the central doctrine of *tikkun* or at least defer it to a remote stage, where it became again a matter of utopianism without immediate impact. How and where is this to be seen?

First of all, in the striking pre-eminence given to the concept of *devekut,* or communion with God.[15] *Devekut* is clearly a contemplative value without Messianic implications and can be realized everywhere and at any time. None of the older Kabbalists who spoke of it with great emphasis as the goal of the mystic's way dreamed of connecting it with Messianism. When the Baal Shem and his pupils made it the very center of Hasidic life, the emphasis was shifted from Luria's stress on the Messianic action of man in the process of *tikkun*—i.e., of the restoration of the broken state of man and the whole universe to its former harmony and unity—toward a strictly personal relation of man to God. The experience of *devekut* destroyed the exile from within, at least for the individual who achieved it—and it is as an experience of the individual and not of the whole community that it is spoken of in Hasidic sources [16]—by a mystical experience of intimacy which, in order to come into its own, did not require the fulfillment of Messianic redemption, which is an essentially public act, consummated by the body of the nation as a whole. The man who has found God by way of *devekut* has worked out his own salvation. He has forestalled redemption on a strictly personal level. The difference between *devekut* in our time and *devekut* on the wider plane where Messianic redemption takes place is not a difference of substance but of degree: in the Messianic era *devekut* will be continuous and everlasting, whereas in exile it cannot endure but comes and goes. But this does not make it, as Tishby rather surprisingly argues,[17] an "eschatological value."

This non-Messianic meaning of *devekut* is brought out with utmost clarity by the highly significant qualification which is given to the Lurianic doctrine of the "lifting up of the sparks." In its original conception there is no connection between this notion and *devekut*. They never appear together, whereas in the classical writings of Hasidism both are so much interwoven that sometimes one might be tempted to take them as almost identical terms, in spite of the great difference in the origin and history of the terms in earlier mystical literature. According to Luria, the vessels destined to contain the divine light broke in the primeval act of the cosmic drama, and the light of divinity became partly scattered throughout all the worlds. To lift up the scattered sparks of light and to restore them to the place they were intended to occupy had not catastrophe intervened—this is the essential task of man in the process of *tikkun*. To fulfill this task is the preparation for Messianic redemption in which each of us plays his part. To understand the special turn this idea has been given by the Baal Shem we have to elaborate a point which would not emerge in full clarity from an analysis of the Hasidic text alone.

Luria knows of two kinds of holy sparks which need to be lifted up from the abyss or prison into which they have fallen. There are the sparks of divinity, of the Shekhinah, which are confined within Creation since the first breaking of the vessels. But there are also the sparks of the soul of Adam, the first man. For after Adam's fall, which intervened when he should have completed the restoration of harmony by lifting up all the sparks from the broken vessels, the great and all-embracing soul that was his was broken too. What formerly had occurred on an onto-logical level was now repeated on an anthropological one. The soul of all mankind was originally contained within Adam. Now, its sparks were scattered throughout the terrestrial universe, and the continued existence of sin has ever more increased their dis-persion. They are in exile and must be led home and restored to their primordial spiritual structure, which is at the same time the structure of Adam and the structure of the Messiah. Everybody must work on this task no less than on that other one of collecting the sparks of the Shekhinah from the husks in which they are held captive by the dark power of the "other," or demonic, side.

Even in Luria's system, it is not always easy to make a clear differentiation between the two kinds of sparks. The light of divinity in all its grades can be reached and lifted up by anyone who takes it upon himself to concentrate on doing so, but the same cannot be said of the sparks of souls. These are connected with each other or organized in an elaborate system, according to the place each one had originally occupied in the ethereal body of Adam. There are "families" of souls, sparks that are attracted to each other by special affinity, because they have what Luria calls the same "root." Nobody can lift up a spark which is not of his own root. It is the task of man to seek out and to search for the sparks of his root—and on the anthropological level he can do no more than that. But it was difficult to be consistent in upholding the difference between these two kinds of activity regarding the sparks. As a matter of fact, the popular literature of later Kabbalism is characterized by its blurring of this dis-tinction. The sparks of the soul and those of the Shekhinah be-come more or less the same and this identification recurs, some-times *expressis verbis,* in Hasidic literature.[18] The emphasis, to be sure, is sometimes more on the human side, and sometimes on the purely mystical and ontological one, and the enormous attraction which the doctrine exercised was enhanced rather than diminished by this combination. The authors of moral tracts, the preach-ers and commentators and the compilers of special prayers appeal-ing to the devout—all of them use the doctrine in the popular blend of its two aspects and frequently great stress is laid on it. Through the intermediary of a very picturesque symbol it epitomized the Messianic mission of man in the broken state into which he had been precipitated by sin. The *Mussar* books, written in the Baal Shem's time but outside his movement, are mostly based on it, a point on which Tishby and I are in agreement.[19]

What is it then that Hasidism has changed in taking over this doctrine? Is there any difference at all between the tenor of a contemporary *Mussar* book and the writing by one of the Baal Shem's pupils? There is indeed a difference although the Hasidic authors do not accentuate it but on the contrary try to efface it. The Rabbi of Polnoye frequently offers the new formulation we are going to consider as just another quotation from the familiar "writings" by which term he and his contemporaries designate the Lurianic literature, which in his time was still largely preserved in manuscript form only. This custom of quoting an essentially new formulation as though it were nothing but the same old stuff is certainly interesting in itself, but it has tended to obscure matters for the student of Hasidism.

The new interpretation of the doctrine consists in the very definite, personal, and intimate turn which it was given, first by the Baal Shem and later on by all the classical writers of Hasidism. I shall quote four of the relevant statements.

1) Jacob Joseph of Polnoye repeatedly quotes the following saying of the Baal Shem which is based on the Kabbalistic tripartition of the soul into the grades: *nefesh, ruah,* and *neshamah.* The three parts of man's soul transmigrate all spheres. *Nefesh,* the force of life, is also incorporated in his servants and domestic animals. If, therefore, man has by his transgression put a flaw on *nefesh,* which corresponds to the [lowest] sphere of action, he causes himself trouble through his servants and animals. *Ruah,* the spirit, is the power of speech. If he has put a flaw on it by gossiping and evil talk, then by such speech he makes enemies who speak disparagingly of him. But the soul proper rests in the brain, of whose substance [according to medieval medicine] the sperm of procreation is made. Therefore, if he puts a flaw on the thought which issues from his brain, he causes himself trouble through his children. A man can indeed lift up the three parts of his soul in every sphere and restore them to his own root by proper action.[20] Here we have the sparks of his soul migrating into parts of his immediate surroundings where they wait for him to be restored to their proper place.

2) More concrete still is the application of this idea in another set of sayings in which the Baal Shem emphasizes that God

takes care to let everyone meet the sparks that belong to his own root. There is a specific sphere in man's environment that mystically belongs to him, and to him alone, and can be touched by nobody else. As a general principle it is quoted, in the name of the Baal Shem, by Ephraim of Sedylkov, his grandson:

I have heard from my grandfather that all that belongs to a man, be it his servants and animals, be it even his household effects—they are all of his sparks which belong to the root of his soul and he has to lift them up to their upper root. For the beginnings of a thing are tied to its ultimate end and even the lowest sparks still have some communion with their beginning, unto the Infinite being. If, then, the man to whose root they belong experiences spiritual uplift they all rise with him, and this is brought about through *devekut,* for *devekut* it is that enables him to lift them up. This is hinted at by the Torah [Exod. 10:9]: "We will go with our young and our old; with our flocks and with our herds will we go"—for all these are holy sparks which are held in capitivity in very low spheres and need to be lifted up.[21]

3) The Rabbi of Polnoye has many extreme formulations of this thesis but he rather surprisingly ascribes them not to the Baal Shem, but to the Lurianic "writings." Thus he says: "It is *well known* from the writings that all that a man eats, and his home, his business transactions, his wife and his contemporaries —all of them come across man as befits his nature, i.e., from his own sparks. If a man deserves it by his good deeds, then he meets the sparks which by his very nature belong to him in order that he may restore them to their rightful place." And similarly: "I say that even a man's food, his clothing, his home and his business— all these belong to the sparks of his own soul which he is called upon to lift up. Even the fact that sometimes he loses in a transaction or brings it to a good conclusion depends on the state of his sparks, as is well known from the [Lurianic] writings. This, then, is the hidden meaning of the verse 'By *all* your ways know Him' [Prov. 3:6]—because everything serves man to concentrate his mind and to lift up the sparks of his own soul which are, at the same time, the sparks of the Shekhinah." [22]

4) The same idea is expressed in the old Hasidic commentary on Psalm 107:5 which, I am inclined to assume for reasons into which I cannot go here, was compiled around 1760 by the preacher Mendel of Bar, a friend and disciple of the Baal Shem, but was later ascribed to the master himself.

There is a great mystery: Why did God create the food and drink for which man longs? The reason is that these are full of sparks of Adam, the first man, which after his fall wrapped themselves up and hid away in all the four spheres of nature, in stones, plants, animals and men, and they strive to return and to cleave unto the sphere of holiness. And whatever a man eats and drinks is actually part of his own sparks which he is under an obligation to restore. It is to this the psalmist alludes in his words: "Hungry and thirsty ones"—i.e., those things for which men are hungry and thirsty, "their soul is wrapping itself into them"—i.e., they are there in exile, in strange forms and clothing. And be it known to you that all things that serve the needs of man are esoterically his own sons who have gone into exile and captivity.[23]

This new turn of the doctrine therefore places on everyone a special responsibility with regard to the sphere of his intimate day-to-day life and his surroundings. As Hillel Zeitlin once said in this respect, in a thoughtful essay: "Every man is the Redeemer of a world that is all his own. He beholds only what he, and only he, ought to behold and feels only what he is personally singled out to feel." [24] No one can do the work of his fellow man, no one can lift a spark which is not his own.

I have called this a new turn, and a highly interesting one at that, because it is exactly the attractive feature of the Hasidic interpretation that is completely lacking in Lurianic literature. The alleged quotations from the old writings are not to be found there: No Kabbalist before Israel Baal Shem ever used such language, as far as I know. I have examined a great many books expounding the doctrine and have always found it couched in terms of a much more general nature. Nowhere earlier is it said that the environment of man is a special world of his sparks, and all the bold formulations about his household effects, his business, and his meals are new. They may have been meant to *paraphrase* the authentic teaching, but in doing so they have deeply *transformed* it.

Let us take, for instance, Hayyim Vital's book on the migrations of the soul which is the main source of this doctrine in its original form. It does not efface the difference between the two categories of sparks, the sparks of the Shekhinah being lifted up by anyone who cares to do so, without any individual limitations, while the other sparks, it is true, can be helped only by kindred souls as ch. 5 of Vital's work explains. "There are sparks which are very near to a man and others which remain at a distance, and all depends on his actions." "You ought to know that a Zaddik is able, by his deeds, to reassemble the sparks of his *nefesh,* his *ruah,* or his *neshamah,* and to lift them up from the depth of the 'husks' "—this indeed goes as far as authentic Lurianic teaching does, but it remains confined to general outlines, and the individual environment is never mentioned as the main medium of man's action. There is an altogether different mood in Lurianism and Hasidism. Of course, the Hasidim speak of *tikkun* too, but its meaning has been qualified by this new turn into the strictly personal sphere of man, where *tikkun* is achieved by *devekut.* The teaching of Luria and Vital is not so much concerned with the fate of the sparks imprisoned in the realms of nature, although it must be said that the legend which rapidly developed around the personality of Luria gave some preponderance to this element. Luria is primarily interested in the exile of the souls and their sparks in the spheres dominated by the power of evil, the *kelipot,* whereas the Baal Shem and his followers emphasize the mystic connection between man and his immediate environment. In other words, the Lurianic doctrine has a more abstract tone, the Hasidic version a more concrete and personal one. For example: The well-known doctrine of the mystical meaning of exile is formulated thus by the Rabbi of Polnoye: "Every single individual in Israel has to go to such places as contain sparks from the root of his own soul in order that he might free them." [25] Such a formulation of the thesis will, however, never be found in the old books where the meaning of exile is explicitly linked with the necessity of redeeming the sparks of the Shekhinah, the remnants of the 'breaking of the vessels,' and not the sparks of the individual souls. By the *mitzvah* which a Jew—any Jew, for that matter—fulfills anywhere in the Galut, the sparks of the Shekhinah in that place are lifted up. As against the metaphysical sphere the emphasis is shifted to the psychological and personal one. The great cosmic vision of the Messianic mission of the Jew in performing the task of *tikkun* has receded into the background and a vision of a different character has taken the stage. I cannot consider this a matter of small importance. I may also mention that the work which later Hasidic tradition considers the Baal Shem's favorite piece of literature, Hayim ibn 'Attar's *'Or ha-Hayim* (1742) knows nothing of this individual turn of the doctrine and never changes the traditional presentation of the subject.[26]

There is no need, in the present context, to go deeper into

a further qualification which the Hasidim were quickly forced to make. There was no general agreement whether everybody or only a Zaddik could perform this lifting up of the sparks. There are several sayings of the Baal Shem's according to which it is not everybody's affair. Only the Zaddik, or he who attains the state of *devekut*, is granted the privilege of meeting the sparks of his own soul. Right at the beginning of the book *Likkutim Yekarim,* the Maggid of Mezritch quotes a dictum of the Baal Shem, pointing out that he who separates himself from God, i.e., who lives without *devekut,* "does not come across the clothes and the food which contain sparks of his own root and has thus no chance of restoring them to their proper place." Sometimes, however, he does not make the lifting up of the sparks dependent upon a special qualification. Objects of daily use, he says, change hands because each one of the respective possessors has to raise some of his sparks from them, and having done so, has no further title to it. And it is made clear that this sentence does not apply to Zaddikim only.[27]

This dilemma is common to all sections of Hasidic doctrine. Whatever is said in one place about man in general is limited in another place to the perfect devout, or Zaddik. It appears that the Hasidim, at the beginning, were not altogether sure whether to apply the doctrine in all its implications to everyone or to limit it to the special category of the elect. There is much shilly-shallying on this point, and the two tendencies clash occasionally rather sharply. We may safely say that the original impulse tended toward the widest possible application of Hasidic principles and rules of behavior, but that in practice the leaders were quickly forced to restrict them to a narrower circle.

The great stress laid on this doctrine of the "lifting up of the holy sparks" in its new version is evident in all Hasidic literature and there is no need to prove it statistically. It is strange that a scholar of Tishby's rank should have sought to deny the striking weakening of the Messianic impulse in the later version which I have analyzed. A text like the classical *No'am Elimelekh* by Rabbi Elimelekh of Lizensk (1786), a most characteristic representative of the novel points of departure in Hasidic doctrine, where this turn is given the greatest possible emphasis, is searched closely by Tishby for material which might be interpreted in the direction of greater Messianic tension. He criticizes an essay by Rivka Shatz who quite correctly had underlined this process of replacing acute Messianism by a personal and mystical concept of salvation.[28] Aside from some traditional formulations which, as I said before, are never completely absent and prove nothing, he comes up with a rather odd argument. He quotes several passages stating that the Zaddik is empowered to bring about even the coming of the Messiah, i.e., that there is in him a potential to bring on redemption. Tishby goes so far as to argue that "the bringing on of the national redemption is considered here as the principal function of the outstanding Zaddik." The truth of the matter is quite different. The stressing of this *potential* capacity of the Zaddik is by no means accidental—for he is expressly forbidden to use it! But this decisive point is not even mentioned by Tishby. The Zaddik has the power to annihilate the forces of severity and rigor by getting *down* to their root and "sweetening" them at their original place. This is a kind of reversal of the lifting up of the sparks: he faces the dark powers at their root and transforms them by meditating on the element of holiness which is inherent even in them. This "restoration" or "sweetening" of the unclean powers, the husks, is the reverse of the usual doctrine that the powers of evil or of rigor are annihilated by lifting up the sparks that are in them and giving them life. (Both doctrines are closely connected.) This, of course, has much to do with the Lurianic doctrine of *tikkun:* if *all* the *dinim,* these powers of rigor, are sweetened, then redemption would come. But the Rabbi of Lizensk warns the Zaddik who wishes to embark on this enterprise of "sweetening" that "he should not exert himself to annihilate the unclean power altogether, *because by this he would cause the immediate coming of the Messiah."* [29] In other words: Messianic exertion is forbidden. Even when there exists a Messianic potentiality in an outstanding personality, it must be be held back and not be actualized. To see in such an idea proof of acute Messianic tension seems strange to me. It is precisely what I call neutralization of the Messianic element.

Returning to the discussion of the implications of the change that occurred regarding the lifting up of the sparks, we must consider the question of the consequences that were drawn by the Hasidim from this shifting of the center of gravity in the original doctrine. The answer is that this doctrine, in authentic Lurianism, was filled with apocalyptic tension; it was seen in direct relation to the consummation of Messianic redemption. Now, for all the Hasidic repetitions of the old formulae, this decisive direct relation has been abolished, a most noteworthy step toward the neutralization of Messianism. How was this done? Simply by introducing a differentiation which in pre-Hasidic Kabbalism was either not mentioned or, if mentioned at all, only in the most marginal way.[30] I am speaking of the differentiation between the two stages of individual and universal redemption, or, in other terms, between redemption of the soul and of the bodies. The idea is the Baal Shem's and may have been current in circles of older Hasidim before his time. It is elaborated in a number of passages in the Rabbi of Polnoye's books and lends a special flavor to his explanations on this point. The "lifting up of the sparks" can accomplish only the ge'ulah peratit, the individual salvation of the soul, which therefore is the task of man and can indeed be wrought by man himself. "All our prayers for redemption"—says the Baal Shem—"are essentially bound to be prayers for the redemption of the individual which is the redemption of the soul, and this is the meaning of the verse [Ps. 69:18]: 'Draw near unto my soul, and redeem it'; it is precisely the soul that is spoken of." [31] Or, in another passage: "The main purpose [of devekut] is to attain personal salvation which belongs to his nefesh, ruah, and neshamah." This is a kind of redemption which "can take place in every man and at every time." [32] The verse of the psalmist on the redemption of the soul is consistently used in Hasidic literature with regard to this idea.

But redemption of the soul without redemption of the social body, i.e., of the nation from its historical exile, of the outward world from its broken state, has never had a Messianic meaning in Judaism. It is a private affair of religious experience and is nowhere spoken of as a Messianic action. One might even say, with greater emphasis, that it is one of the main points where Judaism and Christianity parted ways. In Christianity, redemption of the soul was considered by innumerable writers as the essential accomplishment of the Messiah. This has always been denied by Judaism which saw one of its glories in the rejection of the Messianic character of a redemption on any other than the public, social, and historical plane. The redemption of the soul, of which the psalmist speaks, was not considered by either rabbinism or Kabbalism as having anything to do with Messianism, and it was left to the heretical dialectic of the Sabbatians to introduce into Judaism this notion of a purely mystical redemption without visible historical change. Now the Hasidim came and restored the balance by their emphatic and clear-cut differentiation. Individual redemption is to be strictly separated from the truly Messianic redemption of all. The Rabbi of Polnoye is tireless in expounding the thesis that our whole life is concerned only with the non-Messianic aspect of redemption, the Messianic one being entirely beyond our ken. We can do nothing in that regard, it is wholly up to God.

We are induced to ask why there should be this radical emphasis on the essentially non-Messianic nature of human activity, which many modern writers on Hasidism, in particular Buber and Dinur, have in vain tried to minimize or to obliterate altogether. The answer seems clear to me. It is in deliberate reaction to the dangerous line of Messianism practiced by man, a line leading up to the Sabbatian upheaval, that these ideas were conceived. The Lurianic teaching on the holy sparks was not just thrown out—its appeal was much too strong for that—but it was reinterpreted in a manner that took the dangerous sting of Messianism out of it. Let us accomplish our task of personal salvation, it seems to say, and forget about the Messiah. Maybe that will pave the way for him. The immediate goal of Hasidism in those generations was no longer the redemption of the nation from exile and the redemption of all being. *That* would be Messianism, even after the Sabbatian conflagration. The goal, as formulated in the works of the Rabbi of Polnoye, is the mystical redemption of the individual here and now, i.e., redemption not *from* exile, but *in* exile, or in other words, the destruction of exile by its spiritualization. Sabbatianism, the revolution against exile, had failed. Hasidism, with the destructive consequences of this tragic failure before its eyes, renounced the idea of Messianic revolt and made its peace with exile, a precarious and uneasy peace, it is true, but peace all the same. It did not deny the original doctrine of redemption by the raising of the sparks, but it removed from it the acute Messianic tension. Outwardly this seemed nothing but a small terminological change, but intrinsically it meant a great deal for the structure of Hasidic thought. Now we can also understand the link between the special emphasis on *devekut,* a value, as I said, without eschatological coloring, and on the doctrine of the sparks in its new version. "The meaning of *devekut* is the attainment of that individual redemption which pertains to one's own soul," said the Baal Shem.[33] Mystical and individual redemption thus become identified, in contradistinction to Messianic redemption which lost the concrete and immediate meaning it held for the Lurianic Kabbalist. "Only when everyone attains individual redemption," goes another saying of the

Baal Shem, "will there be universal redemption and Messiah shall arrive." [34] This statement implies a tremendous postponement in the actual arrival of the Messiah, and we feel here the deep emotional difference between Luria's and Israel Baal Shem's approach: Luria might have said the same, but, as far as he was concerned, final redemption was just around the corner, the process of *tikkun* was almost finished. But in the mouth of the Baal Shem it was a deeply melancholic statement. And this brings us back to his letter to his brother-in-law discussed before. Here the liquidation of Messianism as a force of immediate urgency is palpable. The flattering words of the Messiah regarding the preconditions of redemption cause the Baal Shem great pain and sadness. For Messianism has once more receded into the distant future.

IV

Some aspects of this neutralization of Messianism are concerned with the relation between Hasidism and Sabbatianism. It is a curious fact that even today for many authors this question is still heavily loaded with emotion that prevents an unprejudiced discussion.[35] There are however not a few specific problems where the relation between these movements plays an important role. The Podolian milieu, particularly in the small towns and villages where Hasidism had its strongest roots, was heavily tinged with Sabbatian influence.[36] Not only ideas stemming from the heretical theology of the sectarians, but also customs which were destined to occupy a vital place in Hasidic group life would have to be investigated in this connection,[37] but that is beyond the scope of this lecture. I will only indicate some points where it seems evident to me that the Hasidim made use of ideas about the Sabbatian Messiah, but gave them a new and very different turn. It is well known that the Sabbatian Messiology centered around the attempt to explain the destructive paradox of an apostate Messiah, a paradox which in its wake produced other religious paradoxes of an antinomian and nihilistic character. I have spoken of this in many of my studies. Such ideas were widely known in Podolia and polemical reference to them can be found in several classics of Hasidic literature. But the Hasidic polemic against heretical Messianism does not preclude the possibility that some of these ideas were taken up by them and given a reinterpretation which, although still pointing to a religious paradox, took out the heretical sting and transformed them into constructive elements in Hasidic doctrine and life. Some of these have no direct relation to Messianism, such as the teaching of the Baal Shem on the *tikkun* of unholy thoughts which beset man especially during prayer, which would deserve a separate study. It was of outstanding importance in the first two generations of the movement and was later considerably toned down and given a harmless reinterpretation because of the dangerous implications of its original version and the accusations leveled against it by the adversaries of Hasidism.

There is one element, though, which has direct bearing on our topic. This is the doctrine of the Zaddik, the center of the Hasidic community. Three very different elements have gone into the making of this figure and I have spoken of this at length in another paper.[38] They are the older Kabbalistic and rabbinic concept of the Zaddik, the figure of the *mokhiah* or moral preacher whose task was rightly stressed in Joseph Weiss' important study on the origin of Hasidism, and the Sabbatian Messiah. Statements and teachings regarding his mission and vicissitudes, which originated with the Sabbatians and do not occur anywhere in the moral literature of Judaism before the Sabbatian outbreak, turn up quite forcefully in Hasidic literature on the Zaddik. But here they no longer serve to justify the dark career of Sabbatai Zevi, acts of transgression or immoral behavior. They have become, instead, indicative of the high tension essential to the figure of the Zaddik. Many of the characteristic motifs of Sabbatian paradoxes reappear in the works of Jacob Joseph of Polnoye and Baer of Mezritch, who by no stretch of the imagination can be considered as partisans of Sabbatianism. The need for dissimulation on the part of the true Zaddik in order to conquer the realm of evil and impurity is developed precisely along the same line of reasoning and by the same comparisons which the Sabbatians used in their apologies for the mystical apostasy of the Messiah. It is true that the sting of antinomianism has been removed, but the idea that the path of the Zaddik was fraught with danger remained, including the far-reaching conclusion that the danger could not be sidetracked and avoided by any maneuver but ought to be squarely faced.

What Abraham Cardozo says about the mission of the Sabbatian Messiah who must dissimulate like a spy who goes into the enemy camp in order to accomplish his task, is transferred to the Zaddik by the Maggid of Mezritch.[39] The comparison current in Sabbatian literature between the Messiah and the red heifer that "purifies the defiled and defiles the pure" is transferred by the Rabbi of Polnoye and his pupil Gedalya of Linietz to the Hasidic Zaddik.[40] It is quite unthinkable that such a statement could have been made by any Jewish moralist and it clearly shows the impact of Sabbatian thinking. The most striking example of such a metamorphosis is represented by the Hasidic teaching on the necessary and unavoidable fall of the Zaddik, one of the cardinal points of Hasidic teaching. It originates with the Baal Shem himself and is developed in many different directions in all the classical writings of Hasidism. It may be connected with his social task as the center of the community, as in the Rabbi of Lizensk's *No'am Elimelekh,* or with the Zaddik's own inner life, his solitary intercourse with God which cannot be sustained, as in the writings of the Maggid of Mezritch and the Rabbi of Polnoye.[41] It is described with all the fervor the Sabbatian heretics had mustered in their apologies for the fall of their "Zaddik"—and they called him by this name [42]—but now it is given a new turn where it no longer has a Messianic meaning. It has been transferred onto a new plane where the original Messianic meaning of this "fall" has been neutralized. That it is still a dangerous undertaking is well known to the Rabbi of Polnoye: "If you say you have to descend in order to rise, it may be argued that the descent is certain, but the ascent is rather doubtful" and, as he says in another place, apparently referring to the Sabbatians of his generation, "many have remained below." [43] And yet, this is the mission of the true Zaddik. This is what Abraham and Moses did, and, as the Kabbalistic saying has it, every Zaddik has something of Moses in himself. But the Hasidic authors carefully and consciously avoid drawing the parallel between the Zaddik and the Messiah in this respect while in other instances they never tire of emphasizing the task of the Zaddik as a Redeemer of the soul, i.e., an un-Messianic Messiah.

To this process of adapting Sabbatian theses on the Messiah an idea must be related which is often considered as one of the most striking and original ones that Hasidism has produced. I refer to the glorification of the tales of the deeds of Zaddikim. Its classical and extravagant formulation is that "whoever tells tales of the Zaddikim is as if he were studying the mystery of the *merkabah.*" [44] But this sententious pronunciamento is not original. It is a Hasidic restatement of a thesis which was first maintained by Nathan of Gaza, the prophet of Sabbatai Zevi, and is quoted in his name in a number of manuscripts containing a collection of Nathan's rules of Sabbatian behavior put together by one of his pupils in Salonika. "A man who busies himself with matters pertaining to *'Amirah* [our Lord and King, may his Majesty be exalted—the constant term for Sabbatai Zevi in the literature of his followers], even by telling stories only, is reckoned like one who studies the mystery of the *merkabah*." [45] Here we have the true origin of a custom widely seen as typical of Hasidic behavior because of our limited knowledge of Sabbatian sources that have only lately come under the scrutiny of the historians. All the Hasidim had to do was to transfer the thesis from the heretical Messiah to the newfangled figure of the Hasidic Zaddik—and to be sure, on that score they did very well indeed.

In the light of the foregoing exposition we may see the fact that even statements which are in accordance with Luria's Messianic doctrine now have a different ring. Interesting in this connection is the pointed re-formulation of one of the Baal Shem's sayings by Nahum of Tchernobyl, of which much has been made by the defenders of acute Messianism in Hasidism. Whereas authentic sayings of the Baal Shem speak of the structure of the human soul which everybody must build up and reconstruct for himself, this quotation, of which nobody else knows, speaks of the structure of the Messiah: "Everybody in Israel has to restore and to prepare that part of the structure of the Messiah [*komat mashiah*] which belongs to his own soul as is known [in Lurianic Kabbalism] . . . , for the Messiah will be a complete structure composed of all the souls of Israel which are six hundred thousand as they were contained within Adam before the fall. Therefore everyone in Israel should prepare that part corresponding to [his part in the soul] of the Messiah which belongs to his own soul until the whole structure will be restored and established and then there will be a permanent and universal *yihud*, realization of unity." [46] This saying identifies the original structure of Adam's all-comprising soul with the soul of the Messiah in accordance with Kabbalistic teaching on metempsychosis. In the distant future the structure of the Messiah will be built up by all of us, but the present task is to prepare and to perfect our own soul which is all we can do. As far as there is Messianism in this saying, beyond the fulfilling of our own task, it is of a utopian character but makes use of the traditional Lurianic formulation.

A last remark seems appropriate. It concerns the process of spiritualization which biblical or rabbinic terms and concepts have undergone in Hasidic exegesis. This of course is not a novel principle. It is a general trend which has its origins, long before Hasidism started, in the homiletical exercises of the preachers. Even the spiritualization of such notions as Egypt, Zion, Eretz Yisrael, Galut (exile) and *ge'ulah* (redemption) began at an earlier period, especially in Kabbalistic homiletics. What strikes the reader of Hasidic literature, which consists mostly of homiletics, is the radical application, the hypertrophic use of this device. The terms were turned into allegorical catchwords denoting no longer only what they actually mean, but standing for a personal state of mind, for a moral condition, or, as we would say in contemporary jargon, for existential situations of man. Notions like these have lost their concrete historical or geographical meaning, they have no longer to do with the fate and future of the nation but with the individual's struggle for his own salvation. If Egypt, the house of bondage, is a sphere that exists in every man, it is only logical that the same applies to the land of Israel and to the inner redemption. Naturally, there occur often enough repetitions of thoughts where such notions are taken at their face value, but their metaphorical use is overwhelming. The sayings and sermons of the Maggid of Mezritch are the outstanding example of an almost complete transformation of all the spheres comprising the world of Judaism into spheres of the soul, of a revalution of each and every one of its conceptions in terms of the personal life of the individual. But this applies also in a high degree to the writings of the Rabbi of Polnoye and those who took much of their inspiration from him.[47] Messianism was the principal victim of this transformation, because it was its peculiar utopian, historical, and revolutionary flavor that had of necessity to be disposed of on the way. It is obvious that the constant application of this transformation would greatly contribute to the process of neutralization of Messianism with which we are concerned.

Out of the infinite wealth of such neutralizing exegesis I shall quote just one characteristic passage regarding the transformation of exile and redemption into non-eschatological states. This is what Ephraim of Sedylkov has to say on Genesis 28:16: "And Jacob awoke from his sleep, and he said, surely the Lord is in this place, and I knew it not."

It is known that the exile is designated by the word sleep and this refers to the state where God removes Himself and hides His face. And redemption means that God reveals Himself through the light of the Torah through which He is awakened from sleep. And this is the meaning of "I am the Lord thy God" because the word I, 'anokhi which [being the first word of the Ten Commandments] comprises the totality of the Torah, stands for the ineffable name of God who is revealed through the revelation of the light of the Torah. And this is what the verse "and Jacob awoke from his sleep" hints at, namely his awakening from exile which is likened to the state of sleeping, as it is said [about the time of redemption] "we would be like dreamers." It may also be explained by way of the saying of the Zohar according to which the last redemption will be through the fiery flame of the Torah and this will be the complete redemption which will not be followed by exile. And this is the meaning of "he awoke from his sleep" *mishenato* which can be read as if it meant *mimishnato,* through his learning. For the last redemption will come through the flame of the Torah. And redemption consists in God enlightening the eyes that all will see the absolute truth and will depart from exile which is falsehood. And this applies equally to the individual, to each and everybody, in the mystery of the saying of the psalmist "Draw near to my soul, redeem it." [48]

The central position which anti-eschatological exegeses of this type occupy in the classics of Hasidic literature points to the degree to which Messianic terms were transformed and neutralized. It is one of the upshots of this process that the Maggid of Mezritch could produce the extraordinary statement that in exile it is easier to attain the holy spirit and the union with God than in the Land of Israel, a statement for which one would look in vain in any other place.[49]

There is no contradiction in this teaching to the older Lurianic one, but there is a significant difference and shifting of emphasis. The school of Lurianism made every Jew a protagonist in the great Messianic struggle; it did not *allegorize* Messianism into a state of personal life. Hasidism in its most vigorous stages took precisely this step. The one and unique great act of final redemption, "the real thing," if I may say so, was thrown out, i.e., was removed from the sphere of man's immediate responsibility and thrown back into God's inscrutable councils. But let us face the fact: once this has been done, all the mystical talk of a sphere of Messiah in one's own life, wonderful as it may sound, becomes but an allegorical figure of speech. If, as has been remarked by

Hillel Zeitlin, every individual is the Redeemer, the Messiah of his own little world—and I agree that this is the essence of early Hasidism—then Messianism as an actual historic force is liquidated, it has lost its apocalyptic fire, its sense of imminent catastrophe. It may continue to use the old words and symbols as indeed it did, but, for better or worse, it has become a force set on the building of a community of the reborn in exile—a venture very far removed from the Zionist interpretation which nowadays is frequently forced upon early Hasidic teaching. It is not at all surprising that the Hasidic movement, in spite of many modern affirmations to the contrary, could do without the Land of Israel. That some Hasidic groups transferred themselves there around 1788, is a marginal phenomenon and the many letters written by their leaders do not indicate any Messianic intensity of feeling. The creative power of Hasidism was centered on the mystical life, on the revival of the Jew in exile. This may have been a very great thing to achieve. But let us not forget that while Hasidism brought about an unheard-of intensity and intimacy of religious life, it had to pay dearly for its success. It conquered in the realm of inwardness, but it abdicated in the realm of Messianism.

Devekut, or
Communion with God

I

EVERY DISCUSSION of Hasidic doctrine has to start with a basic question, namely: Is there a central point on which Hasidism is focused and from which its special attitude can be developed? I think there can be little doubt that there is, indeed, such a focal point, the discussion of which will take us right into the heart of the problem. This is the doctrine of *devekut*, the practical application of which has determined the spiritual physiognomy of Hasidism.

Devekut, the meaning of which I am going to analyze, is, of course, neither an exclusively Hasidic concept nor a novel invention of the Baal Shem. Exactly where the new departure in its Hasidic application is found will become clear if we proceed to consider both its "prehistory" and its position in Hasidism.

Throughout Kabbalistic literature, *devekut* is frequently mentioned as the highest ideal of the mystical life as the Kabbalists see it. This is not to be wondered at, considering the meaning of the term as used in many books. In general Hebrew usage, *devekut* only means attachment or devoutness, but, since the thirteenth century, it has been used by the mystics in the sense of close and most intimate communion with God. Whereas in Catholic mysticism, "Communion" was not the last step on the mystical way—although a book *De adhaerendo Deo (On Communion with God)*, ascribed to Albert the Great but actually by the Bavarian monk Johannes of Kastl, was one of the outstanding mystical manuals of the later Middle Ages—in Kabbalism it is the last grade of ascent to God. It is not union, because union with God is denied to man even in that mystical upsurge of the soul, according to Kabbalistic theology. But it comes as near to union as a mystical interpretation of Judaism would allow. I have already spoken briefly of this Kabbalistic concept of *devekut* in my former lectures on Jewish mysticism, but I may be permitted to add some remarks on the subject. *Devekut,* or as we may also call it, communion, is characterized in Kabbalistic literature by the following three traits:

1. It is a value without eschatological connotations, i.e., it can be realized in this life, in a direct and personal way, by every individual, and has no Messianic meaning. It is a state of personal bliss which can be attained without having recourse to the vast field of eschatology, utopianism, and Messianism. Being a strictly individual attainment, it is not an experience of the group, the social community of men, as is Messianic redemption, nor is it rooted in a hope or, for that matter, an anticipation of the Hereafter, of the World-to-come. In an eschatological sense, man cannot be redeemed alone, individually. Such individual redemption or salvation carries in Judaism no Messianic meaning. It is essentially a private experience; *devekut* can be reached alone. The only exception, when *devekut* became an experience of the whole community of Israel, was—at least according to some Jewish theologians—the revelation at Mount Sinai, but even then it was more in the nature of a multiplied experience of many single individuals than of the community as an integrated whole.

2. Furthermore, such *devekut,* although attained within the framework of this world, is, for the most part, realized only by the paradoxical means of abnegation and denial of the values of this world. Moses Nahmanides, for instance, speaks of "those who abandon the affairs of this world and pay no regard to this world at all, as though they were not corporeal beings, but all their intent and purpose is fixed on their creator alone, as in the cases of Elijah and Enoch, who live on forever in body and soul, after having attained Communion of their souls with the Great Name" (on Lev. 18:4). The realization of *devekut* means, therefore, a constant being-with-God which is not dependent on death and life after death.

3. For the understanding of the new turn of the idea of *devekut* in Hasidism, however, no passage is more important than Nahmanides' commentary on Deuteronomy 11:22, "To love the Lord your God, to walk in all His ways and to cleave unto Him." The old commentaries are divided on the question of whether this cleaving, which is *devekut,* is to be understood as

a promise held out to the faithful, or as a commandment binding upon everyone. Abraham ibn Ezra is of the first opinion; Nahmanides of the second. He explains the verse as follows:

It warns man not to worship God and somebody beside Him; he is to worship God alone in his heart and his actions. And it is plausible that the meaning of "cleaving" is to remember God and His love constantly, not to divert your thought from Him in all your earthly doings. *Such a man may be talking to other people, but his heart is not with them since he is in the presence of God.* And it is further plausible that those who have attained this rank, *do, even in their earthly life, partake of the eternal life,* because they have made themselves a dwelling place of the Shekhinah.

This statement, by the way, bears a strong resemblance to a similar one by Maimonides about the highest rank of prophecy, at the end of the *Guide of the Perplexed* (III, 51). In Nahmanides' definition, there appears, for the first time, an element which has played no great part in the Kabbalistic doctrine of *devekut,* although it is mentioned often enough in quotations of this classical passage, but which was given great prominence by the Baal Shem, and even more by his followers. I am referring to the combination of earthly action and *devekut.* Of course, it was not Nahmanides' intention to say that *devekut* could be realized in social action and association too. But he clearly thought that it could be sustained even in social intercourse, although such intercourse in itself is considered rather as a hindrance which must be overcome by special effort. *Devekut* is a value of contemplative, not of active life. But Nahmanides' saying could be used to prove the possibility of the coincidence of the two spheres. A man might appear to be with other people, to talk to them and, perhaps, even to participate in their activities, but in reality he is contemplating God. This is the highest attainment in the Kabbalistic scale of values and represents a blend of action and contemplation. For Nahmanides, *devekut* has always the specific meaning of communion with the last of the ten *sefirot* or grades of divine manifestation, namely, with the Shekhinah, but this detail was not retained by other Kabbalists, who keep to the more general definitions of *devekut* given by other members of Nahmanides' circle of Gerona. His older colleague, Rabbi Ezra ben Solomon, already speaks of *devekut,* or communion with the Naught, which is certainly a much higher rank than communion with the Shekhinah, the Naught being the most hidden recess of divinity which contemplation may behold.

This idea of *devekut* as the ultimate fulfillment of the mystic's path permeates the theosophical and ethical literature of the Kabbalists. Isaiah Horovitz connects the state of *hasidut* with that of *devekut*: "Who is a Hasid? He who acts in piety towards God and gives pleasure to his Creator and all of whose intention is bent on cleaving to Him and thereby becoming a chariot for God." Characteristically, it still appears in Moses Hayim Luzzatto's *Path of the Upright* as the last stage of the Path. In the opinion of this contemporary of the Baal Shem, it is a special grace granted to the Hasid, a gift of grace for which man can only prepare himself by incessant striving for knowledge and cognition and by the sanctification of all his actions. It is at the very end of the Path that God Himself takes over his guidance and causes divine holiness to dwell on him. Then only— says Luzzatto—may man succeed in his quest for such *devekut* with God as may last forever, for he may be helped by God to what Nature withholds from him. "If a man attains such spiritual rank, even his earthly actions become actually holy matters, and this is alluded to in the biblical prescriptions on meals made of holy offerings."

Here we find two basic motifs in connection with the doctrine of *devekut* which reappear and are given prominence in the Hasidic teaching of the Baal Shem: (1) the sanctification of the profane sphere in the life of the perfect Hasid, its transformation into one single sphere of holy action which leaves no room for the concept of a separate state of "profane" action; (2) the paradigm of eating in holiness as the perfect example of this supreme state of man. What is generally considered as an earthly performance par excellence, is transformed into a holy, nay, a mystery rite. This paradigm, by the way, is by no means a late addition, nor is it a specific trait of Hasidism, as it is sometimes considered to be. It is common to the whole Kabbalistic renaissance of Safed. The transformation of the profane sphere of human activity is stressed by Luzzatto, who says that he who has attained communion lifts up the earthly things which serve his needs, and does so by the very act of using them. "He raises them up to himself, rather than descending from his rank and state of *devekut* by using them." But Luzzatto draws no social conclusion from this conception of *devekut*. With him, everything connected with it remains wholly within the sphere of contemplation. He only follows in the footsteps of the older masters of Kabbalism by insisting on retreat and withdrawal from social intercourse as the principal means of attaining such "holiness" or "communion" (to him the two terms cover the same meaning). If *devekut* is the last stage on the path of ascetic self-abnegation, it would obviously be difficult to interpret it in terms of social ethics.

Luzzatto's book cannot be considered a literary source of the new Hasidic turn, but rather the opposite. But among the books with which the Baal Shem and the old Hasidic conventicles were undoubtedly conversant, there is the *Sefer Haredim* ("The Book of the God-Fearing"), one of the popular classics of Kabbalistic ethics, composed before 1600 at Safed by Eliezer Azikri. The three highest values which, according to him, the "Hasidim of Israel" cultivate, are "loneliness or retreat from society, asceticism, and *devekut.*" He defines the latter as the fixing of thought on God (ed. 1601, fol.66b). When the Baal Shem's Hasidism, in the eighteenth century, said that *devekut* was more important than study, this thesis aroused considerable hostility and was quoted in all polemical writings against the movement as proof of its subversive and anti-rabbinic tendencies. But it is noteworthy, and has been overlooked, that this fundamental tenet of Hasidism is quoted by Eliezer Azikri in the name of no less an authority of Kabbalism than his teacher, Isaac Luria himself. "These three principles of conduct are seven times more useful to the soul than study," Luria is reported to have said.

The bond between the old Kabbalists of the thirteenth-century school of Gerona and latter-day Hasidism, in their evaluation and elaboration of *devekut* as a mystical state of mind, is proved conclusively by a statement of Eliezer Azikri to which no attention has been paid. This author tells us that the "Hasidim of old times" took off no less than nine hours daily from their study of the Torah

for the spiritual activities of retreat and *devekut* and used to imagine the light of the Shekhinah above their heads, as though it were flowing all around them and they were sitting in the midst of the light, and this is the way I have found it [the meaning of *devekut*] explained in an old manuscript of the ancient ascetics. And while in that [state of meditation], they are all trembling as a natural effect, but [spiritually] rejoicing in trembling.

Azikri's source, the "old manuscript," is known to us. It was my good fortune to discover it some years ago in a lengthy and extremely interesting description of the meaning of Kabbalistic meditation (*kavvanah*) whose author was none else than the great mystic Azriel of Gerona. Through the intermediacy of the sixteenth-century moralist of Safed, this description had come down to the Baal Shem and his followers, and the description of the state of *devekut,* which I quoted in my former set of lectures from a book of one of the Great Maggid's disciples, is taken, albeit without naming the source, from Azikri's work. This little example may serve to demonstrate the hidden after-life of the old Kabbalistic manuscripts, the impact of which is too easily overlooked.

II

But let us return to the crucial point which our discussion of *devekut* has now reached. The questions can now be asked: What is the difference between the old Kabbalistic idea of *devekut* and the Hasidic one? Why could Luria and Azikri, in the sixteenth century, make the statements I have quoted without being attacked, whereas the rabbinical antagonists of Hasidism lost their tempers when they found an essentially identical statement in the writings of Baer of Mezritch and Mendel of Przemyslany? Was it only a question of the different time and environment that made a perfectly orthodox statement sound wicked and heretical two hundred years later? This, of course, would by no means be impossible. The history of religion abounds in examples of such different evaluations of the same tenet under different historical conditions. But the true answer to our problem is to be found in another consideration which, in my opinion, will take us into an even deeper understanding of the essential nature of Hasidism.

It is not so much the meaning of *devekut* that has changed in Hasidism as its place, and this is a most significant change indeed. The novel element is the radical character given to *devekut* by this change. Hasidic *devekut* is no longer an extreme ideal, to be realized by some rare and sublime spirits at the end of the path. It is no longer the last rung in the ladder of ascent, as in Kabbalism, but the first. Everything begins with man's decision to cleave to God. *Devekut* is a starting point and not the end. Everyone is able to realize it instantaneously. All he has to do is to take his monotheistic faith seriously. It is, therefore, small wonder that the Baal Shem identifies *emunah* (faith) and *devekut*. "Faith," he says (*Toledot* 195b), "is the intimate communion of the soul with God." And the first, and most pointed, consequence of this identification is the frequently repeated formula that to fall away from the state of *devekut* is essentially equivalent to separation of the creature from its Creator, nay, to idolatry (*avodah zarah*). God pervades everything, or, as the old adage goes, "no place can be void of the Shekhinah." Therefore, to be aware of this real omnipresence and immanence of God is already the realization of a state of *devekut*. In the opinion of the Baal Shem, to be out of *devekut* is not simply a state of estrangement from God, it rather implies the negation of His oneness and all-pervading presence. This idea is not an accidental obiter dictum of no consequence. It is commonly repeated from the Baal Shem's teaching in all the early writings of Hasidim before 1790. The Baal Shem formulated it in the words of the Torah (Deut. 11:16), *ve-sartem-va-avadtem elohim aherim*, "lest you turn aside and serve other gods," meaning, "once a man turns aside from *devekut* and the fixation of his thought on God, he is considered as one who serves other gods and there is no mediating path."

This change of position in the scale of values explains, to my view, much of the attraction Hasidism has held for the "common Jew." On the one hand, there could be—and, indeed, has been—the continued stress on the mystical implications of the state of *devekut* as an extreme attainment, and Nahmanides' passages on it are frequently quoted by those who consider it ultimate. On the other hand, it could be considered the focal point in the religious life of every Jew. Even if the leaders and saints took *devekut* in its most exalted meaning, this novel turn explains why it could very quickly become externalized when put as a demand to the average man. To be sure, it was a comfort to the masses that to cleave to God was no longer a remote ideal for the few, but there is also the second aspect which cannot be overlooked: if *devekut* was demanded from everybody and, in a way, forced upon the masses, it was bound to assume rather crude and vulgar forms. Once the radical slogan, "Judaism without *devekut* is idolatry," was accepted, its very radicalism already contained the germ of decay, a dialectic typical of radical and spiritualist movements. Since not everyone was able to attain that state of mind by mere introspection and contemplation, external stimulants, even liquor, had to be employed. *Devekut* in its popular and even objectionable forms was not a phenomenon of later degeneration, but was well known from the very beginnings of the newfangled Hasidic conventicles. As Moses of Satanov tells us, *devekut* was practiced about 1740 by rather simple people, who found in it an outlet for their emotional piety.

It is important to note that the same connection between *devekut* and the state of retreat and isolation constantly emphasized in the older literature of Kabbalistic ethics continues to prevail in the writings of eighteenth-century Hasidim. In this respect, there is no difference between the old-fashioned ascetic, such as Moses of Satanov, and the new school of the Baal Shem. *"Devekut"* says the former, "can be mainly attained during the time one spends in solitary retreat, for it is then that the soul actually cleaves to its Creator, for the whole earth is full of His glory." The reason given here that *devekut* is possible because God is everywhere, is exactly the same advanced by the Baal Shem and the Maggid of Mezritch.

III

A closer analysis of the Baal Shem's sayings on *devekut* will enable us better to understand its twofold aspect in Hasidic teaching. We have already mentioned the connection between "faith" and *devekut,* but the authentic dicta of the Baal Shem provide us with several other elucidations which are relevant to our discussion.

As a classical illustration of the meaning of *devekut* and, incidentally, also of the way famous Hasidic dicta have traveled through Hasidic tradition, we have the daring reinterpretation of Psalm 81:10, "There shall be no strange God in thee." These words, said the Baal Shem, can be taken according to the Hebrew sequence of words to mean "God shall not be a stranger to thee." And when is God no longer a stranger to man? When man constantly fulfills the admonition of the psalmist, "I set the Lord always before me." It is the communion with God through *devekut* that makes God an intimate friend of man, instead of a forbidding and remote stranger. This saying, quoted by Gedalya of Linietz, was not, even in Hasidic circles, generally known to belong to the Baal Shem. It is frequently quoted as one of the epigrams of Rabbi Mendel of Kotzk, in the fourth generation after the Baal Shem, who used to translate the biblical passage in a literal manner, *Nit zol zeyn in dir Gott fremd.* The

Rabbi of Kotzk obviously liked the saying, and it is considered by many as one of his great words. Since there was no critical examination of the old and authentic sayings, many of them have, in the course of time, come to be ascribed to later authorities who were wont to quote them.

The performance of the commands is in itself an act of *devekut,* as is shown by an etymological pun. According to the Baal Shem, *mitzvah* means a bond. The talmudic adage, "each good deed brings about another one," is taken to mean that every communion with God leads to ever closer communion. *Devekut* is thus not a state but is in itself a path comprising an infinity of ever more intimate communions.

If the essence of religious action is communion or *devekut,* it follows that leaving this state of communion is the essence of sin. Even he who "falls away from the fixation of his thought on God for a moment only" is called a sinner. But this statement, mentioned by the Baal Shem's grandson, sets such a high standard for *devekut* that it had to be qualified and mitigated, as will be shown presently.

The Maggid Rabbi Mendel of Bar used to quote the following literal translation of Psalm 32:2 in the name of his teacher, the Baal Shem, "Blessed is the man to whom not to think of God is iniquity." Here the primitive radicalism of the demand of *devekut* is somewhat mitigated. Blessed is the man who has no other sin to repent of than his falling or stepping out of *devekut.* It is a sin, but the sin of a blessed man, of the perfect Hasid who has attained a higher level than the rabbinical Zaddik. It is *devekut* as the final stage on the Kabbalist's path that is reflected in this and similar statements. Incidentally, this is the only word of the Baal Shem quoted (though anonymously) in a book of an old-fashioned Hasid like Simhah of Zolozitz, a contemporary of the master.

Of what does that *devekut* consist which is realized in study and prayer? The answer is given in many authentic dicta of the Baal Shem stressing that *devekut* is a spiritual or contemplative act by which a man binds himself to the spiritual element inherent in the letters of Torah and prayer. The words and their element, the letters, are the vessels which contain a priceless jewel, the light of The Boundless *En-sof. Devekut,* in the opinion of the Baal Shem, is communion with this inner light that animates the letters of the Torah or, for that matter, everything. For he accepts the Kabbalistic conception of creation as externalized speech: Everything that exists consists of letters of the divine language. Each of them is only the vessel which contains unfathomable depths of divine light, a light which is not created, but is the light of the Shekhinah herself. What is required, therefore, is to concentrate in study and prayer not on the external figures of speech, nor on the "letter," but on the "spirit" that animates it. That is what *devekut* can perform. Meir Margalioth, the Rabbi of Ostrog, says that it is this special conception of *devekut* that he learned from his master, the Baal Shem, and that he had actually observed how it was practiced by him. This definition, which occurs also in the Baal Shem's authentic letter to his brother-in-law, puts the emphasis on a definite technique of contemplation which the Baal Shem practiced and taught, and there can be no doubt that it goes far beyond the earlier definitions of *devekut* which I have discussed. I am inclined to think that the dialectic of *devekut* to which I have made reference is fully reflected in this conception: It sounds very simple and anyone might start practicing it, but it is extremely difficult to attain as a sustained state of communion. Why should not anyone be able to concentrate on the inwardness of the spiritual element in everything? As a matter of fact, it is a counsel given not to the accomplished Kabbalist at the end of his path, but repeatedly addressed to everybody. Yet, it has the unmistakable ring of a mystical practice which has its esoteric side and is by no means as easy to carry out as it appears to be.

Sometimes the letters and the holy names composed of them are identified with the light that dwells therein, the letters themselves being transformed into the spiritual element, with which communion must be established. In this connection, great interest attaches to the mystical turn the Baal Shem gave to an old Jewish saying which extols the merit of the study of the Torah for its own sake (*torah lishmah*). Several dicta explain the new meaning infused into the old phrase. This high ideal—the Baal Shem is reported to have said—must be understood according to the precise meaning of the phrase, which is "for the sake of its name." It is the name of God, the spiritual element, which is evoked by true study and which should be aimed at in study and worship. Study of the Torah (*lishmah*) is not a principle like "art for art's sake," but reflects the longing to discover the hidden element inherent in the letters and words. There are many variations of this motif among the Baal Shem's sayings, and it is obvious that he used the idea very often. Lurianic Kabbalism

knew of a parallel explanation of *lishmah,* but whereas the Lurianic idea aimed at some theosophic detail in the mechanism of the
Upper Worlds, the Hasidic exegesis of the saying is of a much
more general nature. It is interesting that Jacob Joseph of Polnoye quotes both explanations, the Kabbalistic and the Hasidic;
he senses that there is a difference between them, but he strives
to efface it.

As I have said, this definition of *devekut* as man's binding
himself to the core (*penimiut*) of the letters, the Torah and the
commandments, instead of to their external aspects only, seems
to be a new point made by the Baal Shem. He was in dead earnest
about the religious implications of this thesis. How much so is
shown by one of his sayings, where he infers from this definition
that he who does *not* bind his thought to the "root" or core
of the action which he performs, is positively sinning by introducing separation into the world of spiritual unity and by
"cutting down the trees of Paradise." This is the familiar Hebrew
phrase for falling into heresy. Therefore—and this idea is ham-
mered into the readers of Jacob Joseph of Polnoye's books—he
who keeps the Torah in its externals only, without *devekut,* is
an arch-heretic in the sense of Kabbalism: instead of binding and
uniting things to God, he separates and isolates them from
Him. This, of course, is a radical and essentially spiritual thesis.
It is interesting to observe how early Hasidic authors strove to
discover a Kabbalistic authority for it. The Rabbi of Polnoye
tries to read it into a statement found in Abraham Azulai's *Hesed
le-Abraham* (written about 1640). But Azulai's statement is of
an altogether different nature and lacks the radicalism of the
Hasidic thesis. The fact that it was necessary to twist quite innocu-
ous Kabbalistic sentences in order to extract from them his new
meaning of *devekut,* tends to show that we are dealing here with
a novel departure. This central thesis that the core of every true
worship is *devekut* could not be held by Kabbalists as long as
they placed *devekut* at the end of the Path, and, as a matter of
fact, Azulai never said it. He says only that the prayer of man is
heard if he succeeds in drawing out the spirituality of the supernal
spheres into the letters. This is quite different from discovering
them there as an ever-present reality. And, of course, no mention
is made by Azulai of the absence of *devekut* constituting a sin or
transgression.

Devekut, or "communion," is not "union" in the sense of the
mystical union between God and man of which many mystics

speak. But it leads to a state, or, rather, implies an action which in Hebrew is called *yihud,* which means unification, the realization of union. The term has not always a mystical connotation, and it is not always easy to determine what is meant by it. Sometimes it only means concentration of mind by uniting all its powers on one focal point, sometimes it means even less, namely, the acknowledgement of God's unity. This latter meaning, however, is more or less restricted to non-mystical literature, where it is frequently found, whereas Hasidic literature uses the term in the same special sense given to it by the Kabbalists. If a man binds his thought to the root of the Torah, this is called a *yihud,* both because he concentrates on it and because he breaks down the barriers and brings about unification by making into an organic whole what seemed separated and isolated. He does not become God, but he becomes "united" with Him by the process in which the core of his own being is bound up with the core of all being. There is one saying of the Baal Shem—apparently the only one—stating that the process of *yihud,* which is accomplished through *devekut,* transforms the Ego, or *ani,* into the Naught, or *ain.* This idea, which plays no central part in the Baal Shem's conceptions, was taken up with great vigor by the Maggid of Mezritch who, as a radical mystic, made it one of the cornerstones of his thought. The hidden Naught, an old Kabbalistic symbol of the depths of the Godhead, held no special attraction for the Baal Shem, but it takes on a new vitality in the teachings of Rabbi Baer and his pupils. Many of the classical writings of Hasidism overflow with lucubrations on the communion with "Nothingness" and the path by which man retraces his steps from "aught" to "naught." The strange enthusiasm which characterizes these sermons on a truly paradoxical symbolism wanes after the generation of Rabbi Baer's pupils. But for the first generation after the Baal Shem it held a fascination unequaled in Jewish literature and not easily explained. It seems to express a degree of abandonment to emotionalism that has no precedent, except for the short upsurge of Sabbatianism in 1666, and could find no adequate expression but in the most daring paradoxes of mysticism. The Baal Shem never said that *devekut* represented a state where man was able to stand within the Naught, an idea cherished by the Maggid. Of course, the new departure introduced by Rabbi Baer did not prevent him from using definitions and theses about *devekut* which he had inherited from the Baal Shem.

There is a point in connection with the Baal Shem's conception of *devekut* that deserves further attention. I am referring to the relation between talmudic study of the Torah and the new central virtue. As far as I am aware, it has been overlooked that this shifting of the place of *devekut* in the scale of values, and the new definition given to it, has something to do with the evaluation of talmudic learning in early Hasidism. The old Safed school clearly already knew that the "Hasidim of old" took nine hours off their time of study in order to practice solitude and *devekut*. Now, when *devekut* was no longer considered a final stage for the few, but a demand on anybody who harkened to the voice, this was bound to hasten the clash between a purely talmudic orientation and the new school. If you concentrate on the spiritual core of the Torah, on the mystic light shining through the letters, and if this is *devekut,* it follows that you cannot concentrate with equal fervor on the specific and concrete meaning of the words, and certainly not on the intricacies of talmudic lore and discussion. To penetrate an intricate discussion is one thing, and to contemplate the divine light that pervades the words is another.

The Baal Shem, and still more his main disciples, were fully aware of the gulf between the understanding of the specific detail and the contemplation of the all-enveloping light which transcends human grasp and understanding. They did not think it possible to unite both of them in one and the same act. (The Baal Shem said to the Rabbi of Polnoye that on Sabbath there was almost no time to study, because all of it ought to be devoted to *yihudim,* i.e., contemplation.) Hence the insistence on taking time off from study and devoting it to contemplation and meditation. The two did not go together. Mendel of Przemyslany, who counseled not to devote too much time to talmudic study, only drew the logical conclusion from the basic demands of *devekut*. The famous warning so vehemently assailed in the struggle between the two camps is to be found in a context where special emphasis is laid on the practice of *devekut*. The radicalism of the mystics and protagonists of popular revivalism, which necessarily brought about the clash, had not yet been watered down. Later on, it would be argued, as some Kabbalists, including Moses of Satanov, had done before, that *devekut* and penetrating study were not mutually exclusive and might be practiced together. Honesty requires us to state that Hasidism, in its beginning, was far removed from such an irenic attitude. Talking about *devekut* and contemplation, it meant what it said, and meant it in an uncompromising sense. The emphasis on *devekut* had, of course, two aspects: one for the average man, to whom it opened up a new vista and, especially through the practice of fervent and ecstatic prayer, a path to God; the other, for the learned, from whom it required a new balance between the intellectual and emotional sides of his nature. In both cases, the problem could not have arisen without the afore-mentioned shifting of the place of *devekut* into the center of man's spiritual activity.

So far, we have found in *devekut* a value which, to the Baal Shem no less than to his forerunners, is connected primarily with solitary meditation and prayer. In prayer, even in communal prayer, man is alone with God, much as he may strive to bind himself spiritually to "Catholic Israel." What I said at the beginning of the characteristics of *devekut* in Nahmanides holds emphatically true for the Baal Shem's conception too, in spite of the change I have just been analyzing. The possibility of a social meaning of communion with God begins to show here and there and seems to be based on the practice of the Baal Shem. His disciple, Moses of Dolina, reports in his name that *devekut* can be sustained even in seemingly idle talk and in attending to one's business. But to accomplish this, he says, special zeal and fervor are required. The very close relation between *devekut* and *yihud* is also shown by the fact that the same saying that Moses of Dolina quotes about *devekut* is mentioned by the Baal Shem's grandson in connection with the possibility of performing *yihudim* not only by prayer and contemplation, but by every earthly performance. Even in social intercourse, in attending to business, etc., it is possible to continue the contemplative attitude by binding oneself to the spiritual core of the matter. In other words, *devekut* and *yihudim* are not concerned so much with the concrete as such, but rather with emptying it of its concrete content and discovering in it an ideal aspect that opens a vista into the hidden life which flows everywhere. *Devekut* was not preached as an active realization of the concrete, but as a contemplative realization of the immanence of God in the concrete.

In the teaching of Baer of Mezritch, the re-evaluation of *devekut* has proceeded a step further, in harmony with the general trend of his thought, which could be characterized as a transformation of Kabbalistic theosophy and its terminological apparatus into mystical anthropology. It is remarkable that the central concept of

Lurianic Kabbalism, the idea of *tikkun,* restoration, plays no great part in the first Hasidic writings. Its place is taken by *devekut,* a substitution which I have found nowhere in pre-Hasidic literature, and which, indeed, could never be found there. Why? Because the idea of *tikkun* in Lurianic doctrine had a strong Messianic connotation and implication on which I have dwelt elsewhere. But *devekut* is essentially a non-Messianic and non-eschatological value. When it took the place of *tikkun* in the mending of the "broken vessels," in the restoration of harmony in the broken state of our being, it could do so only because something had fundamentally changed in the outlook of the Hasidim. About this change, namely, the neutralization of Messianism as a driving power, I shall speak at greater length later. Before this liquidation of Messianism had taken place, nobody could have thought of substituting the private and contemplative experience of *devekut* as a healing force for the broad and comprehensive action that was the essential meaning of *tikkun.* This substitution tells much about the real difference between Lurianism and Hasidism.

Rabbi Baer enumerates three factors which may induce the state of *devekut:* retreat from association with other people; the writing down of Kabbalistic mysteries on the Torah; and the practice of *yihudim,* in the sense of special meditations. No special emphasis is laid as yet on the attainment of *devekut* within the group. He does not change the basic meaning of *devekut* as a value of introspection which consists of solitary intercourse with God. It is not a social value. In his opinion, it is a high degree of perfection if a man is "sometimes" able to be alone with himself and God "even when in one room with many other people." It was left to Rabbi Baer's disciples, especially to Elimelekh of Lizensk, to take the final step and demand the realization of *devekut* as a social value. But this could be done only at a high price, namely, by binding *devekut* to the institution of Zaddikism, a connection wholly foreign to primitive Hasidism.

Looking back on our analysis, there is one point which deserves to be amplified. It is remarkable that *devekut,* an essentially emotional value, is linked in a surprisingly large number of sayings of the Baal Shem and his various pupils or associates with a seemingly intellectual effort. *Devekut* is reached by a fixation of one's thought *(mahshavah)* or mind *(sekhel)* on God. True, there are some sayings which mention the souls as a whole, and not only its intellectual power, as the instrument of *devekut.* But the insistence on the use of mind and thought cannot be accidental, even if we concede that "thought" is sometimes used in a rather loose sense. For it does not always mean the purely intellectual and intentional act of the mind, but rather indicates in some places any intentional act of the soul, including its voluntaristic and emotional spheres. I assume, however, that the strong emotional coloring of the "thought" of man in the dicta about *devekut* has something to do with the nature of this act. In fixing all one's attention on God, thought, sunk in contemplation of the ineffable light, loses its definite content as an intellectual act. By the practice of *devekut,* thought is transformed into emotion; it is, if I may be permitted to use the expression, de-intellectualized. In other words, the insight which is won by *devekut* has no rational and intellectual content and, being of a most intimate and emotional character, cannot be translated into rational terms.

This point is very succinctly put forward by Meshullam Feibush Heller, a pupil of the Maggid of Mezritch and the Maggid of Zlotchov. His classic epistle on the fundamentals of Hasidism contains pointed criticism of the contemporary study of Kabbalah. True mystery, he says, is not what can be read and studied by anybody in the printed volumes of Kabbalistic teaching, which is a purely intellectual affair, like so many other studies; there is no point in calling this an "esoteric" knowledge when it is, in truth, as exoteric as any other knowledge that can be imparted by books. The real mystery and esoteric wisdom is that of loving communion with God, *devekut ha-ahavah ba-shem yitbarakh.* It cannot be told or transmitted, and "everyone knows of it only what he has found out for himself, and no more."

It is, however, not without interest that the link between *devekut* and intellectual effort may have come down from Kabbalistic tradition. Joseph Gikatilla (about 1300) defines *devekut* as the process by which man binds his soul to God by way of intellectual thought, and he labors this intellectual view of *devekut* at some length in his book on the Kabbalistic reasons of the commandments.

IV

If Hasidic piety was focused to such a degree on *devekut,* there could be no doubt that the great demand could not be fulfilled continuously. There are two ways in which the Baal Shem dealt with this question in his sayings. Sometimes he admits the necessity of an interruption of *devekut.* The soul, too, must take a rest from the exertions and the emotional strain. By simple and un-strained activities it must gather new strength for the renewed exercises of *devekut* (*Ben Porat,* fol. 34a). Seen in this light, attending to the business of daily life is a necessary interruption and preparation for the adventure of spiritual life, and therefore no reproach attaches to it. In *devekut,* man is cleaving to the spiritual life of all worlds which is the Shekhinah or the imma-nence of God. This vital force, which is aroused by communion, cannot operate without interruption. A "descent," a *yeridah,* from the state of *devekut* is therefore part of human nature. The Baal Shem used to apply to this the verse in Ezekiel 11:14, which he interpreted to mean, "the force of life" *(hiyut),* instead of *hayot* of the text, "runs and returns," i.e., operates not steadily but with interruptions. The meaning of all this, of course, is that the force of life, although it is there, cannot be continuously realized and made conscious. Jacob Joseph of Polnoye mentions twice such a "fallen state" or *yeridah* of the Baal Shem himself when he had gone to another country; it is to be regretted that he gives no further details, but contents himself with the remark that after that he had double power of "ascent," *aliyah.*

But it must be admitted that in the light of his own pro-nouncements, this is not a satisfactory solution. If it is sin, or even heresy, to fall out of *devekut,* how could an explanation such as this one hold good? Out of this dilemma came a fundamental thesis of the Baal Shem, meant as a qualification of the doctrine of *devekut* and which, indeed, played a very important part in early Hasidism. This is the doctrine of *katnut* and *gadlut,* the minor and major states of man.

As a matter of fact, *katnut* and *gadlut* are not only states of man's mind or being, but, according to the Baal Shem, two basic states of every being. "Just as there exists a state of *katnut* and *gadlut* in the supernal *sefirot,* there is a similar state in every thing, even in the clothes that a man wears," his grandson quotes him as saying. We have here another striking example of the metamorphosis of Kabbalistic terms. In Lurianic Kabbalah these terms have a specific theosophic meaning, as states of the divine mind in some of its manifestations. The chapters on these states in Vital's *Etz Hayim* are famous for their difficulty and their daring use of anthropomorphic symbolism. The Baal Shem takes the terms back into the human sphere and gives the theosophic idea a new turn or twist.

With him, *katnut* and *gadlut* are phases of life, everywhere and at all times, from purely natural and even artificial things up to the configuration of the divine *sefirot* where the same rhythm and the same law prevail. *Katnut,* the minor state, is the state of imperfection, even of degradation, whereas *gadlut* means the full development of a thing to its highest state. Everywhere in time, space, and the soul there is the same organic law of the two states, an idea which the Rabbi of Polnoye was tireless in preaching and applying.

There is a higher and lower state in human existence and human affairs, and particularly in worship. But everything depends on the rank a man has reached in his spiritual struggle for perfection. With one, *katnut* may mean an outward and mechanical way of worship "without soul" or, as the Baal Shem was fond of putting it, "without joy." But with another class, it may mean only a lower standard than their customary one. *Katnut,* then, is the time of man's struggle with his lower instincts in order to lift himself up to *gadlut,* a state that knows of no struggle, but only of the enjoyment that comes with victory over the darker side of his nature.

The same verse in Ezekiel I, used by the Baal Shem in support of the interruption of *devekut,* is also adduced by him in connection with this rather different theory. There is a steady flow of life, up and down, and no state is void of its manifestation. There can be a modest form of *devekut* even in the minor state. It is limited and without that exuberance and exhilaration that comes to man only when joy sweeps him off *katnut.* But still, it enables him to keep some sort of communion even in that state of estrangement from God as which *katnut* is frequently pictured. One saying has it that "in the time of *gadlut* man is literally cleaving to God, which cannot be said to apply in the time of *katnut.*" For when man falls into this state—and there is no exception to the law that necessitates this periodic occurrence—he finds himself in melancholy sadness and estrangement. His worship contains an element of compulsion and not those high qualities of pure fear and love which characterize that worship out of an overflowing heart which is essentially what *gadlut* means. Only by constantly striving to overcome this state of separation and to attain anew the higher state, by the very struggle to get oneself out of the spiritual desert, there remains some indirect approach to God. This is the point on which the Baal Shem's defense of his behavior with simple folk is centered. *Katnut* is the time to serve God even through idle talk or story telling! For, even by this means, can man bring about the spiritual concentration which will help him to attain *devekut*. In *katnut,* man should devote himself to external action or worldly talk, but even then the true Hasid will be meditating on the spiritual side of what seems to be a purely material undertaking. Nobody may notice it, yet he transforms the lowest forms of activity into something of a higher order. It is obvious, and I need not labor the point, that this thesis can be as sublime as it may prove dangerous. The mystic content of idle talk—that is certainly a thesis full of perverse possibilities! And a very popular thesis at that. It is constantly emphasized in the doctrinal tradition of early Hasidism and must be considered as an active factor in its propaganda.

Katnut is, therefore, the time of trial through which the perfect man, no less than anybody else, must pass. There is, to be sure, a twofold aspect of *katnut:* it can be the natural relaxation after the strain of *devekut,* but it can also be an intentional descent, because of some hidden purpose. This second aspect plays an important part in Hasidic doctrine. It is connected with the motif of the falling, or stepping down, of the Zaddik, a problem that had a special fascination for the Hasidim. I do not think it could have acquired this importance had it not been for the Sabbatian theories of the necessary fall of the Messiah and its later Podolian metamorphosis. Only after Sabbatianism, the problem of *Nefilat ha-Zaddik* became an acute one that needed to be discussed. Earlier Kabbalistic ethics does not know it as a pressing one. Now, from the Baal Shem's sayings till Elimelekh of Lizensk, it takes on rather astonishing dimensions. In my view, it is a sublimation of an antinomian thesis, on a plane where it was calculated to lose its sting. The deliberate stepping down from holiness into a state of *katnut*—says the Baal Shem—is very dangerous, and there are many who have remained there and could not rise again. This sounds very much like an echo of the Sabbatian turmoil!

Another saying of the Baal Shem has it that, "if it happens to a perfect man that he cannot study or pray, he should realize that this also shows the hand of God who is pushing him back in order that he may come nearer." Here we have essentially the principle which, as far as I can see, was formulated in its final shape by Rabbi Baer of Mezritch, if not by the Baal Shem himself. The formula *yeridah tzorekh aliyah,* "the descent, or stepping down, is necessary in order to ascend to a higher rank"— something perhaps best translated by the French phrase, *reculer pour mieux sauter*—recurs constantly in Rabbi Baer's sayings on the meaning of *katnut*. But he admits two kinds of "stepping down": "Sometimes," he says, "a man falls from his rank because of himself . . . and sometimes the state of the world causes him to fall, and in both cases the descent is for the sake of an ever higher ascent." *Katnut,* then, for all its personal color, is not only a matter of purely personal causation. It may depend on the surroundings of a man, his fellow men, or other factors. This explanation was very frequently used to justify the deliberate or quasi-deliberate stepping down of a perfect man, a Zaddik, in the Hasidic sense of the term. If all the world is in a state of *katnut,* he should join in and associate his efforts with theirs in order to reach *gadlut.* It is in this context that Jacob Joseph of Polnoye uses almost the same formula as the Maggid of Mezritch. (Incidentally, since he uses it immediately before a quotation from the Baal Shem, we may infer that the formula itself was not known to him as a saying of his master; otherwise he would have acknowledged it as such.)

We even have the prescription of the Baal Shem as to which parts of prayer should be said in a state of *katnut* in order to be able to pray the other parts in the ravishment of *devekut*. It is obvious, therefore, that a state which is considered as preparatory to *devekut* does *not* constitute a sin in the sense I have explained before. Of course, there is danger in *katnut,* namely the danger of remaining in what should be only a transitory stage. But the whole teaching of the Baal Shem is centered around this conception of a steady ebb and flow in the spiritual life of man: in *gadlut,* there is communion and even ecstasy, but in *katnut,* there is preparation for it. Understood in this right sense, no fault is to be found in such a state.

V

In the foregoing analysis of *devekut,* I have laid stress on those points which characterize the specific color and significance the term has taken on in Hasidic parlance, and particularly with the Baal Shem. They are more or less typical of the conception of *devekut* in the bulk of Hasidic literature. But there is one further point which I think should be discussed here. I have said that communion, for all its depth and importance, is not union. But is this truly so? Are there no stages of deeper contemplation, ravishment, and ecstasy where one state passes into the other?

Since much has been made of the allegedly pantheistic leanings and doctrines of the Baal Shem and his early pupils, especially by S. A. Horodetzky and Jacob S. Minkin, it may be worth while to go into the matter. All the more so, since Horodetzky uses the term pantheism in a very loose way which tends to make pantheists of a great many inside and outside of the Hasidic camp who might never have so much as dreamed of such a faith as that venerable author ascribes to them. If Creator and Creation are essentially one, then *devekut* may indeed be union. I propose, therefore, to examine this question, if only briefly, in order to reach a better understanding of some shades of the concept of *devekut* which deserve our attention.

As to the Baal Shem himself, there is no proof, in his authentic sayings, of any doctrine which might properly be called pantheistic. In contradistinction to this absence of an identification of God and the universe, of the Creator and Creation, there is full proof of his belief in the immanence of God in every one of His creatures. It is at most what philosophers call "panentheistic" teaching—all Being *in* God, but not all Being God. This sort of teaching was current in Kabbalism, especially in Cordovero's works. If we knew for sure that the Baal Shem had studied Abraham Azulai's *Hesed le-Avraham,* which is an abstract of Cordovero's Kabbalah, we would better understand the genesis of some of his formulas as quoted in the books of the Rabbi of Polnoye. For Azulai sharply accentuates the panentheistic core of Cordovero's teaching. But all we know positively is that this rabbi himself had read the book, which was printed as early as 1685. Whether his master knew it we can only guess. Azulai states, for instance, that man is "in communion with God," because "there is nothing that is separated from Him." But the reason he adduces for the latter statement is perfectly orthodox and non-pantheistic; it is the chain of cause and effect which, in the last resort, links God with His Creation. The formula of the "chain of causes" enables the mystics to reinstate God as the immanent soul or life of all being. And it is only in this quality, and not as the last and transcendent cause, that God appeals to the mind of the Baal Shem. His thinking on this score is very simple and unsophisticated. He repeats the old formulas which every Kabbalist had used before him, and, with one notable exception, without additions of his own: "Everything is full of His glory," "No place is void of Him," "Thou keepest them all alive" (Neh. 9:6), which was frequently understood to mean: Thou art the vital force, *hiyut,* of everything. To this last quotation the Baal Shem made the significant addition, of everything, even of sin, an idea which he repeated in a great many variations.

On the other hand, the Baal Shem was fond of telling a parable which recurs in several variations in the books of his disciples and apparently carries quite a different meaning.

A king had built a glorious palace full of corridors and partitions, but he himself lived in the innermost room. When the palace was completed and his servants came to pay him homage, they found that they could not approach the king because of the devious maze. While they stood and wondered, the king's son came and showed them that those were not real partitions, but only magical illusions, and that the king, in truth, was easily accessible. Push forward bravely and you shall find no obstacle.

The interpretations put on this parable in Hasidic literature differ widely. Its literal sense conveys no pantheistic meaning but rather an "acosmic" one: the world is denied real existence, reality is seen rather as a sort of "veil of Maya." The perfectly devout man, the "son of the king," discovers that there is nothing that separates him from his father. External reality is but an illusion. This is the way the parable is commented on by the Baal Shem's grandson. But others, as for instance the Rabbi of Polnoye, give it a pantheistic turn: "People with true insight know that all the walls and partitions, all the outward clothes and covers are in truth of His own essence, for there is no place void of Him." If the formula alone were decisive, we might safely say that there is, indeed, a pantheistic element to be found, at least in some of the Baal Shem's disciples. But the ideational content of the formula is, almost in every case, limited to a much less radical interpretation, by reading into it either the doctrine of divine immanence or that of the annihilation of reality before the contemplative mind. For if one looks closely into the context of such passages, all that remains of the high-flown formulas is always the omnipresence of the divine influxus, *shefa,* and *hiyut,* the vitalizing power, instead of that of the divine substance. I think that the numerous writers who have compared the Baal Shem's teaching to that of Spinoza have considerably overshot the mark. I, for one, am unable to find any teachings reminiscent of Spinoza in the Baal Shem's doctrinal sayings.

An excellent example of the shifting of emphasis in the use

of extreme formulations is provided by a saying of Pinhas of Koretz on the subject, in his *Midrash Pinhas* (1872f., 9b, 60):

If a man fulfills the commandments of the Torah, such as the commandment of the phylacteries, and says the formula prescribed by the Kabbalists, namely, "In the name of all Israel [I am doing this]" then he lifts up the whole universe to its "root" above, *for the world is really God Himself,* like the locust whose clothing is part of its own self. Therefore, he annihiliates [by his action] the [outward] existence of the whole universe. And if we see that in spite of all this the world is still there, it is because the vital energy of God is always active and the world is incessantly renewed.

Here, then, we have within one sentence the different motives I have just mentioned, and this, I think, should warn us against over-stressing such formulas as "the world is really God Himself." What is particularly interesting in this view is that the performance of the *mitzvah* does not give more meaning and reality to the world, as modern interpretations of Hasidic theology would lead us to expect but, on the contrary, detracts from its apparently illusory reality and leads from the Aught to the verge of the Naught. For the "root" of the world is the Naught which the mystic contemplates, with which he communes and in which he longs to "stand." At their "root" the created things lose their identity as creatures, because all that can be beheld there is God alone. But we should not forget that, to reach that state, Creation as Creation must be "annihilated," which implies that Creation, in its own right, is not what pantheism would declare it to be, namely a mere mode of Infinity. We are indeed, as we may put it, dwelling in God, but we are not God. Also, it should be borne in mind that the "son of the king," who pushes through to his father, sees his father and cleaves to him, but does not become one with him.

This, then, brings us back to the point I have raised: are there, in original Hasidic teaching, more radical formulations of the central doctrine of *devekut* than those we have been considering? The answer is that there is a definite turn toward a more mystical formulation of it in the teaching of the Maggid of Mezritch and some of his pupils. The Baal Shem and Jacob Joseph of Polnoye do not emphasize a "union" or "unity" *(ahdut)* between God and man, and their formulations are much more careful than those current in Rabbi Baer's sayings. This adds further weight to what I have said about the necessity of taking Jacob Joseph's allegedly pantheistic statements with not too small a grain of salt. Comparing the two most conspicuous pupils of the Baal Shem, there can be no doubt that Jacob Joseph is the relatively sober one, whereas Rabbi Baer of Mezritch has gone far on the way of what must be described as mystical intoxication. The difference between the sermons of the two, which have come down to us, is tremendous. I have mentioned the streak of soberness that characterizes the Baal Shem. In Rabbi Baer, this trait has disappeared. He is no longer the friend of God and the simple folk, who roams through the markets. He is the ascetic whose gaze is fixed on, or, I might rather say, lost in God. He is a mystic of unbridled radicalism and singularity of purpose. His predilection for the more paradoxical figures of mystical speech colors his sermons to a degree equaled by few of his predecessors in the history of Jewish mysticism. It is, therefore, not astonishing that he should use the terminology of mystical union in describing some stages of *devekut,* although here, too, it may be wise not to lose ourselves in his terminology, which is radical indeed, but to consider the context of his thought.

It will serve as an illustration of this peculiar mystical bent of Rabbi Baer if I close by summarizing his bold explanation of Numbers 10:2 which, as a description of the ultimate goal of *devekut,* goes as far as anything in early Hasidism. The rather inoffensive prescription of the Torah: "Make thee two trumpets of silver, of a whole piece shall thou make them," gives birth in Rabbi Baer's mind to the following enthusiastic explanation based on a mystical pun, the word *hatzotzerot,* trumpets, being taken as two words, *hatzi-tzurot,* halves of forms. Man and God, he says, are each only a half-finished, incomplete form. Man without God is really not man, *adam,* a sublime and spiritual being, but only *dam,* blood, a biological entity. He is lacking the *a* or *alef,* which is God, *alufo shel olam,* the master of the world. Only when the *alef* and *dam,* God and man, get together, the two form a real unity, and only then does man deserve to be called *adam.* But how is such unity, *ahdut,* accomplished? By *kisuf* which means "the constant striving for union with God." If man casts off all earthly or material elements and ascends through all the worlds and becomes one with God to the degree of losing the feeling of separate existence, then will he be rightly called *adam,* Man, "being transformed into the cosmic figure of the primordial man whose likeness upon the throne Ezekiel beheld." This, according to Baer, is the transfiguration of man which is reached through, or in, the state of *devekut:* man finds himself by losing himself in God, and by giving up his identity he discovers it on a higher plane. Here, and in many other sayings of Rabbi Baer, *devekut* is said to lead not only to communion, but to *ahdut,* union. But —this union is, in fact, not at all the pantheistic obliteration of the self within the divine mind which he likes to call the Naught, but pierces through this state on to the rediscovery of man's spiritual identity. He finds himself because he has found God. This, then, is the deepest meaning of *devekut* of which Hasidism knows, and the radical terms should not blind us to the eminently Jewish and personalistic conception of man which they still cover. After having gone through *devekut* and union, man is still man— nay, he has, in truth, only then started to be man, and it is only logical that only then will he be called upon to fulfill his destiny in the society of men.

Martin Buber's
Interpretation of Hasidism

THERE CAN BE no doubt that Martin Buber has made a decisive contribution to the Western world's knowledge of the Hasidic movement. Before Buber undertook to introduce and interpret Hasidism to Western readers, this movement was all but unknown to the scientific study of religion. This was true despite the fact that since its crystallization in Podolia around the middle of the eighteenth century, it constituted one of the most important factors in the life and thought of East European Jewry. As long as the ideas of the Enlightenment, beginning at the end of the eighteenth century, asserted their influence on Jewish circles, Hasidism for Western Jews seemed essentially an outbreak of extreme obscurantism, allied with all those forces in the Jewish past to which the protagonists of a modern, enlightened Judaism were most sharply opposed.

The great Jewish scholars of the nineteenth century who inaugurated the scientific study of Judaism (men like Heinrich Graetz, Abraham Geiger, and Leopold Zunz) felt the same way. They did not care for mysticism and emotionalism in religion and they repudiated the values which such movements emphatically propagated. Not until the turn of the century did certain Jewish writers and scholars, especially in Russia, attempt to regard this phenomenon without prejudice. This new view was linked to a general revaluation of Jewish history which was now treated as the history of a living people and no longer as the model for an enlightened theology, a model which most scholars measured by the abstract criteria of philosophers and theologians. The new wave of Jewish nationalism which welled up toward the end of the nineteenth century and a romantic impulse to discover the deeper forces at work in the life of the East European Jewish masses played a large role in bringing about this change. Scholars

228

like Simon Dubnow, enthusiasts like Samuel A. Horodetzky, and great poets like Isaac Leib Peretz heralded the new era. Dubnow's pioneering study of the history of Hasidism was conducted in a remarkably cool and reserved manner; however, the discovery of the world of Hasidic legend lent great luster to the movement. This discovery, which was especially due to Peretz and Berdichevsky, possessed tremendous poetic appeal and marked a new era in Jewish literature, especially that in Hebrew, Yiddish, and German.

It is within this context that we must examine Buber's lifelong fascination with the phenomenon of Hasidism and his contribution to its understanding. When in his youthful quest for a living Judaism Buber discovered Hasidism, he was overwhelmed by the message he seemed to find in it. Thereafter he devoted more than fifty years of a distinguished literary career to ever new formulations of this message's meaning. His Zionist credo, which put him on the track of Hasidism, was now interwoven with his conviction of the significance of Hasidic doctrine for the rebirth of Judaism: "No renewal of Judaism is possible which does not bear in itself the elements of Hasidism."

As an often fascinating and always vigorous and spirited writer, Buber made a significant impact with his first books, *The Tales of Rabbi Nachman* and *The Legend of the Baal-Shem*. Since that time we owe to his pen a virtually unending stream of Hasidic material and interpretative analysis which reaches its climax in *Tales of the Hasidim* and other books of a more theoretical character, like *The Message of Hasidism,* which have exercised a lasting influence, especially since the end of World War II.

Buber's influence is not hard to explain. While the enthusiasm of certain other apologists for Hasidic teaching, like Horodetzky's for example, was essentially naïve and their books were an odd mixture of charming simplicity and dullness, in Buber we have a deep and penetrating thinker who not only admires intuition in others but possesses it himself. He has that rare combination of a probing spirit and literary elegance which makes for a great writer. When an author of such stature and such subtlety set down with untiring seriousness what to him seemed the very soul of Hasidism, it was bound to make a deep impression on our age. In one sense or another we are all his disciples. In fact most of us, when we speak about Hasidism, probably think primarily in terms of the concepts that have become familiar through

Buber's philosophical interpretation. Despite Buber's own frequent indications, many authors who have written about him during these years have not in the least been aware that Buber's work *is* an interpretation and that there might be a problem in relating the interpretation to the phenomenon itself. As a thoughtful reader once remarked to me, along with his interpretation of Hasidism Buber has for the first time presented the European and American reader with a canon of what Hasidism is. His interpretation was accompanied by such a wealth of seemingly irrefutable proof in the form of Hasidic legends and sayings that it was bound to silence any critic.

The more than fifty years of Buber's neo-Hasidic activity have evoked a strong response also outside the Jewish world. Competent scholars have been rather reluctant to raise basic questions as to whether this poetic, moving, and beautifully formulated interpretation can stand up to critical and sober analysis. Dubnow did express certain general doubts regarding the all too modern style of the interpretation and said of Buber's books that they were "suited to further contemplation, not research," but he supplied no evidence for this judgment. The emotional (to say nothing of the artistic) appeal of Buber's writings was of course so infinitely greater than that of Dubnow's rather arid discussion of Hasidic ideas that there could be little doubt as to whose arguments would have the greater impact. Yet, while historical research has meanwhile progressed far beyond Dubnow's achievement and has opened up many new perspectives and insights into the origins and developments of Hasidism, Buber's writings—especially those of his later years—have only recently evoked critical analysis. Such analysis now seems to me urgent and very much in order. In taking up this discussion here I will have to restrict myself to several points I consider fundamental.

A critical analysis of Buber's interpretation of Hasidism has to confront certain particular difficulties from the very start. The greatest is that Buber, to whom no one denies possession of an exact knowledge of Hasidic literature, does not write as a scholar who gives clear references to support his contentions. Buber combines facts and quotations to suit his purpose, namely, to present Hasidism as a spiritual phenomenon and not as a historical one. He has often said that he is not interested in history. In the context of our discussion this means two things of equal importance. First, Buber omits a great deal of material which he does not even consider, although it may be of great significance for the understanding of Hasidism as a historical phenomenon. To give only two examples: the magical element, which he consistently explains away or minimizes, and the social character of the Hasidic community. Secondly, the material that he does select he often associates closely with his own interpretation of its meaning. I shall have more to say about this later.

The other great difficulty facing the critical reader of Buber is connected with the circumstances of his development. Buber began as an enthusiastic admirer or even, one might say, adherent of religious mysticism. It was his discovery that there was a mystic kernel of living Judaism in the Hasidic movement which struck him with such force when he first came into contact with Hasidic literature and tradition. At that time he saw Hasidism as the flower of Jewish mysticism, the "Kabbalah become ethos." Thus his early interpretation bears a mystical hue as, for example, in that justly famous chapter "The Life of the Hasidim" with which he introduced *The Legend of the Baal-Shem* in 1908. Several years later, however, his thinking underwent a further development which brought about a deep change in his views. This change is best characterized in his philosophical writings by the distance lying between *Daniel: Dialogues on Realization* (1913) and *I and Thou* (1923). Here he renounced the world of mysticism and took a new stand which brought him into the front rank of what we would today call religious existentialism, even if Buber rather pointedly avoids using the term in his own writings. But in this new phase as well Buber continued to find in Hasidism illustrations for his views. His brief pamphlet *The Way of Man in Hasidic Teaching* is not only a gem of literature but also an extraordinary lesson in religious anthropology, presented in the language of Hasidism and inspired by a large mass of authentic Hasidic sayings. It is precisely to this problem of determining the nature of the inspiration which Buber found in the old texts and the change they underwent when he interpreted them in his own way that I must devote the major part of my discussion.

In this last, mature phase of his selective presentation of Hasidism, Buber no longer stressed the essential identity of Kabbalah and Hasidism, as he had done in his earlier works. Although he still recognizes the strong links between the two phenomena, he was concerned with establishing and maintaining an essential distinction between them. He now likes to refer to the Kabbalah as gnosis, which he no longer regards as a mark of praise. He sees two contradictory forms of religious consciousness at work in Hasidism—even if the creators of the movements may not have been aware of this split. Kabbalistic tradition determined one of them. It aimed at knowledge of divine mysteries, or at least at insight into them, and was bound to lead Hasidism into speculations of a theosophical nature. Buber was perfectly well aware that Hasidism developed within the framework of the Lurianic Kabbalah. He even explicitly adopted my own characterization of the Kabbalah of Isaac Luria as a classic example of a gnostic system within orthodox Judaism, as I set it forth in my *Major Trends in Jewish Mysticism.* But this Kabbalistic Gnosticism was not—and here I agree with Buber—a really creative element in Hasidism. Its conceptual apparatus was used by the great masters of Hasidism, but they transferred its basic meaning from the sphere of divine mysteries to the world of man and his encounter with God. According to Buber, this was the really creative aspect of Hasidism. And since in the last analysis it is the creative impulse which matters, he felt justified in almost completely ignoring the Kabbalistic or "gnostic" element in Hasidism. For him it is nothing more than a kind of umbilical cord which must be severed as soon as the new spiritual creation exists in its own right if we are to see and understand the new phenomenon in its authentic mode of being.

Buber's writings contain numerous formulations of this attitude. I would like to cite only one of them, taken from his debate with Rudolf Pannwitz:

The Hasidic movement takes over from the Kabbalah only what it needs for the theological foundation of an enthusiastic but not over-exalted life in responsibility—the responsibility of each individual for the piece of world entrusted to him. Gnostic theologoumena that are thus taken over are transformed; their ground and their atmosphere are transformed with them. From spiritualities enthroned in the Absolute, they become the core of realizations [*Bewährungen*]. The pneuma has settled down in the blessings of a fervor that fires with enthusiasm the service of the Creator practiced in relation to the creature. Therefore, everything has become different. In place of esoterically regulated meditations has come the unprescribable endowing of each action with strength of intention, arising ever again from the moment. Not in the seclusion of the ascetics and schools of ascetics does the holy now appear, but in the joy in one another of the masters and their communities. And—what was unthinkable in the circles of the old Kabbalah—the "simple man" is held in honor, that is, the man of the original *devotio,* the man by nature at one with himself who lacks the secret knowing as well as the rabbinical knowledge, but can do without both because united he lives the united service. Where the mystical vortex circled, now stretches the way of man.

This statement, though delivered by a voice that demands respect, cannot convince anyone who is familiar with both the Kabbalistic and the Hasidic literature. But in order to understand the extraordinary mixture of truth, error, and oversimplification which it contains, we must direct our attention to the most basic features of Buber's attitude to the phenomenon of Hasidism, namely, his conviction that our main source for the understanding of Hasidism is its legends. Only this conviction, together with Buber's method of selection, can explain assertions like the one quoted above.

Here we must point out that the extensive literature of Hasidism ultimately falls into two categories. First, there is a very large body of theoretical writings which consists mostly of sermons and lectures, commentaries on biblical texts, and tractates on the prayers and on other objects of religious life. The common conception among general readers who draw their knowledge of Hasidism from Buber, namely that Hasidism is the pure "lay mysticism" of unlettered groups, is conclusively refuted by this literature. The most important of these works were written between 1770 and 1815, when Hasidism emerged from bitter polemics as a force in East European Jewry and sought to spread its views and manner of life orally and in writing. These works contain the teachings of the great saints of Hasidism, the Zaddikim, which, by the way, often cite as illustration epigrammatic sayings or short anecdotes. An even more extensive literature of the same type came into being after 1815, but for the most part it contains only variations of the basic motifs that were set forth and developed in the older works; only here and there do we find a few new ideas. This literature embraces well over a thousand volumes.

The second category consists of an equally extensive body of legends, biographies, and tales concerning the miracles of the Zaddikim and of collections of their memorable sayings. This genre of legends developed at the end of the eighteenth century and enjoyed an ever-increasing popularity among the Hasidic masses. It was thought that to tell stories of the saints was just as productive on the spiritual level as the study of divine mysteries. The main features of the Hasidic legends crystallized during the first half of the nineteenth century, in many instances incorporating much earlier legends of different origin, which were then transferred to the great personalities of Hasidism. Since about 1860, several hundred volumes of this genre have appeared, and every single leading Hasidic personality—even of the last generations—has been adorned with such a wreath of legend.

Now it is important to note that Buber's presentation and interpretation of Hasidism is based almost exclusively on this second category of Hasidic literature—on the legends, epigrams, and anecdotes of the Hasidic saints. He writes:

Because Hasidism in the first instance is not a category of teaching, but one of life, our chief source of knowledge of Hasidism is its legends, and only after them comes its theoretical literature. The latter is the commentary, the former the text, even though a text that has been handed down in a state of extreme corruption, one that is incapable of being restored in its purity. It is foolish to protest that the legend does not convey to us the reality of Hasidic life. Naturally, the legend is no chronicle, but it is truer than the chronicle for those who know how to read it.

This consistent emphasis on the pre-eminence of the folk tradition over the theoretical literature shows that Buber employs a methodological principle which seems to me highly dubious. Buber's terminology, of course, is rather inclined to spread confusion. What is a "category of teaching" in contrast to one of "life" when it comes to analyzing a historical phenomenon whose teaching is inextricably bound up with the life which it demands, not separated from it by an abyss? Buber's metaphors about text and commentary are misleading and conceal the historical fact that the so-called commentary was the first and most authoritative presentation of the meaning of this life, long before it was enveloped by legends. The identity of legends and life, which Buber claims, is fictitious. Strictly speaking, these legends are themselves nothing more than a commentary to what, with Buber, one might call life. Life is reflected both in the legend and in the teaching, but it must be emphasized that whereas the origins of this Hasidic life were deeply influenced and shaped by ideas laid down in the theoretical literature, its beginnings were certainly not influenced by legend.

Buber's ambiguous use of the concept of "life" has made him fall into a trap. Naturally, from an aesthetic point of view, the legends possess a considerable advantage and appeal and lend themselves more easily to a subjective interpretation than the theoretical writings in which a train of thought is more carefully developed and carried through. Nonetheless, in my opinion, a discussion of the meaning of Hasidism—even if with Buber we call it "Hasidic life"—must be based essentially on these writings. Now it is very revealing that in the course of the years, as Buber developed and elaborated his existential and subjectivist "philosophy of dialogue," his references to the theoretical literature of Hasidism became ever weaker and more scanty. I would suspect that to many readers of Buber it would not occur that such literature even exists.

Apparently Buber regarded these sources as far too dependent on the older Kabbalistic literature to be regarded as genuinely Hasidic. And this dependence is indeed immediately obvious. Many of them, including some of the most famous Hasidic books, are written totally in the language of the Kabbalah, and it is a basic problem of research to determine exactly where their ideas depart from those of their Kabbalistic predecessors. The Hasidic authors obviously did not believe that they had in any way broken with the gnostic tradition of the Kabbalah and, little as Buber wants to admit it, they wrote clearly and plainly as Gnostics. When Buber claimed that the legends of Hasidism were its truly creative achievement, he put himself into an unusually paradoxical position. He had to contend that the originality of the movement genuinely manifested itself only in a genre of literature which almost entirely came into being nearly fifty years after the period in which Hasidism was in fact creative and in which it produced those theoretical writings which Buber has so decisively shoved aside. Such a position is simply not tenable.

Buber, in short, by making his choice and leaving out whatever is in conflict with its demands, asserts an authority which we cannot concede him. To describe the world of Hasidism, the way of life it propagated, and the teachings of its masters exclusively on the basis of its legends is exactly like trying to present Islamic mysticism by considering only the epigrams of the great Sufis without regard for their extensive theoretical (and likewise "gnostic") literature, or to describe Catholicism by selecting and interpreting the most beautiful sayings of the saints of the Church without regard to its dogmatic theology. Such a procedure is indeed conceivable, and an analysis or even merely a compilation of the sayings of their great spirits would undoubtedly provide wonderful insights into the worlds of Sufism or Catholicism. Such words, reflecting the reaction of a significant individual to the system of thought in which he lives or the way in which he conceives it, of course possess a strong tinge of what we would today call existential meaning. I would be the last to deny that. But the profit and the illumination we would draw from a compilation or even a profound interpretation of such words or legends should by no means seduce us into thinking that they represent the real doctrines of Sufism or Catholicism whose dogmatic features would be all too easily obliterated in a presentation of this kind.

All of this applies precisely to Buber's choice of Hasidic material. These legends and sayings are certainly most impressive and they just as certainly possess a general human interest. However, if we want to know what they really meant in their original context we would still have to revert to those primary sources which Buber pushes aside as merely secondary. We shall presently see how important this original context is when we come to a discussion of the central point in Buber's interpretation of Hasidism. Although his selection entails certain ambiguities, we willingly grant Buber as a writer and even as the advocate of a message the right to choose what appeals to him. But I very much doubt that such a selection can form the basis for a real and scholarly understanding of what most attracted Buber to Hasidism.

Naturally there is some truth to Buber's idea of the relation between Hasidism and Kabbalah. Although one may say that the Hasidim never lost their enthusiasm for the teachings of the *Zohar,* the Bible of the Jewish mystics, and for the Lurianic Kabbalah, and although no page of a Hasidic book can be understood without constant reference to these traditions, it still remains true that, in elaborating the theosophical doctrines of the Kabbalah, the Hasidic writers did not prove themselves particularly creative. All students of Hasidism are agreed that its most valuable contribution lies somewhere else. The Hasidic writers use the old formulas, concepts, and ideas, only giving them a new twist. Buber is also completely right in saying that gnostic theologoumena, which are taken over by the Hasidim, are often transformed. Into what are they transformed? Into assertions about man and his way to God. Hasidic writers are fond of reinterpreting the conceptual language of the Kabbalah, which originally referred to the mysteries of the Godhead, in such a manner that it seems to concern the personal life of man and his relation to God. A great deal of emphasis is placed on this "moral" reinterpretation of the old theosophical vocabulary. In the writings of Rabbi Dov Baer of Mezritch—the student of the Baal Shem who first organized the movement (died 1772) —we find page after page in which he almost systematically takes up individual Kabbalistic concepts in order to explain their meaning as key-words for the personal life of the pious. They do not for this reason lose their original meaning, which in fact continues likewise to appear, but they gain an additional level.

To this point I would agree with Buber. But again he carries his claims too far when he juxtaposes the ideal of the Kabbalist who is initiated into the divine mysteries to that of the simple man who, though he lacks rabbinic and gnostic knowledge, has achieved "unity" in his life. This seems a false set of alternatives. The Kabbalists never excluded the possibility that a simple and unlettered man could reach the highest spiritual perfection, nor did Hasidism declare such a "simple man" its highest ideal. He may appear here and there in Hasidic legend, which in just this respect has adopted a much older pre-Hasidic Jewish tradition, but Hasidic teaching knows nothing of his representing the highest ideal which the disciple is to realize. Quite to the contrary, it tirelessly repeats the teaching of the necessary reciprocal relationship between the truly spiritual man—who always appears as a gnostic initiate—and the simple people. These two types of men can bring about the true Hasidic community, which needs both of them, only by binding themselves to their common "roots" in the spiritual world. The Hasidic legends honoring the faith of the unlettered are essentially the same as those found in all great religions; only in the rarest instances do they shed light on the specific guiding values which Hasidic literature sets up as normative and on the methods which it prescribes for achieving intimate communion with God. This latter concern, achieving *communio* with God, is the heart of Hasidism.

I agree with Buber when he says:

What Hasidism is striving for in relation to the Kabbalah is the deschematization of the mystery. The old-new principle that it represented, restored in purified form, is that of the cosmic-metacosmic power and responsibility of man. "All worlds depend on his works, all await and long for the teaching and the good deed of man." This principle, by virtue of its pure intensity, enabled Hasidism to become a religious *meeting*. It is not a new element of teaching. . . . Only here it has become the center of a way of life and of a community.

The idea that man's action represents a meeting with God is without doubt and quite justifiably central to Buber's point of view. It takes on enormous dimensions in his Hasidic writings, but raises the question: Does his interpretation of this principle, as he claims, really penetrate to the core of Hasidism?

Hasidism does indeed teach that man meets God in the concreteness of his dealings in the world. But what did the Hasidim mean by that? The answer is clear: According to the great mythos of exile and redemption which is the Lurianic Kabbalah, "sparks" of the divine life and light were scattered in exile over the entire world, and they long through the actions of man to be "lifted up" and restored to their original place in the divine harmony of all being. This Kabbalistic mythos, whose intricate details need not be presented here—I have dealt with the subject at length in *Major Trends in Jewish Mysticism*—is probably the most important legacy of the Kabbalah to Hasidism. The many variations to which Hasidism subjected this mythos all held that since these "holy sparks" were to be found everywhere without exception, Hasidism denied in principle the existence of a purely secular sphere of life which would have no significance for the religious task of man. Even what is profane and seems irrelevant to the religious sphere, in fact contains a specific religious challenge to man. Everywhere there is an opportunity, yea a necessity, to lift up the "holy sparks," and everywhere lurks the danger of failure. Thus religion is not a beaten track in a narrowly circumscribed course. New paths open up in all directions, and God stands at the end of every path. The contemplative mind can discover the "spark" in every sphere of life and thereby transform even what is essentially profane into something that possesses immediate religious significance.

The motto for this attitude was provided by Proverbs 3:6, "In all thy ways acknowledge Him," which the Hasidim interpreted to mean: Through every single action in which you are engaged you are enabled to gain knowledge of God, you are enabled to meet Him. As a matter of fact, the Talmud already calls this verse "a short word on which all of the chief points of the Torah depend." During the Middle Ages some commentators tried to set aside this rather bold principle by seeking to interpret it as narrowly as possible; Hasidism, in its own mystical way, restored it in its full significance. The following remark is attributed to Rabbi Pinhas of Koretz: "How then is it possible to know God in *all* ways? It is, because when God gave the Torah, the whole world was filled with the Torah. Thus there is nothing which did not contain Torah, and this is the meaning of the verse. Whoever says that the Torah is one thing and the profane sphere another is a heretic." Since the beginnings of Hasidism this doctrine has always been regarded as one of its basic principles.

The Hasidic writers placed special emphasis on such "forgotten" realms of simple and insignificant action, and Hasidism's transformation of them into vehicles for the sacred was one of the most original aspects of the movement. True to their native radicalism—and it is as radicals in temperament that the Hasidim have their place in Jewish history—they were not afraid to formulate their position in paradoxes. "Small talk with one's neighbor can be the vehicle of deep meditation," said the Baal Shem. "The main point of divine worship," says another leader of Hasidism, "lies precisely in serving Him by means of profane and non-spiritual things." "Even by political gossip and conversation about the wars of the gentiles—the ultimate in idle talk and wasted time in the eyes of contemporary Jewish moralists!—may a man be able to attain an intimate connection with God," says a third. And this amazing statement is by no means a simple exaggeration—its author gives detailed advice on how to perform the feat. The Rabbi of Polnoye, a disciple of the Baal Shem, sums it up this way: "There is nothing in the world, large or small, which is isolated from God, for He is present in all things. Therefore, the perfect man can perform deep meditations and contemplative acts of 'unification' even in such earthly actions as eating, drinking, and sexual intercourse, yes, even in business transactions." The contemplative acts of mystical spiritual concentration, which in Kabbalistic terminology are called unifications (in Hebrew: *yihudim;* singular: *yihud*), need no longer be performed in solitude and retreat from the world; they can also be done in the market place and precisely in those places which seem most removed from the realm of the spirit. It is here that the true Hasid finds the perfect arena for a perfectly paradoxical achievement.

But is this achievement really paradoxical? At this point we must come to grips with the central principle of Buber's interpretation of Hasidism. The teaching which I have just discussed is a fact of intellectual history. But how is it to be understood? What kind of contact with the concrete reality of things does man, following this radically mystical theory, achieve by lifting up the holy sparks? Does he in fact arrive at an intimate acquaintance with the concrete in its actual concreteness, i.e., with "life as it is"? In using this phrase, I am quoting Buber who says with great clarity and conviction that Hasidism "kindled in its followers a joy in the world *as it is,* in life *as it is,* in every hour of life in this world as that hour is," and that it taught a "constant, undaunted, and enthusiastic joy in the here and now."

This far-reaching thesis constitutes the basis of Buber's existentialist interpretation of Hasidism as a teaching of the complete realization of the here and now. It seems to me we can gain a more precise understanding of the truly dialectical nature of the Hasidic teaching if we clarify for ourselves what makes Buber's thesis so dubious. Of course Hasidism in a certain sense knows joy and affirmation of reality—a fact that has never eluded the attention of the many writers on Hasidism. However, the Hasidic doctrine of relation to the "concrete" is more complicated and seems to me far removed from Buber's interpretation. This is quite clear in regard to the twist which Hasidic authors gave to the Kabbalistic doctrine of the uplifting of the sparks, which I should now like to explain with the utmost possible precision.

The teaching of the uplifting of the sparks through human activity does in fact mean that there is an element in reality with which man can and should establish a positive connection, but the exposure or realization of this element simultaneously *annihilates* reality, insofar as "reality" signifies, as it does for Buber, the here and now. For the "undaunted and enthusiastic joy," which, to be sure, Hasidism did demand of its adherents, is not a joy in the here and now. In joy—and we may say with Buber: in all that he does with full concentration—man does not enter into relation with the here and now (as Buber conceives it) but with what is *hidden* in the essentially irrelevant garment of the here and now. Buber's joy in life as it is and in the world as it is seems to me a rather modern idea, and I must say that the Hasidic expressions seem to me to convey a totally different mood. They do not teach us to enjoy life as it is; rather, they advise us—better: demand of us—to extract, I am tempted to say distill, from "life as it is" the perpetual life of God. But this is the salient point: the "extraction" is an act of abstraction. It is not the fleeting here and now to which joy is directed, but the eternal unity and presence of transcendence. Now of course it is just this concept of abstraction in regard to joy and to the uplifting of the sparks to which Buber's interpretation of Hasidism objects. He does away with it because it runs counter to his essential interest in Hasidism as an anti-Platonic, existentialist teaching. Buber says: "Here where we stand the hidden divine life must be made to shine forth." This formula does in fact convey authentic Hasidic teaching, but with an ambiguity of which Buber's readers cannot become aware. For precisely in that act in which we let the hidden life shine forth we destroy the here and now, instead of—as Buber would have it—realizing it in its full concreteness.

Interestingly enough, Buber's statement may be found almost word for word in Kabbalistic writers such as Moses Cordovero, and represents a gnostic thesis whose meaning Hasidic teaching did not alter in the least. When you see a beautiful woman, says Rabbi Dov Baer of Mezritch whom I have already mentioned, you should by no means think of her beauty in its concrete tangible form—i.e., as it exists in the concrete here and now—but disregard its concrete reality and direct your spirit to the divine beauty which shines forth from the concrete phenomenon. Then you will no longer behold the beautiful and seductive here and now which is this woman, but the ideal and eternal quality of beauty itself which is one of God's attributes and one of the spheres of His manifestation; from there you will progress to the contemplation of the source of all beauty in God Himself. Statements of this kind in Hasidic literature are legion. They use the concrete meeting of man with reality as a springboard to transcend reality, not to fulfill it. Their Platonic ring sounds rather different from Buber's exaltation of the here and now, and Hasidic mysticism is not half as this-worldly as Buber's readers must be inclined to suppose. The here and now is transcended and disappears when the divine element makes its appearance in contemplation, and the Hasidim were tireless in deriving this moral from their dicta. As so often in the history of mysticism, here, too, human action is laden with contemplative meaning and thus transformed into a vehicle of the mystical deed.

Moreover, the Hasidic conception of the realization of the concrete, which in the final analysis is what concerns us here, contains an essential element of destruction of which Buber's analysis, as far as I can determine, understandably fails to take notice. The Baal Shem and his followers, however, were quite clearly aware of this element, which recurs again and again in the classical literature. Let me quote only one particularly characteristic statement that is ascribed to the Baal Shem to make clear what is at issue. It was transmitted by Rabbi Wolf of Zhitomir.

The Baal Shem once asked an outstanding scholar about his relation to prayer: "What do you do and where do you direct your thoughts when you pray?" He answered: "I bind myself to everything of individual vitality which is present in all created things. For in each and every created thing there must be a vitality which it derives from the divine effluence. I unite with them when I direct my words to God in order by my prayer to penetrate the highest regions." Then the Baal Shem said to him: "If that is what you do, you destroy the world, for in extracting its vitality and raising it to a higher level, you leave the individual created things without their vitality." He said to him: "But since I bind myself to them, how could I extract their vitality from them?" The Baal Shem replied: "Your own words indicate that your prayer cannot carry much weight, for you do not believe that you have the power to lift their vitality out of them."

Here, then, we have the clear and radical thesis: The actual and final realization of such a communion has a destructive quality. And the solution the author suggests for this dilemma points up the dialectical character of these concepts of communion and lifting up. This act, in which all that is alive in individual things is raised to a higher level, belongs only to the moment and may not last. At the same instant in which the vital force is extracted from things it must flow back into them. Or, as so many Hasidic writers like to put it: It is necessary to reduce things to their nothingness in order to restore them to their true nature. Only genuine adepts are able to perform this esoteric action, as the author is well aware. Buber's opinion that Hasidism renounced esotericism is not at all supported by an analysis of the sayings of the Baal Shem. Nor does such an action, as Buber claims, result in the realization of the concrete in its concreteness. For, as is clearly indicated by the statements of the Baal Shem, it is not of the essence of this act that it is momentary and without duration. That it must be broken off is only accidental, caused by man's decision to discontinue it or his weakness and inability to sustain such a destructive penetration and communion.

As such, this penetration is much more likely to empty the concrete than to fill it totally with concreteness, as Buber would have it. We might perhaps say that the dialogue which the Hasidic author reports could be understood rather well as a dialogue between the Baal Shem and Buber.

The classical literature of Hasidism—the writings of the great disciples of the Baal Shem—contradicts Buber's interpretation also in another way: It consistently treats the individual and concrete existence or phenomenon quite disdainfully. The Hebrew expressions for the concrete, totally in contradiction to what Buber would lead us to suspect, always have a disparaging nuance. Only thus can we also understand why the "stripping off of corporeality," quite in the spirit of mysticism but not at all in the spirit of Buber's interpretation, serves as a high ideal which can be achieved in prayer or meditation. The here and now does indeed present a valuable opportunity for meeting between God and man, but such meeting can occur only where man tears open another dimension in the here and now—an act which makes the "concrete" disappear. In other words, the concrete in Buber's sense does not even exist in Hasidism. The here and now of created existence is not identical with that which shines forth from it once it has become transparent. The assumption of such an identity contradicts the real Hasidic teaching which makes perceiving the divine kernel of all existence dependent precisely on emptying the concrete phenomenon of its own weight and individual significance.

Buber's formulations always blur this essential difference. On the other hand, he establishes a distinction between the Platonic lifting up of the concrete into the realm of ideas and the existential seizing of the holy sparks hidden in all things. But this distinction belongs entirely to Buber's personal interpretation and is by no means as clear-cut in the Hasidic texts. For the Hasidim, realization, the seizing of reality, was a precarious enterprise. Under the strain of such realization, as is contained in the teaching of the lifting up of the sparks, "reality" itself might break apart. For it is not the *concrete* reality of things that appears as the ideal result of the mystic's action, but something of the *Messianic* reality in which all things have been restored to their proper place in the scheme of creation and thereby been deeply transformed and transfigured. Thus, concepts like reality and concreteness mean something totally different for Buber than for the Hasidim. He sometimes uses these terms both for the realm of the here and now and for the realm of transformed existence—a circumstance which has tended to render indistinct the problem posed by his interpretation. Since, in addition, the Hasidim laid great stress on the teaching that human activity is not able to really bring about or reveal the Messianic world—a point which likewise remains unclear in Buber's writings—they were left, in their own view, only with prescribing ways and means for the individual to use the concrete as a vehicle to the abstract and thereby to the ultimate source of all being. Though couched in the language of very personal religion, this may be conventional theology and not nearly as exciting as the new interpretation which Buber has read into it; in any case, it is what Hasidism stood for.

Yet one should not underestimate the possibility that the teaching of the lifting up of the sparks was in practice understood by many Hasidim in a less dialectical fashion than originally intended. Hasidic theory, as presented by the Baal Shem himself and the most significant among the first generations of disciples, never lost its awareness of the destructive consequences which flow from this doctrine and sought to devise ways and means to avoid them. But the complaints of both friend and foe alike testify that the practice was often more primitive than the theory. For many Hasidim lifting up the sparks did in fact mean living a fuller life. They were not concerned with emptying the real by removing the sparks, but with filling it by bringing them in. Here the holy sparks no longer appear as metaphysical elements of divine being, but as subjective feelings of joy and affirmation which are projected into the relation between man and his environment. This, however, is a view that derives not from the theology of the founders of Hasidism but from the mood of some of its followers. And of course it is this popular or vulgar version, which is sometimes (by no means always!) reflected in the world of Hasidic legend, which provides the relative justification for Buber's highly simplified view. But to call this the message of Hasidism seems to me far from the truth.

I have here dealt in detail with one central point in Buber's interpretation of Hasidism. Were we to analyze other important concepts we would face the same task of testing Buber's statements by reference to the theoretical literature of Hasidism. We would then find that the curiously vague and ambiguous terms Buber uses are always almost, but never quite, Hasidic. I can hardly think of a better illustration for this than the following sentence: "In the Hasidic message the separation between 'life in God' and 'life in the world,' the primal evil of all 'religion,' is overcome in genuine, concrete unity." This sentence seems to indicate that man's responsibility is infinitely more important than the dogmatic formulations of rigid institutional religion. But it is a fact that what Buber calls "the primal evil of all religion" asserts itself at the center of Hasidic teaching. Buber's "concrete unity," when applied to Hasidism, is a fiction, for "life in the world" is no longer life in the world when its divine roots appear in contemplation and thereby transform it into "life in God." It is naturally not surprising that, contrary to Buber, the Hasidic writings maintain that fundamental separation which so embitters Buber.

This brings us to a point that is crucial for Buber's interpretation and for the difference between him and the historical phenomenon of Hasidism. To put it bluntly, Buber is a religious anarchist and his teaching is religious anarchism. By that I mean the following: Buber's philosophy demands of man that he set himself a direction and reach a decision, but it says nothing about which direction and which decision. Rather, he says explicitly that such direction and decision can be formulated only in the world of It in which the world of the living I and Thou is objectified and dies. But in the world of living relation nothing can be formulated and there are no commandments. Whether right or wrong, Hasidism could not share this essentially anarchical view since it remained obligated to Jewish tradition. And this tradition presents a teaching in which directions and decisions could be formulated, i.e., a teaching concerning *what* should be done. Only against this background can we understand in its true context the certainly emphatic interest of Hasidism in the *how* of such action. For Buber this world of the *how* is all that has remained. "No longer the established act but the consecration of all action becomes decisive." It is this concept of consecration, which often recurs in Buber's writings, that furnishes the key for his specific type of religious anarchism. This "consecration" is the moral intensity and responsibility which determine the *how* in the relation between man and his action, but not its content. With admirable consistency Buber has always refused to pin himself down on any content of such action, on any *what*. We can therefore understand why references to the Torah and the commandments, which for the Hasidim still meant everything, in Buber's presentation become extremely nebulous. To be sure, Jewish mysticism, which developed a certain conception of the meaning of revelation, greatly expanded the realm to which the Torah, as an ultimate value system, has reference. But it is still identifiable as Torah and that separation, of which Buber speaks so disparagingly, is preserved even in Hasidism. Where the separation of the realms is overcome, it occurs at the expense of "life in the world," as the saying of Rabbi Pinhas of Koretz quoted above shows clearly. Buber's interpretation of the meaning of such Hasidic concepts as "intention" and the "quality of fervor," which accompany man's actions and are supposed to permeate them, may represent a significant and humanly impressive formulation of the basic principle of religious anarchism; but in connection with his interpretation of Hasidism this interpretation isolates a moment, which has its meaning only in the context of other considerations that Buber has neglected, and dissolves it in the completely undetermined and indeterminable.

Buber's interpretation stresses the uniqueness of the task confronting every single individual. "All men have access to God, but each has a different one." This is certainly true, but it is not a new statement of personal religion introduced by Hasidism. Rather, this idea comes originally from the Lurianic Kabbalah, i.e., from that very gnosis at which Buber in his later writings looks so askance. It holds that each individual is enjoined to raise the holy sparks which belong specifically to his spiritual root in the great soul of Adam, the common soul of all mankind. For at one time every soul and soul-root had its special place in this soul of Adam. All that Hasidism did was to formulate this theory in a popular manner and thereby give it an even more personal turn. Thus the Hasidic teaching of the sparks, which in the social and personal environment of man await meeting with him and being lifted up by him, really represents "Kabbalah become ethos."

Another example of the peculiar vagueness in Buber's use of Hasidic concepts is presented by his use of the word *yihud* ("unification"), which he considers of great importance. Following Kabbalistic parlance, the Hasidim use *yihud* to mean a contemplative act by which man binds himself to the spiritual element by concentrating his mind on the holy letters of the Torah, which is also the holy book of nature. Buber, however, asserts that in Hasidism *yihud* is no longer a magic formula or procedure as it is in the Kabbalah. Rather it is "none other than the normal life of man, only concentrated and directed toward the goal of unification." There may also still have been *yihud* in the older sense, but "this magical component never touched the center of Hasidic teaching." Yet I must say that I have been unable to find in the Hasidic writings any new shade in the meaning of this concept. In the older Hebrew literature it always had two meanings, and neither has undergone any change in the Hasidic literature. The first derives from the Kabbalists and always designates some special meditation which is to accompany a specific act, a meditation in which one unites himself with a spiritual reality—be it the soul of a departed saint or its sparks, or be it a name of God or of one of his hypostatized attributes. In this usage the concept also designates the result achieved by such meditation. The second meaning of *yihud,* however, derives above all from the once very famous ethical work of Bahya ibn Pakuda, *The Duties of the Heart,* where it refers to the directing of awareness or of action toward God. In this sense the concept is always used only in the singular. Where it occurs in the plural, it can only have the Kabbalistic meaning which has to do exclusively with contemplation and not, as Buber would have it, with the concrete unity of human life achieved by the intensity of concentration. Such acts of *yihud* are achieved by contemplative communion with the inwardness of the "letters" which are imprinted in all being. In all the sayings of the Baal Shem of which I am aware, the term is used in this precise and technical sense. Thus Buber's translations of many passages on *yihud* are very modern, appealing, and suggestive, but they are not acceptable.

To sum up, the merits of Buber's presentation of Hasidic legends and sayings are indeed very great. Precisely in the mature form of the anecdote, which dominates his later writings, this presentation will in large measure stand the test of time. But the spiritual message he has read into these writings is far too closely tied to assumptions that derive from his own philosophy of religious anarchism and existentialism and have no roots in the texts themselves. Too much is left out in this description of Hasidism, and what is included is overloaded with very personal speculations. Their character may be exalted and they may appeal deeply to the modern mind. But if we would understand the real phenomenon of Hasidism, both in its grandeur and in its decay (which are in many ways connected), we shall have to start again from the beginning.

POSTSCRIPT

When the above analysis was first published, Buber wrote a short reply which appeared at the end of his *Schriften zum Chassidismus* (1963, pp. 991-98). Here he once again commented on the relation of teaching and legend to the life of the community in the history of religions. The following is my response.

I

Buber's statements—which insofar as they touch upon general issues will scarcely encounter any basic opposition—miss the main point in our discussion. The teaching of Hasidism was developed by the immediate disciples of the Baal Shem and the Maggid of Mezritch, using concepts which the first masters had employed themselves—and these were Kabbalistic concepts. At the same time these disciples wrote under the full impact of the new group life, which to a great extent they themselves had helped to create. There is no basis whatever in the Hasidic tradition for the attempt to construct a possible contradiction between the specifics of this group life and the concepts through which it unfolded. Just those writings, in which what Buber calls the epigonic element is least prominent and the original effective impulse attains undistorted expression, characteristically reproduce many maxims of the Baal Shem (quite clearly distinguishable from the style of the disciples), but they are not legends in Buber's sense of the term. The salient point of my critique is that these writings thoroughly contradict Buber's assertions regarding the meaning of Hasidic life as he formulated them in his later writings, and that he silently passes over this contradiction in order to rely on anecdotes which are more susceptible to his own reinterpretation. To be sure, he attempts to make it plausible that these anecdotes could perhaps be as old as the theoretical writings, but this can only rarely be shown, while in many instances just the opposite is demonstrable. It is precisely the analysis of the oldest sources of Hasidic legend which makes this clear. The older and more authentic the historical and social framework within which many of these oldest legends move or are enclosed, the less do they stand in real contradiction to the theoretical writings, produced in the same milieu, at the same time or considerably earlier. Naturally I do not say that the legends are worthless as evidence. What I do say is that Buber's interpretation must be false when for anyone familiar with the texts this interpretation establishes such a contradiction—and this applies to crucial points. Buber's reference to the special task which he has set himself and which has determined his selection of the material and his attitude to the sources makes no difference. Buber does not like it when the obvious subjectivity of his selection is emphasized, and in reply refers to the "reliability of the chooser in carrying out his special task." I am convinced that his selection corresponds as much as possible to the sense of his own message. I am not convinced that the sense of his message, as he formulated it, is that of Hasidism.

II

I should like to add a word about the parallels which Buber draws in his reply between the Hasidic anecdotes and the Zen stories. I do not believe that these parallels can be drawn. The Zen stories are not legends at all, but rather—and this does not appear in Buber's statements—exercises for meditation, and thus they belong to a completely different genre. That they are clothed in the form of a tale does not make them legends. They are exclusively statements which are at first glance totally senseless or in the highest degree paradoxical. The disciples are instructed to meditate on them for weeks or months in order thereby to drive forward to illumination. They transmit a mystical reality which, since it cannot be grasped by maxims, revels in the assertion of ultimate paradoxes. But the Hasidic anecdote, precisely as it has been so masterfully canonized in Buber's new formulations, is an entirely different matter. Its sense and meaning are immediately revealed and they transmit something which can be transmitted. Thus it moves in a totally different sphere of religious experience. I cannot believe that this juxtaposition provides any greater understanding of the specific character of the Hasidic stories. The anecdotal garb of the *koan,* which mentions names and events, is more closely related to the form in which the great teachers of jurisprudence used to give their students seminar assignments than it is to religious legend.

In order to make it clear how little Buber's selection of the Hasidic material may be compared to the category of the provocative and unintelligible Zen utterances, I would like to tell a little story which deals with Buber himself. I once asked Buber why in his writings he had suppressed the significant and unfathomable words regarding the Messianic age that were transmitted in the name of Rabbi Israel of Rizhin (they are quoted in part in the essay "Toward an Understanding of the Messianic Idea in Judaism" in this volume). I shall always remember his reply. He said: because I do not understand them.

The Tradition of the
Thirty-Six Hidden Just Men

THE PUBLICATION of André Schwarz-Bart's novel, *The Last of the Just*, which by its theme and its development gripped so many readers, has directed attention to the Jewish folk legend which forms the basis of the book. This legend, widespread in Jewish folklore, speaks of thirty-six Zaddikim, or just men, on whom—though they are unknown or hidden—rests the fate of the world. The author of this novel gives that tradition a most imaginative twist. According to some Talmudists, he says, it goes back to ancient times. As a novelist Schwarz-Bart is not bound by scholarly conventions and can give free reign to his speculative fantasy. But many readers of the book may have asked themselves what in fact is the source of this legend and what evidence is there for it. The theme has exercised a special attraction on Jewish writers of recent generations, above all on those writing in Hebrew and Yiddish.

What are the historical origins of this legend and how did it develop? It is curious that, despite the wide popularity of this idea in Jewish circles, no scholarly studies of any kind have been written on its development. To be sure, this is less surprising than it may seem at first glance. For as a conception of Jewish folk religion it took definite shape only quite late and one would search for it in vain in the many volumes of inspirational and moralistic literature of the Middle Ages, which were intended to introduce the simple Jew to the message of Judaism.

In the ancient Jewish sources of the tradition, the motif of the thirty-six just men is quite separate from that of the existence of hidden just men. Already in the biblical Proverbs of Solomon we find the saying that the just man is the foundation of the world (Prov. 10:25) and therefore, as it were, supports it. The talmudic tradition has various expressions according to which there are a number of just men in each generation who are equal in dignity to Abraham, Isaac, and Jacob. Most frequently thirty just men are mentioned, a number derived from the mystical numerical interpretation of a word in Genesis 18:18. According to this exegesis, God swore to the patriarch Abraham that the world would never be without thirty men as just as he. Dicta of this kind were ascribed to various Palestinian and Babylonian scholars of the second to fourth centuries, above all to the famous Rabbi Simeon ben Yohai. One of these authorities, Joshua ben Levi, expressed the opinion that if Israel were worthy of it, eighteen of these thirty just men would live in the land of Israel and twelve outside it. Others held the view that it was the non-Jewish peoples that were maintained on account of these thirty just men who either emerged from the Gentiles or at least dwelt among them. These just men protect the world as Abraham did in his day. Other traditions in the Babylonian Talmud refer to forty-five just men who perform this function.

A Babylonian teacher of the fourth century, Abbaye, was the first to introduce the number thirty-six: "The world is never without thirty-six just men who daily receive the Divine Countenance." Here the motif of perceiving divinity, which is granted these just men, replaces that of preserving the world. The explanation for the number thirty-six is also drawn from number mysticism. It rests on an interpretation of the numerical value of a word in Isaiah 30:18: "Happy are they that hope for Him." The numerical value of the Hebrew word "him"—in Hebrew every letter possesses also a numerical value—is thirty-six, so that the verse could be understood as well to mean: "Happy are they who hope for the thirty-six," i.e., who rely on these thirty-six just men.

The exegesis that produced this number of thirty-six just men, which later became so popular, is manifestly so artificial as to cast doubt upon whether Abbaye really derived it from the verse in Isaiah. More likely he took an idea known to him from other sources or views and in this way read it into Scripture in order to find further support for it there. Sofia Amaisenova was the first to express the suspicion—perhaps not to be dismissed out of hand—that this number originates in ancient astrology where the 360 degrees of the heavenly circle are divided into thirty-six units of ten, so-called "deans." A dean-divinity ruled over each segment of the thus divided circle of the zodiac, holding sway over ten days of the year or, in another variation, over ten degrees of the zodiac. Egyptian Hellenistic sources, especially, have provided us with a rich literature concerning the deans and dean-gods. Here the deans were regarded also as watchmen and custodians of the universe, and it is quite conceivable that the number thirty-six, which Abbaye read into Scripture, no longer represented these cosmological powers or forces but rather human figures. A Hebrew manuscript in Munich, which contains astrological inquiries addressed to the figures of the zodiac, proves that in the Middle Ages certain Jewish authors recognized such a relationship of the two spheres. Each sign of the zodiac is divided into three "faces," which produces the classical number of thirty-six deans; each dean is named for one of thirty-six biblical characters from Adam and Enoch to Daniel and Ezra.

During the Middle Ages, in any case, this number thirty-six supplanted all other, older numbers and was also taken over by the Kabbalistic literature. But in neither the ancient Jewish legend nor the later rabbinic and Kabbalistic literature up to the eighteenth century do these thirty-six Zaddikim appear as unknown and hidden. Even where there is a reference to pious individuals who do their work entirely in secret, no connection is established with the motif of the world's preservation by the thirty-six just men. Such legends, concerning just or pious men whose good deeds remain unknown to their fellow men or who practice their virtues under a more or less paradoxical disguise, are very old. The oldest such legend comes from the third century and is recounted in the tractate of the Palestinian Talmud dealing with fast days:

Rabbi Abbahu saw in a dream that if a certain Pentakaka would pray for rain it would fall. The rabbi summoned him and asked: What is your occupation? He answered: Every day I commit five sins (hence probably the name Pentakaka, from the Greek word penta-kaka: five bad deeds). I rent out whores, clean the theater, carry the whores' clothes to the bathhouse for them and dance while beating a drum in front of them. The rabbi asked: And what good have you done? He answered: Once while I was cleaning the theater a woman came and stood behind a pillar weeping. I asked her: What is the matter? She answered: My husband is in prison and I would like to ransom him. So I sold my bed and my blanket and gave her the proceeds with the words: Here is some money, ransom your husband and don't become a whore. The rabbi spoke to him: You are indeed worthy of praying and having your prayer heard.

This ancient legend is the prototype for many stories which were told in the Middle Ages. They are contained, for example, in the collection of legends composed by Nissim ben Jacob in eleventh-century Kairouan in North Africa or in the *Book of the Pious* of Rabbi Judah the Pious who lived in Regensburg and Speyer in the twelfth century. But nowhere in these stories do you find any indication that their heroes belong to a special category of just men whose hiddenness is essential for the fulfillment of their function.

It is however quite possible that this conception arose very early and was transmitted in popular versions of the legend of the thirty-six just men, even though it did not come down to us in written form. As Rudolf Mach first noted, it appears in the Islamic mystical tradition, particularly in places which took over this Jewish conception and in their own way developed it further. According to this tradition God ordained that the saints direct the world. As early as the tenth and eleventh centuries we find in the writings of Islamic mystics that among these saints there are four thousand who are hidden and do not know each other. According to a treatise of the eleventh-century Persian mystic Hudjwiri, they are not even aware of the special distinction of their rank; invariably they are hidden from themselves and from mankind. Still older Islamic sources mention the number of forty saints, who constitute a special category. They live unrecognized by their fellow men while contributing to the continued maintenance of the world through their good deeds. For the present we cannot determine whether this conception originated in a Jewish tradition which had already taken on new form when it penetrated Islamic circles or whether the metamorphosis occurred in Islam and then the tradition returned to Judaism in this new form at an as yet undetermined time. Precisely those Jewish oriental sources which would be most likely to reflect such influence on account of their proximity to Islam afford us no evidence for the presence of this idea. There are just men who conceal their mode of life but nowhere do we find that the continued maintenance of the world depends especially upon them.

On the other hand, it is entirely conceivable that the conception of the hidden just men derives from the folk heritage of the great religious movement which swept German Jewry in the thirteenth century and which is designated German Hasidism (in contrast to the much later Polish variety). The crystallization of the idea would definitely fit in with this group's entire attitude toward life. In any case, it first appears among the

German and Polish Jews, the so-called Ashkenazic Jews of the east. The Yiddish language has even coined a special word for these hidden just men who in popular speech are called "Lamed-vovniks." *Lamed-vav* is the Hebrew numeral for thirty-six. When the Hasidic movement arose in Poland in the eighteenth century this conception was already widespread. Hasidic authors speak frequently of the two categories of Zaddikim: those who are hidden and keep to themselves, and those who are known to their fellow men and to some extent fulfill their task under the critical eye of the public. The just man of the first type is called *nistar,* i.e., hidden; the one of the second type *mefursam,* i.e., known. The hidden just men belong to a higher order because they are not subject to the temptation of conceit which is virtually inseparable from public life. Some of them devote special effort to presenting their fellow men an image of themselves which is in the starkest contrast to their real nature. Others may not themselves be aware of their own nature; they radiate their holiness and righteousness in hidden deeds without even knowing that they belong to those chosen thirty-six. Jewish folklore of the eighteenth and nineteenth centuries, especially in Eastern Europe, was untiring in its elaboration of these aspects of the conception—and the more paradoxical, the better. From this tradition, for example, stem many of the stories which Ernst Bloch tells of such hidden just men in his *Traces.* According to several of these legends, one of the thirty-six hidden men is the Messiah. If the age were worthy of it, he would reveal himself as such. According to other legends, a hidden just man dies the moment he is discovered. There are some wonderful tales of this kind in the writings of the great Hebrew storyteller S. Y. Agnon. It was said of one of the most famous Hasidic saints of the eighteenth century, Rabbi Leib Sores (i.e., the son of Sarah), that he was in secret contact with the hidden just men and provided for their most pressing material needs. Still later this motif was transferred to the founder of the Hasidic movement itself, Israel the Baal Shem.

We know of at least two Kabbalistic books of the eighteenth century whose authors were reputed to belong to the hidden just men: Rabbi Neta of Szinawa and Rabbi Eisik who lived as a ritual slaughterer in the little village of Zurawitz near Przemyšl. In the introductions to their writings, which of course were published only after their deaths, their contemporaries tell of the rumors which circulated regarding their true character. When about fifty years ago some enthusiastic Hasidim in Russia forged an entire correspondence of the Baal Shem in order to provide, as it were, authentic material for the legends surrounding him, they did not forget to include more or less moving letters which were supposedly exchanged between the master and several of the hidden just men. All in all, the collections of Hasidic legends from the nineteenth century have preserved for us a considerable number of such traditions and anecdotes concerning the Lamedvovniks. Naturally nothing could be further removed from this tradition than the conception which Schwarz-Bart devised with poetic license according to which the condition of belonging to the thirty-six just men can be a family inheritance (and conscious at that!) which is passed on from father to son. There are no families of hidden just men. The hidden just man—if he is anything at all—is your neighbor and mine whose true nature we can never fathom; the conception cautions us against passing any moral judgment on him. It is a warning which is even more impressive because it is sustained by a somewhat anarchic morality: Your neighbor may be one of the hidden just men.

The Star of David:
History of a Symbol

SYMBOLS arise and grow out of the fruitful soil of human emotion. When a man's world possesses spiritual meaning for him, when all of his relations to the world around him are conditioned by the living content of this meaning—then, and only then, does this meaning crystallize and manifest itself in symbols. A reality without tension, a reality which in the eye of the beholder contains no specific intent, cannot address him in the language of symbols. It remains mute, unformed matter. Certainly a very high degree of tension is required in order to crystallize the variegated phenomena of this world into simple, unitary, and characteristic forms. Something of the secret of man is poured into his symbols; his very being demands concrete expression. The great symbols serve to express the unity of his world.

If this be true for the individual, it is true to an even greater extent for the symbols which are used by a group, a community, or a people. A symbol which expresses the temper of a community encompasses that particular world. Anything in that world can become a symbol; it need only have something of the spiritual "charge," of the intuitive heritage which lends the world meaning, gives it character, and reveals its mystery. The community lays hold of some detail of its world, apprehends the totality in it, and derives from it and through it that totality and its content. The more such a detail contains within it of the specific character of that community's world, the more is it suited in the eyes of the community to become a symbol.

From this it follows that a symbol must be directly comprehensible. Research and examination must not be necessary in order to understand it. It is precisely the fact that this meaning appears through the symbol, in the most compact form and yet in its totality, that makes it a symbol. Despite all their profundity, symbols may not pose riddles. A symbol is not worthy of its name if it appears to a person, especially one within the community, who participates in its emotional life, as a riddle which must be solved and commented on. Such a symbol does not fulfill its function of transmitting to the beholder an entire world or an entire tradition in the language of intuition and metaphor. A symbol which possesses some of the qualities of a secret code, which becomes comprehensible only to those who delve into it with the tools of research, may be of interest to antiquarians and lovers of complex allegories; but it is doubtful whether it can speak to a living group and awaken within it that impulse which is released neither by logical interpretation nor assiduous meditation, but by lightning-like illumination.

Symbols contain emotional force even when they crystallize and encompass a world view which is essentially and basically rational, like, for example, the hammer and sickle which are the emblem of the Soviet Union. Just that utmost concentration of meaning which is achieved in concrete representation lends the symbol an emotional note even when the meaning expressed by it is proudly acclaimed for its thoroughgoing rationality. Thus the symbol transmits something of the emotional life crystallized within it to the consciousness of those who regard it with the eyes of believers. Conversely, it is also able to gain for itself an additional and ever deepening meaning from the living emotion of those whom it addresses. Perhaps one may even conjecture that symbols, which do not possess any meaning within a particular historical or spiritual context and therefore seem inappropriate to express symbolically the life of a community, receive a certain secondary meaning as a result of the intensity with which people under certain circumstances become attached to them.

Such considerations are forced upon us in view of the recent debates regarding the *magen david,* the Shield of David or Star of David. The question was raised whether this symbol should be incorporated into the flag of the new State of Israel, a state which derives its meaning as much from the Jews' vision of their future as from the unspeakable horrors of their most recent past.

This subject of the Shield of David seems problematic in every way. The scholarly and popular literature which has dealt with it consists of a chaos of assertions, some correct and others fantastic. Unfortunately, one cannot rely at all on previous writers, who mix their own, in part highly fanciful, explanations with

the actual tradition of the Shield of David. Since they lack a
clear idea of the real tradition, each one interprets it to his own
liking. One says: We have before us a symbol of Judaism, i.e.,
of the religious content and intellectual world of monotheism;
another says: It is nothing but a symbol of Jewish "statehood"
or "sovereignty," and just for this reason it deserves a place in
the emblem of the State of Israel. One declares it a distinctive
mark of the wars of David's kingdom, the other considers it a
symbol of harmony and eternal peace, the union of opposites
and their neutralization in the principle of unity. All they have
in common is the confusion they fall into when they try to prove
an alleged traditional meaning for this symbol. They all get lost
in idle talk and endless speculations which correspond to nothing
in the Jewish tradition. To be sure, the Shield of David is a
peculiar symbol which invites meditation, and praised be he who
has not locked the gates of association.

II

What, then, is the true history of the Star of David in Jewish
tradition? Is it rooted in that tradition? Did it for larger or
smaller circles possess dignity as the symbol of Judaism, or at
least as a Jewish symbol? And if not—when did it receive this
function and status, and as a result of what circumstances? If
we seek to clarify these questions, we must distinguish between
the appearance of the sign itself, i.e., the figure of the two interlocked equilateral triangles, and the history of the designation
which it bears today as the Shield of David. The symbol and
its designation were not always connected. The history of the
symbol, its career and its reception by Judaism, are however
of great interest, especially if we remove the inventions and fantasies which certain recent Jewish scholars have woven around it.

   The hexagram is not a Jewish symbol, much less "the symbol
of Judaism." None of the marks of a true symbol nor its manner
of origin, described above, apply to it. It expresses no "idea,"
awakens no primeval associations which have become entwined
with the roots of our experiences, and it does not spontaneously
comprise any spiritual reality. It calls to mind nothing of biblical
or rabbinical Judaism; it arouses no hopes. Insofar as it had
any connection at all with the emotional world of a pious Jew
it was on the level of fears which might be overcome by magic.
Until the middle of the nineteenth century no scholar or Kab-

balist got the idea of trying of detect in the Star anything like
the secret of its Jewish meaning. It does not appear at all in
books on the religious life nor in the entire literature of Hasidism.
And this was the case not because such meaning was assumed
and not considered problematical, but rather because no one even
dreamt of such meaning.

The figure of the hexagram, with its two interlocked triangles, is to be found among many peoples and is often associated
with another figure, the pentagram or five-pointed star. In 1918
the Portuguese ethnographer J. Leite de Vasconcellos published
a monograph, which has remained nearly unknown, entitled *Sig-
num Salomonis.* He gathered rich material regarding this dissemination of the Seal of Solomon in a wide variety of cultures
and ages outside the sphere of Judaism, whether it was used as
a protective sign in magic or as a simple ornament. The fact that
it occasionally appears in such ornamental fashion on Jewish
monuments still does not make it a "Jewish symbol." Even as
decoration it rarely appears on Jewish antiquities. Its first certain
occurrence can be established on the seal of one Joshua ben
Asaiah, which dates from the late monarchical period (about 600
B.C.). The hexagram next appears—with a clearly indicated point
at its center—only much later among the various ornamental
motifs on a frieze that decorates the well-known synagogue of
Capernaum (second or third century). But the same frieze
displays a swastika right next to it, and no one will on that
account claim that the swastika might be a Jewish symbol. The
hexagram also appears in conjunction with the pentagram as a
geometrical ornament on the ruins of the old Galilean synagogue
of Tell Hum. Assyrian, and later also Phoenician and Hebrew,
seals often display a six-pointed star with six rays beaming forth
from its center, leading some authors to confuse it with the hexagram which geometrically represents a completely different configuration. Such seals also contain pentagrams and other signs and
figures, none of which can be regarded as a specifically Jewish
symbol. What is supposedly a hexagram has been discovered
chiseled into the wall of a shrine at Megiddo from the period of
the Kingdom of Israel. But the photograph shows the emblem
has suffered so much weather damage that it is quite possible to
ascribe this interpretation to the fantasy of those who unearthed
it or to a false reconstruction. On the other hand, there is a
genuine pentagram which appears on the seals of oil cruses of the
fifth century B.C., which may have belonged to the treasury of the

Jerusalem Temple. It is impossible to say whether this has some specific significance.

A large number of Jewish emblems appearing in different contexts have been preserved from the Hellenistic Age where they always refer back to biblical rituals or have been developed from them. (They are discussed at length in Erwin Goodenough's monumental work, *Jewish Symbols in the Greco-Roman Period.*) But the pentagram and the hexagram are both totally absent. And it is exactly here that we can speak of real Jewish symbolism, dominated by the Menorah, the seven-branched candelabrum which more than any other is a genuine and widespread symbol of Judaism. This awareness of the towering symbolic significance of the Menorah was preserved also in later centuries. Yet, a second emblem, whose origins need not be discussed here, appears ever more clearly by its side. It is that of the two lions holding onto the Tree of Life or the Ark of the Torah which is associated with it. These emblems possess a living relationship to the spontaneously apprehensible contents of Jewish imagination. As for the hexagram, it appears as a decorative motif—not as a Christian symbol—on a fairly large number of Christian churches of the early Middle Ages. But it hardly ever occurs on medieval synagogues or on Jewish ritual objects of this period. Precisely this appearance of the sign on Christian churches long before its appearance on synagogues should serve as a warning to members of the far-flung clan of "Interpretobold Symbolizetti Allegoriovitch Mystificinski." We can therefore understand the sigh uttered by Jacob Reifmann, one of the greatest scholars of the Jewish Enlightenment, when nearly one hundred years ago he began to suspect that the Shield of David was a foreign shoot in the vineyard of Israel. To such symbolism he applied the verse from Scripture: "They mingled themselves with the nations and learned their works" (Ps. 106:35).

There has never been any lack of attempts to provide the Shield of David with a distinguished genealogy. Thus Moses Gaster claimed that it was introduced into Judaism by Rabbi Akiba, the greatest rabbi of the second century. Akiba allegedly used it as a Messianic symbol in the war of liberation conducted by Bar Kokhba, the "son of a star," against the Emperor Hadrian. This is as much a product of fantasy as the views which trace it back to the *Zohar* of the thirteenth century or to the great sixteenth-century Kabbalist Isaac Luria. In reality this emblem does not appear at all in these writings, let alone as a symbol of Judaism. In the extensive Lurianic literature the hexagram, designated as "Seal of Solomon," appears only once. It occurs on an amulet where it is in no way connected with the ideas developed in these writings. Regardless, the common reference works on Judaism are full of nonsense about how the general use of the Shield of David originated with the Lurianic Kabbalah. Max Grunwald, who has spun out many fantasies concerning this emblem, writes in 1923: "This international sign was not accepted as a specifically Jewish symbol until Isaac Luria. He sees in it the image of the *adam kadmon* [the primeval man in the world of the divine ten spheres or *sefirot*]: the six triangles plus the hexagon in the center represent the seven lower spheres while the upper three are to be conceived as lying above it." One wonders in vain where he got this arrangement; nothing in any Kabbalistic text corresponds to it. Béla Vajda even tries to convince us that "the meaning of the Shield of David, as it is described in the *Zohar* [which has no reference to it at all!], strongly influenced Luria's powerful fantasy; he found that it depicted his world view with amazing force." Such nonsense is copied from one book to another and one wonders why nobody took the trouble to open the Lurianic writings themselves and look there for the symbol and its alleged interpretation. Of course that would have meant discovering that all these discussions were built on air.

The answer to the question of how these scholars came to confound their own interpretations with Lurianic ideas is clear, simple, and a bit funny. They claim that when Luria was prescribing the ritual for the Seder, which inaugurates the Passover holiday, he determined that the objects on the Seder plate recalling the Egyptian slavery be arranged in such a manner that they form a hexagram. The truth of the matter is that this text says something quite different, without making the least reference to the Shield of David. The six objects on the plate, which for Luria correspond to six of the divine powers, are to be arranged in the form of two triangles, one under the other, as in the hierarchical order of the so-called *sefirot*-tree. They are not intertwined at all, but simply arranged in parallel fashion vertically, so that there is no similarity whatever to a hexagram. But when in the nineteenth century the Shield of David began to be used to an ever-increasing extent on nearly every Jewish cultic object, "artistic" Seder plates were also produced according to modern taste. The arrangement introduced by Luria (which is also mentioned in many editions of the Seder ritual, the so-called

Passover Haggadah) was then quite arbitrarily transposed into the form of a hexagram. The emblem is entirely missing on older Seder plates as well as on those that date from the eighteenth century. Instead there are very different decorative elements, such as for example the favorite twelve signs of the zodiac, the twelve tribes of Israel, and the like. The modern pseudo-historians of the Shield of David confused the real Lurianic conceptions with the modern design on the Seder plate which became quite popular in the nineteenth century; they then projected the modern arrangement and its representation in the form of a hexagram back onto the Lurianic Kabbalah.

III

The real history of the Shield of David and its emergence in Judaism is to be found in a totally different sphere from the conceptual realm of Kabbalistic theosophy and symbolism. In part it leads us back into the world of Jewish magic, which, to be sure, later enjoyed the designation "practical Kabbalah," but which was always only very loosely and externally linked with the conceptual realm and the theoretical doctrines of the Kabbalists. I am here using the term "practical Kabbalah" in accordance with the linguistic usage of the Kabbalistic literature itself; during the last two generations too many authors have applied it to the Lurianic system in a totally distorted and derivative sense, attempting to distinguish it from the allegedly speculative Kabbalah of Luria's contemporary and teacher Moses Cordovero. Jewish magic, which employs amulets and talismans, is of course much older than the theosophical speculations of the actual Kabbalah.

In this area there was always a powerful reciprocal influence between Jews and non-Jews, for nothing is more international than magic. Magic signs and figures travel from one people to another just as "holy," i.e., incomprehensible, names and their combinations in learned and popular magic wander back and forth among the nations and religions, often distorted beyond the point of recognition. Such magic figures—sometimes of a totally expressionistic character, as in *Dr. Faustus' Hell-Charm*—are mostly known in the magic literature of the Near East and of Europe as "seals." This is due both to their early use on signet rings—the production of such magic rings at one time constituted an entire métier, for which we still possess manuals—and to the widespread conception that with the help of such signs a person could "seal" himself and gain protection from the attacks of spirits and demons.

Two of the most important figures to be "charged" with such magic were the hexagram ✡ and the pentagram ☆ . In practice the transition from one to the other was extremely easy. Various specimens of the same amulet will often bear in the same place at one time a pentagram and at another a hexagram. It is difficult to say for how long certain definite names have been used for several of the most common seals. The Arabs, who in general took a stupendous interest in all occult sciences, made many such terms especially popular, just as they also dealt systematically with magic before the "practical Kabbalists." But just these names, Seal of Solomon and Shield of David, which are often used interchangeably for the two emblems, go back to pre-Islamic Jewish magic. They did not originate among the Arabs who, incidentally, know only the designation Seal of Solomon.

The Seal of Solomon is manifestly connected with the legend (already attested in Josephus) concerning Solomon's dominion over the spirits. This legend also speaks early of a Solomonic signet ring on which originally, to be sure, was engraved not a magic emblem but the ineffable name of God, the tetragrammaton. The power of this signet ring is described with great aplomb in texts of Jewish—and later also Christian—magic, such as the *Testament of Solomon,* a Greek manual of Jewish and Judeo-Christian magic which in its original elements is very old. As yet we cannot say for sure when the inscription on this wondrous signet ring was replaced by one of the two figures. We only know this much for certain: It happened before the sixth century, i.e., before the rise of Islam. Karl Preisendanz has described an amulet of which copies exist in the British Museum and in Leningrad. The Christian pictures on the obverse side enable us to date it fairly exactly in the sixth century. The reverse side depicts among other things two lions which hold a very well executed hexagram; on the obverse side this hexagram is specifically referred to as "Seal of Solomon." The picture of the two lions is an originally Jewish motif, which was then also taken over by Christians. It cannot yet be determined whether this name for the hexagram appeared here for the first time among Jews or among Christians, from whom the Arabs then adopted it.

But about the same time the series of conceptions may already have been familiar which connected the hexagram with the

name of David. The basis for this is the inscription on a tombstone in Taranto in Southern Italy which certainly originated no
later than the sixth century. There, according to the inscription,
lies the grave of the wife of one "Leon son of David," and a hexagram is chiseled in front of the name David. It would be difficult
to assume that this is a mere coincidence. On the other hand, the
sign does not recur on any other Jewish tombstone of the Middle
Ages, not even in connection with the name David. A double
pentagram occurs at the end of the first line on the monument
of a Spanish Jewess of Tortosa, which belongs to approximately
the same period, but its significance in the context remains
unclear.

What the nature of the connection between the hexagram and
the name of King David may have been can be easily explained.
We possess a number of medieval Jewish magical texts which
speak of a shield of David which provided him with magic protection. The oldest of these texts probably originates in the
Orient or in Southern Italy. It contains an explanation of a
secret alphabet in the so-called "star-script" often used for amulets. This particular alphabet is supposed to be that of Metatron,
the highest of all the angelic princes. It has been preserved in a
number of Hebrew manuscripts. One of these letters, which
looks like this 𝖵 (similar to a Latin V which has three small
circles at its three corners), is said to have been constructed in
the manner of a shield "for King David had a shield on which
the Great Name of God containing seventy-two letters—a combination of holy names which according to an ancient Jewish
legend made possible Israel's redemption from Egypt—was engraved and which helped him to win all of his wars." Furthermore, it says here that a verse from the Bible was also engraved
on it, in which the first letters of each word made up the name
Maccabee. This shield was then passed on until it reached Judah
the Maccabee, hero of the Maccabean wars. Of a similar nature
are other magic texts in circulation among German Jews in the
thirteenth century. For example, there is an explanation of the
seventy secret names of Metatron, which however varies in that
under the Great Name of God another name is inscribed: Taftafiyah, one of these secret names of Metatron. "And when you go
out to war and your enemies attack you, pronounce this name
and you will remain unharmed." At what point this name,
whether as Maccabee or as Taftafiyah, was conjoined with the
figure of the hexagram, thus explaining its designation as Shield

of David, we cannot determine on the basis of the sparse material which has so far become known. That tombstone in Taranto could be the earliest evidence of such an association. It remains strange that, as we shall see, nearly 700 years passed before the designation as Shield of David could be unequivocably attested for the hexagram from Hebrew literature.

But whatever the name may have been under which the pentagram or the hexagram was known, it had one and only one purpose in its career as magic: to serve as protection against demons. In this connection it also appears in the magic versions of the *mezuzah* which circulated widely from earliest medieval times down into the fourteenth century. The *mezuzah* is a capsule which contains a certain passage from the Torah written on a strip of parchment. Following a rabbinic prescription which goes back long before the Christian era, it has been attached to the doorposts of every Jewish household. Although, to begin with, scarcely intended for magic protection, at the hands of adepts in magic the *mezuzah* could easily be made to take over this function as well. Rabbi Eliezer of Metz (twelfth century) reports that it is a "common practice to add seals and the names of angels at the end of the Bible verses contained in the *mezuzah* for the sake of the increased security of the home. This is neither commanded nor prohibited; it simply serves as additional protection." But there were also other authorities who unhesitatingly decided that the *mezuzah* must be written with these additions in magic style. Maimonides vigorously attacks the extremists who inscribe the names and seals not only at the edges of the actual text of the *mezuzah* but even interpose them in the text and between the lines. According to him, they have lost their prospect for salvation "because they have perverted the great commandment regarding the proclamation of God's unity, the honor and love of Him [of which the text in the *mezuzah* speaks] to the end of making it an amulet for selfish purposes." However, the seals in these magic versions of the *mezuzah,* a number of which have been preserved, are mostly nothing more than drawings of a hexagram; sometimes, as in the case of a *mezuzah,* from the Elkan Adler collection, there are up to twelve such hexagrams.

Thus, this emblem began its career in larger Jewish circles not as a symbol of monotheism but as a magic talisman against evil spirits. Among the masses, that remained its principal significance down to the first half of the nineteenth century. The above-mentioned magic version of the *mezuzah* no doubt originated in

Babylonia or Palestine of the early Middle Ages, although we cannot determine in which of the two lands. No document of this period which describes the preparation of the magic *mezuzah* uses a particular name for the seal, neither Seal of Solomon nor Shield of David. Although all reference works insist that the Karaite scholar Judah Hadasi (mid-twelfth century) first called the hexagram Shield of David, this particular designation is in fact an addition of the printer who published Hadasi's work in Southern Russia in 1836.

In the course of time the magic *mezuzah* fell into desuetude. But the two forms of the Seal of Solomon, the pentagram and the hexagram, were preserved in the occult literature of all three monotheistic religions. A glance at manuals of sorcery from the Renaissance, such as the *Clavicula Salomonis* or *Dr. Faustus' Hell-Charm* and similar products of the Faustus literature, shows that they were used in many connections. Until the seventeenth century the hexagram does not appear very frequently, by either of its two names, on Jewish amulets or in the descriptions of such amulets in occult manuscripts. A manuscript of such instructions, which was put together in Italy about 1550, contains on the title page a figure which displays two intertwined hearts and several Shields of David. Only a little later (already in a manuscript of 1586) the tradition of Isaac Luria's students in Safed knows of a "general talisman" which it describes as a hexagram and designates as the Seal of Solomon. Yet a Judeo-German manuscript written about 1600 (now in Jerusalem) calls the pentagram the "Shield of David with five points"—which shows the continuing instability of the terminology. Beginning in the sixteenth century, many such amulets displaying a hexagram achieved considerable popularity. This was especially true of a talisman to ward off fires, which appears again and again in all kinds of places, in literature as well as on old houses and the like; its occurrences have often been described.

IV

Aside from its uses for magic, the hexagram was also employed since early Arabic times purely for decoration. This was quite in keeping with the tradition of ornamentation so beloved by the Arabs. The *Masorah* (the traditions concerning the text of the Bible) in oriental Bible manuscripts is sometimes presented in such figures. In addition to the figure of the Menorah, which represents a genuine Jewish symbol, a hexagram or an octogram are also used. D. Günzburg and V. Stassof in their work *L'orne-ment hébraïque* (Berlin, 1905) reproduced such ornaments, written in miniature script. The validity of the editors' ascription of these texts to the ninth century remains doubtful; more likely they originated in Egypt and belong to the early eleventh century.

From the Orient such ornaments in Bible manuscripts traveled also to Europe. Thus we have a Hebrew Bible written in Germany in 1298 that belongs to the Paris National Library and was displayed in 1960 at the "Synagogua" exhibition in Recklinghausen; it contains at the end of the manuscript a hexagram in highly intertwined form. The Middle Ages displayed a peculiar preference for presenting the hexagram in a sloping position. This is true both for its ornamental use on Christian churches (for example on the marble bishop's throne in the cathedral built in Anagni about 1226) and also in Hebrew manuscripts. In this position it appears splendidly executed among the geometrical ornaments on a special page at the end of the so-called Kennicott Bible of the Bodleian in Oxford, which was written shortly before the expulsion of the Jews from Spain and was illustrated by a Jewish artist, Joseph ibn Hayyim.

The emblem was also used as an ornament for the seals which public officials sometimes added to their signature on documents. But this is true in equal measure of Jews and Christians. The earliest evidence of such use comes from the instance of a Christian notary in Barcelona in 1190. Documents of 1226 regarding transactions of Aragonese Jews are signed by a Christian notary of the city with a hexagram. The same is done there in 1248 by a Jewish financial official (bailiff). Since his name was Vidal Solomon, we may suppose that he selected this sign as Seal of Solomon. Without any connection with names of David or Solomon, it also appears on the seal of a German Jew who performed the official function of financier for the Archbishop of Trier; his seal occurs on a document from the year 1347. The name Jacob ben Rabbi Nethanel (in the Latin text: Daniel) is written around a circle containing a hexagram which at its center has a star shining with six rays. It is the only example as yet known of this usage on the seals of German Jews of the period.

Until the thirteenth century there is no unequivocal evidence that the hexagram was brought into connection with the legend of David's shield mentioned above. But it can be shown with certainty from its first provable appearance in Jewish literature that the new terminology arose out of this connection. The first Kabbalist to speak of the Shield of David in connection with David's wars and to refer overtly to that legend is Joseph Gikatilla in his *Gates of Righteousness* (1280-90). Like the old source, Gikatilla in a very popular old Jewish prayer also juxtaposes this magic shield with the predicate of God as "Shield of David." But he gives no description of its appearance. This changes a few years later. Shortly after 1300 a Kabbalistic work was composed in Spain by the name of *Sefer ha-Gevul* (*The Book of the Border*). Its author was David ben Judah, on his father's side a grandson of the great Catalan Kabbalist Moses ben Nahman, and on his mother's side a descendant of Judah the Pious, the famed leader of medieval German Hasidism. His work has survived only in manscript; it is a commentary to a part of the *Zohar.* Here we find the figure of the hexagram in two places, both times designated in the superscription explicitly as Shield of David. Beneath the drawing is the magic name Taftafiyah, just as in the above-mentioned descriptions of the Shield of David in the occult texts of German Jewry from the thirteenth century. Some of the manuscripts of the book have in this place pentagrams instead of hexagrams. On the other hand, this connection of the hexagram with the angelic name Taftafiyah has been preserved in collections of magical instructions and amulets from the fifteenth to seventeenth centuries. Such is the case, for example, in the manuscripts of the encyclopedia of the practical Kabbalah which the Italian Kabbalist Moses Zacuto compiled in the seventeenth century, and in which the emblem otherwise plays no role. Later on, the angelic name was often replaced by the divine name Shaddai, and silver amulets with this drawing and inscription were very common among oriental and European Jews. But the relationship between the emblem and the Shield of David derives from the connection with the older form.

It is of interest in this regard that in the late Middle Ages an entirely different tradition began to circulate about the emblem on King David's shield. Isaac Arama, a famous Spanish Jewish writer, in 1470 claimed that Psalm 67 was engraved in the form of a Menorah on David's escutcheon. So here we have the noteworthy combination of the Menorah with the motif of the Shield of David, though not in the sense in which that term is used later. Nonetheless, one gets the feeling here that the Shield of David must have become as legitimate a symbolic representation of Judaism as the Menorah. Beginning in the fifteenth century the custom of writing Psalm 67 in the form of a seven-branched candelabrum became very widespread. Often it is even referred to as the Menorah Psalm. It began to appear, written in this form, in a great variety of places, for example on the front of the precentor's desk in the synagogue; the Kabbalists rapturously praised its specific effect as a protective talisman. About 1580 a booklet appeared in Prague entitled *The Golden Menorah*. At the end it says: "This psalm, together with the Menorah, alludes to great things . . . and when King David went out to war, he used to carry on his shield this psalm in the form of a Menorah engraved on a golden tablet and he used to meditate on its secret; and thus he was victorious." But it seems that the hexagram as a sign charged with magic exercised a greater attraction on the Shield of David until it finally defeated the Menorah on the battlefield of modern Jewish symbolism.

The great attraction of the Shield of David for the mystics is further indicated by the later legend which the Egyptian chronicler Joseph Sambari relates as late as 1676, concerning David Reubeni. Posing as the representative of independent Jewish tribes in Arabia, Reubeni around 1530 made such a great impression on the Jews of Italy because he sought to combine Messianism with worldly, even military, exploits. "He made flags and produced a shield on which holy names were written and declared it the shield of David, the king of Israel, which he had used to wage God's wars. It is said that this shield is still today preserved in the synagogue of Bologna." But we do not learn the form in which the "holy names" were arranged on the shield and we have no proof that the shape of this shield of David was the one we know today.

After its first appearance about 1300, we find the designation Shield of David in place of Seal of Solomon here and there in manuscript collections of "practical Kabbalah" even before the expulsion from Spain. In 1506 the author of *Shushan Sodot,* a Kabbalistic compilation made from earlier sources, mentions the preparation of a magic ring bearing the "figure of the Shield of David." He does not indicate what the figure looks like, apparently because the shape is already familiar to his readers. The sign appears frequently on the amulets of a famous magician in Poland, Rabbi Joel Baal-Shem (ca. 1650), and he is familiar with its name as well. Eventually it also became known among the Christians, especially in Germany and Italy, insofar as they were interested in Jewish things. Perhaps the rise of the new designation also influenced the gradually increasing differentiation in terminology, as the Seal of Solomon comes to designate the pentagram, whereas previously it could be used for both figures. As late as 1674, the Christian Hebraist Johann Christoph Wagenseil maintained that in the linguistic usage of German Jews the hexagram was considered the Seal of Solomon. Since the beginning of the eighteenth century, however, we find the expression Shield of David with its fixed meaning, and even Christians begin to employ it in this sense.

In 1708 two disputations by David Theodor Lehmann appear in Wittenberg, entitled *de Clypeo Davidis*. Latin and German pamphlets of the period present allegorical interpretations in the spirit of the alchemists, such as *Naturae naturantis et naturatae Mysterium or The Secret of Nature in the Shield of David,* published in 1724 in Berleburg, a well-known center of Christian theosophy. Such explanations were further suggested by the use of alchemistic symbolism. The one triangle was regarded as a sign for water and the reverse triangle as a sign for fire; the interpenetrating triangles could then represent the harmony of opposing elements. Many alchemists were of the opinion that this interpenetration produces "fiery water" (*esh-mayyim*), and used the old talmudic pun on the Hebrew word for heaven, *shamayyim*. Christian theosophists of this period, who enjoy using the language of alchemy, speak a great deal of this "fiery water" in connection with the formation of the Shield of David or "signet-star."

Such interpretations, however, were not common among the Jewish authors of the time. Instead we find that they employ interpretations which make this sign the distinctive mark of the Davidic house and thus connect magic with the Kabbalistic symbolism of the "kingdom of David." Among the Kabbalists this "kingdom" is a symbol of the tenth *sefirah* in the tree of the ten emanations or potencies by which the Godhead manifests itself. This *sefirah* is represented in the upper world by the corpus mysticum of the "Congregation of Israel," in the lower, however, by the "kingdom of David." Abraham Hayyim Cohen of Nikolsburg, a Moravian Kabbalist of the first half of the eighteenth century and the son of an influential Sabbatian preacher, writes that there was a difference between the escutcheon of the kings of the Northern Kingdom of Israel and that of the Davidic House in Judah. While the former had a simple triangle as their coat of arms, the kings of the House of David had a hexagram, thereby indicating that they belonged to the sphere of "kingdom."

This symbolism now recurs in a most peculiar connection. The career of the Shield of David as magic not only reaches its height, but it moves beyond the realm of magic to become a symbol of the vision of the Messianic redemption, which the followers of the Kabbalistic Messiah Sabbatai Zevi believed they had already begun to detect. This new shift is most evident in the famous amulets from Metz and Hamburg written by Rabbi Jonathan Eibeschütz. After 1750 they caused a real scandal within Central European Jewry. It seemed simply incredible that one of the greatest talmudic scholars of the age should have given these cryptographically sealed amulets to pregnant women and thereby declared himself an adherent of the mystical heresy of the followers of Sabbatai Zevi. (This debate still divides and excites a lot of people today!) Insofar as they became known and were published by his critics, all of these amulets contain the Shield of David; in fact it is the only emblem that appears. In its center there are various inscriptions such as simply the word "Seal," or "Seal of MBD," "Seal of the God of Israel," and the like. In his defense, Rabbi Jonathan tried to hide behind a purely magical interpretation of the amulets; he denied both their Messianic symbolism and that his cryptograms could be deciphered as Sabbatian confessions. He retreated to the claim that all of the words are only magical names derived from old sacred texts without meaning or import. They may not be deciphered and interpreted as complete sentences in order to obtain some conceivable connection of meaning. His critics, however, saw the matter very differently. They ascribed Rabbi Jonathan's predilection for the Shield of David on his amulets to his regarding it a Messianic symbol of the arrival of redemption embodied in Sabbatai Zevi. They compared the variant forms of the inscriptions on the amulets and explained signs like MBD as an abbreviation of Messiah ben David and the like. It can hardly be denied that the interpretations of the amulets in this sense are downright convincing, just as it is not surprising that Rabbi Jonathan, like most Sabbatians, did not want to reveal his secret and therefore denied the reproaches. So we have two alternatives: If Rabbi Jonathan was not a secret Sabbatian, then his amulets have no symbolic significance whatever and represent only a pitiful hocus-pocus. But if he was a Sabbatian, then we would have to admit that the Shield of David was a very significant symbol for his secret vision of redemption, even if, for the time being, it remained a very private and esoteric symbol. It was not only the seal or escutcheon of David, but also that of the "Son of David," who is the Messiah. We have the identical symbolism of the Shield of David in the same period also in the work of a Polish Kabbalist, Isaiah the son of Joel Baal-Shem.

We may say that this transition to a new meaning of the Shield of David has been rather exciting to present-day observers. The modern interpretation of the emblem as a symbol of redemption, which still determined the title (and the title-page drawing) of Franz Rosenzweig's *Star of Redemption,* owes its initial rise to the stammerings of the Sabbatians about the redemption to which letter permutations on these amulets bear secret witness. It is more than doubtful whether the fathers of the Zionist movement, when they emblazoned the Shield of David on the flag of Jewish rebirth, had any idea that in this respect as well they were in harmony with the secret intentions of those great Sabbatians for whom orthodoxy and heresy were so strongly intertwined. Again and again their opponents badgered the Zionists about their alleged pseudo-Messianism and compared their venture to that of the Sabbatians. Thus I am sure the discovery of this secret family tree of their symbol would have been a thorn in the side of many Zionists also, though others, who took no offense at such a tie, would more likely have found it a mark of honor. In any case, the adherents of dialectics—which operates also in the growth of symbols—should be very pleased.

V

The second line of development, which has played a role in the dissemination of the Shield of David to wider circles, ran a very different course. It is connected with the already mentioned ornamental use of the sign, and especially with its utilization on the official seals of several Jewish communities. Here also belongs its use as a printer's mark, which A. Yaari studied in detail in his work on Hebrew printer's marks. This usage, too, was at first not very common. Until the beginning of the nineteenth century, it appears only in a few places. About 1492 Eliezer Toledano used it in a Lisbon edition of the Pentateuch, which only recently has been recognized as an incunabulum. The printer David ibn Nahmias in Constantinople used it beginning in 1493, and not necessarily on account of its association with his own name. Above all it appears in Prague on several of the earliest

Hebrew publications, for example on the title page of the first such book which was published there at the end of 1512. All kinds of figures appear on this title page: the water pitcher of the Levites, lions, a stag, and a very large Shield of David which takes up the most space. Above it and beneath it is a regal crown. Likewise, the title page of a 1522 Prague prayer book for the festivals (*mahzor*) bears the escutcheon of the city next to a second coat of arms inscribed with a curved Shield of David. On a book printed there in 1540, a cherub holds in his hand such a coat of arms with a straight-lined Shield of David. All of this may already be connected with the particular function which the emblem had received in the Prague community. In addition, it appears as a printer's mark especially in the Foa family, which was active in Italy and Holland for many generations. A Foa in Sabionetta used such a mark as early as 1551. It depicts a Shield of David between the branches of a palm tree which, in turn, is supported by two lions—no doubt the usual symbol of the Tree of Life and the two lions with which we have already become acquainted. Until 1804 it is in evidence on many publications of this family which manifestly had a special relationship to the emblem since it recurs on the synagogue established by them in Italy and on the ritual objects that were used there. Whether in this case it served purely as an ornament or whether it had some particular significance we do not know. The name David plays no special role here. No other printer used it in this period, and it is evident that no one considered it a sign of general Jewish significance. When a Russian printer, Israel Jaffe in Kopys, used it in 1804, he simply copied his printer's mark from that of the Foa family, which he must have come to like after seeing it on many printed works. Other printers of the early eighteenth century, as for example those in the small Jewish community of Wilhermsdorf in Franconia, also imitated the sign of the Foa family, but they left out precisely the Shield of David while keeping the remaining emblems. Apparently they did not care for it at all.

Continuing the oriental tradition, the hexagram appears occasionally—even before the rise of printing—in Hebrew manuscripts that were written in Italy and Germany in the fourteenth century. Thus the Schocken Library in Jerusalem owns an illustrated Haggadah of the early fifteenth century (probably from Northwestern Germany) which, in the proper context, contains the drawing of a man holding a circular *matzah* inscribed with a very elaborately executed, double-lined and intertwined Shield of David. The same motif recurs in other illustrations for the Seder ritual in Italian manuscripts of the middle of the fifteenth century and is still retained in certain late printed editions of the Seder Haggadah, such as a Venetian Haggadah of the eighteenth century which I have seen.

Although the above is more indicative of playful ornamentation, a hexagram with crooked bases does appear on the attic window of a medieval house which still stands in Hameln and is known to have once been a synagogue. Here then, as far as we know for the first time, the ornamentation which occurs in so many Gothic churches has been transferred to a Jewish house of worship. The emblem has not until now been attested in other old synagogues, except in Bohemia. There it is found on the walls of the synagogue of Budweis, discovered during an excavation. The Jews of Budweis were expelled as early as 1506, and the structure probably belongs to the fourteenth century. But this brings us to the special meaning which the sign received among the Jews of Bohemia.

For the "official" use of the hexagram as the insignia of a Jewish community had its origins in Prague. From there it was transplanted, especially in the seventeenth and eighteenth centuries, to other communities and areas in the East and the West. We can no longer determine whether the Jews themselves chose this sign for their flags and seals or whether it was imposed on them by the Christian authorities. Either is possible. But even if it was a matter of coercion, it soon became an established custom. Popularly always referred to by the Jews of Prague as Shield of David (*magen david*), it became a great favorite of the Jews of Bohemia and Moravia.

Regesta of old documents concerning the history of the Jews in Prague—the originals were burned nearly 250 years ago—mention the fact that the Emperor Charles IV in 1354, as a token of his special benevolence, gave the Jews of Prague the privilege of displaying a flag. This Jewish flag is by no means legendary; it is mentioned on numerous occasions in the history of Prague Jewry as something quite well known. When in 1527 Emperor Ferdinand I entered Prague, the municipal authorities ordained that the Jews were to march out toward him "with their flag." Now this flag contained a large Shield of David—not however, as some books would have it, together with a pentagram or witch's foot. If the Jews of Prague already at that time saw the emblem as the escutcheon of King David, in keeping with the afore-mentioned old magical tradition common among German Jews, then one might assume that they chose it themselves and raised it on their banner, so to speak, with great pride. In view of the continuous tradition of the sign among the Jews of Prague, we may certainly presume that it in fact represented a conscious emblem of Jewish pride and a memory of past glory, which was nourished by that magical tradition. The old flag has not been preserved. But when in the course of time it was damaged, it was replaced in 1716 by a new one which since then has been kept in the "Altneuschul" of Prague and is still shown in the synagogue to this day. According to the present inscription, it was originally bestowed in the year 1357, not 1354. In an act of favor of 1598, Emperor Rudolph II granted the distinguished Prague Jew Mordecai Meisel the right to "prepare a duplicate of the flag of King David, on the model of the one in the old synagogue, and to display it publicly in processions" in the new house of worship he had built. The authorities manifestly paid no less respect to the flag with the Shield of David than did the Jews: In 1716 the leaders of the community even received a monetary fine because they had not taken sufficient care of the old flag and had allowed it to deteriorate!

We hear of a similar Jewish flag in connection with the entry into Budapest of Matthias Corvinus, King of Hungary, in 1476. There, as the chronicler reports, the Jews marched out toward him with a red flag on which was depicted "a five-pointed witch's foot above two gold stars with a Jew's hat underneath." It remains unclear whether the gold stars might have been hexagrams, though it is possible that they were. The Jew's hat, here pictured under them, was in Prague later transferred into the inner space of the Shield of David and seems to have been falsely interpreted by Prague Jewish legend as a Swede's hat. Here too the juxtaposition of pentagram and hexagram on Jewish flags unfolded on official occasions is characteristic. No decision on a final selection of one of the two signs had yet been reached.

In Prague, however, a firm tradition was preserved, apparently from the beginning, in which the hexagram maintained preponderance over the pentagram. I have already mentioned the use of the Shield of David on the title page of the oldest work printed in Prague. After more than a thousand years it reappears for the first time on a tombstone in the old Jewish cemetery where the grave of the once very famous chronicler David Gans, who died in 1613, bears a large Shield of David. This is not too surprising, as his last book, which appeared in 1612, was called *Shield of David*. Otherwise the sign is not common on tombstones even in Prague. However, probably in keeping with its use on the flag, it must have early been appropriated for the community seal. In 1627 Emperor Ferdinand II confirmed this old seal on which the six consonants of the Hebrew word *magen david* are inscribed between the angles of the two triangles. Although the letters are quite distinct on the photographs of this old seal, it has not deterred some hyper-clever scholars from reading the consonants as MGSDRD and trying to find the word "magistrate" in it! Beginning about 1600, the insignia is also used in Prague for various public purposes and appears in all manner of places. We find it on the seals of Jewish organizations and individuals, as decorations on the iron grating around the *almemor* (the raised reading desk for the Torah in the center of the synagogue), on the tower of the Jewish city hall, and the like. But still in 1622, when the Emperor granted a coat of arms to Jacob Bassevi von Treuenberg, the first Jew of Prague, and of the Habsburg Empire as such, to be given a patent of nobility, Bassevi did not receive a Shield of David but three pentagrams on a diagonal band running across the coat of arms. The pentagram must thus still have been competing with the Shield of David as a type of Jewish insignia. According to the tradition of Prague Jewry, in 1648 they received permission from the Emperor to place the Swede's hat into the center of the Shield of David, supposedly in reward for their help in repulsing the Swedish attacks on the city during the Thirty Years' War. Hebrew community documents displayed in Prague now bear the seal in this form. We have it, for example, on a document concerning the appointment of the great bibliophile Rabbi David Oppenheim to be chief rabbi (May 24, 1702); its Hebrew original was part of the (second) S. Kirschstein Collection and was reproduced in its catalogue (1932).

Use of the Shield of David as a heraldic sign spread from Prague to the Jewish communities of Austria, Bohemia, and Moravia. This dissemination really begins in the seventeenth century. It appears for the first time on the seal of the Jewish community of Vienna in a document of 1655. In 1656 we also find the first instance of a clear juxtaposition of the Cross and the Shield of David as signs of the two religions. The boundary stone between the Jewish section of Vienna and the Christian section has been preserved; it does not juxtapose the Shield of

David with the coat of arms of the city of Vienna but with the Cross, and both are chiseled into the stone in equal size. Here then, as Paul Diamant has noted, it appears for the first time as a symbol of "Judaism" juxtaposed to the symbol of Christianity, not merely as the emblem of a single community. When the Jews of Vienna were expelled in 1670 and scattered over Moravia, Southern Germany, and Prussia, they often took their insignia with them to their new domiciles. The influences from Vienna and Prague, which tended in the same direction, reinforced each other. The exiles from Vienna introduced the Shield of David in Nikolsburg and Kremsier; we find it not much later in other Moravian communities, such as Weiskirchen and Eibeschütz. Some of these seals carry the Shield of David by itself while on others it is held by a lion, harking back to the older motif which we encountered earlier. After 1680 the Shield of David, emanating from Prague and Vienna, also reaches the large Jewish center in Amsterdam where the Ashkenazic (German-Polish), though not the Sephardic (Portuguese), community uses it on its seal from the eighteenth century onward. The form is that of Prague, with a tilted Swede's hat in the center. Likewise, in communities of Southern Germany it is often employed for community seals beginning in the early eighteenth century, as in Kriegshaber near Augsburg. It is also used in synagogues such as those at Schwabach, Sulzbach, Altenkundstadt and Gellenhausen for which photographs have been published especially in Alfred Grotte's *Deutsche . . . Synagogentypen . . . bis Anfang des 19. Jahrhunderts* (Leipzig, 1915).

The travel of the insignia eastward seems to have taken place more slowly. Here it does not occur at all on community seals of the seventeenth and eighteenth centuries, i.e., it was not used officially, even though it appears here and there as an ornament on synagogue objects. From Breslau, which had a Jewish community that originated in Moravia, we have an embroidered Torah mantle (ca. 1720) which bears a large Shield of David on a white background, with rosettes in the center and in the six angles. A drapery in front of the ark, dating from 1751, has two large Shields of David, on the top and the bottom, thus very visibly displaying them to the congregation. The sign is preserved from a still earlier period among the wood carvings above the ark of the 1643 wooden synagogue of Volpa near Grodno where many other Jewish motifs are also represented. But this seems a strictly isolated instance. We meet the emblem in other Polish wooden synagogues only in the eighteenth century; for example, in the window of the shabby wooden synagogue of Uzlen in White Russia where quite a few such Shields of David are inscribed in a circle on the center post of the window. Otherwise the sign may be found in Poland—as among the Jews of Egypt and Morocco—only in contexts related to, or stemming from, magic. Here and there the magical and the representative functions, which we have discussed, run together. This is true of the tombstone of a great magician from Podolia, "Doctor Falk," who achieved great fame in his time and was called the "Baal-Shem of London," which is where he died in 1782. The initials of his name, Samuel Jacob Hayyim, are there inscribed in a large Shield of David. Such utilization of the sign on monuments was still very rare at this time and became popular only much later. On the cemetery of the Portuguese Jews of Hamburg, for example, it does not appear before 1828.

This, more or less, was the history of the Shield of David until the beginning of the nineteenth century. The great dissemination of the emblem which then began was without question principally motivated by the drive to imitate. The Jews of the emancipation period were looking for a "symbol of Judaism" to match the symbol of Christianity which they saw everywhere before them. If Judaism was nothing more than an "Israelite persuasion," it seemed only proper that, like the other religions and confessions, it should have a visible distinguishing sign. In this process the construction of synagogues played a special role. Alfred Grotte, in his day one of the most famous synagogue builders, wrote in 1922:

When in the nineteenth century the construction of architecturally significant synagogues was begun, the mostly non-Jewish architects strove to build these houses of worship according to the model of church construction. They believed they had to look around for a symbol which corresponded to the symbol of the churches, and they hit upon the hexagram. In view of the total helplessness (of even learned Jewish theologians) regarding the material of Jewish symbolism, the *magen david* was exalted as the visible insignia of Judaism. As its geometrical shape lent itself easily to all structural and ornamental purposes, it has now been for more than three generations an established fact, already hallowed by tradition, that the *magen david* for the Jews is the same kind of holy symbol that the Cross and the Crescent are for the other monotheistic faiths.

About the same time, the first half of the nineteenth century, the Shield of David began to be customary also on ceremonial objects of all kinds, and this usage spread from Central and Western Europe to Poland and Russia. Since utilization of the sign on amulets was at that time still widespread, the pious of the old school did not call it into question. The imitation, which lay in the act of choosing a symbol for the Jewish religion as such, was for them concealed by the magic nature of the sign which was familiar to them—especially to the simple people—from numerous amulets. As late as 1854, Gerson Wolf in Vienna, a scholar thoroughly acquainted with the spiritual state of Moravian Jewry, wrote that all the trust which the pious Jew has in the Shield of David rests on the feeling it gives him of protection and security from hostile powers. Wolf knew nothing of this same Jew's also finding a symbol for his Judaism in it. And this very quality, which the sign lacked in the living consciousness of the Jew, could scarcely be lent to it by the well-intentioned but nebulous homiletics of later allegorists. Even so, there is no lack of examples for the special effectiveness of this symbolism among "enlightened" Jews. Heinrich Heine, who regarded his baptism with total cynicism, from 1840 on used the Shield of David in place of his name when signing his Paris reports in the *Augsburger Allgemeine Zeitung*, remarkable and significant evidence of that "Confessio Judaica" which permeates his biography. The sign is by no means an addition of the editors, but may be found on the originals of the essays, a good many of which are presently in the Bibliotèque Nationale in Paris.

Thus one may say: Just at the time of its greatest dissemination in the nineteenth century the Shield of David served as the empty symbol of a Judaism which itself was more and more falling into meaninglessness. The sermons of the preachers were not sufficient to breathe new life into the symbol. The brilliant and empty career of the *magen david* in the nineteenth century is itself a sign of Jewish decay.

Then came the Zionists. Their endeavors were directed not only to the re-establishment of the old glory, but even more to the transformation and renewal of their people. The very first issue of the movement's periodical, *Die Welt*, which appeared June 4, 1897, published by Theodor Herzl, bore the emblem on its masthead. When the Zionists chose it as their insignia at the Basle congress, it possessed two qualities which had to recommend it to men in search of a new symbol. In the first place, it was known to everyone because of its general dissemination through the centuries, its appearance on every new synagogue, on the seals of the communities, the philanthropic societies, and the like. Secondly, in contemporary consciousness it lacked any clear connection with religious conceptions and associations. This fault became a virtue: rather than calling to mind past glory, it addressed hopes for the future, for redemption.

But far more than the Zionists have done to provide the Shield of David with the sanctity of a genuine symbol has been done by those who made it for millions into a mark of shame and degradation. The yellow Jewish star, as a sign of exclusion and ultimately of annihilation, has accompanied the Jews on their path of humiliation and horror, of battle and heroic resistance. Under this sign they were murdered; under this sign they came to Israel. If there is a fertile soil of historical experience from which symbols draw their meaning, it would seem to be given here. Some have been of the opinion that the sign which marked the way to annihilation and to the gas chambers should be replaced by a sign of life. But it is possible to think quite the opposite: the sign which in our own days has been sanctified by suffering and dread has become worthy of illuminating the path to life and reconstruction. Before ascending, the path led down into the abyss; there the symbol received its ultimate humiliation and there it won its greatness.

Revelation and Tradition as Religious Categories in Judaism

JUDAISM, AS IT HAS constituted itself in distinct historical forms over the last two thousand years, is properly recognized in the history of religions as a classical example of religious traditionalism. For present purposes it is of no consequence whether this is an advantage or a disadvantage; our intent is not to evaluate, but to understand. Moreover, what tradition has meant in the household of Judaism—and to a high degree still continues to mean—eminently merits our attention, especially where we intend to discuss in general, human terms the function of creativity and spontaneity in relation to that which is given. What directs a man or what can enable him to direct his life's work is, after all, manifestly dependent on his ideas about his place in the world or his total orientation to life. Thus a discussion of the meaning of tradition is one of the most enlightening aspects under which the theme of our conference can be regarded. For within all human groups tradition demands an absolutely central position, even as the creative impulse, which insinuates itself into every tradition, calls our attention to the living relationship of giving and receiving. We desire to understand how the given and the spontaneous—that which newly flows into the stream of tradition—are combined in passing on the patrimony of each generation to the next.

It may be in order if at the beginning of this discussion—to indicate its climate, as it were—I tell you a little story which the Talmud, not entirely without tongue in cheek, relates of Moses and Rabbi Akiba. In this connection you must know that Akiba developed from an illiterate shepherd into the greatest scholar of his generation who died as a martyr during the Hadrianic persecutions. In the history of Judaism he is one of the most significant representatives of that conception of tradition whose spiritual foundations and implications we shall here try to explicate. It was he, more than any other single great teacher in Judaism, who helped to crystallize rabbinic Judaism as a religious system of sheer indestructible vitality. A hundred years after his death the following was told:

When Moses ascended onto the heights [to receive the Torah], he found the Holy One, blessed be He, sitting there tying wreaths [or crowns] to the letters. He said to Him: "Master of the Universe, who is holding You back?" [That is, why are You not satisfied with the letters as they are, so that You add crowns to them, i.e., the little flourishes which occur on certain letters of the Torah scrolls?] He answered him: "There is a man who will arise after many generations by the name of Akiba ben Joseph; he will expound heaps and heaps of laws upon every tittle." Then he said to Him: "Master of the Universe, show him to me." He replied: "Turn around." Then Moses went and sat down behind eight rows [of the students of Akiba]. But he did not understand what they were talking about. Thereupon his strength left him [i.e., he was perplexed because he was unable to follow discourses concerning the Torah which he himself had written]. When Akiba came to a certain matter where his students asked him how he knew it, he said to them: "It is a teaching given to Moses at Sinai." Then he [Moses] was comforted and returned to the Holy One, blessed be He. He said to Him: "Master of the Universe, You have a man like that and You give the Torah by me?!" He replied: "Be silent, for this is the way I have determined it." Then Moses said: "Master of the Universe, You have shown me his knowledge of the Torah, show me also his reward." He answered: "Turn around." He turned around and saw that Akiba's flesh was being weighed at the market stalls [his flesh was torn by the tortures of the executioners]. Then he said to Him: "Master of the Universe, this is the Torah and this is its reward?" He replied: "Be silent, for this is the way I have determined it." [1]

This story, in its own way magnificent, contains *in nuce* many of the questions which will concern us here.

In considering the problem of tradition, we must distinguish between two questions. The first is historical: How did a tradition endowed with religious dignity come to be formed? The other question is: How was this tradition understood once it had been accepted as a religious phenomenon? For the faithful promptly discard the historical question once they have accepted a tradition; this is the usual process in the establishment of religious systems. Yet for the historian the historical question remains fundamental: In order to understand the meaning of what the faithful simply accept, the historian is not bound to accept fictions that veil more than they reveal concerning the origins of the accepted faith. Thus, tradition as a special aspect of revelation is historically a product of the process that formed rabbinic Judaism between the fourth or third pre-Christian centuries and the second century of the Common Era.

In all religions, the acceptance of a divine revelation originally referred to the concrete communication of positive, substantive, and expressible content. It never occurred to the bearers of such a revelation to question or to limit the specific quality and closely delineated content of the communication they had received. Where, as in Judaism, such revelation is set down in holy writings and is accepted in that form, it initially constitutes concrete communication, factual content, and nothing else. But inasmuch as such revelation, once set down in Holy Scriptures, takes on authoritative character, an essential change takes place. For one thing, new historical circumstances require that the communication, whose authoritativeness has been granted, be applied to ever changing conditions. Furthermore, the spontaneous force of human productivity seizes this communication and expands it beyond its original scope. "Tradition" thus comes into being. It embodies the realization of the effectiveness of the Word in every concrete state and relationship entered into by a society.

At this point begins the process in which two questions gain importance: How can revelation be preserved as a concrete communication, i.e., how can it be passed on from generation to generation? (This is a virtually impossible undertaking by itself.) And, with ever greater urgency: Can this revelation be applied at all, and if so, how? With this second question, spontaneity has burst into the nascent tradition. In the process of this renewed productivity, Holy Scriptures themselves are sometimes enlarged; new written communications take their place alongside the old ones. A sort of no-man's-land is created between the original revelation and the tradition. Precisely this happened in Judaism, for example, as the Torah, to which the quality of revelation was originally confined, was "expanded" to include other writings of the biblical canon that had at first been subsumed, completely and emphatically, under the heading of tradition and considered merely repositories of this. Later, the boundaries often shifted: the canon, as Holy Writ, confronted tradition, and within the tradition itself similar processes of differentiation between written and oral elements were repeated.

J. F. Molitor has excellently presented these problems of the written and oral tradition:

Scripture crystallizes incessantly flowing time and sets forth the evanescent word as a perpetual present with firm and lasting features. In this respect it is the best and surest medium of all tradition. To be sure, Scripture, on account of its faithfulness and greater reliability (since in its case falsification is less possible), deserves preference over oral tradition. But every written formulation is only an abstracted general picture of reality which totally lacks all the concreteness and individual dimension of real life and therefore is subject to every kind of misinterpretation. The spoken word, as well as life and practice, must therefore be the constant companions and interpreters of the written word, which otherwise remains a dead, abstract concept in the mind, lacking all vitality and tangible content.

In modern times, where reflection threatens to swallow up all of life, where everything has been reduced to dead, abstract concepts, and it has been thought possible to educate men by theory alone, that old inherent reciprocal relationship between the written and spoken word, between theory and practice, has been totally displaced. When everything practical is incorporated into theory, when everything transmitted orally is put into writing and nothing left over for life, true theory along with genuine practice in life are lost. In the ancient world, however, where men still related to each other in much simpler, more natural ways, this natural relationship of the written to the spoken word, of theory to practice, was likewise much more properly observed.[2]

The process which is considered here occurred in Judaism at the time of the Second Temple. For our purposes, it does not matter whether the Torah as revealed law was promulgated in the earliest period or only later. But changed circumstances, especially the impact of the Hellenic world, produced a vigorous ferment which seized the theocratic community acknowledging the Torah; it created a Judaism which as a historical phenomenon differentiated itself from a number of other, in part very vibrant, groups within the Jewish people. Tradition now asserted itself ever more emphatically as a new religious value and as a category of religious thought. It becomes the medium through which creative forces express themselves. By the side of the Written Torah tradition arraigns itself, and it is called Oral Torah from approximately the first Christian century on. Tradition is not simply the totality of that which the community possesses as its cultural patrimony and which it bequeathes to its posterity; it is a specific selection from this patrimony, which is elevated and garbed with religious authority. It proclaims certain things, sentences, or insights to be Torah, and thus connects them with the revelation. In the process, the original meaning of revelation as a unique, positively established, and clearly delineated realm of propositions is put in doubt—and thus a development as fruitful as it is unpredictable begins which is highly instructive for the religious problematic of the concept of tradition.

At first it seems as if the Written and Oral Torah stand side by side, as if two different sources of authority were both given in revelation: one which could be written down, and one which could be, or was allowed to be, transmitted only orally by the living word. But that was not the end of the matter, as we shall see shortly. It is this Oral Torah of which is written at the beginning of the *Ethics of the Fathers* in the Mishnah: "Moses received the Torah from Sinai and transmitted it to Joshua, and Joshua to the elders, and the elders to the prophets, and the prophets transmitted it to the men of the Great Synagogue." This Great Synagogue was a group which for a long period, under Persian rule, presumably conducted the affairs of the community which had returned from exile. In fact, this nebulous group may well have been a historical construction, invented by much later generations on the basis of the last biblical reports regarding arrangements in Judea which are found in the books of Ezra and Nehemiah. We do not know whether the dogmatic concept of the Oral Law goes back to the period which is assumed for this group, even if the concept of a "fence around the Torah" (preventive measures intended to assure observance of the Torah) is ascribed to it. In any event, reference to the Oral Law is already common in the first century before the Common Era.

The content and range of this most important concept fluctuated, and with the advancing consolidation of rabbinic Judaism it underwent an expansion. At first this tradition, appearing as Torah, was limited to statutes or ordinances not contained in the Torah available to everyone. It made no difference whether Moses himself had received this Torah—which was now in written form —orally, and later had written it down or whether he had it dictated to him, so to speak, from the pre-existing heavenly master copy—both conceptions are attested in the rabbinic and apocryphal literature. Thus, in the course of generations, many statutes circulated which were designated as "*Halakhah* to Moses from Sinai." [3] Soon, however, the scope of the concept's application was enlarged. Everything that was discussed by the scribes and transmitted in the academies—whether legal, historical, ethical, or homiletical—was implanted into the fruitful realm of tradition, which now became an extraordinarily lively spiritual phenomenon.

I spoke a moment ago of the "scribes"—and this brings us to the salient point for an understanding of the relationship of the new, Oral Torah to the received, Written one. Efforts are begun to understand Scripture ever more exactly, making it the object of research, of exegetical probing into its implications (in Hebrew: Midrash). The Oral Torah no longer simply runs parallel to the Written; the task now is to derive it and deduce it from Scripture.

The unfolding of the truths, statements, and circumstances that are given in or accompany revelation becomes the function of the Oral Torah, which creates in the process a new type of religious person. In the history of religion, this type has evoked admiration as much as rejection and derision, and not without reason. The biblical scholar perceives revelation not as a unique and clearly delineated occurrence, but rather as a phenomenon of eternal fruitfulness to be unearthed and examined: "Turn it and turn it again, for everything is in it." Thus the achievement of these scholars, who established a tradition rooted in the Torah and growing out of it, is a prime example of spontaneity in receptivity. They are leaders because they know themselves to be led. Out of the religious tradition they bring forth something entirely new, something that itself commands religious dignity: commentary. Revelation needs commentary in order to be rightly understood and applied—this is the far from self-evident religious doctrine out of which grew both the phenomenon of biblical exegesis and the Jewish tradition which it created.

This inner law of development of the concept of revelation is also traceable in other religions which accept the authority of revelation. The process under discussion here is therefore of general significance for the phenomenology of religion. Judaism experienced this process in a peculiarly vigorous and consequential form, and its agents examined it with great thoroughness. This will make our consideration of the present complex of problems especially illuminating and far-reaching.

A creative process begins to operate which will permeate and alter tradition—the Midrash: the more regulated *halakhic* and the somewhat freer aggadic exegesis of Scriptures, and the views of the biblical scholars in their various schools, are regarded as implicitly contained in the Written Torah. No longer only old and carefully guarded sentences but now also analyses of Scriptures by the scholars themselves lay claim to being tradition. The desire for historical continuity which is of the very essence of tradition is translated into a historical construction whose fictitious character cannot be doubted but which serves the believing mind as a crutch of external authentication. Especially peculiar in this historical construction is the metamorphosis of the prophets into bearers of tradition—a very characteristic, albeit to our minds a very paradoxical, transformation. Originally only the last of the prophets, Haggai, Zechariah, and Malachi, had been meant by this proposition, for they possess special importance in the doctrine of the uninterrupted chain of tradition[4]: the last of the prophets are, not without all justification, regarded as the first of the scribes and "men of the Great Assembly." Subsequently, also the older prophets are designated as links in the chain, which would otherwise have had to be invisible.

This leads to the viewpoint expressed daringly in talmudic writings, namely, that the total substance of the Oral Torah, which had in fact been the achievement of the scholars, comes from the same source as the Written Torah, and that it was therefore basically always known. The saying "turn it . . ." reflects this viewpoint. But underneath this fiction, the details of which do not concern us here, there lies a religious attitude which is interesting and which had significant results. I refer to the distinctive notion of revelation including within itself as sacred tradition the later commentary concerning its own meaning. This was the beginning of a road which, with a full measure of inherent logic, was to lead to the establishment of mystical theses concerning the character of revelation as well as the character of tradition.

Here we immediately encounter a significant tension in the religious consciousness of the scholars themselves, between the process by which the tradition actually developed and the interpretation of that process. On the one hand, there was the blossoming productivity of the academies where the Scriptures were explored and examined in ever greater detail—the spontaneous achievement of the generations upon whom, in turn, was bestowed such authority as was transmitted by the great teachers and the tradition. On the other hand, there arose the claim apparently flowing from the dogma of the revealed nature of the Oral Law. What this claim amounted to was that all this was somehow part of revelation itself—and more: not only was it given along with

revelation, but it was given in a special, timeless sphere of revelation in which all generations were gathered together; everything really had been made explicit to Moses, the first and most
comprehensive recipient of Torah. The achievement of every
generation, its contribution to tradition, was projected back into
the eternal present of the revelation at Sinai. This, of course, is
something which no longer has anything in common with the
notion of revelation with which we began, namely, revelation as
unequivocal, clear, and understandable communication. According
to this new doctrine, revelation comprises everything that will
ever be legitimately offered to interpret its meaning.

The patent absurdity of this claim reveals a religious assumption that must be taken all the more seriously. The rabbis
did not hesitate to express this assumption in rather extravagant
formulations. In the forty days that Moses spent on Mount Sinai
(Exod. 34:28), he learned the Torah with all its implications.[5]
Rabbi Joshua ben Levi (a third-century Palestinian teacher)
said: "Torah, Mishnah, Talmud, and Aggadah—indeed even
the comments some bright student will one day make to his
teacher—were already given to Moses on Mount Sinai"—and
even the questions that such a bright student will some day ask
his teacher![6] In our context, statements such as these are highly
suggestive. They make absolute the concept of tradition in which
the meaning of revelation unfolds in the course of historical
time—but only because everything that can come to be known
has already been deposited in a timeless substratum. In other
words, we have arrived at an assumption concerning the nature
of truth which is characteristic of rabbinic Judaism (and probably
of traditional religious establishment): Truth is given once and
for all, and it is laid down with precision. Fundamentally, truth
merely needs to be transmitted. The originality of the exploring
scholar has two aspects. In his spontaneity, he develops and
explains that which was transmitted at Sinai, no matter whether
it was always known or whether it was forgotten and had to be
rediscovered. The effort of the seeker after truth consists not in
having new ideas but rather in subordinating himself to the
continuity of the tradition of the divine word and in laying open
what he receives from it in the context of his own time. In other
words: Not system but *commentary* is the legitimate form through
which truth is approached.

This is a most important principle indeed for the kind of
productivity we encounter in Jewish literature. Truth must be

laid bare in a text in which it already pre-exists. We shall deal later with the nature of this pre-existent givenness. In any case, truth must be brought forth from the text. Commentary thus became the characteristic expression of Jewish thinking about truth, which is another way of describing the rabbinic genius. Under the influence of Greek thought, there were also explications and attempts at system-construction within Judaism. But its innermost life is to be found where holy texts received commentary, no matter how remote from the text itself these commentaries and their ideas may appear to the present-day critical reader. There is, of course, a striking contrast between the awe of the text, founded on the assumption that everything already exists in it, and the presumptuousness of imposing the truth upon ancient texts. The commentator, who is truly the biblical scholar, always combines both attitudes.

Tradition as a living force produces in its unfolding another problem. What had originally been believed to be consistent, unified and self-enclosed now becomes diversified, multifold, and full of contradictions. It is precisely the wealth of contradictions, of differing views, which is encompassed and unqualifiedly affirmed by tradition. There were many possibilities of interpreting the Torah, and tradition claimed to comprise them all.[7] It maintains the contradictory views with astounding seriousness and intrepidity, as if to say that one can never know whether a view at one time rejected may not one day become the cornerstone of an entirely new edifice. In Jewish tradition the views of the schools of Hillel and Shammai, two teachers who lived shortly before Jesus, play an important part. Their mutually contradictory attitudes toward theoretical and practical problems are codified by the Talmud with great thoroughness, although the rule is that in the application of the law the views of Hillel's school are decisive. But the rejected views are stated no less carefully than the accepted ones. The Talmudists formulated no ultimate thesis concerning the unity of these contradictions, concerning dialectical relationships within the tradition. It was only one of the latest Kabbalists who formulated the daring and, at first blush, surprising thesis, which has since been often reiterated, that the *Halakhah* would be decided according to the now rejected view of the school of Shammai in the Messianic era. That is to say, the conception of the meaning and of the applicability of the Torah which is unacceptable at any given time within history in reality anticipates a Messianic condition in which it will have its legitimate function—and thereby the unity of the Torah, which embraces all of this, is fully sealed.[8]

Thus, tradition is concerned with the realization, the enactment of the divine task which is set in the revelation. It demands application, execution, and decision, and at the same time it is, indeed, "true growth and unfolding from within." It constitutes a living organism, whose religious authority was asserted with as much emphasis as is at all possible within this system of thought.

Nothing demonstrates this authority, the authority of commentary over author, more triumphantly than the story of the oven of Akhnai which is told in the Talmud. Rabbi Eliezer ben Hyrkanos and the sages disputed about whether or not this oven, which had a particular type of construction, was subject to impurity in the sense of the Torah. Finally, against the opinion of Rabbi Eliezer, a majority declared it subject to impurification. On this matter the talmudic account, which represents one of the most famous passages in Jewish literature, then continues:

On that day Rabbi Eliezer brought forward all the arguments in the world, but they were not accepted. He said to them: "If the *Halakhah* [the proper decision] agrees with me, let this carob tree prove it." Thereupon the carob tree was uprooted a hundred cubits from its place; some say, four hundred cubits. They replied: "No proof may be brought from a carob tree." Then he said: "If the *Halakhah* agrees with me, let this stream of water prove it." Thereupon the stream of water flowed backwards. They replied: "No proof may be brought from a stream of water." Then he said: "If the *Halakhah* agrees with me, let the walls of the schoolhouse prove it." Thereupon the walls of the schoolhouse began to totter. But Rabbi Joshua rebuked them and said: "When scholars are engaged in *halakhic* dispute, what concern is it of yours?" Thus the walls did not topple, in honor of Rabbi Joshua, but neither did they return to their upright position, in honor of Rabbi Eliezer; still today they stand inclined. Then he said: "If the *Halakhah* agrees with me, let it be proved from Heaven." Thereupon a heavenly voice was heard saying: "Why do you dispute with Rabbi Eliezer? The *Halakhah* always agrees with him." But Rabbi Joshua arose and said (Deut. 30:12): "It is not in heaven." What did he mean by that? Rabbi Jeremiah replied: "The Torah has already been given at Mount Sinai [and is thus no longer in Heaven]. We pay no heed to any heavenly voice, because already at Mount Sinai You wrote in the Torah (Exod. 23:2): 'One must incline after the majority.' " Rabbi Nathan met the prophet Elijah and asked him: "What did the Holy One, blessed be He, do in that hour?" He replied: "God smiled and said: My children have defeated Me, My children have defeated Me." [9]

The question remains: Does tradition keep its freshness in such a view, or does it freeze into Alexandrianism and lose its organic ability to grow when too much is demanded of it? At what point does deadly decay lurk? The question is as important as it is hard to answer. As long as there is a living relationship between religious consciousness and revelation there is no danger to the tradition from within. But when this relationship dies tradition ceases to be a living force. To be sure, this looks very different to an outside observer. Everyone who studies the tradition of any religious community is aware of this antinomy. For example: For the Church Fathers the rabbinical students of Scripture were still guardians of a valuable tradition; to later Christendom, they appeared incomprehensible and rather terrifying—and this at a time when the tradition enjoyed a very active inner life. For tradition omnipotence and impotence dwell closely together; all is in the eye of the beholder.

In Judaism, tradition becomes the reflective impulse that intervenes between the absoluteness of the divine word—revelation—and its receiver. Tradition thus raises a question about the possibility of immediacy in man's relationship to the divine, even though it has been incorporated in revelation. To put it another way: Can the divine word confront us without mediation? And, can it be fulfilled without mediation? Or, given the assumption of the Jewish tradition which we have formulated, does the divine word rather not require just such mediation by tradition in order to be apprehensible and therefore fulfillable? For rabbinic Judaism, the answer is in the affirmative. Every religious experience after revelation is a mediated one. It is the experience of the voice of God rather than the experience of God. But all reference to the "voice of God" is highly anthropomorphic—a fact from which theologians have always carefully tried to escape. And here we face questions which, in Judaism, have been thought through only in the mystic doctrines of the Kabbalists.

II

The Kabbalists were in no sense of the word heretics. Rather they strove to penetrate, more deeply than their predecessors, into the meaning of Jewish concepts. They took the step from the tradition of the Talmudists to mystical tradition. In order to understand the mystical concept of tradition, we must take a step backward and try to visualize the Kabbalists' concept of Torah as revelation and as the word of God. The Kabbalists sought to unlock the innermost core of the Torah, to decode the text, so to speak. (Here we have a new concept of tradition: after all, the Hebrew word *kabbalah* means "the receiving of the tradition.") This goes far beyond what had been thought about these questions in exoteric Judaism, and yet the Kabbalists' thinking remains specifically Jewish. In a way, they have merely drawn the final consequence from the assumption of the Talmudists concerning revelation and tradition as religious categories.

The first question which presented itself to the Kabbalists in this connection concerned the nature of that Torah which is known as the Written Torah. What is it that God can actually reveal, and of what does the so-called word of God consist that is given to the recipients of revelation? The answer is: God reveals nothing but Himself as He becomes speech and voice. The expression through which the divine power presents itself to man in manifestation, no matter how concealed and how inward, is the name of God. It is this that is expressed and given voice in Scripture and revelation, no matter how hieroglyphically. It is encoded in every so-called communication that revelation makes to man. "For the Holy Scriptures, the great mysterium of the revelation of God, containing all within all, is a hieroglyph of unending hieroglyphs, an eternal spring of mysteries, inexhaustible, pouring forth without end, ever new and glorious." [10] To be sure, those secret signatures (*rishumim*) that God had placed upon things are as much concealments of His revelation as revelation of His concealment. The script of these signatures differs from what we view as Torah, as revealed Scripture, only in the unconditional, undistracted concentration in which these are here collected. The language, which lives in things as their creative principle, is the same; but here, concentrated upon its own essence, it is not (or at most thinly) concealed by the creaturely existence in which it appears. Thus, revelation is revelation of the name or names of God, which are perhaps the different modes of His active being. God's language has no grammar; it consists only of names. The oldest Kabbalists— Nahmanides, for example—profess to have received as tradition this understanding of the structure of the Torah. It is clear, however, that this was originally a tradition of magical character, now transposed into a mystical tradition.

The creative force thus concentrated in the name of God, which is the essential word that God sends forth from Himself, is far greater than any human expression, than any creaturely word can grasp. It is never exhausted by the finite, human word. It represents an absolute which, resting in itself—one might as well say: self-moved—sends its rays through everything that seeks expression and form in all worlds and through all languages. Thus, the Torah is a texture (Hebrew: *arigah*) fashioned out of the names of God and, as the earliest Spanish Kabbalists already put it, out of the great, absolute name of God, which is the final signature of all things. It constitutes a mysterious whole, whose primary purpose is not to transmit a specific sense, to "mean" something, but rather to express the force of the divinity itself which is concentrated in this "name." This conception has nothing to do with any rational understanding of the possible social function of a name; this Name cannot, after all, even be pronounced. The Torah is built up out of this Name, just as a tree grows out of its root, or, to use another favorite image of the Kabbalists, just as a building is erected out of an artistic interweaving of bricks that ultimately also consist of one basic material. This is the thesis repeated in every possible form in the classical writings of the Kabbalah: "The whole Torah is nothing but the great name of God." As Joseph Gikatilla has set forth in great detail, in the Torah the living texture constructed out of the tetragrammaton is seen as an infinitely subtle braiding of the permutations and combinations of its consonants; these in turn were subjected to more such processes of combination, and so on *ad infinitum,* until they finally appear to us in the form of the Hebrew sentences of the Torah. Thus, the very words that we read in the Written Torah and that constitute the audible "word of God" and communicate a comprehensible message, are in reality mediations through which the absolute word, incomprehensible to us, is offered. This absolute word is originally communicated in its limitless fullness, but—and that is the key point—this communication is incomprehensible! It is not a communication which provides comprehension; being basically nothing but the expression of essence, it becomes a comprehensible communication only when it is mediated.

This strictly mystical view of the nature of revelation is basic to any analysis of tradition. It has significant consequences. One of them is so radical that it was taught only in veiled, symbolical terminology. It amounted to the assertion that there was no such thing as a Written Torah in the sense of an immediate revelation of the divine word. For such a revelation is contained in the Wisdom of God, where it forms an "Ur-Torah" in which the "word" rests as yet completely undeveloped in a mode of being in which no differentiation of the individual elements into sounds and letters takes place. The sphere in which this "Ur-Torah" (*torah kelulah*) comes to articulate itself into the so-called Written Torah, where signs (the forms of the consonants) or sounds and expressions exist—that sphere itself is already interpretation. An old dictum of the Midrash, according to which the pre-existent Torah was written before God with black fire upon white fire, was given the esoteric interpretation that the white fire is the Written Torah in which the letters are not yet formed; only by means of the black fire, which is the Oral Torah, do the letters acquire form. The black fire is likened to the ink on the parchment of the Torah scroll. This would imply that what we on earth call the Written Torah has already gone through the medium of the Oral Torah and has taken on a perceptible form in that process. The Written Torah is not really the blackness of the inked writing (already a specification), but the mystic whiteness of the letters on the parchment of the scroll on which we see nothing at all. According to this, the Written Torah is a purely mystical concept, understood only by prophets who can penetrate to this level. As for us, we can perceive revelation only as unfolding oral tradition.

While this notion was only rarely hinted at, there was general acceptance of another conclusion drawn from the principle of the Torah as the name of God, and this one is central to our discussion. It is the thesis that the word of God carries infinite meaning, however it may be defined. Even that which has already become a sign in the strict sense, and is already a mediated word, retains the character of the absolute. But if there is such a thing as God's word, it must, of course, be totally different from the human word. It is far-reaching, all-embracing, and, unlike a human word, cannot be applied to a specific context of meaning. In other words: God's word is infinitely interpretable; indeed, it is *the* object of interpretation par excellence. Saying that, we have indeed moved far away from the origin of our consideration, i.e., from the original historical notions of revelation as a specific and positive communication. In this new perspective, the old notions are but the exoteric garments of an insight that probes far deeper. Here revelation, which has yet no specific meaning, is that in the word which gives an infinite wealth of meaning. Itself without meaning, it is the very essence of interpretability. For mystical theology, this is a decisive criterion of revelation. In every word there now shines an infinite multitude of lights. The primeval light of the Torah that shines in the holy letters refracts on the unending facets of "meaning." In this connection, the Kabbalists always speak of the "seventy faces of the Torah"; the number seventy simply represents the inexhaustible totality and meaning of the divine word.

We now face the problem of tradition as it presented itself to the Kabbalists. If the conception of revelation as absolute and meaning-giving but in itself meaningless is correct, then it must also be true that revelation will come to unfold its infinite meaning (which cannot be confined to the unique event of revelation) only in its constant relationship to history, the arena in which tradition unfolds. Theologians have described the word of God as the "absolutely concrete." But the absolutely concrete is, at the same time, the simply unfulfillable—it is that which in no way can be put into practice. The Kabbalistic idea of tradition is founded upon the dialectic tension of precisely this paradox: it is precisely the absoluteness that effects the unending reflections in the contingencies of fulfillment. Only in the mirrorings in which it reflects itself does revelation become practicable and accessible to human action as something concrete. There is no immediate, undialectic application of the divine word. If there were, it would be destructive. From this point of view, so-called concreteness— which has so many admirers these days and whose glorification is the labor of a whole philosophical school—is something mediated and reflected, something that has gone through many refractions. It is the tradition of the word of God—for the Kabbalists the basis of any possible action that deserves the name of action— that permits its application in history. Tradition undergoes changes with the times, new facets of its meaning shining forth and lighting its way. Tradition, according to its mystical sense, is Oral Torah, precisely because every stabilization in the text would hinder and destroy the infinitely moving, the constantly progressing and unfolding element within it, which would otherwise become petrified. The writing down and codification of the Oral Torah, undertaken in order to save it from being forgotten, was therefore as much a protective as (in the deeper sense) a pernicious act. Demanded by the historical circumstance of exile, it was profoundly problematic for the living growth and continuance of the tradition in its original sense. It is therefore not surprising that, according to talmudic report,[11] it was originally prohibited to write down the Oral Torah; and it is not surprising that great Kabbalists (Nathan Adler in Frankfurt, for example) are said not to have committed their learning to writing because, since he and his students were keeping tradition from being forgotten, the prohibition against writing it down continued to be valid for him.

The understanding of tradition as a process that creates productivity through receptivity can now be seen clearly. Talmudic literature recognizes two types of men who preserve the tradition. One is the man who was useful in the Houses of Study, who could recite from memory the texts of all the old traditions of the schools—mere receptacles who preserved tradition without augmenting it in the slightest by their own inquiry. But this man, a conduit for tradition, is at best an expedient, virtually an oral book. The truly learned man is the one who is bound to tradition through his inquiries. So far as the consciousness of future generations is concerned, only the men of the second type are the true carriers of tradition, for tradition is living creativity in the context of revelation. Precisely because tradition perceives, receives, and unfolds that which lives in the word, it is the force within which contradictions and tensions are not destructive but rather stimulating and creative. For those who stand within the tradition it is easy to see the organic unity of these contradictions, precisely because it presents a dialectic relationship in which the word of revelation is developed. Without contradictions it would not perform this function.

The scholar and commentator, therefore, fulfills a set task: to make the Torah concrete at the point where he stands, to make it applicable *hic at nunc,* and, moreover, to fashion his specific form of concretization in such a manner that it may be transmitted. The later Kabbalah formulated a widely accepted dictum: that the Torah turns a special face to every single Jew, meant only for him and apprehensible only by him, and that a Jew therefore fulfills his true purpose only when he comes to see this face and is able to incorporate it into the tradition. The "chain of tradition" is never broken; it is the translation of the inexhaustible word of God into the human and attainable sphere; it is the transcription of the voice sounding from Sinai in an unending richness of sound. The musician who plays a symphony has not composed it; still, he participates in significant measure in its production. This, of course, is valid only for those who assume a metaphysical contemporaneity for all tradition. For those, on the other hand, who see tradition as the creature of history, in whose course revelation is reflected, tradition legitimately represents the greatest

creation of Judaism, which when properly understood is constituted only within this tradition.

For the Kabbalists the voice from Sinai was the constant
medium, the foundation for the continuing existence of tradition.
The unique event called revelation—in just the sense analyzed
here—is juxtaposed to the continuity of the voice. Every carrier
of tradition refers back to it, as is emphasized by the texts I shall
now examine. These texts attempt to unify the exoteric concept
of tradition as developed by the Talmudists with the mystical
concept that was conditioned by the assumptions of the Kabbalists
concerning the nature of revelation. They are extracts from two of
the most important works of later Kabbalistic literature and to
me seem highly important for our considerations.

In this literature, the most extensive discussion concerning the
nature of tradition is found in the work *Avodat ha-Kodesh,*
written in 1531 in Turkey by Meir ben Gabbai.[12] He set out to
prove that tradition is not a profane achievement of human thought
and deliberation, but that it is precisely "Oral Torah" and a
re-sounding of the voice (in the sense adduced earlier). At the
same time, Meir ben Gabbai tried to answer the question of how
it was possible, even necessary, for the tradition to offer such
differing conceptions concerning the observance of the Torah,
since the Torah, perfect within itself, is after all the revelation
of the divine will. I quote here one of his very detailed explications:

The highest wisdom [the *sophia* of God, which is the second
sefirah] contains as the foundation of all emanations pouring forth out
of the hidden Eden the true fountain from which the Written and the
Oral Torah emanate and are impressed [upon the forms of the celestial
letters and signatures]. This fountain is never interrupted; it gushes
forth in constant production. Were it to be interrupted for even a
moment, all creatures would sink back into their non-being; for the
gushing forth is the cause of God's great name appearing in its oneness and in its glory [as depicted by this emanation]. On this fountain
rests the continued existence of all creatures; it is said of it (Ps.
36:10): "For with Thee is the fountain of life." And this is a life
that has no measure and no end, no death or dissolution. Now, since
the nature of the original source is also preserved in what was formed
from it, it necessarily follows that the Torah, arising out of this source,
also never has an interruption within itself. Rather, its fountain always
gushes forth, to indicate the source whence it was formed [literally:
"hewed out"]. We learn this from the prayer which designates God
as The One Who "gives the Torah" [present tense]. For that great

voice with which He gave it has not ceased. After He gave us His holy words and caused us to hear them as the very essence of the whole Torah, He did not cease to let us hear its details through His prophet, the trusted one of His house [i.e., Moses]. This is what Onkelos meant when he interpreted the Hebrew text of Deuteronomy 5:19 on the voice of God at the revelation [which, if taken literally, can more readily have the opposite interpretation] as "a great voice that did not cease speaking." That great voice sounds forth without interruption; it calls with that eternal duration that is its nature; whatever the prophets and scholars of all generations have taught, proclaimed, and produced, they have received precisely out of that voice which never ceases, in which all regulations, determinations, and decisions are implicitly contained, as well as everything new that may ever be said in any future. In all generations, these men stand in the same relationship to that voice as the trumpet to the mouth of a man who blows into it and brings forth a sound. In that process, there is no production from their own sense and understanding. Instead, they bring out of potentiality into actuality that which they received from that voice when they stood at Sinai. And when the Scriptures say: All these words God spoke to your congregation, a great voice that does not cease speaking, everything is thus contained in it. . . . Not only did all the prophets receive their prophecy [out of this voice] at Sinai, but also all the sages who arose in every generation. Everyone received that which is his from Sinai, from that continuous voice, and certainly not according to his human understanding and reckoning. And this is so because the completion of the unity has been entrusted into the hands of man, as the Scriptural verse says (Isa. 43:10): "If ye are my witnesses, says the Eternal One, I am God." All words that can ever be said in a new way have thus been placed into this fundament which is the divine voice; the Master of the world desired that they receive actuality through men of this earth who form and fulfill God's name. That great voice is the gate and the portal for all other voices, and that is [the meaning of] "fence of unity," and the reference of the verse in the Psalms: "This is the gate of the Lord," the gate representing the Oral Law which leads to God, Who is the Written Torah, guarded by the Oral Torah. This is the reason for the fences and limitations with which the scholars enclose the Torah. But since that voice is never interrupted and that fountain always gushes forth, the deliberations of the scholars in the Talmud were necessary; Rabina and Rab Ashi, its redactors, refrained from interrupting that stream [which flows and becomes visible in those deliberations]. And this is also the path walked by scholars of all generations, and there is no fulfillment of the Torah except on that path. If new teachings [regarding the understanding of the Torah] are produced daily, this proves that the fountain ever gushes and that the great voice sounds forth without interruption. For that reason, the deliberations upon the Torah may not suffer any interruptions, nor the production of new teachings and laws and incisive discussion. But the authority of the prophets and scholars who know the secret is nothing but the authority of that voice from which they have received all they have produced and taught, which in no way arose out of their own mind and out of their rational investigations (III, ch. 23).

Later on in this disquisition, we discover how Meir ben Gabbai explains the conflicts of opinion that appear in the tradition from this Kabbalistic point of view. He holds them to be facets of revelation:

That ever-flowing fountain [of emanation from which the Torah originates] has different sides, a front and a back; from this stem the differences and the conflicts and the varying conceptions regarding the clean and the unclean, the prohibited and the permitted, the usable and the unusable, as it is known to the mystics. The great, continuing voice contains all these diverse ways of interpretation, for in that voice there can be nothing missing. According to the size and strength of that voice the opposing interpretations appear within it and confront one another. For the one has seen the face of that voice as it was turned toward him and made his decision for purity, the other one for impurity, each according to the place where he stood and where he received it. But all originates from one place and goes [despite all apparent contradictions] to the one place, as is explained in the Zohar (III, 6b). For the differences and contradictions do not originate out of different realms, but out of the one place in which no difference and no contradiction is possible. The implicit meaning of this secret is that it lets every scholar insist on his own opinion and cite proofs for it from the Torah; for only in this manner and in no other way is the unity [of the various aspects of the one stream of revelation] achieved. Therefore it is incumbent upon us to hear the different opinions, and this is the sense of "these and those are the words of the living God." For all depend ultimately upon the divine wisdom that unites them in their origin, even though this is incomprehensible for us and the last portal remained closed to Moses. For that reason, these things appear contradictory and different to us, but only as seen from our own standpoint—for we are unable to penetrate to those points where the contradictions are resolved. And it is only because we are unable to maintain two contradictory teachings at the same time that the Halakhah is established according to one of these two teachings; for all is one from the side of the Giver. But from our side it appears as manifold and different opinions, and the Halakhah is established according to the teaching of the school of Hillel.

This interpretation achieved its widest dissemination above all through the authority of Isaiah Horovitz (ca. 1565-1630), who presented an unexcelled synopsis of rabbinic and Kabbalistic Judaism in his great work *The Two Tables of the Covenant*. Drawing upon the disquisition just quoted, he develops the religious dignity of the creative tradition by proceeding from the explanation of a particularly pointed talmudic saying which states: "The Holy One, blessed be He, speaks Torah out of the mouths of all rabbis.[13] Horovitz comments:

Some interpret this saying in reference to the petition which we express in the prayer "Give us our share in Thy Torah," which is taken to mean: Give us a share in the Torah which God Himself studies; or else: May we become worthy of having Him say a teaching in our name. And this is the situation: the scholars produce new words [in the understanding of the Torah] or derive them through the power of their insight. But all of it was contained in the power of that voice that was heard at the revelation; and now the time has come for them to bring it from potentiality into actuality through the efforts of their meditation. But God is great and mighty in power, and there is no limit to His understanding. His potentiality permits no interruption [in this voice]; rather, it is boundless and endless, and all this [that the sages hear in the voice] is guided by the measure of renewal and the origin of souls in every generation as well as the ability of man to arouse the higher power. It thus follows that while we say of God that "He has given the Torah" [in the past], He can also be designated at the same time [in every present time] as "the One Who gives the Torah." At every hour and time the fountain gushes forth without interruption, and what He gives at any time was potentially contained in what He gave [at Sinai]. Let me explain the essence of this matter further. We know that the domain of what is made more stringent [in the law by the rabbis] becomes enlarged in every generation. In the days of our teacher Moses the only prohibitions were those which he had expressly received at Sinai. Nevertheless, he added ordinances here and there for special purposes as they arose; and so did the prophets after him, and the scribes, and every generation with its scholars. For the more the snake's poison spreads, the more is the protecting fence needed, as is said (Eccles. 10:8): "He who breaks the fence is bitten by the snake." The Holy One, blessed be He, gave us 365 prohibitions [in the Torah] in order to prevent the snake's poison from taking effect. The more this poison spreads within a generation, the larger must the realm of prohibition become. If this had been so at the time when the Torah was given, then all these prohibitions would have been written into the Torah. As it is, all this is contained by implication in the Torah's prohibitions; for in all this, there is only one point [namely, fighting the snake's poison]. Therefore God commanded: Set a watch upon the watch,[14] which means: act according to the prevailing conditions. Thus, all the additional stringencies [in fulfilling the

Torah] that had to be added in every generation derive from the authority of the Torah. As the snake's poison spreads, and more of its potential becomes actual, the statement [15] that God created the evil inclination as well as the antidote to it becomes valid. Then we need stimulation from above in order to translate the [additional] prohibitions from potentiality into actuality as well, until [at the time of redemption] we shall again be reunited with the highest fountain of all fountains [which will then nullify the prohibitions].

I must reveal further secrets which are related to this matter in order to make plain that all the words of the wise men are words of the living God [and thus have religious dignity]. The words of the Talmud in Tractate Erubin (13b) will thereby become understandable: "Rabbi Akiba said in the name of Rabbi Samuel: For three years the school of Shammai and the school of Hillel engaged in argument. The one said the *Halakhah* is according to us, and the other one said the *Halakhah* is according to us. A divine voice then sounded forth and said: Both these and those are the words of the living God, but the *Halakhah* is to be decided according to the school of Hillel." Rabbi Yomtov ben Abraham of Seville reported in his commentary that the rabbis of France had raised the question: How is it possible that both are the words of the living God when one prohibits what the other one permits? Their answer was that when Moses ascended the heights in order to receive the Torah he was shown forty-nine reasons for a prohibition and forty-nine reasons for a permission for every problem. He asked God about this and was told that this would be left to the sages of Israel of every generation, and that the decision was theirs to make. And this—so says the scholar from Seville—is correct according to the Talmud; but according to the Kabbalah there is a special reason for this. It appears to me that the expression of the Talmud "These and those are the words of the living God" is justified *prima facie* only where it is possible to hold that the words of both parties are valid at the same time. This applies, for example, to the place in the Talmud (Gittin, 6b) which refers to the unfaithfulness of the concubine in Gibea (Judg. 19:2): "Once when Rabbi Ebiathar met the prophet Elijah and asked him what the Holy One, blessed be He, was thinking about, Elijah answered: "About the story of the concubine in Gibea" [about which Ebiathar and his colleague Jonathan had expressed different opinions]. "What did he say about it?" [asked the rabbi]. "My son Ebiathar says thus, and my son Jonathan says thus." The rabbi said: "Is it possible for God to have doubt?" Elijah answered: "These and those are the words of the living God." For it is possible to consider the sayings of both valid. But in a situation where one prohibits something which the other permits, it is clearly impossible to consider both of their sayings valid. For the decision supports the one, and we do not accept the validity of the words of the other. But if these words are also considered words of the living God, how can one word of His be invalid? The full import, therefore, cannot rest with the words of the French rabbis, since they are insufficient in this case. But it can rest with the reason and the secret that apply here according to the Kabbalistic tradition, as indicated by the rabbi from Seville. The verse in Ecclesiastes 12:11: "The words of the wise are as goads, and as nails well fastened are those that are composed in collections, they are given from one shepherd" is interpreted in the Tractate Hagigah (3b) as follows: "Composed in collections," this refers to the biblical scholars who sit in assemblies and occupy themselves with the Torah; some declare a matter unclean, and others declare it clean; some prohibit, others permit; some declare it unusable, and others declare it usable. Someone might say: If this is so, how can I study the Law? Therefore Scripture continues: "They are given by *one* shepherd; One God gave them, one spokesman [Moses] said them out of the mouth of the Lord of all actions, praised be He, as is said (Exod. 20:1): 'And God spoke all these words.'" You, too, turn your ear into a funnel and fashion for yourself an understanding heart in order to understand the words of those who declare as unclean and the words of those who declare as clean, the words of those who prohibit and the words of those who permit, the words of those who declare as unusable and the words of those who declare as usable. We have here the affirmation that all differences of opinion and viewpoint that contradict one another were given by one God and said by one spokesman. This seems to be very alien to human understanding, and man's nature would be unable to grasp it were it not for the help given to him by the prepared way of God, the pathway upon which dwells the light of the Kabbalah.[16]

In the Jewish conception, therefore, genuine tradition, like everything that is creative, is not the achievement of human productivity alone. It derives from a bedrock foundation. Max Scheler is reported to have said: "The artist is merely the mother of the work of art; God is the father." The tradition is one of the great achievements in which relationship of human life to its foundation is realized. It is the living contact in which man takes hold of ancient truth and is bound to it, across all generations, in the dialogue of giving and taking. Goethe's word applies to it:

> The truth that long ago was found,
> Has all noble spirits bound,
> The ancient truth, take hold of it.

> (Das Wahre war schon längst gefunden,
> Hat edle Geisterschaft verbunden,
> Das alte Wahre, fass es an.)

The Science of Judaism
—Then and Now

To COMMENT ON the question of the Science of Judaism [*Wissenschaft vom Judentum*] in the half hour I have been allotted—or even in two hours—is a presumptuous venture. It has the allure of being at the very least daring, if not actually reckless. It is of course far beyond my ability to discuss this question properly in such a short address. I would therefore like to sketch only a few rather private notions which may, however, yield a picture of what has actually changed in the Science of Judaism. The picture can also show us where we stand today and what lies in store for us. The problem itself is eminently significant for us; it is a problem that preys on our minds.

The Science of Judaism emanated from Germany. Leopold Zunz, his first co-workers, and the great founders of the Science of Judaism who followed in his footsteps during the nineteenth century, set out to establish it as a discipline. From Germany its influence spread to all the lands where Jews have settled. This heritage of German Jewry remains alive today even where recent decisive changes are destined to transform the nature of the structure extensively. For us the Science of Judaism means an understanding of our character and history. That, in a word, is the main concern.

This understanding of our own character and history has undergone extensive change. For the Science of Judaism did not develop in a vacuum; rather, it served historical functions. In its most important formative period it played the role of a real historical force in Judaism for wide circles of the Jewish community. The function of this discipline is to move the viewer to thought, sometimes to overpower him, sometimes drive him to despair, but at other times perhaps fill him with quiet, slight hope.

When it came into being, the Science of Judaism was a powerful and very active force in Berlin, Galicia, Prague, and other centers open to the influence of early nineteenth-century German culture. To be sure, the function it exercised had always been of a questionable nature; it always had a twilight quality. It arose and took effect under the influence of antiquarian, ideal, and romantic conceptions. Its first proponents were deeply, if not indirectly, influenced by the conceptions of the romantics. What motivated the German romantics, however, was the active comprehension of the organism of their own history in the sense of a positive, nationally oriented perspective and future. They wanted to further their own cause. The first great difficulty, the onerous heritage which the Science of Judaism has bequeathed us since its beginning, has been the large opposite tendencies that were active in it during and after its establishment. The attempt to disregard the most vital aspects of the Jewish people as a collective entity dominated in particular the work of the most significant representatives of the Science of Judaism. That attempt to reduce Judaism to a purely spiritual, ideal phenomenon, which, moreover, was evaluated according to certain time-bound estimations and judgments, necessarily pushed into the background those features which were not relevant if viewed from the perspective of such spiritualization. These eminent scholars and great personalities have left us all a great and positive heritage for which each of us can never be sufficiently grateful, for it forms the foundation of our work; but their bias represents a form of censorship of the Jewish past.

The Jewish people as a whole was very much alive; it was more than some fixed structure, let alone something defined or definable by a theological formula. This Jewish people presented a problem that went far beyond the tasks the theologians of Judaism set for themselves. And we cannot and must not forget that with two very prominent exceptions, truly central figures, nearly all of the creators and co-workers in the domains of Jewish historiography and Science of Judaism were theologians. The rabbinic share in both the positive and the problematic is enormous; it cannot be overestimated. These rabbis, who unlocked the sources, were the first to make possible precise inquiries and historical criticism. But at the same time, especially due to the influence of the nineteenth century, they brought with them a certain tendency, shared about equally by all the "denominations": to water down Judaism and to spiritualize it. The exceptions I mentioned were Leopold Zunz and Moritz Steinschneider. Although of theological rabbinical backgrounds, they achieved a strictly untheological attitude and proclaimed it clearly in their life's work. In the case of Moritz Steinschneider, one of the most significant scholars the Jewish people ever produced, the attitude was even downright anti-theological. But their students were rabbis. Under the conditions prevailing in the nineteenth or early twentieth century no one else had the opportunity to devote his leisure to such studies—in the way a university professor can devote his life to serious inquiries and responsible investigations, certain that other obligations will not deter him from their completion.

Today some of us, at least, have different opportunities to devote ourselves to such scholarly problems, and we easily fail to appreciate the difficulties with which our forefathers, the founders of the discipline, had to struggle. Then there was no institution devoted to pure scholarship unrelated to some religious tendency, be it orthodox, liberal, or conservative (the differences between the three do not really matter in their scholarly work; they are much less than one would think). No institution approached scholarly inquiry free of the determining influence of such theological points of view. This shortcoming scarcely allowed for creation of the major comprehensive works which the study of Judaism as a living organism—and not as a variously defined idea—demands. In 1825, at the very inception of the Science of Judaism, Zunz developed a grand, youthful program for a genuine folklore of the Jews which, in his view, embraced everything that is part of a living organism. He found hardly any successors to carry out this splendid plan, which he had conceived before any really detailed work had yet been undertaken. Only in the last two generations has the project been seized upon in earnest.

However, two tendencies were competing in the construction of the Science of Judaism from the very beginning. The one was set upon the liquidation of Judaism as a living organism. Its goal was "de-Judaization" as Zalman Rubashov called it in the title of his article, "First Fruits of De-Judaization," which dealt with the first programmatic statements of Zunz's Society for Culture and Science of the Jews. The other was directed toward its transfiguration. These destructive and constructive tendencies stand in a peculiar dialectical relationship. The great representatives of German romanticism, whom Zunz took as his models, were emotionally attached to the living peoplehood (the "genius" of the people). But for this the proponents of the Science of Judaism had little (if any) interest. Theirs was a completely different attitude.

Gotthold Weil, an early Zionist, was one of the last students of Moritz Steinschneider (who died in 1907 at more than ninety years of age). After his teacher's death, Weil recalled a conversation he had held with the aged Steinschneider upon a visit to him in his library toward the end of a life devoted for seventy years to researching the details of Jewish bibliography, literature, and culture. With youthful enthusiasm—he had probably just been freshly inspired by the Jewish Students' League—Weil gushed forth before the old man the ideas of the Jewish renaissance and the reconstruction of Judaism as a living entity. But old Steinschneider regarded this as nonsense. Pointing toward his bookcases with an inimitable gesture he said, "We have only one task left: to give the remains of Judaism a decent burial." Not everyone expressed it as radically and precisely as Moritz Steinschneider, who never minced words in expressing his convictions. However—a breath of the funereal did in fact cling to the atmosphere of this discipline for a century; occasionally there is something ghostlike about this literature. Yet at the same time the positive element quite unintentionally asserts itself. In many of these scholars, romantic enthusiasm overcomes their original intention of liquidating, spiritualizing, and de-actualizing Judaism. It drives them on to positive insight far removed from what they originally envisioned.

This tendency of the Science of Judaism in the nineteenth century, moreover, cast a kind of spell over Jewish history itself, a spell which expressed itself in a certain type of idyll, a peculiar etherealization. The ancient Jewish books, forgotten and betrayed by a few generations, had become opaque for this nineteenth century. They were often regarded as possessing only antiquarian interest. They no longer sent their rays outward but, as it were, radiated only into themselves; they had become invisible. Yet there is life hidden in this Judaism. It awaits the breaking of the spell and the release which are often missing in the great works of the Science of Judaism. A living relationship to the realities of Jewish literature existed only insofar as it lent itself to timely exploitation for the political and apologetic battle of the Jews in Europe, especially in Western Europe. Beyond this there is scarcely a direct, living relationship to these things. It is one of the peculiarities of our past that it is practically impossible today to read with enjoyment the translations of Hebrew poetry and the great works of significant prose which were produced in these circles during the nineteenth century. They are all under a certain spell and possess a peculiar Jewish sentimentalism which is entirely foreign to the original. The originals are often quite un-bourgeois. They are amazingly full of life and radiate an atmosphere that trembles in awe of the past. But in these translations, which I first read as a young man, they gave me an eerie feeling.

The position and function of the Science of Judaism has radically changed. For a long time apologetics played an enormous role, a distinctly positive role, which we should not forget. The struggle for equal rights, which was of decisive importance for the Science of Judaism, forced the Jews to select certain themes. The determination of what was worth dealing with and what was not, in itself presented a great achievement, regardless of how questionable the principles of selection may seem to us today. We must not forget that the highly significant work which first raised the Science of Judaism to the rank of a scholarly discipline, Zunz's great opus, *The Liturgic Addresses of the Jews* (1832), was written out of apologetic motives. It was intended to prove that the German sermon, which at the time was a subject of bitter controversy in the Jewish communities, had historical justification. Thus a project in apologetics, directed no less to the Jewish authorities than to the organs of government, produced one of the greatest achievements of the Science of Judaism. Today it is still universally regarded as one of its high points.

Apologetics was the great stimulus in a battle waged against old and new anti-Semitism, a battle against all kinds of political tendencies, including some within the Jewish community; scholarship was used in furthering such political purposes. The Science of Judaism was a force in this battle—often a decisive weapon— as we can recognize by looking back on it today. Yet at the same time this attitude contained the danger of one-sided concentration of interest on those matters which possessed apologetic value. Many of us know that there were large areas which seemed downright obdurate from an apologetic point of view. Naturally the Science of Judaism therefore regarded such fields with the gravest suspicion, with aversion, and even with open enmity. This is true for large segments of Jewish literature and Jewish life and culture. From the point of view of the Enlightenment-minded, purified, rational Judaism of the nineteenth century they seemed not properly usable and hence were thrown out as un-Jewish or, at the least, half pagan. Such was the case with all phenomena of Jewish mysticism—to the study of which I have devoted my own work—as well as other related areas. The inability to deal with material things or to present spiritual phenomena outside the realm of a refined theology capable of also pleasing rationally inclined Gentiles—all this led to keeping such areas beyond reach. And this applies not only to such great spiritual manifestations as Hasidism and the Kabbalah. It applies also to quite tangible concrete manifestations of Jewish life, as shown by the horror with which the Science of Judaism reacted to the question of the Jewish underworld of the eighteenth and nineteenth centuries: thieves, robbers, and the like. Only non-Jews dealt with this question, either from anti-Semitic motives or from a completely impartial point of view. The theme was strictly taboo in the Science of Judaism although it considered presentation of the relations between Jews and the surrounding non-Jewish world a problem of the first magnitude and much in need of formulation. But this matter received attention only in its most "genteel" aspects. What went on in the cellar was scrupulously avoided. These scholars considered only the intellectual relations of the salon: the Bible and Luther, Hermann Cohen and Kant, Steinthal and Wilhelm von Humboldt. They took no notice of the fact that in the most diverse areas exactly the same relations existed in the "basement." These relations were extraordinarily real, though of a kind not always or not all appropriate for discussion in the "salon." Such matters were simply disregarded. Today we have to collect them with the greatest difficulty in order to gain a reasonably complete picture of how the Jewish organism functioned in relation to its actual environment. We must determine on which of the various levels, from the most refined to the most despised, there existed a vital intercourse—whether or not we happen to like it. In those days such matters naturally and quite understandably fell victim to self-censorship.

Where do we stand today? As much as apologetics can accomplish—and I think it can accomplish a great deal—we have today experienced a change, taken a new turn that is expressed above all in three developments. The Zionist movement—in agreement with Zunz's view at the very beginning—again understood Judaism as a living organism and not merely as an idea. It could

therefore apply criteria of value entirely different from those of
a purely philosophical and theological view of what Judaism
represented as a historical phenomenon. Zionism brought about
the first basic change, although in the first twenty or thirty years
of the movement it scarcely influenced scholarly work itself. Many
scholars became Zionists, but very few of them drew radical
consequences from it for their work or for the problematics of
their area of research. Nonetheless, this change produced something new: it became possible for people to devote themselves
fully to the Science of Judaism as a result of their Zionist commitment. These men had no theological attachments and did not
approach the subject because of rabbinical interests. While in
one respect this may have been a disadvantage, it had the advantage of perhaps providing a more comprehensive perspective
when dealing with the living whole. Zionism regarded Jewish
history as an organic process of confrontation between the Jewish
and non-Jewish worlds. The new valuations of Zionism brought
a breath of fresh air into a house that seemed to have been all
too carefully set in order by the nineteenth century. This ventila-
tion was good for us. Within the framework of the rebuilding of
Palestine it led to the foundation of centers like the Hebrew
University in Jerusalem where Judaic studies, although central, are
pursued without any ideological coloring. Everyone is free to say
and to teach whatever corresponds to his scholarly opinion without
being bound to any religious (or anti-religious) tendency. As a
result, great opportunities lay open to treat Jewish sources, the
Jewish past, and Jewish spiritual life with new profundity and
liveliness.

To be sure, the two other developments are no less significant, although we have not the time to do them justice today. I
refer to the holocaust we have all witnessed, and the establishment
of the State of Israel. The significance of these two developments
for the Science of Judaism cannot be overestimated. Never again
shall we be able to regard Jewish history and the conditions of
Jewish community life with the same eyes. The holocaust has
finally and irrevocably removed a view which was possible only
until then. Henceforth Judaism can be regarded solely as the
continuity of a social whole, which certainly struggled under
the inspiration of great ideas, but was never completely ruled or
directed by them. However, at the same time, the holocaust
sawed off the branch we were sitting on. The great reservoir
of strength, the rising generation, the hope of an enthusiastic

youth which would be drawn to the idea of a newly visible, inclusive image of Judaism and would turn its attention to a new Jewish historiography—that generation died in Auschwitz and similar places. It is idle to have any illusions about it. We have suffered a loss of blood which has indeterminable consequences for our spiritual and scholarly creativity. We ourselves—considering our close proximity to the events—have as yet scarcely been able to rationalize and understand in a scholarly manner the meaning of what we ourselves have lived and suffered through. It is simply not possible to draw the consequences this soon. The great catastrophe of the Jewish expulsion from Spain in 1492 provides a historical precedent. This community was one of the largest and most flourishing, spiritually significant branches of the living tree of Judaism. When it suddenly was broken off the Jewish people needed a very long time before it could render itself account and come to grips with what had happened. Two generations passed until it reached that point in the course of the sixteenth century. The situation today is not very different. I do not believe that we, the generation that experienced this event—which affected all that was dear to us—either directly ourselves or through our neighbors, can be in a position to draw the consequences as yet. However, the meaning of the holocaust must remain of overwhelming significance for the problematics of the Science of Judaism and, in my opinion, cannot be assessed too highly.

The establishment of the State of Israel, as yet the only visible positive result of the holocaust, falls into the same category. Taken together, they somehow represent two sides of a single vast historical event. The significance of this occurrence lies in a tremendous prospect: that the Jewish people can try to solve its problems without any squinting to the left or right; it can pose the question of confrontation of Jews and non-Jews; it can approach the clarification of all the historical and spiritual issues pending between Jews and Gentiles. Such problems can now be taken up and discussed, independent of what anyone else may have to say on the subject and without any regard for external considerations. As always, a productive, positive prospect, which sets forth such possibilities, also has a corresponding great danger. All of us, especially those who work in Israel and have tied their research to life there, know that dangers exist as well. Judaism as a whole is more than an idea—however potent—that motivates us. There is no getting away from the danger that Jewish history may now be regarded one-sidedly as a process brought into line with a Zionist point of view. The heritage of an apologetics in reverse, an apologetics which now, so to speak, has revised everythink in terms of Zionism, has produced notable examples in our scholarly work. In reality we have yet to free ourselves from such an inheritance; perhaps in a living process it may not be possible to do so overnight. We have not yet overcome what is amateurish, one-sided, and idyllic, or the exclusive emphasis on narrow social perspectives. Anyone who wants to become melancholy about the Science of Judaism need only read the last twenty volumes of the *Jewish Quarterly Review* (published in the United States), and he will lose his faith in Jewish scholarship. Or let him read another document of our time, the Hebrew periodical *Sinai* (published in Jerusalem); its study will, for entirely different reasons, produce the same melancholy in any reader who is committed to the scholarly way of thinking. It is not true that everything is now revealed and out in the open. Yet great perspectives have been laid open as a result of this, if I may say so, utopian retreat of the Jewish people to its own existence and the decision to engage this existence to the fullest extent—perspectives that obviously influence research. The secularized view of Judaism opens up an enormously positive potentiality. Seen from a theological point of view, it may in a quite different fashion lead to a new manner of religious inquiry which will then not be determined simply by formulas inherited from an earlier generation.

The major centers of activity are now in Israel and America, to which the center of the one-time European Jewish scholarly enterprise has been transferred. The natural tensions between them will continue to exist and will remain fruitful. To be sure, we still have great individual Jewish scholars everywhere in the world. But it seems unlikely that active centers will develop outside these two large Jewries. Whatever happens in these two, the products of these two centers will always stand in some relation of tension, for tension is the natural relation between living things. We must and shall hope that great individuals will accomplish achievements made possible by the new perspective, the new view of the Jewish past and of Jewish character. Our generation has no reason to complain: a Fritz [Yitzhak] Baer in Jerusalem is not inferior to Graetz; Baron is not less than Dubnow, Saul Lieberman not less than Zacharias Frankel; Julius Guttmann and Harry A. Wolfson are not less than David Neumark and David Kaufmann. We have men who are re-creating a scholarly heritage in our generation. They have set out to produce not reassurance but reflection and further thought. This ·renewed heritage, with its vitality and impetus to inquiry, is the equal of anything in the past.

This is our situation today. We have renounced the bottled product which in the past so often constituted the Science of Judaism. We have committed ourselves to the task of investigating what is alive in Judaism, of undertaking an empirically oriented impartial enterprise instead of an antiquarian history of literature. Achievements of this sort can already be seen in the fields of Talmud and the history of religion, medieval Hebrew poetry (which only in our own generation has been revealed in all its beauty and significance), and the previously untouched area of folk literature. Thus we have today some conception of important matters which await more thorough study. The great works of Jewish literature have not yet been scientifically evaluated. An aesthetics of Jewish literature is still totally lacking; only very few scholars have been able to determine what constitutes the formal aspect in the literary products of our past. I said that we are all at a great turning point which sets us a task. It is a task to which the heirs of German Jewry should also apply themselves with full devotion. By genuine scholarly immersion into facts and circumstances we may be able to reorganize and reconstruct the whole from its smallest parts. Such an immersion must not shrink from the insight expressed in the magnificent saying ascribed to Aby Warburg: *Der liebe Gott lebt im Detail* (It is in the minutiae that God can be found).

At the Completion
of Buber's Translation
of the Bible

MY DEAR MARTIN BUBER, somewhat like a traditional Jewish *siyyum* marking the completion of a course of study, we have gathered today in your house to celebrate the notable occasion of the conclusion of your German Bible translation. It provides us with a significant opportunity to look back on this your work, its intent, and its achievement. Some of us have witnessed and followed the development of this work from its inception and we can well understand the feeling of satisfaction which must accompany its conclusion.

You are a man who has always brought great perseverance and endurance to his tasks. Fifty years and more you devoted to the completion of your Hasidic œuvre, which accompanied you most of your life. And, if I am not mistaken, thirty-five years have now passed since we received the first volume of the translation by you and Franz Rosenzweig. I do not know exactly the circumstances which in 1924 or 1925 made you decide to begin this project together with Rosenzweig. I was already in Palestine at the time. I believe it was—as sometimes happens—a providential impulse, the kind of pure coincidence which is never entirely coincidental, that a young publisher, Lambert Schneider, came to you and said he would like you to do a Bible translation. When you decided to undertake this project and gained the collaboration of Franz Rosenzweig, you probably did not expect this task to occupy you more than a few years. And yet, as it turned out, for more than a generation—with a few interruptions —you have devoted to it a large portion of your energy and, I would add, of your creative powers. It must have been a challenge for you to deal with a text which as Holy Writ demands more than the effort of the artist and the precision of the philologist, especially from people who, like Rosenzweig and yourself, approached this text from a definite spiritual point of view and felt addressed by it. And so you put much of your own self into this work, even when you could express it only through the medium of the most faithful translation.

When I received the Genesis volume, or rather the book called "In the Beginning," I wrote you a long letter in which I set forth all kinds of considerations. I do not recall exactly what I wrote, but I still have your reply in which you said that you had found in my letter the only serious criticism you had thus far received. Since then your work has done more than pass through the crucible of criticism. It has established itself as a historical accomplishment and proven itself a special kind of *Gastgeschenk*. But more of that later. You yourself have been the most severe, stubborn, and determined critic of your own work, the artist, master of the language, and homo religiosus who constantly struggled for the precision and richness of expression that would satisfy your intention.

If I consider what in fact you and Rosenzweig might have primarily intended by this project, I am tempted to say that it was an appeal to the reader: Go and learn Hebrew! For your translation is in no sense an attempt to raise the Bible, through the medium of the German language, to a level of clear comprehensibility, beyond all difficulties. Rather, you took special care not to make the Bible simpler than it is. What is clear remains clear, what is difficult remains difficult, and what is incomprehensible remains incomprehensible. You do not take the reader in and you make no concessions. The reader is constantly referred back to his own reflection and must ask himself—precisely as you intended—what it is that here seeks expression. You smoothed out nothing, nor made things easier. Quite the contrary: You had a special sense for the obstacles and difficulties which lie hidden in even the seemingly unproblematic flow of prose or poetry. I almost said: You made the text rougher in order to let the words affect the reader with that much more immediacy. The method which you found useful was to strive for the utmost literality, a literality that seemed at times to go to the limits and beyond. You had a definite conception of the rough-hewn structure of the Hebrew language and sought to express it in your translation. No fill-in words, no transitions where none exist in Hebrew. No trifling with the sublime but letting it stand in its own rough greatness.

And there is something else. I do not know if you realized at the time what the effect of your method in all its severity would be. But I believe I have found the right word for it in your own most recent writings. A few days ago I read your brief but significant philosophical reflections on the meaning of the "Spoken Word," which you wrote in 1960 as an authentic summary of your thinking in terms of language (*Sprachdenken*). I became aware that what mattered to you in your translation was the spoken word. You were not interested in translating the Bible as literature; not the literary quality was important to you, not what the reader could pick up with his eyes, but the realm of the living, spoken word. It is a unique feature of your translation that it uses every means to force the reader to read the text aloud. By its syntax and choice of words, and even more by its separation of sentence parts into "breathing units," it forces him, as much as a written text possibly can, to read it out loud. The sentences are printed in such a way as to divide them into lines according to the natural breathing cycle. Thus in your work you provided one of the most significant illustrations for the notion of structure in literary discourse, which in those days when you and Rosenzweig began your task was becoming known as colometry. The biblical word as spoken word, as recitative, was always before your eyes— or rather before your ears—and in this no translator has ever surpassed you. This unimposing faithfulness to the original carries another blessing with it. For your translation is not merely a translation; without adding a word of explanation per se it is also a commentary. Time and again when we have encountered difficult sections of the Bible many of us have asked ourselves: What does Buber have to say about this? Not so very different from our asking ourselves: What does Rashi say? This incorporation of commentary even into the strictest literality of the translation itself seems to me one of the greatest achievements of your work.

The long interruption which followed the publication of the major portion of your translation by Lambert Schneider and Schocken gave you the opportunity to rework it in recent years for the definitive and complete new edition; you have brought it into harmony with the new sense for language as well as the exegetical knowledge of your mature years. I have not compared these two versions throughout, but I have read enough of them to venture the following remark: If I had to characterize the difference between the two versions, the old and the new, I would speak—if you will allow me the term—of the extraordinary urbanity of the later version. What I mean is this: the first version, in all its grandeur, contains also an element of fanaticism. This fanaticism, it seemed to us, was inseparable from your endeavor. It aimed at driving words to their limit, extracting— I almost said chiseling out—from the language an extreme, yes, an excess of toughness and precision. It was not always easy to recover the melodic presentation of great texts, the *niggun* of the language. And yet just this was the goal you set for the reader. Though, as you know, I have nothing against fanatics, certainly not against those of language, the distinct urbanity of your new version seems to me the greater virtue. Without giving up the purpose and method of your translation, you achieved something both very engaging and pleasing. It is possible now to read many of the sentences without a feeling of anxiety; precision has not been sacrificed, but there are signs of a kind of retreat to a more civil, measured way of speech, of the spoken word. It indicates a mastery which no longer has need of extravagance but is able to make its point even with discretion. The words of biblical discourse no longer stand in that state of tension with their melos which we sometimes felt in the earlier translation. It is a marvelous dispensation that you have been able to complete a work of such maturity, of such exegetical wisdom and linguistic faithfulness.

Finally, there is one last consideration which has determined the special character of your translation in both versions. It is one of the grand paradoxes of this undertaking that in a translation which in the final analysis renders the Bible as the word of God the name of God as such should not appear. It is replaced by the emphatic and prominent use of I, Thou, and He. By these pronouns alone may we apprehend God, with great clarity, though only mediately as befits us. This is not the least significant of the numerous and bold innovations of the translation. It rests on the conviction that in a book that speaks of the rule of God in creation and in history the name of God which was available to the ancient authors need only appear indirectly. In this way you found a creative compromise between the traditional Jewish awe that forbids the pronouncing of the name of God and the obligation to make the biblical word readable, i.e., audible.

So much for my appreciation and expression of gratitude to you for your work. You have spared no pains to study commentaries and supercommentaries, German and Hebrew dictionaries, philologists both good and bad. In your final choice of words you took a stand without using the medium of translation to exercise criticism. And so we may express to you our thanks and congratulations on the completion of your work.

And yet I am not able to close without saying a word about the historical context of your work, which must remain a question and a very concerned question. When you and Rosenzweig began this undertaking there was a German Jewry; your work was intended to have a vital influence on them, to arouse them and lead them to the original. There also was a German language in which you could find a link with great traditions and achievements, and with significant developments of this language. You yourselves could hope to raise this language to a new level by your work. There was a utopian element in your endeavor. For the language into which you translated was not that of everyday speech nor that of German literature of the 1920's. You aimed at a German which, drawing sustenance from earlier tendencies, was present potentially in the language, and it was just this utopianism which made your translation so very exciting and stimulating. Now whether you consciously so intended it or not, your translation—which came from the association of a Zionist and a non-Zionist—was a kind of *Gastgeschenk* which German Jewry gave to the German people, a symbolic act of gratitude upon departure. And what *Gastgeschenk* of the Jews to Germany could be as historically meaningful as a Bible translation? But events took a different course. I fear (or hope?) I shall provoke your contradiction and yet I cannot refrain from asking: For whom is this translation now intended and whom will it influence? Seen historically, it is no longer a *Gastgeschenk* of the Jews to the Germans but rather—and it is not easy for me to say this—the tombstone of a relationship that was extinguished in unspeakable horror. The Jews for whom you translated are no more. Their children, who have escaped from this horror, will no longer read German. The German language itself has profoundly changed in this generation, as everyone knows who in recent years has had contact with the new German language. And it has not developed in the direction of that language utopia to which your endeavor bears such impressive witness. The contrast between the common language of 1925 and your translation has not decreased in the last thirty-five years; it has become greater.

As to what the Germans will do with your translation, who can venture to say? For more has happened to the Germans than Hölderlin foresaw when he said:

> it is not ill if certain things are lost,
> and living sound from discourse fade away.

> (und nicht Übel ist, wenn einiges
> verloren gehet, und von der Rede
> verhallet der lebendige Laut.)

For many of us the living sound which you tried to evoke in the German language has faded away. Will anyone be found to take it up again?

On the 1930 Edition of
Rosenzweig's Star of Redemption

TEN YEARS AFTER it was first published we have before us a
second edition of Franz Rosenzweig's *Star of Redemption*. Even
today, it is not easy to say in which respect it has exercised the
greatest influence. Perhaps the reason for this is that the *Star of
Redemption* belongs to that peculiar genre of books whose significance, from the moment of publication, was entirely undisputed.
Subtly yet noticeably these books emanated a healing and
harmonizing power, but in a mysterious way seemed to provoke
an analysis of their most basic contents while at the same time
making such analysis impossible. Here was a rigorously theistic
system which drew a rather new insight into the world of Judaism
and its theology from yet unused sources of religious thought.
Who would deny that coming to terms with it was then, and
still is, an urgent concern? Does it not seem all the more astonishing that as yet it has received no serious treatment? The enthusiasts,
of which there were quite a few, were no doubt blinded by its rays.
Thoughtful readers of the book could not overlook the imperious
aggressiveness with which certain ideas, especially large sections
of the second and third parts—the doctrine of revelation, the
discussion of Christianity, and the theologia mystica of truth
(of the "Star")—tore into the taut world of medieval classical
Jewish theology, to say nothing of the settled idyllic world of
"liberal" of "orthodox" Jewish theology at the time of World
War I. To be sure, it was impossible to plot the course of this
new star by the coordinates of existing religious tendencies. But
should not the obvious impossibility of recognizing the realms of
orthodoxy or liberalism in Rosenzweig's world have rather called
forth the desire for serious analysis and clearer definition of the
problematic elements which are inevitably present in this as in
any theology? Instead of stimulating analysis it seems to have

hindered it. The awareness that a star has seldom shown forth from such depth and run its course has driven contemporaries completely away from critical discussion, let alone polemics. This is true despite the fact that few works have been as provocative since the appearance of the *Guide of the Perplexed* or the *Zohar*. Therefore it can hardly be doubted that in the long run this work will need ever increasing critical attention. Perhaps also the enigmatic pensiveness of the work exercised magical power. The first generation of its readers seems to have given this quality especially intense attention as the reverse side of its aggressiveness. The early effect of the work was thus largely banished into the stillness where the fire of this star burnt inward.

In order to determine the secret of this effect it may also be proper to recall the contemporary situation. I think one can say without disrespect that hardly ever had there been a Jewish theology of such vacuity and insignificance as existed in the decades before World War I. The inability to penetrate religious reality with rigorous concepts as well as the lack of readiness to perceive the religious world of Judaism in its totality were apparent equally in all the movements; they determined the inherent weakness manifest in the products of those years. Since the collapse of the Kabbalah and the last efforts to describe the reality of Judaism from this point of view—attempts such as those of Solomon Plessner and Elijah Benamozegh only showed the complete decay of this movement—othodox theology has suffered from what one might call "Kabbalah-phobia." It had decided to abrogate any deeper speculation which in a new and positive way might have led back to that world of the Kabbalah. This decision had most disastrous and destructive results in the theology of Samson Raphael Hirsch who—a classical instance of the "frustrated mystic"—preferred to construct a highly questionable and nearly coarse symbolism of his own design just to avoid any reference back to the world which he had forbidden himself: the world of the Kabbalah. And what healthy chunks the liberal theologians took out of Judaism! For the sake of an abstraction they had more or less to eliminate the realities of language, land, and peoplehood from their theories. In Moritz Lazarus' *Ethics of Judaism*, for example, their most fruitful and clearest intuitions no longer made sense in terms of this abstraction and were extinguished by the artificial vacuum surrounding them. Finally, Zionism with its seemingly secularizing tendencies was as yet unable to contribute to a theology that on account of its weakness was incapable of recognizing, let alone of grasping, the religious problematics, only incompletely and ineffectually concealed by that secularization.

Given this situation, we found in Rosenzweig's work something new which in an unanticipated way addressed us from the center of our hopes for renewal. It challenged us and, why not admit it, perplexed us. What paradox could move us more deeply than this one: the re-establishment of a connection with the traditional Jewish view of the world, which had once been great but became indeterminable, achieved and developed not from an analysis of its earlier components but directly from a completely different approach. It was obtained by philosophical penetration into the order of a world which would be able to survive the catastrophic collapse of [German] idealism as the structural principle of the world—which would in fact grow out of this catastrophe. The seductive illusion of man's moral autonomy determined the theology of Jewish liberalism, which had its origins essentially in idealism. From here no path lay open, except for a radical reversal in direction, back toward the mysteries of revelation that constituted the basis of Rosenzweig's new world, which turned out to be the most ancient world of all. Yet the new interpretation of this world stands in opposition even more to the classical theology of a Maimonides or a Hasdai Crescas. To begin with, it moves from the positions of reason to a theistic mysticism and gives support to strictly mystical theologoumena (in counterpoint to the bitter polemic against the mysticism of apocalyptic prayer which opens Part III of the *Star*). More important, it dares as well to set in the center of its theological anthropology a comparative analysis of Judaism and Christianity which ends in a *non liquet,* and therefore with a dictum that from the point of view of orthodoxy must seem rash and nearly blasphemous.

This basic understanding of Judaism seemed to have little or nothing in common with the themes familiar to us in such endeavors, and that made it at once attractive and problematic. The thinker, who by his personal reflections had ripped open the abyss in which the substance of Judaism lies hidden, had sealed it again with new names. Whether or not the attempt to deduce the two possibilities for theocratic modes of life in Judaism and Christianity from the dialectics of the concept of redemption could in fact determine the true place of each one may remain in dispute, though this is one of the principal points in the *Star,* which most unavoidably calls for serious analysis. There is no dispute, however, regarding the significance of Rosenzweig's metaphysical-pragmatic method of discovering the secrets contained in the liturgical structure of religious realities. To be sure, by his use of the doctrine of the anticipation of redemption in Jewish life, a concept as fascinating as it is problematic, Rosenzweig took a decided and hostile stand against the one open door in the otherwise very neatly ordered house of Judaism. He opposed the theory of catastrophes contained in Messianic apocalypticism which might be considered the point at which even today theocratic and bourgeois modes of life stand irreconcilably opposed. The deep-seated tendency to remove the apocalyptic thorn from the organism of Judaism makes Rosenzweig the last and certainly one of the most vigorous exponents of a very old and very powerful movement in Judaism, which crystallized in a variety of forms. This tendency is probably also responsible for the strangely church-like aspect which Judaism unexpectedly sometimes takes on here. Apocalypticism, as a doubtlessly anarchic element, provided some fresh air in the house of Judaism; it provided a recognition of the catastrophic potential of all historical order in an unredeemed world. Here, in a mode of thought deeply concerned for order, it underwent metamorphosis. The power of redemption seems to be built into the clockwork of life lived in the light of revelation, though more as restlessness than as potential destructiveness. For a thinker of Rosenzweig's rank could never remain oblivious to the truth that redemption possesses not only a liberating but also a destructive force—a truth which only too many Jewish theologians are loath to consider and which a whole literature takes pains to avoid. Rosenzweig sought at least to neutralize it in a higher order of truth. If it be true that the lightning of redemption directs the universe of Judaism, then in Rosenzweig's work the life of the Jew must be seen as the lightning rod whose task it is to render harmless its destructive power.

Ten years are a short time in the life of a work which is destined to undergo change and to endure. It was an attempt, mystical in the strictest sense, to construct that which did not allow of construction, the star of redemption. (In mystical astronomy—which is what one could call Rosenzweig's symbolic world—there is likewise really no other mode of description except by construction.) This work will disclose its enduring content only to a generation that will no longer feel itself addressed in such immediate fashion by the themes most pertinent to the present time (which need not always be its most central themes) as did that generation which at the time of its appearance had just gone through World War I. Only when the enchanting beauty of its language will have worn off and the figure of the martyr, which for us contemporaries is inseparably part of it, will have withdrawn to cast an aura of its own—only then shall this testimony to God be able to assert itself in its undisguised intent.

The Politics of Mysticism:
Isaac Breuer's New Kuzari

I

IN THE WAVERING twilight in which we live, few lights are burning. Judah Halevi's *Kuzari,* one of the rare unforgotten documents of our religious thought, has paled in its glory and relevance. In a different way we again confront the old questions, but only few know how to approach them. Isaac Breuer (*Der neue Kuzari: Ein Weg zum Judentum*) does so with self-confidence: [1] since he knows the truth (which not everyone can claim) and believes in it (which is not at all self-evident in respect to this truth) he can dare to raise the pretension which is, after all, expressed by such a title. And since, one may well say, he belongs to the category of those zealous for the Lord, passionate appeal and polemics cannot here be lacking.

In fact, no thoughtful reader will be able to put down this book without the most conflicting emotions. As eccentric and obstinate, as totally unrepresentative as it appears to be, the book nonetheless contains something like a genuine testimony to the baroque situation of German Jewry in the night of its catastrophe. An author speaks here whose readiness for paradox, no less than his determination to express a conviction regarding religion and political history in all of its most ambiguous elements, deserves our respect and even, in regard to certain aspects, our admiration. The boldness of taking a step even beyond the sublime, which a forensic pathos fed by an overstrained imagination cannot resist, is not the worst and certainly not the least hopeful form of civil courage. Here is a writer who with the eloquent flow of his historiosophy and theosophy navigates the rapids of abstruseness with an ease and naïveté that could lead one to believe he is not entirely clear on the risk of his venture. Yet that would be to

325

underestimate his insight. He knows what is at stake and is not at a loss for weapons. He picks up whatever comes within his reach and then lashes out with it in all directions. The reader, easily benumbed and bedazzled by so much offensive spirit and verbal fencing, finishes the book rather breathless. When he looks back on this field of combat, glances over this "Battle of the Torah," and imagines the arsenal from which the weapons scattered here could have come, he may be overwhelmed by a vague dread; the scenery is that ghostly.

What is the battle in this *New Kuzari* all about? By calling itself "a path to Judaism," it renders a distorted, and in this very distortion a characteristic, testimony to itself. The true situation is highly incongruous with the embellished literary form in which the author presents it. This contradiction between appearance and reality, which has always been a special danger for the dialogue as a literary category, permeates the book in a disturbing way and robs it of form. Seemingly we are shown the path to Judaism; in reality we see one of its strangest variants, consigned to oblivion, desperately struggling to hold its ground. Seemingly we follow the path which Alfred Roden alias Rosenstock, by background a "German citizen of total Jewish non-belief," struggles to attain. In a series of biting dialogues, in which the partners turn toward us their by no means purely allegorical profiles in their full ambiguity, complexity, and vacillation, this young man storms past members of the *Centralverein*, liberals, Zionists, members of the Mizrahi and of Community Orthodoxy, straightway toward the true path to Judaism. In Rabbi S. R. Hirsch's separatist congregation [2] (the abundantly imperfect to be sure, but according to its inner significance legitimate seed of a theocracy in the Diaspora) this path leads on from step to step without break, blessed by the wellsprings of Bible and prayer, Talmud and Kabbalah. Finally it reaches that utopian point of Jewish history at which Alfred Roden, i.e., Isaac Breuer, at the turn of the era erects the banner of the movement of "tideyism." * And thus, whether in Frankfurt or in Jerusalem, he prepares to correct "the much misunderstood phrase *torah im derekh eretz* in the sense of tideyism," i.e., of the new watchword *torah im derekh Eretz Yisrael*, and thus counterpoise the "national-bound socialism of theocracy" in the Holy Land to the apostate slogans of the Zionists. So much for the approach of the

---

* An ism based on the intial letters of *torah im derekh Eretz Yisrael*.

author, who presents his conception of such a Judaism in further didactic conversations of his alter ego (who now appears as a reformer of the strictest German-Jewish orthodoxy) and in the more lengthy chapters, giving information and arguments, which interrupt and then conclude these dialogues. The diction of the dialogues in no way belies the significant talent of their author for pointed, drastic, even lawyer-like formulation (and for malice, *nota bene*).

But all of this, once again, is appearance. The true physiognomy of the book and its inner, totally opposite rhythm break through it. For, in all seriousness, this path to Judaism in just those respects which are of most decisive consequence to the author—the paradoxical and nearly grotesque metaphysics of a separatism that has lost itself in a dream of power and dominion spun out of intoxicated mysticism—is by no means built so soundly and solidly that it could draw to itself any travelers other than the most foolhardy: those who, fleeing a collapsing house, jump for their lives. It is not in the least likely that all who mutely listen to that dialogue on the necessity of withdrawal from the Jewish community, which is about to degenerate completely into a national community as in Palestine, will capitulate as helplessly and naïvely as that doughty orthodox community rabbi of the dialogue. But as essential as this may be to the author, it is not central. It would not be worth spending any time on this book if it were nothing more than the renewed expression of a certain conviction regarding the organizational structure of the Jewish community. Such a conviction would deserve the respect of those who think differently even where it cannot be debated or where, as a result of its definite and inescapable contradictions and forced sophisms, it has long become doubtful. All of this the author has already expressed just as sharply and perhaps with even greater force in his earlier writings, especially in *The Jewish National Home*,[3] which deserves a special niche in anti-Zionist literature. Likewise, there seems nothing new in his inclination to follow into its most sinister consequences the conception of the Torah as divine law and of the covenant as a religious legal fact by employing the most radical of juridical categories. Indeed, the reader becomes aware of their metaphysical character a good deal faster than is conducive to the author's intentions.

But there is a great deal in this book which is novel and astonishing, and it will be worth while from the start to indicate clearly where we stand, what it is here that tempts us. This novelty takes two forms: a new historical formula and its new theological proof. What is the author really trying to rescue and what is the new incantation with which the magician-legalist exorcizes us bothersome Zionist demons?

II

As I have already indicated, what is really under consideration here is not the way to Judaism but rather a sortie made from a beleaguered fortress, a true battle of desperation to rescue a world which is falling to pieces, a world which for the author is identical with the Torah. Attack is the best means of defense. That the author has made this attempt to liberate an endangered fortress through a daring surprise onslaught, for the most part evidently undertaken still before the radical change of 1933, does all honor to his clairvoyance. Let me make it perfectly clear: in the year 1933 German Jewish orthodoxy too, lame and idle as it was, lost a highly consequential battle, as did, in no small measure, that portion of orthodoxy which likes to call itself "independent." It happened at a great historical moment when the chances of the old Torah were greater than they had been for 150 years. But looking at the question of historical responsibility as a whole, we can ascribe the guilt for this lost battle to an individual under whose banners and by whose slogans (which proved to be not beacon lights but insubstantial delusions) the cause was lost. The true loser of this battle—and this aggressive book was in fact written to save him—has a name and, one might say, an address in history. His name is Samson Raphael Hirsch and he lives where Joseph Karo, Friedrich Schiller, and Judah Halevi were supposed to have met. (Some are of the opinion that the meeting is a spiritual fact of Jewish history, while others stoutly maintain that it was too windy, even a bit too spooky at that corner, and it was not possible to observe the scene any too closely.) It is the complete breakdown of the spiritual world of Samson Raphael Hirsch which has become apparent in our time. To save it, this *New Kuzari* finds no paradox too bold, no argument worth sparing, and no mysticism too obscure. I shall not here detract in the slightest from the great historical significance of Hirsch for a bygone age of bourgeois accommodation of an orthodox kind, even if I regard it as ominous. But it is remarkable how timidly the spiritual stature of this man is still treated, even by a generation which, though long in possession of criteria for a critique, only too seldom finds the courage to use them. Thus a kind of veneration for Hirsch has maintained itself down to our days and confronts us with "immediate" claims—not the least of them in Isaac Breuer's book—which have a ghost-like, musty aura about them.

But the time has come to finally say no. Torah-true Judaism in Germany has paid dearly for the slogan with which the ghastly accommodation theology of Hirsch and his school was allowed to demoralize its Jewish substance: that equivocal *torah im derekh eretz*. A number of things took place under this banner for which today, when the time of reckoning has come, no one wants any longer to accept responsibility. It was one of those formulas that reveal their hidden life too late, after their dialectic has turned against their proponents. In its beginnings in that bleak "world of progress," it was a concept which was intended to ease the accommodation of the old-style orthodox to that which was strangest for them, but it fulfilled its function all too well. It became the vehicle of an assimilation which would require a Jewish Balzac to describe fully in terms of its demonic triumphs within the orthodox camp. The slogan, which was supposed to strengthen the Jewish backbone of the pious in a changed world, contributed more than any other to breaking it for him. Today nearly a hundred years have passed since the appearance of the *Nineteen Letters on Judaism*,[4] which gave this development its first cue. The bright view of that slogan has long been replaced by a dark one which naturally no one wanted to see and the bankruptcy has become apparent. Few slogans of historical significance have been led *ad absurdum* in such horribly drastic fashion; few appear as chimerical today as does this one. Breuer calls it a "much misunderstood phrase," as if this were not just its tragedy, that we have understood it so thoroughly—not to say suffered from it—in its historical, naked reality, unconcealed by any complexity of expression. Even Breuer, who not only praises the mystical fullness of this formula but also develops it further, seems toward the end suddenly no longer completely satisfied with it. One really does not know why. It seems as if a breeze from the infamous world of secular history blew in on him on April 1, 1933. And since he is fond of paradoxes, and no doubt knows also that successful magic requires contact with the soil, he prepares to replace the formula *torah im derekh eretz*— which has after all been robbed of a significance it had acquired only surreptitiously—with another one. What a pretty symbol of the recurrent sense for the renewal of our ancient tongue even in these circles that within the word combinations that are normally called Hebrew it has absolutely no meaning: *torah im derekh Eretz Yisrael*! This magical new formula (totally untouched by the genius of the language) seems somehow to include the soil of our land within the range of the old formula which now became obsolete. It means—in German the orthodox terminology is quite a bit clearer—the battle for "national emancipation," naturally not in the sense of the Zionist betrayal of God, but in the sense of "tideyism." "Tideyism" is supposed to mean the conquest of Palestine for the phantom world created by Hirsch which threatens to evaporate in a Galut that now shows a less favorable side than those "mild aspects" from which it emerged. It is well known, to be sure, that Hirsch wanted nothing to do with the task of building up Palestine; he desired, as our author says with such exquisite care, "nothing more, even in the Diaspora, than to settle you today in God's kingdom of the future." But this settlement, we may say it openly, has miscarried —and for good reason. It is difficult to live by an apocalypse, especially one which does not take itself seriously and which is all set on denying its inherently catastrophic nature.

Zionism, which in these days must hold fast against related, though quite differently expressed, temptations, has the great advantage of never having appropriated such hopelessly compromised slogans. While it has not yet apprehended its religious problematics, it has acknowledged its secularism without a lot of silly excuses. No equivocal phraseologies have hindered the encounter with itself and with its genius that arises from the midst of such secularism. That genius will confront it with those questions which, we may be sure, the Jewish people is unable to escape. On Samson Raphael Hirsch one of the few great chances for Jewish renewal was wagered and lost. The battle of the Torah in our land will not be possible under his banner. And, as a matter of fact, this is no longer even the same flag that Isaac Breuer is now waving, even if he does assure us it has only been renovated slightly. Oh no, it has been materially transformed, transformed by none other than that devilish damnable Zionism which irresistibly attracts the metaphysician of separatism and which nonetheless correctly appears to his conscious political sensibilities as the most powerful threat to his world. Since the old slogans do not work any longer in the orthodox camp—any more than they do for the liberals—and since our people has perceived *history* and wills history in both its most profane and most sacred realms, a string of ideologies has come into being that seeks to turn aside this claim by presenting weighty paradoxes and absurdities. In Breuer's book we see the strictly orthodox variant of these attempts. As much as it might seem worth fighting against, it deserves respect for its clear rejection—at least in principle [5]—of those unbearable, longing, furtive glances into the realm of German history, which make the pompous theology of suffering of "German-Jewish existence," propagated from the other side, so totally unpalatable. The Jew of this *New Kuzari* wants to be a Jew and nothing but a Jew—but in a long, and certainly extremely dubious interpretation of the theocratic claim to sovereignty, he is forbidden to exist within the realm of secular history. However, we trust in the immanent power of a movement which cannot be held back by such artificial prohibitions, derivable from our literature only by forced interpretation. Alfred Roden's students may yet travel as far as Jaffa under the flag of "tideyism"—let us hope that they do it soon. But a transformed world will speedily transform them along with it. The arcane magic of the new slogan, if indeed it possesses any (for its palpable "meaning" will not bring anyone even to Jaffa), will claim victory over the intentions of its master who has undertaken to conjure up the spirits of the land. There are few things —the prophecy is not difficult to make—which Alfred Roden may be as certain of as the loss of his students to those spirits which arise from the earth there. His identification of them with the phantoms that populate the world of Rabbi Hirsch is for us, let us be frank, a welcome, fruitful error.

III

However, this inclination to rescue the world of Samson Raphael Hirsch (which even the author realizes is endangered) by means of a transforming interpretation which could lend it aggressiveness and power is not expressed just in regard to this point, to the ideology of "tideyism" and the polemic against Zionism as a betrayal of the divine kingdom. Entirely different pillars of Hirsch's world have begun to totter! Even if in historical perspective that *torah im derekh eretz* which embitters us so much today has proven the strongest pillar of his fame, it still was no more than the formal summary of a content which was of much greater concern to its author. This content has been analyzed perceptively by Max Wiener in his excellent book *Jewish Religion in the Age of the Emancipation*.[6] Even without the author's formulating it explicitly, the analysis led also to a rather devastating critique. For some time this most pretentious side of Hirsch's theology—which indeed was least able to gain influence—has been recognized as a realm. of the most unrestrained allegorizing (which, as was customary then, mistakenly considered itself symbolism). It was an allegorizing which logically and earnestly forbade itself access to mysticism and genuine symbols (in which not just any old "ideas" are realized, but something which cannot be expressed or carried out).

Hirsch's liberal opponents, who possessed a great deal more historical instinct for what was distasteful to them than he did, already seventy years ago sensed in this rationalistic and humanistic allegory the distant echo of a mysticism which had so decidedly belied itself in this man's thought. Fear of Kabbalah was the nightmare of that generation of Jewish orthodoxy in Germany which felt the horrors of the Eibeschütz scandal [7] (they were still more familiar with its secret history than we are) deep in its bones. Fear of Kabbalah—that was the hidden motive behind Hirsch's efforts to probe the depths of the Torah, efforts which got stuck in the spheres of a super-mystical humanism glistening with allegory because this Philo of the nineteenth century wanted at any price to protect his world from being compromised, as it doubtlessly would have been, by any reference to Kabbalah. Thus his world remained lifeless and unreal. Only now and then one or another more deeply penetrating sentence, like a light from a hidden outside source, would illuminate it with a genuinely mystical radiance. Hirsch's pronounced affinity for the Torah commentary of Nahmanides, in which he ignored the Kabbalistic passages with ironclad determination, tells us a great deal about the man himself as well as his buried potentialities.

But the grandson found his way back home: only what can be transformed can be saved. After sixty years, Hirsch's world has become threadbare and unsightly. It was a world that combined material ease with an inner standard of life, but it seems destined to oblivion, to sinking into the morass of pseudo-profundity which once was its reflection. Its ideals no longer uplift us, even if we do not explicitly repudiate them—like that *torah im derekh eretz*. This world needs "saving" in an idea or—for the theosopher more likely—in a symbol. *Keneset Yisrael*, the "Kingdom" of Israel's "meta-history," serves as such a symbol. With growing astonishment the reader perceives how the author employs expressions of pious reverence and ever bolder interpretations to cast aside the world of Hirsch's allegories; grand symbols, powerful, unfathomable, take their place. Half attracted and dazed, half outraged by the obscure presentation, the reader cannot remember having read in S. R. Hirsch's writings these curious and remarkable expositions and theologoumena concerning the essence of Torah, the community of Israel, the First Cause and the soul, the "Kingdom" and its king, the nature of miracles, and many other grand themes. Then suddenly he realizes that he is in the midst of the world of mysticism and theosophical speculation. What is happening here is a most triumphant re-entry of Kabbalah into orthodox thought, a most resolute effort to recover that rejected cornerstone. The Kabbalah so completely dominates the religious conceptions which here support— if they do not actually replace—the tottering foundations of Hirsch's world that the master's capitulation is astonishing. Infinite profundity unfolds, magically concentrated in a few key words. To be sure, only at one point does the author indicate clearly that Kabbalah is involved and whoever does not know it anyhow (and not many will) won't learn it. Perhaps the reason for this curious reticence of our most recent esotericist may be sought in his awareness that the paraphrases he uses are, after all, only his own very modern formulations, which need not so readily correspond to the legitimate sense of the underlying Kabbalistic, in part profoundly mystical, dicta. In fact, one could register some very serious misgivings. But let us leave aside the question whether a philologically tenable interpretation of Kabbalistic doctrines is presented here, whether in particular the unlimited mysticism in the theory of the "meta-history" of *Keneset Yisrael*, which dominates the whole book, really does grasp that great Kabbalistic symbol out of which it is obviously developed: the "Kingdom" or the "spoken Torah." It is enough that the author has deduced it from his sources (reading it reminds one strongly of the mystical passages in Nahmanides, Gikatilla, and Isaiah Horovitz).

The purpose of Breuer's undertaking is to transform the world of Hirsch back into the more substantial world of the Kabbalah (which it never ought to have renounced) and thereby to cancel it—and thus in the Platonic sense to "rescue" it; but at the same time he also wants to take from the unfathomable depths of our ancient mysticism some metaphysical grist for the mill of his "tideyistic" anti-Zionism. It is only a pity that he seems to have overlooked what the *Zohar* teaches: that "mill which stands at the edge of the great abyss" is the fixed abode—if not the national home—of demons. These demons make a fool of their master. One may confidently assert that the Kabbalah in its new-style function as a weapon against Zionism is a remarkably two-edged sword. The Kabbalah lends itself to such a stubborn battle only under duress. The politics of mysticism, all too laden with contradiction, has time and time again turned against its protagonists. All these shiny paradoxes regarding history and meta-history, with a slight dialectical shift of emphasis easily made in their employment, may be used just as readily to support Zionism. Somehow, the author seems to have sensed this himself: for in the perhaps most provocative passage of his book he tries to come to terms with the highly annoying providential confirmation of Zionism with the help of an absolutely amazing, meaningless theory of "God's historical miracle in the Balfour Declaration." If, as the author pointedly and with bitterness formulates it, Zionism is not only "treason against Torah and the Torah-people, but also, mildly put (!!), a singular stupidity," its historical claim "the most outrageous insolence that ever raised its head," its path a "bloody irony," then why—a harmless Kabbalist might ask himself—is it the bearer of the "clearest of all God's historical miracles?" Here, just at the desired point, providence intercedes; inexplicably and paradoxically it makes use of such "traitors" as Herzl and Weizmann—instead of God knows who else. Here, indeed, all discussion comes to an end. Nobody likes to argue with a mystic who uses providence to cover up the weakness of his politics or to cut through the Gordian knot in which he got them entangled. Surely without transformation there can be no mastery of the future: Zionism needs badly to be mindful of its religious problems; it needs historical consciousness and criticism of its activities and slogans. But just as it will not find its salvation, its *tikkun,* in the wild apocalypticism of the Revisionists, it must not give way to a politics of mysticism which uses the most profound symbols of our inner life to usurp a power which others have fought for and have sacrificed themselves to firmly establish— which uses these symbols to subjugate a way of life whose development the adherents of that politics have followed with nothing but excommunications, maledictions, and hate.

The Golem of Prague
and the Golem of Rehovot [1]

ONCE UPON A TIME there was a great rabbi in Prague. His name
was Rabbi Judah Loew ben Bezalel and he is known in Jewish
tradition as the Maharal of Prague. A famous scholar and mystic,
he is credited by Jewish popular tradition with the creation of a
Golem—a creature produced by the magical power of man and
taking on human shape. Rabbi Loew's robot was made of clay and
given a sort of life by being infused with the concentrated power
of the rabbi's mind. This great human power is, however, nothing
but a reflection of God's own creative power, and therefore, after
having gone through all the necessary procedures in building his
Golem, the rabbi finally put a slip of paper into its mouth with
the mystic and ineffable Name of God written on it. So long as
this seal remained in his mouth, the Golem was alive—if you can
call such a state alive. For the Golem could work and do the bidding of his master and perform all kinds of chores for him,
helping him and the Jews of Prague in many ways. But the poor
creature could not speak. He could respond to orders and he could
sort them out, but no more than that.

All this went very well for a time; the Golem was even
given his day of rest on the Sabbath, when God's creatures are not
supposed to do any work. Every Sabbath the rabbi would remove
the slip of paper with the Name of God on it, and the Golem
would become inanimate for the day, nothing but a massive con-
glomerate of clay cells (in those days they were not yet speaking
of "little gray cells"). One Friday afternoon, however, Rabbi
Loew forgot to remove the Name from the Golem's mouth and
went to the Great Synagogue of Prague to pray with the community and to receive the Sabbath. The day had barely drawn to a
close and the people were getting ready for the ushering in of the
holy day, when the Golem began to get restive. He grew in

335

stature and, like one mad, began tearing about in the Ghetto, threatening to destroy everything. The people did not know how to stop him from running amok. A report of the panic soon reached the "Altneuschul" where Rabbi Loew was praying. The rabbi rushed out into the street to confront his own creature which seemed to have outgrown him and become a destructive power on its own. With a last effort he stretched out his arm and tore the Holy Name out of the Golem's mouth, whereupon the Golem fell to the ground and turned into a mass of lifeless clay.

In another version of the same legend, which is recounted of a great rabbi in sixteenth-century Poland, the rabbi is successful in stopping the Golem, but the heap of clay falls upon and kills him. However, the most famous version in Jewish lore of the idea of the Golem as a human creature on a subhuman plane is the one involving Rabbi Loew. It is only appropriate to mention that Rabbi Loew was not only the spiritual, but also the actual, ancestor of the great mathematician Theodor von Karman who, I recall, was extremely proud of this ancestor of his in whom he saw the first genius of applied mathematics in his family. But we may safely say that Rabbi Loew was also the spiritual ancestor of two other departed Jews—I mean John von Neumann and Norbert Wiener—who contributed more than anyone else to the magic that has produced the modern Golem. It is the latest embodiment of this magic which we are privileged to dedicate today, the Golem of Rehovot. And, indeed, the Golem of Rehovot can well compete with the Golem of Prague.

Now, this idea of the Golem is deeply ingrained in the thinking of the Jewish mystics of the Middle Ages known as the Kabbalists. I want to give you at least an inkling of what lies behind the idea. It may be far removed from what the modern electronic engineer and applied mathematician have in mind when they concoct their own species of Golem—and yet, all theological trappings notwithstanding, there is a straight line linking the two developments.

As a matter of fact, the Golem—a creature created by human intelligence and concentration, which is controlled by its creator and performs tasks set by him, but which at the same time may have a dangerous tendency to outgrow that control and develop destructive potentialities—is nothing but a replica of Adam, the first Man himself. God could create Man from a heap of clay and invest him with a spark of His divine life force and intelligence (this, in the last analysis, is the "divine image" in which

Man was created). Without this intelligence and the spontaneous creativity of the human mind, Adam would have been nothing but a Golem—as, indeed, he is called in some of the old rabbinic stories interpreting the biblical account. When there was only the combination and culmination of natural and material forces, and before that all-important divine spark was breathed into him, Adam was nothing but a Golem. Only when a tiny bit of God's creative power was passed on did he become Man, in the image of God. Is it, then, any wonder that Man should try to do in his own small way what God did in the beginning?

There is, however, a hitch: Man can assemble the forces of nature—identified by him as the basic forces of material creation —and combine them into a semblance of the human pattern. But there is one thing he cannot give to his product: speech, which to the biblical mind is identical with reason and intuition. The Talmud tells a little story: "Rabha created a man and sent him to Rabbi Zera. The rabbi spoke to him but he did not answer. Whereupon the rabbi said: You must have been made by my colleagues of the academy; return to your dust." In Aramaic, the language of the Talmud, the academic colleagues are denoted by the same word that is used for magicians: quite a nice ambiguity. Just as the human mind remains infinitely inferior to the all-encompassing divine intelligence of God, so does the Golem's intelligence lag behind the human—that is to say, it lacks that spontaneity which alone makes Man what he is. But still, even on a subhuman plane, there is in the Golem a representation of Man's creative power. The universe, so the Kabbalists tell us, is built essentially on the prime elements of numbers and letters, because the letters of God's language reflected in human language are nothing but concentrations of His creative energy. Thus, by assembling these elements in all their possible combinations and permutations, the Kabbalist who contemplates the mysteries of Creation radiates some of this elementary power into the Golem. The creation of a Golem is then in some way an affirmation of the productive and creative power of Man. It repeats, on however small a scale, the work of creation.

But there is a more sinister side to this too. According to one of the first texts we have on the Golem, the prophet Jeremiah was busying himself alone with the *Sefer Yetzirah* ("The Book of Creation") when a heavenly voice went forth and said: "Take a companion." Jeremiah, obeying, chose his son Sira, and they studied the book together for three years. Afterward, they set about combining the alphabets in accordance with the Kabbalistic principles of combination, grouping, and word formation, and a man was created to them, on whose forehead stood the letters, *YHWH Elohim Emet,* meaning: God the Lord is Truth. But this newly created man had a knife in his hand, with which he erased the letter *alef* from the word *emet* ("truth"); there remained the word *met* ("dead"). Then Jeremiah rent his garments (because of the blasphemy, God is dead, now implied in the inscription) and said: "Why have you erased the *alef* from *emet?*" He replied: "I will tell you a parable. An architect built many houses, cities, and squares, but no one could copy his art and compete with him in knowledge and skill until two men persuaded him to teach them the secret of the art. When they had learned how to do everything in the right way, they began to anger him with words. Finally, they broke with him and became architects on their own, except that what he charged a guinea for, they did for ten shillings. When people noticed this, they ceased honoring the artist and instead gave their commissions to his renegade pupils. So God has made you in His image and in His shape and form. But now that you have created a man like Him, people will say: There is no God in the world beside these two! Then Jeremiah said: "What solution is there?" He said: "Write the alphabets backward with intense concentration on the earth. Only do not meditate in the sense of building up, as you did before, but the other way around." So they did, and the man became dust and ashes before their eyes.

It is indeed significant that Nietzsche's famous cry, "God is dead," should have gone up first in a Kabbalistic text warning against the making of a Golem and linking the death of God to the realization of the idea of the Golem.

In the development of this conception the Golem has always existed on two quite separate planes. The one was the plane of ecstatic experience where the figure of clay, infused with all those radiations of the human mind which are the combinations of the alphabet, became alive for the fleeting moment of ecstasy, but not beyond it. The other was the legendary plane where Jewish folk tradition, having heard of the Kabbalistic speculations on the spiritual plane, translated them into down-to-earth tales and traditions like the ones I quoted at the beginning. The Golem, instead of being a spiritual experience of man, became a technical servant of man's needs, controlled by him in an uneasy and precarious equilibrium.

This is where we may well ask some questions, comparing the Golem of Prague with that of Rehovot, the work of Rabbi Judah Loew with the work of Professor—or should I say, Rabbi?—Chaim Pekeris.

1. Have they a basic conception in common? I should say, yes. The old Golem was based on a mystical combination of the twenty-two letters of the Hebrew alphabet, which are the elements and building stones of the world. The new Golem is based on a simpler, and at the same time more intricate, system. Instead of twenty-two elements, it knows only of two, the two numbers 0 and 1, constituting the binary system of representation. Everything can be translated, or transposed, into these two basic signs, and what cannot be so expressed cannot be fed as information to the Golem. I dare say the old Kabbalists would have been glad to learn of this simplification of their own system. This is progress.

2. What makes the Golem work? In both cases it is energy. In the old Golem it was the energy of speech, in the new one it is electronic energy. In the case of the Kabbalists it was the *Shem ha-Meforash,* the fully interpreted and expressed and differentiated name of God. Now, it is still differentiation according to a given system and interpretation of signs and ciphers which makes the Golem work.

3. What about human shape? Here I must admit to some qualms. Certainly the Prague Golem was never very attractive as a human being, but he seems to have borne some resemblance to the human countenance—which, I am sorry to state, cannot be said of our present Golem of Rehovot. It still has a long way to go, to be molded into an acceptable shape. You can say, of course, that these external shapes are optical illusions and deceit, and that what counts, after all, is the mind at work. And here the Golem of Rehovot may be at an advantage. External beauty has been denied to him. What kind of spiritual beauties lurk inside, we shall learn in due time, I hope.

4. Can the new Golem grow in stature and productivity? He certainly can, although with growing productivity we rather expect the Golem of Rehovot to shrink in size and to take on a more attractive and becoming exterior. Whether the Golem of Prague could correct his mistakes, I doubt. The new Golem seems to be able, in some ways, to learn and to improve himself. This makes the modern Kabbalists more successful than the ancient ones, and I may congratulate them on this score. There is even more to it. The old Golem, we learn, served his master by bringing

water to the house. The new one serves his rabbi, Chaim Pekeris, by calculating the movement of the ocean tides—a somewhat more progressive type of activity, so far as water is concerned.

5. What about memory and the faculty of speech? As for memory, we don't know how the old Golem scored. The new one certainly shows a great improvement—although he has, I am sorry to say, occasional lapses of memory and other momentary weaknesses which cause trouble to his makers. The progress of the new Golem is thus linked to a certain regression from the previous state. Adam never fell ill, according to the rabbis, and the same goes for the old Golem of the Kabbalists. The new one, alas, shows a deplorable propensity in this direction. And as for speech, and all that it implies—I mean the spontaneity of intelligence— both the old and the new Golem are found to be sadly lacking. Everybody speculates about what is to become of the more advanced forms of the Golem. But it seems that for the time being, and for quite some time to come, we are saddled with a Golem that will only do what he is told. There is still a long, long stretch ahead to that utopian figure of a Golem, about whom the famous cartoon in the *New Yorker* spoke. It showed two scientists standing in great embarrassment before this end-of-days Golem as they scanned the tape giving out his latest information. The caption read: "The damned thing says: *Cogito, ergo sum.*"

6. And this brings me to my last question: Can the Golem love? In an old book we read some sayings about the Golem attributed to the rabbi of Prague. Here is one of them: "The Golem was never ill, for he was immune to every impulse to do evil, from which all illness stems. And the Golem had to be created without the sexual urge; for, if he had had that instinct, no woman would have been safe from him." Now I have to leave it to you to answer this query. For I am really at a loss what to think.

All my days I have been complaining that the Weizmann Institute has not mobilized the funds to build up the Institute for Experimental Demonology and Magic which I have for so long proposed to establish there. They preferred what they call Applied Mathematics and its sinister possibilities to my more direct magical approach. Little did they know, when they preferred Chaim Pekeris to me, what they were letting themselves in for. So I resign myself and say to the Golem and its creator: develop peacefully and don't destroy the world. *Shalom.*

Notes

TOWARD AN UNDERSTANDING
OF THE MESSIANIC IDEA IN JUDAISM

1. Cf. Joseph Klausner, *The Messianic Idea in Israel from its Beginning to the Completion of the Mishnah* (New York, 1955); Hugo Gressmann, *Der Messias* (Göttingen, 1929); Lorenz Dürr, *Ursprung und Ausbau der israelitisch-jüdischen Heilandserwartung* (Berlin, 1925); Willi Staerk, *Die Erlösererwartung in den östlichen Religionen* (Stuttgart, 1938); Sigmund Mowinckel, *He That Cometh: The Messianic Concept in the Old Testament and Later Judaism* (Oxford, 1956).

2. For the concept of the utopian, as discussed in the following, see above all the analyses of this category presented by Ernst Bloch in his two works: *Geist der Utopie* (Munich, 1918) and *Das Prinzip Hoffnung* (Berlin, 1954-59). Although many of Bloch's suggestions elicit great reservations, one must admire the energy and insight with which he has approached and carried through his discussion of utopianism. The elaborate Marxist montage of his second work stands in poorly concealed contradiction to the mystical inspiration which is basically responsible for Bloch's best insights. Not without a measure of courage, he has managed to draw his insights safely through a veritable jungle of Marxist rhapsodies.

3. Flavius Josephus, *Antiquities,* I, 70.

4. *Midrash Tanhuma,* Section *Mas'e,* Paragraph 4; *Midrash Bereshit Rabba,* ed. Theodor, p. 445.

5. Cf. G. G. Scholem, *Major Trends in Jewish Mysticism* (New York and London, 1946), p. 72.

6. *Midrash Shir ha-Shirim Rabba,* VI, 10.

7. Sanhedrin 97a.

8. *Exodus Rabba,* XXV, 16.

9. *Midrash Tehillim* to Psalm 45:3.

10. Sanhedrin 98a.

11. Cf. the synoptical compilation of the pertinent material in Strack-Billerbeck, *Kommentar zum Neuen Testament aus Talmud und Midrasch,* IV, 977-86.

12. End of the Mishnah tractate Sota.

13. Sanhedrin 98a.

14. *Shir ha-Shirim Rabba,* II, 7 (Cf. Ketubot 110a).

15. This legend, which for some strange reason is missing from M. J. Bin Gorion's *Der Born Judas,* was often printed as a small popular book. Cf. also my essay concerning it in *Zion,* V (Jerusalem, 1933), 124-30, as well as Z. Rubashov, "The Legend of Rabbi Joseph de la Reyna in the Sabbatian Tradition" (Hebrew), in *Eder Yakar* (Tel Aviv, 1947), pp. 97-118.

16. Karl Bornhausen, *Der Erlöser* (Leipzig, 1927), p. 74.

17. Siegmund Hurwitz, *Die Gestalt des sterbenden Messias* (Zurich, 1958).

18. Berakhot 34b.

19. An excellent discussion of the various nuances of this conception of the Messianic Torah in the Talmud and Midrash is contained in the monograph of W. D. Davies, *Torah in the Messianic Age* (Philadelphia, 1952).

20. Cf. the detailed presentation of the individual stages of this development in Joseph Sarachek, *The Messianic Ideal in Medieval Jewish Literature* (New York, 1932).

21. In the Thirteen Principles which Maimonides set forth in the introduction to Sanhedrin, Ch. 10, of his Mishnah commentary, we find the following: "The twelfth principle concerns the Days of the Messiah. It consists of believing and recognizing as true that he will come and not thinking that he will delay. 'Though he tarry, wait for him.' And one must not determine a time for him nor speculate on biblical verses in order to bring about his coming. And the sages said: 'May the spirit of those who calculate the End be extinguished.' One should rather believe in him . . . magnify and love him, and pray for him, in accordance with the words of all the prophets from Moses to Malachi. And whoever is in doubt concerning him or belittles his glory, he has denied the Torah which explicitly promises his coming."

22. Cf. the German translation by Moritz Zobel in his excellent compilation, *Der Messias und die messianische Zeit in Talmud und Midrasch* (Berlin, 1938), pp. 90-91.

23. Sanhedrin 91b.

24. The word can mean: as a fundamental principle; but also (in Zobel's view): as an important object of attention.

25. In his *Epistle to Yemen,* where Maimonides pays great heed to the eschatological requirements of the tradition which he later eliminates, this element of miracle still has its place, though it is presented in very sober fashion. With manifest conservative regard for his Yemenite readers, Maimonides here formulates the difference between the prophetic rank of the Messiah and that of the other prophets from Moses to Malachi in this way: "But his unique characteristic is that when he appears God will cause all the kings of the earth to tremble

and be afraid at the report of him. Their kingdoms will fall; they will be unable to stand up against him, neither by the sword nor by revolt. They will neither defame nor slander him, but they will be frightened into silence when they behold his miracles and wonders. He will slay anyone who tries to kill him and none shall escape or be saved from him. . . . That king will be very mighty. All peoples will maintain peace with him, all nations will serve him on account of the great justice and the miracles which issue from his hand. All the words of Scripture testify to his success and to our success with him." (*Iggeret Teman,* ed. David Hollub [Vienna, 1875], p. 48.)

26. Abraham Cardozo, the very differently oriented follower of Sabbatai Zevi, surprisingly referred to this discussion of Maimonides even after his apostasy. He sought to support his thesis that it is in the nature of the Messiah for him to behave in such fashion as to nurture doubts regarding the legitimacy of his mission until his authority is finally established.

27. The conception of the Last Judgment plays no role at all in Maimonides' writings. There is no future retribution in the sense of eschatological reward and punishment.

28. Of course he also excludes conceptions like that of the pre-existence of the Messiah and of the Messiah ben Joseph.

29. *Megillat ha-Megalle,* ed. Adolf Poznanski and Julius Guttmann (Berlin, 1924).

30. Cf. Scholem, *op. cit.,* p. 248.

31. Cf. also *ibid.,* pp. 244-51, 278-86, and *Eranos Jahrbuch,* XVII, 325-33.

32. This conception, especially prevalent in the Lurianic School, was earlier developed by Moses Cordovero in his *Elima Rabbati* (Brody, 1881), ff.46c/d. In the older Kabbalah it is especially the now uninterrupted *hieros gamos* of *tiferet* and *malkhut* which characterizes the mystical aspect of the Messianic age.

33. As a citation from the *Zohar* in Benjamin of Zlasitz, *Ture Zahav* (Mohilev, 1816), ff. 56b. The formulation makes more pointed a passage in *Zohar,* II, 12b.

THE CRISIS OF TRADITION
IN JEWISH MESSIANISM

1. Cf. "Revelation and Tradition as Religious Categories in Judaism" (this volume, pp. 282-303).

2. Victor Aptowitzer, *Parteipolitik der Hasmonäerzeit im rabbinischen und pseudoepigraphischen Schrifttum* (Vienna, 1927).

3. Aage Bentzen, *Messias, Moses Redivivus* (Zurich, 1948).

4. George Foot Moore, *Judaism in the First Centuries of the Christian Era* (Cambridge, Mass., 1927), I, 271. Despite the profound

and justified misgivings which have been expressed regarding Moore's conception of these developments, his book remains one of the few significant attempts to portray the process by which rabbinic Judaism came into being.

5. W. D. Davies, *Torah in the Messianic Age* (Philadelphia, 1952).

6. On this central question compare the chapter "The Meaning of the Torah in Jewish Mysticism" in G. G. Scholem, *On the Kabbalah and Its Symbolism* (New York and London, 1965), pp. 32-86.

7. Davies, *op. cit.*, pp. 52-53.

8. *Midrash Vayikra Rabba,* IX, 7.

9. *Yalkut* (as well as *Midrash Mishle*) to Prov. 9:2.

10. *Midrash Tehillim* to Psalm 146:7, ed. Solomon Buber, p. 535. The conclusion of this passage shows even more clearly the purely speculative character of these considerations. Here we find: "Some say that even cohabitation will one day be forbidden. For this the reason is given that if God, according to Exodus 19:15, prohibited cohabitation for three days preceding the one day of the Sinaitic revelation, how could He not prohibit it completely in the Messianic age when the Shekhinah will dwell among them in continuous revelation?"

11. *Midrash Vayikra Rabba,* XIII.3, ed. M. Margulies, p. 278, with highly characteristic attenuation in the variants. Cf. also Davies, *op. cit.*, pp. 59-61.

12. *Yalkut* to Isa. 26:2, para. 429.

13. Cf. Gerson D. Cohen, *Messianic Postures of Ashkenazim and Sephardim (Prior to Sabbatai Zevi).* Leo Baeck Memorial Lecture IX (New York, 1967).

14. The sources for this movement have been gathered and discussed in the Hebrew volume by A. Z. Aescoly, *Jewish Messianic Movements, Sources and Documents* (Jerusalem, 1956), pp. 164-78.

15. Cf. Scholem, *op. cit.*, Ch. 7.

16. I have dealt with this subject at length in *Sabbatai Zevi and the Sabbatian Movement during his Lifetime* (in Hebrew, Tel Aviv, 1957).

17. More on this subject in "The Crypto-Jewish Sect of the Dönmeh (Sabbatians) in Turkey" (this volume, pp. 142-66).

18. I have published long sections from this work in my *Be'ikvot Mashiah* (Jerusalem, 1944), pp. 88-128. There I recognized that it belonged to the corpus of the writings of Nathan of Gaza but not that it was identical with his book *Zemir Aritzim,* which is completely extant, for example, in a manuscript in the British Museum (Or. 4536, pp. 13-76).

19. I have published the text of the *Iggeret Magen Abraham* in the collection *Kobetz al Yad,* XII (Jerusalem, 1937), 121-55. Despite my original doubts (expressed in my book *Sabbatai Zevi*), Cardozo's authorship has since been definitely proven.

20. The text is to be found in the manuscript of David Kaufmann, #255 in the Academy of Sciences in Budapest. I have dealt with it in detail in the Festschrift *Ale Ayin* for Salman Schocken (Jerusalem, 1952), pp. 157-211.

21. Cf. the document in Jacob Emden, *Torat ha-Kena'ot* (Lvov, 1870), p. 53. Its true character and value has now been determined by M. Benayahu in *Studies in Mysticism and Religion Presented to G. G. Scholem* (Jerusalem, 1967), Hebrew Section, pp. 33-40. There we also find numerous examples of such violations of the law committed by Sabbatai Zevi.

22. Cardozo, *Magen Abraham,* p. 134.

23. All these citations, *ibid.,* pp. 132-33.

24. See the detailed discussion in Scholem, *On the Kabbalah and Its Symbolism,* pp. 71-77.

25. *Midrash Kohelet Rabba* XII, 9, recasting a passage in the Talmud, Sanhedrin 99a.

26. *Magen Abraham,* p. 134.

27. On the sources of these three typologies, which do not appear in the main portion of the *Zohar,* cf. the detailed discussion by I. Tishby, *Mishnat ha-Zohar* (Jerusalem, 1961), II, 375-98, esp. 387-90.

28. On this subject, cf. G. G. Scholem, *Von der mystischen Gestalt der Gottheit* (Zurich, 1962), Chapter 2: "Gut und Böse in der Kabbala."

29. Tractate Avot VI, 2.

30. Cf. the passages dealing with Israel at Sinai and with the first tablets in *Be'ikvot Mashiah,* pp. 93 and 100.

31. *Magen Abraham,* pp. 134-35.

32. These ideas are stressed in *Zemir Aritzim* and in other of Nathan's writings, especially in the *Sefer ha-Beriya* and in the *Drush Raza de-Malka.* Cf. also Scholem, *Sabbatai Zevi,* II, 695.

33. *Magen Abraham,* p. 144.

34. Erubin 100b.

35. The thirty-six prohibitions which fall into this category are enumerated in the Mishnah Keritot, I, 1.

36. Cf. my Hebrew article on Baruchya in *Zion,* VII (1941), 136-37, 140-41.

37. Cf. Scholem, *On the Kabbalah and Its Symbolism,* pp. 66, 83-86; Tishby, II, 387.

38. Cf. the article mentioned in Note 20; p. 191.

39. Cf. "Redemption Through Sin" (this volume, pp. 78-141); also, "Die Metamorphose des häretischen Messianismus der Sabbatianer im religiösen Nihilismus im 18. Jahrhundert," in *Zeugnisse; Theodor W. Adorno zum 60. Geburtstag* (Frankfurt am Main, 1963), pp. 20-32.

40. Cf. my study "Le mouvement sabbataiste en Pologne," *Revue de l'histoire des religions,* CXLIV (1953-54), 62.

REDEMPTION THROUGH SIN

1. Fritz Mauthner, *Erinnerungen* (Munich, 1918), p. 306. The author's mother was the daughter of a former "believer" who hailed from the small Bohemian community of Horosiz and was educated at the Frankist "court" in Offenbach.

2. Meir Balaban, *Le-Toledot ha-Tenu'ah ha-Frankit,* 2 vols. (Tel Aviv, 1934-35), p. 265, cites the words of the Frankist Eliezer from Jeżierzany, who said to Rabbi Hayyim Rappaport of Lvov at the disputation's end: "Hayyim, we have given you blood for blood! You meant to make [the shedding of] our blood lawful, and now you have been given blood for blood!"

3. Rabbi Mordecai Ashkenazi, a pupil of the prominent Sabbatian Rabbi Abraham Rovigo. Cf. G. G. Scholem, *The Dreams of R. Mordecai Ashkenazi* (in Hebrew, Jerusalem, 1938), p. 80.

4. The views that follow are to be found in Nathan's and Cardozo's epistles, in many places in the *Sefer Inyanei Shabtai Zevi* (ed. A. Freimann, Berlin, 1913), and, most systematically, in Cardozo's "Iggeret Magen Abraham," published by me in *Kobetz al Yad,* XII (Jerusalem, 1937). From Sasportas' *Sefer Kitzur Zitzat Novel Zevi* (1867, p. 64) it emerges that Sabbatai Zevi himself defended his apostasy with similar arguments.

5. *Inyanei Shabtai Zevi* (ed. A. Freimann, 1913), p. 88.

6. *Ibid.,* p. 90, from Cardozo's epistle to his brother-in-law.

7. The phrase comes from the *Tikkunei ha-Zohar, tikkun* 60.

8. Cardozo and Nathan of Gaza cite a manuscript containing the revelations of a *maggid* ("spiritual intelligence") to Rabbi Joseph Taitatsak as their authority for this statement.

9. *Inyanei Shabtai Zevi,* p. 91.

10. Jacob Emden, *Torat ha-Kena'ot* (Lvov, 1870), p. 53.

11. One might particularly cite in this connection the puzzling case of the great talmudic scholar Rabbi Jonathan Eibeschütz, a psychological enigma that still needs badly to be unraveled, although here is not the place to do so. I cannot conceal the fact, however, that after thoroughly examining both Eibeschütz' own Kabbalistic writings and all the polemical works that they engendered I have been forced to conclude that he was indeed a Sabbatian, as both Jacob Emden and, in a later age, Heinrich Graetz insisted.

12. David Kahana, *Toledot ha-Mekuballim, ha-Shabta'im, ve-ha-Hasidim* (Odessa, 1913–14), I, 69.

13. *Inyanei Shabtai Zevi,* p. 84; cf. also pp. 93, 95, 107. The belief that one should restrict one's studies to the *Zohar* and not read the writings of the Lurianic School at all was still widespread among the "radicals" in the movement as late as the time of Jacob Frank, as can

be seen from Baruch Kossover's introduction to the *Sefer Yesod ha-Emunah*, written in 1761.

14. Both these *kavvanot* and the theory behind them are explained in a *tikkun* currently in the Elkan Adler Collection in The Jewish Theological Seminary in New York, MS. 1653.

15. According to Cardozo, "Despite the fact that it remains as true as ever, the learned Sabbatai Zevi completely rejected the wisdom of Rabbi Isaac Luria" (see Cardozo's manuscript on "the mystery of the Godhead" published by I. H. Weiss in his *Bet ha-Midrash* [1865], p. 67). Elsewhere, in his *Derush Raza de-Razin* (MS. Jewish Theological Seminary, art. 153), he states: "The learned Sabbatai Zevi was in the habit of saying about Rabbi Isaac Luria that he built a fine chariot [*merkabah*] in his day but neglected to say who was riding on it."

16. On the origins of this document see my article in *Zion*, III, 173. The tract was published (Berlin, 1713) under the title *Mehemanuta de-Khola* in the *Sefer Oz Lelohim* of Nehemiah Hayon, who gave it his own peculiar interpretation.

17. Many of Cardozo's writings that have so far appeared in print touch on this question. See his treatment of "the mystery of the Godhead" published by H. Weiss; Bernheimer's article on his homily *Ani ha-Mekhuneh*, published in *Jewish Quarterly Review*, XVIII, 97–129; and my Hebrew article "New Information on Abraham Cardozo" published in the memorial volume *Ma'amarim le-Zikhron Rav Zevi Peretz Hiyyot Zal* (Vienna, 1933), pp. 223–50.

18. This was the opinion of Cardozo, and of Abraham Rovigo who writes: "I think that there are still several *kavvanot* that I could employ even now, notwithstanding that the mystery of the Godhead has been made known." Elsewhere in the same manuscript he comments: "The mystery of the Godhead is still unbeknown to anyone."

19. This important book was published in 1891 in Vienna, but despite the lateness of the date there can be no serious doubt of its authenticity, some recent attempts at raising such doubts notwithstanding.

20. See the *Sefer Zitzat Novel Zevi*, p. 65.

21. See G. G. Scholem, *On the Kabbalah and Its Symbolism* (New York and London, 1965), pp. 66 ff.

22. The *Tikkunei ha-Zohar*, for example, asserts (*tikkun* 69): "Above [i.e., in heaven] there are no laws of incest." Another commonly cited support for this belief was Leviticus 20:17 (which is devoted almost entirely to an enumeration of incestuous transgressions). "And if a man shall take his sister, his father's daughter, or his mother's daughter, and see her nakedness, and she see his nakedness, it is a shameful thing," in which the Hebrew for "shameful thing," *hesed,* is the same word that is ordinarily used in the Bible in the sense of "loving-kindness."

23. Among anti-Sabbatian Kabbalists there were a number of attempts to explain this monstrous perversion, as it seemed, of sacred writings. In his *Divrei Sofrim* ([1913], p. 32d), for example, R. Zadok Hacohen of Lublin cites an unidentified "book written by a saintly man" as his authority for asserting that the Sabbatians "came to the end that they came to because they engaged in the study of the Kabbalah with their hearts full of lust and therefore materialized much [of its spiritual meaning]; and in consequence of the fact that they saw references to copulation, kissing, embracing, and so forth [in what they read], they yielded to lascivious passions, may God preserve us from the same, and committed great evil." In much the same vein, Rabbi Zevi of Żydaczow, one of the great Kabbalists of the Hasidic movement and possibly none other than Rabbi Zadok Hacohen's "saintly man" himself, writes in his *Sur me-Ra va-Aseh Tov:* "I once heard my teacher [the Seer of Lublin] comment on certain students by mentioning the case of that well-known sect. . . . It [i.e., Sabbatian antinomianism] happened because they desired to achieve the revelation of Elijah and to prophesy by the Holy Spirit . . . without troubling to discipline their natures or their material selves; and so, being unworthy and without caution, they overreached themselves by attempting to probe the Unity [of God] without [first] purifying their material natures; and by imagining divine forms [with sexual attributes] under the chariot [*merkabah*], their lascivious passions were aroused, may God preserve us from the same, and what happened happened. . . . And he [the Seer of Lublin] quoted the Baal Shem Tov as saying that because the fools studied this wisdom [the Kabbalah] without application and without the slightest fear of Heaven, they materialized [its teachings] and lapsed."

24. See the testimony cited in Jacob Emden's *Torat ha-Kena'ot* (Lvov, 1870), p. 53, and Jacob Frank's remarks on Baruchya in A. Kraushar, *Frank i Frankiscy Polscy* (Cracow, 1895), II, 26.

25. *Al Tilei Beit Frank* (Berlin, 1923), p. 18.

26. Kraushar, *op. cit.,* I, 214.

27. See Daniel Chwolson, *Die Saabier und der Sabismus,* I (1856), 229, who refers to several passages on this subject in Karl Ritter's *Erdkunde,* vol. IX.

28. Details on the nature of this practice can be found in Abraham Galanté's *Nouveaux documents sur Sabbatai Sevi* (Constantinople, 1935), pp. 50-53.

29. Abraham Danon, *Études Sabbatiennes* (Paris, 1910).

30. Solomon Rosanes, *Korot ha-Yehudim be-Turkiah ve-Artsot ha-Kedem,* Part IV (Sofia, 1934), especially pp. 462-77.

31. See Berl Bolechover, *Sefer Divrei Binah,* quoted by I. Braver in *Hashiloah,* XXXIII, 332.

32. Jacob Emden, *Edut be-Ya'akov,* fol. 48b.

33. *Ibid.*

34. The quotation is from the anti-Sabbatian pamphlet *Lehishat Saraf*, published in 1726, fol. 2.

35. Emden, *op. cit.*, fol. 50b. The story is also told in Emden's *Torat ha-Kena'ot*, where the accused is quoted as saying in addition that to suffer shame for the sake of Sabbatai Zevi is a great *tikkun* for the soul.

36. Jacob Emden, *Hit'abbekut* (Lvov, 1877), fol. 6a. The author of this eye-opening Aggadah, obviously no anti-Sabbatian fabrication, was none other than Nathan Neta, Jonathan Eibeschütz' son.

37. This important manuscript, formerly the possession of Dr. Hayyim Brody, is now in the Schocken Library in Jerusalem. It is a commentary on *En Ya'akov* (a very popular collection of talmudic Aggadot) written by the Frankist Löw von Hönigsberg.

38. *Divrei Nehemiah* (Berlin, 1713), pp. 81–82.

39. This verse was generally interpreted by the Kabbalists as referring to a time when the Devil (called Adam Belial, the demon in the figure of a man) dominates the soul of a man (especially a pious one).

40. See G. G. Scholem, *Halomotav shel ha-Shabtai R. Mordekhai Ashkenazi,* Schocken Library: Studies and Texts . . . , I (Jerusalem, 1938), 64.

41. Such a reappearance was also predicted for 1706, the fortieth year after Sabbatai Zevi's apostasy, and for 1716, the fortieth year after his death.

42. Jacob Emden's books contain a great deal of material on this subject that is not to be lightly dismissed.

43. A section of this sermon, taking as its text Zechariah 4:10, "Not by might, nor by power, but by My spirit, saith the Lord of Hosts," reads as follows: "For the Messiah will not perform great miracles, nor do battle with the enemies of Israel, nor gather the exiles of Israel back to their Land; rather will they become objects of grace among the nations by virtue of the King Messiah's great wisdom . . . Yea, verily, it will be well for the Community of Israel wheresoever it dwelleth among the peoples of the earth." That there continued to be Sabbatians in Altona after Eibeschütz' death is beyond doubt, as is proved by a Frankist document in which mention is made of a letter addressed to Frank by a group of "believers" in Altona in 1777 (Kraushar, *op. cit.*, II, 33).

44. By this phrase *(adonenu malkenu yarum hodo)* Sabbatai Zevi was regularly referred to in Sabbatian literature.

45. Cardozo, in the manuscript published by I. H. Weiss, *Bet ha-Midrash*, p. 65.

46. See the discussion of Cardozo's doctrine of the Godhead above in chapter 4.

47. The Spanish term used to denote Baruchya of Salonika in the sect of his followers who saw in him the reborn Sabbatai Zevi and God incarnate.

48. Jacob Emden, *Sefer Shimmush*, 7a.

49. This motif, repeated many times in *The Sayings of the Lord,* first occurs in a letter addressed by the Frankists to the king and the bishop of Lvov in 1759.

50. Frank's sayings were never published in Hebrew because the Hebrew translation of the second volume of Kraushar's history, in which they appear, was prevented from going to press at the last minute by the news of Kraushar's conversion to Catholicism, which shocked the Jewish public. I am deeply indebted to my friend Miss Hadassah Goldgart (Tel Aviv) for furnishing me with an exact version of the original Polish text.

51. *The Sayings of the Lord,* no. 1211. The attitudes expressed here are unique in the history of Sabbatianism.

52. *Ibid.,* no. 1157. The numbering follows Kraushar. On the whole I have tried to refrain from citing more than one saying to illustrate a given point so as not to needlessly multiply quotations and notes.

53. *Ibid.,* no. 1773.

54. *Ibid.,* no. 1565.

55. *Ibid.,* no. 406.

56. *Ibid.,* no. 2164.

57. See Kraushar, *The Sayings of the Lord,* II, pp. 47–50.

58. Kraushar, *op. cit.,* no. 1790. See also H. Graetz, *Frank und die Frankisten* (Breslau, 1868), p. 71.

59. Kraushar, *op. cit.,* no. 1892.

60. *Ibid.,* no. 1825. (This is obviously an allusion to Ezek. 20:25.)

61. *Ibid.,* no. 851. An allusion to the stories in Genesis.

62. *Ibid.,* no. 2190.

63. *Ibid.,* no. 1776 (II, 50). Elsewhere, however, Frank's appraisal of Sabbatai Zevi's activities is more positive. See especially no. 1267.

64. *Ibid.,* no. 211.

65. *Ibid.,* no. 561.

66. *Ibid.,* no. 219 (II, 268).

67. *Ibid.,* II, 25.

68. *Ibid.,* no. 2146 (II, 132).

69. *Ibid.,* no. 2152.

70. *Ibid.,* no. 1419.

71. *Ibid.,* no. 1974.

72. *Ibid.,* no. 1279.

73. *Ibid.,* nos. 157, 159.

74. *Ibid.,* no. 1294.

75. *Ibid.,* no. 1452.

76. According to Frank, this was the mystic meaning of the phrase in Proverbs 30:18, "There are three things which are too wonderful for me."

77. Kraushar, *op. cit.,* I, no. 1776.

78. *Ibid.,* no. 1122.

79. *Ibid.,* no. 2043.

80. *Ibid.,* no. 1109.

81. *Ibid.,* no. 1416.

82. *Ibid.,* no. 358.

83. *Ibid.,* no. 858.

84. *Ibid.,* no. 2091. The word *Das* or *Daas* in the Polish text does not mean "religion" (Hebrew *dat, das* in the Ashkenazic pronounciation), as was believed by Graetz, but rather "knowledge" in the sense of *gnosis (da'at, da'as)*. This is the spelling used throughout in the Frankist commentary on the *En Ya'akov* in the phrase "the holy gnosis" *(ha-da'as ha-kedoshah)*. The Hebrew text of the "Red Epistle," on the other hand (see below), does speak of "the holy religion" *(ha-das ha-kedoshah)*.

85. *Ibid.,* no. 805.

86. *Ibid.,* no. 1743.

87. *Ibid.,* no. 1784.

88. *Ibid.,* no. 772; see also no. 2164.

89. *Ibid.,* no. 240.

90. *Ibid.,* no. 154. The phrase comes from the *Zohar,* II, 95a.

91. *Ibid.,* no. 1046.

92. *Ibid.,* no. 1776.

93. *Ibid.,* no. 255.

94. *Ibid.,* no. 1185.

95. *Ibid.,* no. 1271.

96. *Ibid.,* no. 1755. This question was asked in a famous Kabbalistic book, the *Sefer ha-Kanah.*

97. *Ibid.,* no. 1810.

98. *Ibid.,* nos. 1263, 1543, 1751.

99. Hans Jonas, *Gnosis und spätantiker Geist* (1934), I, 234.

100. Parts of this work were published by A. Kraushar, *op. cit.,* II, 186–218.

101. *Orient,* XII (1851), 534–43, 568–74. The complete manuscript has recently been discovered by me in Jerusalem.

102. Peter Beer, *Geschichte, Lehren und Meinungen aller . . . Sekten der Juden,* II (1823), 343-401.

103. The full text of this piece has now been published by me in the Yitzhak F. Baer Jubilee Volume (Jerusalem, 1960), 409-30.

104. This was testified to by witnesses who appeared before the rabbinical court of Fürth in the year 1800. The entire proceedings were published by N. Gelber in *Historishe Shriften* (Vilna: YIVO, 1929), p. 290.

105. See Beer, *op. cit.,* pp. 343, 374.

106. See Kraushar, *op. cit.,* no. 1983.

107. See, for instance, the sermon on the *alenu* hymn (*Orient,* XII, 583, 540), which was given at a gathering of "believers" in Prague in 1803.

108. The text of the epistle was published by Porges in *Revue des Études Juives* (XXIX, 283-86), and again by Mark Wischnitzer, *Mémoires de l'académie impériale des sciences* (St. Petersburg, 1914), who was unaware of its previous appearance.

109. This verse is also cited in this connection in the tractate Sanhedrin 97a.

110. The passage in the *Sefer Zror ha-Mor* is as follows: "And herein [in Lev. 13:13] is an allusion to the fact that when the human race has gone so far astray that the white [i.e., human purity or innocence] has become red [*adom*] with sin, then he [the Messiah] is pure and his servants are pure, for he is his [their?] Messiah."

[Two apparent incongruities provide the basis for this exegesis: first of all the fact that white, generally the symbol of purity, is repeatedly spoken of in Leviticus as one of the telltale signs of leprosy; and secondly, the seemingly paradoxical statement in Leviticus 13:13 that "the priest shall look (at the diseased man); and, behold, if the leprosy have covered all his flesh, he shall pronounce him clean that hath the plague; it is all turned white: he is clean"—Tr. Note.]

111. The Bible makes no mention of Jacob's ever having fulfilled this promise to come to the place of Esau. The Palestinian Talmud (Avodah Zarah II, 5) says that this will happen at the End of Days.

112. Jacob is spoken of in this fashion in the Kabbalah because he was supposed by the Kabbalists to have combined in his person the two opposing qualities of divine rigor *(din)* and divine mercy *(hesed)* and to have served as an intermediary between them; here, however, the meaning is that Jacob Frank is able to grasp hold of the opposites of Judaism and Christianity and unite them.

113. In the Talmud (Ta'anit 5b) there is a statement that "our father Jacob did not die."

114. The text reads "religion" *(das)* rather than—as we would have reason to expect (see above, n. 84)—"knowledge" *(da'as),* but since this version appears in all known copies of the epistle there can be no question of its being the result of an erroneous transcription: it was an intended play on words.

115. The reference is to two distinct passages, one in the *Zohar* proper (I, 147a) and the other in the *Sitrei Torah* (I, 147b–148a). Exegeses of the Abraham and Isaac narratives can be found there too.

116. To the best of my knowledge there is no such statement in the *Zohar,* but it is quoted several times in Frankist writing and was used as a mystical slogan.

117. According to the *Zohar* the well is the home of the Shekhinah. Therefore, he who rolls the stone (to the epistler a symbol of the dead weight of the law) from its mouth finds "the Virgin."

118. They are the powers of evil which instead of freeing the world from the bondage of laws restored their domination which the patriarchs had attempted to end.

119. The *Zohar* (III, 138a), in commenting on the reason for

God's repetition of Jacob's name in Genesis 46:2, observes: " 'Jacob, Jacob'—the last [Jacob] was perfect (i.e., lacking in nothing), the first was not perfect since he had not yet heard the tidings about Joseph."

120. The passage in the *Zohar* (I, 145b) reads as follows: "When the serpent had subverted Adam and his wife, and infected her with impurity, the world was polluted and was laid under a curse. . . . Therefore the world must wait until a woman comes after the pattern of Eve and a man after the pattern of Adam who will circumvent and outwit the evil serpent."

121. The true faith in the redeeming power of subversion should not be revealed.

122. In other words, just as Isaiah speaks of light being brought forth from darkness (a prophecy that is naturally understood here in a Frankist sense), as Jacob worshiped his God by going into the impure Land of Haran and by fulfilling his mission there—an explanation consistent with the allegorical interpretation of his journey given above.

123. *Seder Eliyahu Zuta,* chap. 19. The passage is deliberately misquoted.

124. E. Ringelblum, in the literary supplement to *Davar* of the 7th of Shevat, 1935.

125. From the commentary on the *En Ya'akov* (II, 42b in the MS).

126. The quotation is from a polemical pamphlet against the sectarians in Prague and entitled (in Hebrew) "A Debate Between 1800 and 1801" (Prague, 1800), p. 23. Wehle is alluded to by means of a Hebrew pun.

BIBLIOGRAPHICAL NOTES:

THE CRYPTO-JEWISH SECT OF THE

DÖNMEH (SABBATIANS) IN TURKEY

Attias, Moshe and Scholem, Gershom G. *Sefer shirot ve-tishbahot shel ha-shabtaim* (Book of the Sabbatian Songs and Hymns; with an introduction by Itzhak Ben-Zvi). Tel Aviv, 1948.

———. "Piyyut u-tefillah le-simhat torah meha-payyetan ha-shabtai rabbi Yehuda Levi Toba" ("Song and Prayer for Simhat Torah by the Sabbatian Poet Judah Levi Toba"), *Sefunot, Annual for Research on the Jewish Communities in the East,* I (Jerusalem, 1956), 128-40.

———. "Piyyut shabtai be-mivta ashkenazi" ("A Sabbatian Song in the Hebrew Pronunciation of Central and Eastern Europe"), *Mahberet, Les cahiers de l'alliance Israélite Universelle,* VII (Jerusalem, 1958), 176.

Bendt, Theodor. "Die Dönmes oder Mamin in Salonichi," *Ausland,* LXI (1888), 186-90, 206-9.

Ben-Zvi, Yitzhak. "The Sabbateans of Salonica" in *The Exiled and the Redeemed*. Philadelphia, 1957. Pp. 131-53.

———. "Ha-shabtaim bi-zemanenu" ("The Sabbatians in Our Time"), *Metzudah,* VII (London, 1954), 331-38.

———. "Kuntres be-kabbalah me-hugo shel Barukhya" ("A Kabbalistic Pamphlet from the Circle of Baruchya"), *Sefunot,* III-IV (Jerusalem, 1960), 349-94.

Brawer, Abraham Jacob. "Zur Kenntnis der Donmäh in Saloniki," *Archiv für jüdische Familienforschung,* II, No. 4-6 (Vienna, 1916), 14-16.

Carlebach, Azriel. "Dönmehs" in *Exotische Juden*. Berlin, 1932. Pp. 154-56.

Danon, Abraham. "Une secte judéo-musulmane en Turquie," *Revue des études juives,* XXXV (1897), 264-81.

———. "Une secte judéo-musulmane en Turquie," *Actes du XIème Congrès des Orientalistes,* 3ème section (Paris, 1899), 57-84.

Galanté, Abraham. *Nouveaux documents sur Sabbetai Sevi; organisation et us et coutumes de ses adeptes*. Istanbul, 1935.

Gordlevsky, Vladimir. "Zur Frage über die 'Dönme' (Die Rolle der Juden in den Religionssekten Vorderasiens)," *Islamica,* II (Leipzig, 1926), 200-18.

Gövsa, Ibrahim Alâettin. *Sabatay Sevi*. Istanbul, n.d. [1938 or 1939].

Graetz, Heinrich. "Überbleibsel der Sabbatianer in Salonichi," *Monatsschrift für Geschichte und Wissenschaft des Judentums,* XXVI (1876), 130-32.

———. "Überbleibsel der sabbatianischen Sekte in Salonichi," *ibid.,* XXXIII (1884), 49-63.

Molkho, Yitzhak R. "Homer le-toldot Shabtai Tsevi veha-donmin asher be-Salonik" ("Material for the History of Sabbatai Zevi and of the Dönmeh in Salonika"), *Reshumot,* VI (Tel Aviv, 1930), 537-43 and supplements in *Zion,* XI (Jerusalem, 1946), 150-51.

———. "Lidmuto ve-zehuto shel Barukhya Russo hu Osman Baba" ("On the Character and Identity of Baruchya Russo or Osman Baba"), *Mahberet, Les cahiers de l'alliance Israélite Universelle,* II (Jerusalem, 1953), 86, 97-99.

———. "Midrash ne'elam al parashat lekh lekha" ("A Mystical Homily on the Torah Section *lekh lekha*") in *Hommage à Abraham en l'honneur de Abraham Elmaleh à l'occasion de son 70ème anniversaire*. Jerusalem, 1959. Pp. 56-65.

Molkho, Y. R. and Shatz, Rivka. "Perush lekh lekha" ("A Commentary on the Torah Section *lekh lekha*"), *Sefunot,* III-IV (Jerusalem, 1960), 433-521.

Nehamah, Joseph. "Sabbatai Zévi et les Sabbatéens de Salonique," *Revue des écoles de l'alliance Israélite* (Paris, 1902), 289-323. (It is signed only as "N." This article appeared under his full name as a pamphlet in Judaeo-Spanish: *Sabbetai Zvi y los Maminim*. Salonika, 1932).

Rosanes, Solomon. *Korot ha-yehudim be-Turkia* (History of the Jews in Turkey), vol. IV. Sofia, 1935. Pp. 462-77.

Schaufler, W. "Shabbathai Zevi and his Followers," *Journal of the American Oriental Society,* II (1851), 3-26.

Scholem, Gershom G. *"Barukhya rosh ha-shabataim be-Saloniki"* ("Baruchya, the Leader of the Sabbatians in Salonika"), *Zion,* VI (1941), 119-47, 181-202.

———. *"Seder tefillot shel ha-Dönmeh me-Izmir"* ("A Prayerbook of the Dönmeh from Izmir") *Kiryat Sefer,* XVIII (Jerusalem, 1941), 298-312, 394-408; XIX, 58-64.

———. *Shabtai Zvi veha-tenuah ha-shabtait biyme hayyav* (Sabbatai Zevi and the Sabbatian Movement up to his Death), 2 vols. Tel Aviv, 1957. An English version will be published by Princeton University Press (in the Bollingen Series) in 1972.

Shatz, Rivka. "Lidmutah shel ahat ha-kittot ha-shabtaiyyot" ("On the Intellectual Structure of one of the Sabbatian Sects"), *Sefunot,* III-IV (Jerusalem, 1960), 395-431.

Slousch, Nahum. "Les Deunmeh, une secte judéo-musulmane de Salonique," *Revue du monde musulman,* VI (1908), 483-95.

Struck, Adolf. "Die verborgenjüdische Sekte der Dönmé in Salonik," *Globus,* LXXXI (1902), 219-24.

von Hahn, J. G. "Über die Bevölkerung von Salonik und die dortige Sekte der Dönmé," *Reise durch die Gebiete des Drin und Wardar (Denkschriften der kaiserlichen Akademie der Wissenschaften in Wien. Philosophisch-historische Klasse,* XVI (1869), 154-55.

Anonymous. "Tarihin esrarengiz bir sahifesi" (Turkish: "A Mysterious Page from History"). This is a history of the Dönmeh based primarily on oral reports which the author, who signs himself as "historian," emphasizes have been carefully checked. In the daily paper *Vatan* (Istanbul, 1924), in ten installments, nos. 272-95.

A SABBATIAN WILL FROM NEW YORK

1. Porges' memoirs have been published in a Yiddish translation from the German original text by Dr. N. M. Gelber in *Historische Schriften fun YIVO,* I (1929), cols. 253-96.

2. "Communication on the Frankist Sect," published by Dr. Stein in the German-Jewish yearbook *Achawa,* IV (1868), 154-66, in particular p. 159.

3. The miniature was given by Eva Frank to Gottlieb Wehle's father in 1816, shortly before her death, as this year is inscribed on the small leather case in which this miniature was kept all the time. It has been presented by the Misses Goldmark to the Schwadron collection of portraits and autographs in the Hebrew University Library. There is ample testimony to the effect that families who were active in the sect were given copies of this painting as a sort of spiritual reward.

4. There is no basic difference between the terms Sabbatianism and

Frankism which, by the way, were never used by the adherents of the sect who always called themselves only *ma'aminim,* i.e., "believers," namely, in the Messiahship of Sabbatai Zevi, or in the new revelation that came through him in his later incarnations including Frank. The Jewish opponents of the sect called them *Shebslach;* the name Frankists was first used by Polish writers when speaking of the group which embraced Catholicism in 1760 under Jacob Frank's leadership. Most of the sectarians, however, remained in the Jewish fold even though they accepted Frank's spiritual guidance. The Sabbatians who followed Frank did not, by their acceptance of Frankism, renounce the basic teachings of Sabbatianism, although they transformed them, not inconsiderably, according to Frank's new interpretations.

5. According to valuable oral traditions about the Prague Sabbatians which Dr. Klein, a former pupil of the Talmudic Academy there (1829-32) collected and published in a place where nobody would expect to find them—as a consequence they have never been taken into account by historians of Sabbatianism—cf. *Literaturblatt des Orients,* 1848, col. 528. On the Wehle and Bondi families, see cols. 526 and 540.

6. *The Jewish Expositor* (London), IV (1819), 30-32.

7. P. Beer: *Geschichte, Lehren und Meinungen aller . . . Sekten der Juden,* II (1823), 343-401.

8. Jacob Emden, *Torat ha-Kena'ot* (Amsterdam, 1752), fol. 60a.

9. Jonah Landsopher was an intimate friend and admirer of Jonathan Eibeschütz who was considered by the Sabbatians one of their great men—and rightly so as has been recently proved conclusively by M. A. Perlmutter in his full-length study *R. Jonathan Eibeschütz' Relation to Sabbatianism* (1947, in Hebrew). Other details regarding Jonah Landsopher's activities about the year 1760 are given in Emden's polemical pamphlet *Bet Jonathan Hasopher,* 6b.

10. On the reasons for this reluctance to admit Sabbatian ancestry, see "Sabbatianism and Mystical Heresy" in G. G. Scholem, *Major Trends in Jewish Mysticism* (New York and London, 1946).

11. *Cf.* Fritz Mauthner, *Erinnerungen* (Munich, 1918), p. 306, and Porges' communication to Dr. Stein in *Achawa,* IV, 160.

12. W. Wessely, in *Zeitschrift für historische Theologie,* 1845, p. 137, reprinted in Fürst's *Orient,* XII (1851), col. 535.

Notes on the Text of the Will

1. Rosi Porges was the daughter of Gottlieb Wehle's aunt, Schoendel Wehle, who was married to Meyer Porges, himself an enthusiastic member of the sect. Cf. Žáček, in *Jahrbuch für die Geschichte der Juden in der czechoslovakischen Republik,* IX (1938), 406.

2. Dr. Dembitz, the grandfather of Louis D. Brandeis, was the last neophyte of Sabbatianism of whom we know. Peter Beer, *op. cit.,*

p. 340, tells that he joined the sect only one year before he wrote his account of the "Zoharites,"i.e., sometime between 1818 and 1822. He denotes him only by his initial "D., a very gifted young man who was studying medicine at the Prague University," but in the copy of Beer's book in the University Library in Prague his full name is given in a manuscript note, cf. Žáček, op. cit., p. 400. Later he was a physician in Germany. His son, Louis Naphtali D. (1833-1900), who came to America in the same group as the author of the will, became a champion of Jewish orthodoxy in the U.S.A., one of the very rare cases of return to orthodoxy in Sabbatian families.

3. Gottlieb Wehle was born on July 27, 1802.

4. Aaron Beer and his brother Jonas Wehle are buried in the same plot and have only one tombstone, which indicates that both died about the same time and indeed, as I have been informed by Dr. O. Muneles (Prague), Jonas W. died on December 12, 1823.

5. Her name was Esther (1772-1838). She was Wehle's second wife and was married to him in 1791.

6. He was the grandfather of Zacharias Frankel and died in 1811. Aaron Beer Wehle was, at the time of the marriage, already an active member of the sect and the question arises whether his father-in-law had not some sympathy with it. The Frankel-Spiros were, indeed, one of the most important families in Prague. Moses Porges, in his oral communication about the sect, told Dr. Stein about "secret conventicles" of the Sabbatians "to which the heads of the richest families used to go." As a matter of fact, already Jacob Emden accused the widow of the "Primator" Simon Frankel of Sabbatian leanings, cf. his Hit'abbekut (Lvov, 1877), f. 45b, but Emden's accusations alone would not carry sufficient weight as a number of them are quite baseless.

7. Jonah ben Mendel (Emanuel) Landsopher, the friend of Jonathan Eibeschütz, is not to be confused with his grandfather Jonah ben Elijahu L. (1678–1712), a famous rabbinical scholar and ascetic. The second Jonah was a steady opponent of Ezekiel Landau, the chief rabbi of Prague. His daughter was called Malkah and is said, in the Wehle genealogy, to have lived ninety-six years.

8. He died on February 3, 1791.

9. He was a distinguished scholar in Prague and a great admirer of Jonathan Eibeschütz.

10. The writer's wife was Eleanora Feigl (born 1805), a daughter of Babette Wehli (1785–1856) and Abraham Feigl (1781–1831). This branch of the family called itself Wehli instead of the original Wehle.

11. These two uncles of the writer were the outstanding personalities in Bohemian Sabbatianism about the year 1800. Both sent their children to the Frankist "court" at Offenbach where Moses Porges met them. Jonas Wehle is mentioned in all the documents as the leader of the Prague group and the synagogue of the sectarians was, after 1799,

in his house. My colleague Julius Guttmann has drawn my attention to a review of Heinrich Graetz' monograph on the Frankists written in 1868 by Zacharias Frankel (Cf. *Monatsschrift für Geschichte und Wissenschaft des Judentums,* XVII, 75-79), which has preserved some of his personal recollections of Jonas Wehle and his group which the historians have failed to notice. The documents published recently by Žáček (cf. note 1) paint a very vivid picture of his activities around the year 1800. Zacharias Frankel's remark that "none of these Sabbatians has ever abandoned Judaism and their children, too, have remained within the Jewish faith" needs qualification. He did not know, apparently, that some of Jonas and Emanuel Wehle's children were baptized (in Offenbach?) and their family name changed to Klarenberg "for mystical reasons" as the genealogy of the family puts it.

12. These three were educated at Offenbach. Porges tells us that their Jewish names were Abraham, Joseph, and Akiba and that they were "renamed" Joseph, Ludwig, and Max, like all the other youngsters who were sent to Offenbach, even those who were not baptized.

13. She seems to have been an enthusiastic member of the sect. She is the last Sabbatian of this group who is known to have participated in antinomian and repulsive practices on the Day of Atonement, 1799. In view of our present knowledge about Sabbatian practice it is difficult to disbelieve the protocols about these incidents which are based not on malignant rumors of the enemies of the sect but on the narratives of Moses and Loeb Porges on their return from Offenbach. Cf. the Appendix to Gelber's edition of Porges' recollections (quoted in note 1 above), col. 290.

14. It appears that the writer confused Jonas Landsopher with his grandfather (cf. note 7) and Ephraim Wehle with the much older Ephraim Lentshitz, of Prague, the author of *Olelot Efrayim,* a well-known collection of homilies.

15. This passage introduces his ancestors as Kabbalists and Sabbatians.

16. It follows from the context that the writer is speaking of the Kabbalistic systems and ideas.

17. The writer obviously aims at the Prague rabbi Eleazar Fleckeles whose "sensational" sermon against the Sabbatians in his community was published in Prague in 1800 under the title *Ahavat David.* Cf. also Žáček's afore-mentioned essay, p. 386, where the petition of another influential member of the sect against Fleckeles' preaching is analyzed. The author of this petition was an ennobled Jew, Loew Hoenig von Hoenigsberg, the son-in-law of Jonas Wehle and himself a pilgrim to Offenbach.

18. They had in view the doctrine of incarnation which the sectarians held.

19. The correct spelling is *Sohariten,* followers of the *Zohar.* The Frankists sometimes used this name in their dealings with the Polish and Church authorities. An English translation of Peter Beer's chapter

on the Frankists has been published as a (very ràre) pamphlet. It is entitled by the plagiarist: *M. J. Mayers, A Brief Account of the Zoharite Jews* (Cambridge, 1826).

20. This statement cannot stand the critical test; as a matter of fact, the sectarians did appeal to the Bohemian authorities through the above-mentioned Loew von Hoenigsberg whose petition is as bitter a denunciation of the "Rabonim" as any polemical writing could be expected to be. The full text of this document has not been published by Žáček but a copy of it is in the Schocken Library in Jerusalem.

21. This testimonial to their virtues is actually found in Fleckeles' bitter attack on the sectarians.

22. Friends and foes agree that this was one of the main preoccupations of the Bohemian Sabbatians who indulged in numerary mysticism and speculations about the near time of the "end."

23. The ceremonial law.

24. The quotation marks in the manuscript suggest that the writer quotes more or less literally from the teachings of the sect.

25. This, at least as regards the formulation used, is a mitigation of the Sabbatian doctrine of incarnation. Sabbatai Zevi, Baruchya of Salonika, and Jacob Frank were considered the incarnations of some of the ten *sefirot,* the mystical attributes of God. It is obvious from Wehle's careful formulation that the Messiah is a vicar or deputy of God which, by implication, may, or may not, mean incarnation. But there can be no doubt, especially on the basis of Jonas Wehle's letters and manuscripts, that the Prague group, like the other Frankists, actually taught incarnation. It was this doctrine which was considered by their rabbinical opponents as a most objectionable element of Jewish-Christian syncretism in their teaching.

26. We know from Porges' recollections that everybody in Offenbach was taught that he might be chosen as one of the elect among whom the last Messiah will be born. In Wehle's formulation we have a moralistic generalization of this idea: everybody may be one of the elect, i.e., one of those chosen as "instruments of Providence" without any direct reference to the original eschatological and Messianic meaning of the principle.

27. Amalie, the widow of Baruch Petschotsch, whom we have found as Gottlieb Wehle's teacher in the principles of Sabbatianism. She died in 1864.

THE NEUTRALIZATION OF THE
MESSIANIC ELEMENT IN EARLY HASIDISM

1. Simon Dubnow, *Geschichte des Chassidismus* I (Berlin, 1931), p. 108; and Martin Buber, *The Origin and Meaning of Hasidism,* trans. by Maurice Friedman (New York, 1960), pp. 107 and 111.

2. Ben Zion Dinur, *Bemifne ha-Dorot* (Jerusalem, 1955), pp.

181-227. This study was first published in *Zion,* 1943-45. In a similar vein, Yitzhak Alfassi says in a recent book: "The very core of Hasidism is the redemption of Israel," cf. *Hasidut: Pirke Toladah u-Mehkar* (Tel Aviv, 1969), p. 192.

3. Isaiah Tishby in *Zion,* XXXII (1967), 1-45. Tishby and I differ greatly in the evaluation of the same quotations. He goes to great length to stress traditional formulae to be found, sometimes quite frequently, in the sources, which in my opinion has led him astray, causing him to take routine phrases as highly meaningful.

4. Cf. J. G. Weiss in *Zion,* XVI (1951), 46-105, and especially his essay in *Journal of Jewish Studies,* IV (1953), 28, where he says on Baer of Mezritch's contemplative school of mysticism that "it abolishes the intense interest in the Messiah and his collective redemption. . . . The lack of all Messianic tension is a characteristic feature of its contemplative piety." This view is also taken by Rivka Shatz, *"Ha-Yesod ha-Meshihi be-Mahshevet ha-Hasidut,"* in *Molad,* New Series, I (1967), 105-11.

5. G. G. Scholem, *Major Trends in Jewish Mysticism* (New York and London, 1946), pp. 328-30. I am limiting myself to the operative sentences of my exposition against which Tishby has come out by using a method of stressing irrelevant elements, a method with which I fundamentally disagree.

6. Tishby, *op. cit.,* p. 29, and in the English resumé of his paper.

7. Dubnow, *op. cit.,* p. 104.

8. It is found in *Mikhtavim meha-Besht* (Lvov, 1923), pp. 1-5.

9. At the end of his book *Ben Porat Yosef* (Koretz, 1781), f. 100a/b. The fact that there are two different versions of the letter deserves closer study, as I have pointed out elsewhere; cf. *Molad,* XVIII (1960), 348. I consider the longer version the authentic one.

10. This seems to be the meaning of Tishby's remark, *op. cit.,* p. 32.

11. *Ibid.,* p. 33.

12. As cases in point I would mention Mordecai Dato's *Migdal David* (on 1575 as the year of redemption) in MS, Oxford 2515, and possibly Isaak Vita Cantarini's *Et Ketz* (fixing redemption on 1740) (Venice, 1710).

13. This holds partly true for the authors discussed at great length by Tishby in the first part of his paper, pp. 8-24. These have no direct bearing on the present discussion, having been written outside the Hasidic camp.

14. In chapters VII and VIII of *Major Trends in Jewish Mysticism* and in my work on Sabbatai Zevi, an English translation of which is scheduled to be published in 1971 or 1972, by Princeton University Press.

15. For additional discussion of *devekut* in early Hasidic doctrine see this volume, pp. 203-26.

16. In some earlier sources, including the writings of Nathan of Gaza, the Revelation on Mount Sinai is seen as the only occasion on which the whole community of Israel reached *devekut* as a collective experience in the past.

17. Tishby, *op. cit.,* pp. 36-37.

18. Cf. e.g., *Toledot,* f. 846, quoted further on.

19. G. G. Scholem, *Von der mystischen Gestalt der Gottheit* (Zurich, 1962), p. 241. In the following I make use of my remarks in this book, pp. 241-46.

20. *Toledot Yaakov Yosef* (in the following notes abridged to *Toledot*) (Koretz, 1780), f. 15a.

21. *Degel Mahane Efrayim* (Koretz, 1810), f. 38a.

22. *Toledot,* ff. 90b and 84b.

23. The commentary on Psalm 107 *Perush al Hodu* has been printed innumerable times.

24. H. Zeitlin, *Ha-Hasidut* (Warsaw, 1910), p. 29.

25. *Ketonet Passim* (Lvov, 1866), ff. 35a/b.

26. Incidentally, I am not altogether convinced of the reliability of the tradition concerning the Baal Shem's predilection for the book of the Moroccan sage. Neither in the Baal Shem's authentic sayings nor in the copious writings of the Rabbi of Polnoye, who is very liberal in quoting other authors, is there any trace of its influence, and it is only the disciples of the Maggid of Mezritch who started the habit of quoting it.

27. *Likkutim Yekarim* (1792), f. 1, col. b, without any reference to the Zaddik.

28. Cf. Rivka Shatz, *Le-Mahuto shel Zaddik ba-Hasidut,* in *Molad,* XVIII (1960), 365-78, particularly 376, and Tishby's remarks in his paper, pp. 36-37.

29. *No'am Elimelekh* (Lvov, 1786), f. 54b (section *vayikra*).

30. The terms *ge'ulah peratit* and *ge'ulah kelalit* are used in some Lurianic writings not in the later Hasidic sense but in order to designate the redemption from Egypt in contradistinction to the Messianic one. The redemption from Egypt pertains only to a specific place and could therefore be considered *peratit,* meaning in this context a *special* redemption, not an *individual* one. In the earliest Hasidic writings the bridge between this usage of the term and the later one can still be seen clearly: the redemption from Egypt is sometimes said to be the prototype of the individual redemption. Moreover, Lurianic Kabbalah drew a distinction between "original souls" which are root-souls *(neshamot mekoriot)* and "particular souls" or "individual souls" *(neshamot peratiot)* which need a *tikkun* destined for them only. Cf., e.g., in Moses Zakkuto's commentary on *Zohar,* III, 18a, printed in Shalom Busaglo's *Mikdash Melekh* (Amsterdam, 1750), f. 28a. The transition from *tikkun perati* to *ge'ulah peratit* was an easy one.

31. *Teshuot Hen* (Berditchev, 1816), f. 13a, which seems to be

composed of the two sayings of the Baal Shem in *Toledot,* ff. 27b and 35b.

32. *Toledot* ff. 79a and 67b.

33. *Toledot* f. 198a.

34. *Teshuot Hen,* f. 43b.

35. When I first took up the question of specific points in which Hasidism was influenced by Sabbatian groups, I was the target of a poisonous attack by Eliezer Steinmann, a Hebrew writer who has published several volumes glorifying Hasidism, who accused me of "looking for *hametz* in Hasidism," cf. his article *"Bedikat Hametz be-Mishnat ha-Hasidim,"* in *Molad,* XI (1951), 259-67.

36. Cf. my essay in *Bet Yisrael be-Polin* (ed. Israel Halpern), Vol. II (Jerusalem, 1949), p. 64, and p. 59 on the common emotional background of the Russian Khlysti and the Sabbatians.

37. This holds true for such customs as dancing, violent gestures during prayer, and probably also for the Sabbath meal. The extraordinary statements of Yafa Eliach in this connection, maintaining that these things, as well as the substance of Hasidic teaching, came originally from the Russian sect of the Khlysti, are entirely without foundation. Cf. *Proceedings, American Academy for Jewish Research,* XXXVI (1968), 53-83. This paper and all its hypotheses are a deplorable example of scholarly irresponsibility, leaving the reader wondering about the state of Jewish studies.

38. Cf. Scholem, *Von der mystischen Gestalt der Gottheit,* pp. 110-34.

39. Cf. *Likkutim Yekarim* (Lvov, 1864), ff. 14a/b, and *Or Torah* (Koretz, 1804), f. 146b (without pagination). The same Sabbatian paradox referring to Moses' stay at Pharaoh's court as a necessary step of dissimulation and outwitting the power of evil in its own realm, which is so frequently mentioned in apologies for Sabbatai Zevi, was taken up by the Rabbi of Polnoye and given a Hasidic twist. Cf. *Teshuot Hen* f. 6a (in the name of the Rabbi of Polnoye).

40. *Toledot* f. 145b (section *hukkat*).

41. On this point cf. G. Nigal, *Manhig va-Edah* (1962), pp. 96-109, and S. H. Dresner, *The Zaddik . . . according to the writings of Rabbi Jaakov Yosef of Polnoye* (London and New York, 1960), pp. 148-221, who deals with the whole problem of the descent of the Zaddik and its dangers at length.

42. All the statements about the Zaddik in Psalms are explained as statements on Sabbatai Zevi in Israel Hazan's commentary on a large part of the Book of Psalms, composed 1679.

43. *Toledot,* ff. 16a and 17a.

44. *Shivhe ha-Besht* (Kopys, 1815), f. 28a.

45. E.g., MS. Guenzburg 517, f. 79b.

46. *Meor Enayim* (Slavita, 1798), f. 91b; cf. also Tishby, *op. cit.,* p. 35.

47. Such writers are, e.g., Gedalya of Linietz, Benjamin of Zaloście, and Ephraim of Sedylkov.

48. *Degel Mahane Efrayim* (Koretz, 1810), f. 17a.

49. *Maggid Devarav le-Yaakov* (Koretz, 1781), f. 9b.

REVELATION AND TRADITION
AS RELIGIOUS CATEGORIES IN JUDAISM

1. Menahoth 29b.

2. J. F. Molitor, *Philosophie der Geschichte oder Ueber die Tradition,* I (1857), p. 4.

3. Cf. the compilation of these statutes in Wilhelm Bacher, *Tradition und Tradenten* (Leipzig, 1914), pp. 33-46.

4. *Ibid.,* pp. 27-31.

5. *Midrash Tanhuma,* ed. Solomon Buber, II, 60a.

6. *Ibid.,* p. 58b.

7. Of Rabbi Meir it is said in Erubin 13b: "He pronounces the impure pure and proves it and the pure impure and proves this" (in order to force the scholars to think through the problems most conscientiously before arriving at a decision). Of his disciple Symmachos it is there reported that he adduced 48 reasons for the impurity of each impure object and 48 reasons for the purity of each pure object. In the same place the Talmud reports very soberly the tradition, which must be particularly disquieting to a pious mind, that in Jabneh there was even an acute student who was able to adduce 150 reasons why a crawling animal is pure—whereas in fact the Torah explicitly and unambiguously prohibits it.

8. This thesis seems first to have been stated by Moses Graf of Prague; see his *Vayakhel Moshe* (Dessau, 1699), pp. 45b and 54a.

9. Baba Metzia 59b.

10. Molitor, *op. cit.,* p. 47.

11. Gittin 60b.

12. *Avodat ha-Kodesh* (Lvov, 1857), I, chs. 21 and 22; also III, chs. 20-24.

13. Hagigah 15b.

14. Yebamot 21a, as an interpretation of Leviticus 18:30.

15. Baba Batra 16a.

16. Cf. Isaiah Horovitz, *Shene Luhot ha-Berit* (Amsterdam, 1689), pp. 25b-26a.

THE POLITICS OF MYSTICISM:
ISAAC BREUER's *New Kuzari*

1. Isaac Breuer, *Der neue Kuzari. Ein Weg zum Judentum* (Frankfurt am Main: Rabbiner-Hirsch-Gesellschaft, 1934).
[Isaac Breuer (1883-1946), lawyer, leader of Orthodox Jewry; grandson of Samson Raphael Hirsch; lived in Frankfurt am Main and settled in Palestine in 1936.—Ed.]

2. [Samson Raphael Hirsch advocated the separation of his followers from the existing Jewish communities and the formation of independent orthodox communities. In 1876 the German government made this legal.—Ed.]

3. *Das jüdische Nationalheim* (Frankfurt am Main, 1925).

4. *Neunzehn Briefe über Judenthum* (Altona, 1836).

5. I say: in principle at least. For what is so strange, and perhaps part of the many wonders of the *torah im derekh eretz* world, is this: These "independent" orthodox, who can draw from the deepest wells of *Halakhah* and Kabbalah, who with so much fervor unmask Zionism as an abomination spawned by the worst—because the most internalized—assimilation, employ a style, a terminology, that is rather startling: not only is it replete with the entire Zionist vocabulary, delicately draped in orthodoxy, but lately it also teems with terms like *Front* and *Führer,* nationalist socialism and the third *yishuv*—and that in purely inner-Jewish contexts. Some, who have a sense of shame and are sensitive to the sound of such expressions—borrowed from another world—out of the mouths of Jews, must sometimes have silently hidden their faces when they read the Frankfurt *Israelit* and other literary products of the Hirsch school.

6. *Jüdische Religion im Zeitalter der Emanzipation* (Berlin, 1933).

7. [Jonathan Eibeschütz, eighteenth-century Talmudist and mystic, was suspected of being a follower of the pseudo-Messiah Sabbatai Zevi. His denial led to a widespread controversy. See "Redemption Through Sin" in this volume, Note 11 (p. 346)—Ed.]

THE GOLEM OF PRAGUE
AND THE GOLEM OF REHOVOT

1. [When Gershom Scholem heard that the Weizmann Institute at Rehovot had completed the building of a new computer, he told Dr. Chaim Pekeris, who "fathered" the computer, that in his opinion the most appropriate name for it would be Golem No. 1 *(Golem Alef).* Dr. Pekeris agreed, on condition that Scholem would dedicate the computer and explain why it should be so named.—Ed.]

Sources and Acknowledgments

Toward an Understanding of the Messianic Idea in Judaism. Lecture, Eranos Conference, 1959. *Eranos Jahrbuch,* XXVIII (1959), 193-239 (in German). *Judaica* (Frankfurt am Main, 1963), pp. 7-74. Trans. Michael A. Meyer.

The Messianic Idea in Kabbalism. *Commentary,* XXV, 4 (1958), under the title "Jewish Messianism and the Idea of Progress: Exile and Redemption in the Cabbala," trans. Moses Hadas.

The Crisis of Tradition in Jewish Messianism. Lecture, Eranos Conference, 1968. *Eranos Jahrbuch,* XXXIX (1970; in German).

Redemption Through Sin. *Keneset,* II (1937), 347-92 (in Hebrew). Trans. Hillel Halkin.

The Crypto-Jewish Sect of the Dönmeh (Sabbatians) in Turkey. Paper read at the Tenth Congress of the International Association for the History of Religions. Marburg, Germany, September 1960. *Numen,* VII (1960), 93-122 (in German). Trans. Michael A. Meyer.

A Sabbatian Will from New York. *Miscellanies of the Jewish Historical Society of England,* V (1948), 193-211 (in English). Reprinted by permission of the Jewish Historical Society of England.

The Neutralization of the Messianic Element in Early Hasidism. Memorial lecture for Joseph G. Weiss, at the Institute of Jewish Studies, University College, London, March 18, 1970 (in English). *Journal of Jewish Studies* (London, Fall 1970).

Devekut, or Communion with God. From a series of lectures held at Hebrew Union College–Jewish Institute of Religion, New York School, March 1949. *Review of Religion,* XIV (1949–50), 115-39. Copyright 1950 by Columbia University Press.

Martin Buber's Interpretation of Hasidism. Based on a lecture at the Institute of Jewish Studies, University College, London, 1961. *Neue Zürcher Zeitung* (May 20 and 27, 1962). *Judaica* (Frankfurt am Main, 1963), pp. 165-206. *Commentary,* XXII (1961), 305-16. Trans. Michael A. Meyer.

The Tradition of the Thirty-Six Hidden Just Men. *Theater, Wahrheit und Wirklichkeit* (Festschrift for Kurt Hirschfeld [Zurich, 1962], 115-22. *Judaica* (Frankfurt am Main, 1963), pp. 216-25. Trans. Michael A. Meyer.

The Star of David: History of a Symbol. *Luah Haaretz* (Tel Aviv, 1948), 148-63 (in Hebrew). Expanded in *Judaica* (Frankfurt am Main, 1963), pp. 75-118 (in German). Trans. Michael A. Meyer.

Revelation and Tradition as Religious Categories in Judaism. *Eranos Jahrbuch,* XXXI (1962), 19-48 (in German). *Judaism,* XV (1966), 1, 23-29, published by the American Jewish Congress, trans. by Henry Schwarzschild, under the title "Tradition and Commentary as Religious Categories in Judaism." Expanded and adjusted to the full text in *Eranos Jahrbuch* by Michael A. Meyer.

The Science of Judaism—Then and Now. Lecture, Leo Baeck Institute, London, September 7, 1959. *Bulletin, Leo Baeck Institute,* III (Tel Aviv, 1960), 10-20 (in German). *Judaica* (Frankfurt am Main, 1963), pp. 147-64. Trans. Michael A. Meyer.

At the Completion of Buber's Translation of the Bible. Speech at a gathering in Jerusalem celebrating the completion of Martin Buber's (and Franz Rosenzweig's) Bible translation, February 1961. *Neue Zürcher Zeitung* (March 31, 1963). *Judaica* (Frankfurt am Main, 1963), 207-15. Trans. Michael A. Meyer.

On the 1930 Edition of Rosenzweig's *Star of Redemption. Frankfurter Israelitisches Gemeindeblatt,* X (1931), 15-17. *Judaica* (Frankfurt am Main, 1963), pp. 226-34. Trans. Michael A. Meyer.

The Politics of Mysticism: Isaac Breuer's *New Kuzari. Jüdische Rundschau,* XXXIX (July 17, 1934, in German). Trans. Michael A. Meyer.

The Golem of Prague and the Golem of Rehovot. Speech delivered at the Weizmann Institute, in Rehovot, on June 17, 1965, when a new computer was dedicated. *Jerusalem Post* (June 18, 1965, under the title "Prague and Rehovot. Tale of Two Golems"). *Commentary,* XLI, 1 (1966), 62-65.

Index